AA

Book of Britain's Coastal WALKS

Foreword by Nicholas Crane

There's nothing like a walk by the sea. I didn't realise how much the coast mattered until I took a long walk inland, from one end of England to the other. I followed the line of longitude marked on maps as two degrees west. The Ordnance Survey shows the line crossing the coast of Northumberland just short of the Scottish border and then running ruler-straight through the centre of England to the English Channel. For the first few days I found it impossible to pull myself away from the coast. I lingered on grassy cliff tops, gazing wistfully at the North Sea (it was a sunny August and it looked Aegean), and I dallied on the beaches and Tudor ramparts of Berwick-upon-Tweed – one of the most stunning coastal towns in the UK. Eventually, I re-orientated my willpower and compass, turned my back on the calm ocean and headed for the green, enfolded hills. I missed the sea. Nearly two months later, I climbed my last range of hills, a double-fold of downland on the Isle of Purbeck. Those final miles are still one of my favourite coastal walks. After snaking through the whispering pines of Newton Heath, the path scrambles up to the airy heights of Nine Barrow Down, where the spirits of ancient Britons survey a green vale and the last, gentle climb over turfed limestone reveals, step-by-step, the wide, blue horizon.

A Walkers' Coast

Why is it that we love walking by the sea? You only have to visit the Tomb of the Eagles in Orkney, or the Stones of Calanais on the Isle of Lewis, or read about the oak circle of 'Seahenge' which appeared one autumn between the tidelines of north Norfolk, to realise that the edge of our islands have had a unique meaning for thousands of years. That 'sacred' quality was recognised by the communities who raised their sanctuaries on the islands of Iona, and Lindisfarne and St Michael's Mount. The coast was a place for escape, for contemplation, for ritual. The seaside resorts which grew like exotic corals beside the sandy beaches of Victorian Britain were sanctuaries too, where sea breezes and a frolic in the waves washed away all thoughts of factory floor and monotonous office life. Now the coast has a broader meaning. We've learned to value its tranquility, its wildness, its nature and history; its sense of fun.

It's a walkers' coast. Our temperate archipelago is sprinkled across the sea between the latitudes of Norway and France, and we have everything from 300-foot cliffs to smiling beaches. Hiking our island perimeter is a form of ancestor-worship. History is layered so generously around our shores that you step to and fro through the centuries like a restless time-lord, passing Tudor castles, Victorian piers, Saxon churches, concrete pillboxes, Martello Towers and promontory forts from the Iron Age. On secluded estuaries and salt marshes, nature reserves and RSPB sanctuaries open windows on worlds we've forgotten how to notice.

Exploring Britain

The coast has opened up for all; it has become a national project. Coast paths run around most of our shores, and are extending by the year. The National Trust now cares for nearly one thousand miles of UK coastline. Bodies such as the Campaign to Protect Rural England, who led the fight for National Parks, strive to preserve the once-and-only purity of our island fringe and monitor the coastal effects of power stations and windfarms. New marine conservation zones are planned to restore the biodiversity of offshore deserts, and the RSPB has recently announced that it wants to reach out beyond its traditional nature reserves and restore disappearing species to huge swathes of the coast. Things have never looked better for a walk by the coast. The Ordnance Survey reckon that mainland Britain is surrounded by 11,073 miles of coastline, so there's plenty out there to explore.

Using this Book

The *Book of Britain's Coastal Walks* divides the country into six regions with up to 19 walks per region. The route of each walk is shown on a map, and clear directions help you follow the walk. Each route is accompanied by background information about the walk and the area.

Route Information

A panel with each walk details the total distance, terrain, conditions underfoot, parking, public toilets and any special conditions that apply, such as restricted access or level of dog friendliness. The minimum time suggested for the walk is for reasonably fit walkers and doesn't allow for stops. An indication of the gradients you will encounter is shown by the rating ▲▲▲ (no steep slopes) to ▲▲▲ (several very steep slopes). Walks are also rated for their difficulty – those rated ●●● are usually shorter and easier with little total ascent. The hardest walks are marked ●●●.

Parking and Getting Started

Many of the car parks suggested are public, but occasionally you may find you have to park on the roadside or in a lay-by. Please be considerate when you leave your car, ensuring that access roads or gates are not blocked and that other vehicles can pass safely. The start of each walk is given as a six-figure grid reference prefixed by two letters indicating the 100-km square of the National Grid to which it refers. Each walk has a suggested Ordnance Survey Explorer map where you'll find more information on using grid references.

Dog Friendliness

Keep your dog under control at all times, especially around livestock, and obey local bylaws and other dog control notices. Remember, it is against the law to let your dog foul in many public areas, especially in villages and towns.

The route information often contains specific advice regarding the dog friendliness of the walk. Not all routes are appropriate for dog walkers so read the advice provided before setting out.

Map Legend

- - ➝ - -	Walk Route		Built-up Area
1	Route Waypoint		Woodland Area
– – – –	Adjoining Path		Toilet
	Viewpoint	P	Car Park
•	Place of Interest		Picnic Area
	Steep Section	)(	Bridge

Walking in Safety

All these walks are suitable for any reasonably fit person, but less experienced walkers should try the easier walks first. Although each walk here has been researched with a view to minimising the risks to the walkers who follow its route, no walk in the countryside can be considered to be completely free from risk. Walking will always require a degree of common sense and judgement to ensure that it is as safe as possible.

❑ Be particularly careful on cliff paths and in upland terrain, where the consequences of a slip can be very serious.

❑ Remember always to check tidal conditions before walking along the seashore.

❑ Some sections of route are by, or cross, busy roads. Take care and remember traffic is a danger even on minor country lanes.

❑ Be careful around farmyard machinery and livestock, especially if you have children with you.

❑ Be aware of the consequences of changes in the weather and check the forecast before you set out. Carry spare clothing and a torch if you are walking in the winter months. Remember that the weather can change very quickly at any time of the year, and in moorland and heathland areas, mist and fog can make route finding much harder. Don't set out in these conditions unless you are confident of your navigation skills in poor visibility. In summer, remember to take account of the heat and sun; wear a hat and sunscreen, and carry spare water.

❑ On walks away from centres of population, you should carry a whistle and survival bag. If you do have an accident requiring the emergency services, make a note of your position as accurately as possible and dial 999.

Right: Sand dunes at Formby Point, Lancashire, northwest England

Page 6: Coast path near St David's in Pembrokeshire, Wales

Southwest England

Southwest England

The coast of Southwest England enthrals visitors with its beauty and great variety. As well as sandy beaches and rocky headlands, there are pretty coves and wide estuaries, picturesque villages with crowded harbours, steep-sided valleys and even stretches of mud flatland and of moor rich in ancient woodland.

There are hundreds of miles of breathtaking coastal walking along the Southwest Coast Path, which runs all the way from Minehead in Somerset to South Haven Point, near Poole in Dorset. Covering no less than 630 miles (1,014km), this is Britain's longest National Trail and encompasses parts of the Somerset seaboard, the whole of the Devon and Cornwall coastline and parts of the Dorset coast. Stretches of the path have their origin in tracks used in the 19th century by coastguards whose job was to watch out for and foil the activities of 'freetraders' or smugglers. They needed to be able to see into each inlet and cove, so the path stuck as close as possible to the shore.

Between St Ives and St Just on the north coast of the Land's End peninsula, for example, Walk 1 runs along stretches of beautiful coastline tracks once patrolled by coastguards. Walk 10 leads onto the

headland of Pencarrow in southeast Cornwall and provides the chance to look down on the dramatic Lantic Bay, surely once a setting for smugglers' derring-do and the landing of illicit cargoes.

Indeed, Walk 10 gives a sense of life as it was lived in 'Old Cornwall'. The area near Polruan overlooking the estuary of the river Fowey was inhabited in prehistoric times, and medieval chapels were established there, then in the 14th and 15th centuries the place became known above all for the brilliant seamanship of the 'Fowey Gallants', vessels that burst from the harbour at Fowey to raid enemy shipping.

Previous pages: Many millions of years old, Hobarrow Bay in Dorset is part of the World Heritage Site of the Jurassic Coast

Left: A stream flowing across the cove at Heddon's Mouth, Exmoor National Park.

Below: The sandstone headland and sandbar at Hengistbury Head in Dorset enclose Christchurch Harbour from the south

Main image: The village of Polruan sits at the mouth of the Fowey estuary in Cornwall

Historic Port, Ancient Remains

Up and down the coast the walks take you to places of great interest and some importance in local and national history. Walk 12 leads along Devon cliffs to Blackstone Point and to 15th-century Dartmouth Castle, providing a fascinating introduction to

the historic port of Dartmouth. Established as a seaport and shipbuilding town as early as the 12th century, Dartmouth became an important centre of the wine trade in the 14th century; its castle was built in 1481-95, and replaced an earlier coastal fort raised in 1388 by John Hawley, privateer and mayor of Dartmouth. The castle incorporates the Gothic-style St Petrock's Church built in 1641–42.

For those interested in more ancient history, Walk 17 visits Kimmeridge Bay, Dorset, where Iron Age tribes quarried bituminous shale, while on Walk 19 you may see remains of a Stone Age camp and an Iron Age trading centre on Hengistbury Head, Dorset, as well as agricultural land at Barn Field that is largely unchanged since the Roman occupation that ended in AD 410. On some areas of the coast, natural growth has been preserved still longer: remnants of ancient wildwood, dating back to the period after the last Ice Age, are found on the Exmoor coast. At Hawk Combe in Somerset, for example, oak woods and native shrubs including the whitebeam and the hazel are to be found, which provide a natural habitat for insects and birds including the pied flycatcher (see Walk 7).

In the Age of the Dinosaurs

The Southwest Coast also contains all of the Jurassic Coast, 95 miles (153km) of English Channel coastline between Old Harry Rocks (near Swanage, in East Dorset) and Orcombe Point (near Exmouth, Devon). Designated by the United Nations Educational, Scientific and Cultural Organization (UNESCO) as a World Heritage Site in 2001, the Jurassic Coast contains cliffs from the Triassic, Jurassic and Cretaceous periods of the Mesozoic Era (roughly 250 to 65 million years ago).

Walk 16 visits two of the Coast's most celebrated features, the beautiful Lulworth Cove and the natural limestone arch of Durdle Door, which are close to one another in Dorset. Walk 15 climbs the high orange sandstone hill known as the Golden Cap between Charmouth and Bridport in Dorset – at 627 feet (191 metres), this is the highest spot on the Jurassic Coast and on the entire south coast of England, with breathtaking sea views.

Beautiful Beaches, Steep Ascents

In addition to the views, one of the many benefits of coastal walking is the chance to enjoy a rest, a sandwich and a paddle on beaches that beckon enticingly from the path. Not least among these is Studland Bay in Dorset (Walk 18), celebrated for its glorious, pale golden sands. However, walkers may also associate coast paths with steep climbs and vertiginous descents. The walks in this book certainly provide opportunities to work off a few pounds – especially in rugged stretches of North Cornwall, where the path from Port Isaac around Kellan Head to Port Quin (see Walk 3) is a particularly strenuous outing. But in both these and other cases in the book, you are richly rewarded for your hard work with breathtaking views of sea and coast, and you gain access to relatively remote spots.

And while enjoying the surroundings, you may like to console yourself with the knowledge that if you walked the whole length of the path – according to figures released by the South West Coast Path Association – you would need roughly 8 weeks, walking seven days a week and covering an average of 11–12 miles a day, and would use no fewer than 26,719 steps while climbing and descending a vertical distance of 115,000 feet (35,000 metres), almost four times the height of the world's tallest mountain, Mount Everest.

Opposite, top left: The pretty quayside in Dartmouth, Devon, was used to film the BBC series *The Onedin Line* in the 1970s

Opposite, lower left: Part of the Long Groyne at Hengistbury Head, Dorset, built in the 1930s to protect the beach from erosion

Left: Clifftop walking with breathtaking views – Bat's Head and Swyre Head, Dorset

Best of the Rest

Heddon Valley

This peaceful, deep and lushly wooded valley lies within the Exmoor National Park, and leads down to the beach and dramatic cliffs at Heddon's Mouth (see Walk 6). There are spectacular views, and in the valley you can visit a restored Victorian lime kiln or explore ancient oak woods. The valley is a particular haven for butterflies, but you should also be on the lookout for woodpeckers and deer.

Cadgwith and The Devil's Frying Pan

This picturesque fishing village (see Walk 9) lies on the eastern side of the Lizard Peninsula in Cornwall. A centre for fishermen from the 12th century onwards, Cadgwith had developed into a village by the 16th century, and today could be said to be the archetype of the Cornish fishing village – with whitewashed, often thatched cottages on both sides of a narrow valley and a stream running down to a sand and shingle beach on which boats are drawn up. From here the walk visits the Devil's Frying Pan, a vast hollow in the cliff thought to have been formed when the roof of a sea cave collapsed, then proceeds to the originally medieval Church of the Holy Cross at Grade, and the ancient St Ruan's Well.

Bantam and Burgh Island

A ramble between Bantam and Bigbury-on-Sea in South Devon (see Walk 11) delivers dunes and wide beaches and introduces visitors to the intriguing Burgh Island, a tidal island 307 yards (282 metres) from the beach at Bigbury-on-Sea. The island once bore a chapel dedicated to St Michael and was a centre for pilchard fishing, but is today known for its gorgeous Art Deco hotel. Music hall singer George Chirgwin built the first hotel on the site in 1895, and this was supplemented by a much larger and more glamorous building constructed in the late 1920s by filmmaker and industrialist Archie Nettlefold and reworked in the early 1930s by Paul Roseveare. The hotel has a glamorous past, with numerous connections to political, literary and musical figures. Tradition has it that British prime minister Winston Churchill and US general Dwight D Eisenhower used the hotel when planning the Allies' 'D-Day' invasion of German-held Normandy in 1944. The hotel was a haunt of Noel Coward and inspired the setting of Agatha Christie's novels *And Then There Were None* and *Evil Under the Sun*; in the 1960s, the Beatles were visitors and the 1965 film *Catch Us If You Can*, starring the Dave Clark Five, ended on the island.

Bedruthan Steps

In north Cornwall Walk 2 delivers magnificent views of pounding surf and slate stacks on the mile-long Bedruthan Steps beach – according to 19th-century tradition, the stacks were put in place by a giant named Bedruthan to use as stepping stones. At one time locals descended to the beach using steps cut into the majestic 300ft (90m) cliffs, to gather seaweed and also to mine for lead, tin and copper in tunnels at the base of the cliffs; today a secure staircase is provided if you wish to take a detour from the walk onto the sands. Swimming is not safe here, because of powerful rip tides, but at low tide the expansive, sea-washed sands are a wonderful place for a stroll or a game of beach cricket. Keep an eye on the incoming tides since there's a chance you may be cut off from the steps.

Otter Estuary Nature Reserve

Designated a Site of Special Scientific Interest (SSSI), the 57-acre (23ha) nature reserve in East Devon (see Walk 13) is a haven for waders such as the oystercatcher and dunlin, as well as ducks including the wigeon. The walk includes a stretch along the Jurassic Coast near Budleigh Salterton and offers views of the pretty village of Otterton with its substantial St Michael and All Angels Church.

Branscombe

Set in the East Devon Area of Outstanding Natural Beauty, the village of Branscombe (see Walk 14) stands behind the shingle beach of Branscombe Mouth on the Jurassic Coast. Traditionally a centre for fishing, flint manufacture and the making of handmade lace, Branscombe boasts a splendid 12th-century church, St Winifred's, with surviving Norman tower and remains of medieval paintings; among many family memorials inside is one to Nicholas Wadham, whose fortune was used, following his death in 1609, to establish Wadham College in the University of Oxford.

1 Church and Coastguard Ways at St Ives

A delightful walk westwards from St Ives leads along a remote and wild coastline once watched assiduously by government 'revenue men' and coastguards

Above: Our walk starts from the picturesque harbour front at St Ives

Right: Situated behind Porthmeor Beach, Tate St Ives art gallery presents modern art created in or connected to Cornwall

In the days before modern transport, the scenic road from St Ives to St Just, along the north coast of the Land's End peninsula, was a rough track used for carrying loads by cart and wagon, horse or donkey. Before the track was made, people travelled more easily on foot along the coastal belt below the hills, through what is still today a palimpsest of ancient fields, first carved out by Bronze and Iron Age farmers. Until the early 20th century the field paths, with their sturdy punctuation marks of granite stiles, were used by locals to visit each other, to travel to church and to go to the St Ives market.

The coastal paths on the outer edge of this mosaic of ancient fields barely existed in earlier times. They were used by those heading to individual farms inland and were often mere links between paths down to coves.

In the Footsteps of 'Revenue Men'

As commerce and foreign wars increased, however, the coastline of southwest England came under much closer official scrutiny. When 19th-century smuggling was at its height, government 'revenue men' patrolled the wilder reaches of the coast to foil the 'freetraders'. In later years, the coastguard service also patrolled the coast on foot until

there were few sections that were not passable, by footpath at least. Linking these paths to create a continuous route for the walker was the final stage in the evolution of today's coastal footpath.

This walk heads along a remote and wild part of the West Cornwall coast, through a landscape of exquisite colours in spring and summer. The steep cliffs are not breached until the narrow Treveal Valley breaks through to the sea at River Cove. Here the route turns inland and plunges into lush green countryside. Field paths lead back towards St Ives over a sequence of granite stiles reminding you of a different world – one in which this journey was an everyday event for Cornish folk.

1 Church and Coastguard Ways at St Ives

Follow paths dating from a time when people travelled on foot out of necessity

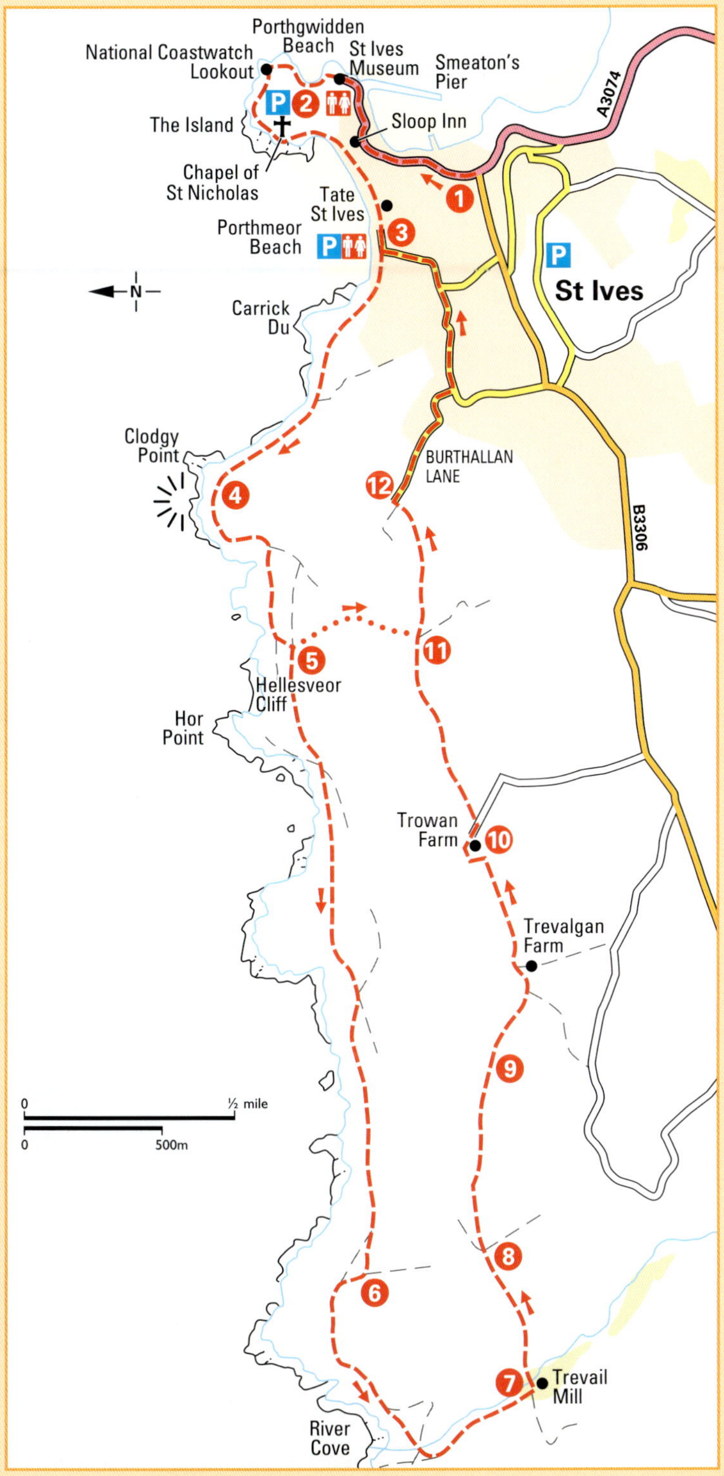

Distance 8 miles (12.9km)

Minimum Time 4hrs

Ascent/Gradient 394ft (120m) ▲▲▲

Level of Difficulty ●●●

Paths Coastal path can be quite rocky. Field paths, many stiles

Landscape Very scenic coast and small inland fields

Suggested Map OS Explorer 102 Land's End

Start/Finish Grid reference: SW 522408

Dog Friendliness Dogs on lead through grazed areas

Parking The Island car park, St Ives

Public Toilets Smeaton's Pier, Porthgwidden Beach or Porthmeor car park

1 Walk along the harbourfront, turning left before Smeaton's Pier, signed to 'St Ives Museum'. Where the road bends, go straight then right past St Ives Museum to Porthgwidden Beach.

2 Cross the car park, go down steps behind the National Coastwatch lookout, then follow a footway to Porthmeor Beach. Go along the beach. At the beach end, go up to the car park.

3 Go up steps beside the public toilets, then right past bowling and putting greens to the headlands of Carrick Du and Clodgy Point.

4 From Clodgy Point walk uphill and to the right. In about 0.5 mile (800m) go left by a small acorn signpost and lichened boulder.

5 Just past a sign for 'Hellesveor Cliff', turn right and follow the coast path. (A shorter version of the walk goes left to Point 11 here.)

6 Keep right at a junction to River Cove. On the other side of the cove, climb to where the path levels off and follow the inland path.

7 At a junction with a track, go left through a kissing gate, then follow signs past Trevail Mill. Go through another kissing gate and climb.

8 Cross a track and follow the hedged-in path. In about 40yds (36m) go left over a stile. Follow field-edges ahead over intervening stiles.

9 Keep in the field with a granite upright. Go over a stile, and where the field hedge bends right, head across to gates. Cross a stile and continue to another at Trevalgan Farm. Go between buildings; in 50yds (46m) turn left at a gate. Go right, cross a stile and on to Trowan Farm.

10 At Trowan Farm, pass a granite post; continue between houses, then go through a field gate. Follow field paths over stiles.

11 Cross a lane, then a stile and follow field edges. Pass a field gap on the left and turn left before a rusty gate. Go over two stiles and between hedges to a surfaced lane.

12 Turn right (Burthallan Lane) to a T-junction with the main road. Turn left and follow the road downhill to Porthmeor Beach.

2 Giant Steps and Staircases at Bedruthan

A tramp along this dramatic stretch of Cornish coastline leads past great sea stacks identified by the Victorians as the stepping stones of a giant

Below: Mussels growing on rocks at Bedruthan Steps

Bottom left: Steep steps down to the beach need to be used with care – but the descent is well worth the trouble

Bottom right: The stepping stones of the giant Bedruthan

The unremarkable countryside that lies inland from Bedruthan Steps belies the stupendous nature of the area's coastline. Green fields run to the sliced-off edges of 300ft (90m) cliffs. At the foot of the cliffs lie rock islands that at high tide are besieged by crashing waves and at low tide, spring from a smooth expanse of golden, sea-damp sand.

This was Victorian 'picturesque' at its most melodramatic and the area was popular with 'excursionists' in the late 19th century. The islands, or stacks, are portrayed as being the stepping stones of a legendary giant called Bedruthan, but this conceit blew in with the first of the Victorian tourists. The stacks acquired picturesque names such as 'The Queen Bess Rock', which, before losing its head to erosion, was said to resemble the figure of Elizabeth I, who never lost her head in any sense.

For many years, before tourists and tall tales of giants, there were flights of steps cut into the cliff faces, probably used by local people descending to collect seaweed and to land cargoes, legitimate or otherwise. Miners may also have sought access to the beach. There was 19th-century mining at Carnewas – the National Trust shop and tea room are housed in old mine buildings – and tin, copper and lead may have originally been extracted from tunnels, known as 'adits', at the base of the cliffs.

Iron Age fortresses

Today you can reach Bedruthan Beach down a secure staircase reached from the coast path, part way along the walk. From the top of the steps the coast path leads north towards Park Head, passing on the way the remains of Redcliff Castle, an Iron Age fortified settlement. From beyond Redcliff Castle, one of the finest views of Bedruthan Beach can be had; but do not go too close to the cliff edge.

The circuit of Park Head, via the pleasant cove of Porth Mear, rounds off the walk. You can walk out to the promontory of Park Head itself passing through the defensive banks of another Iron Age fortified settlement across the neck of the headland. From here the coast path leads back past Redcliff Castle and then on towards Carnewas.

2 Giant Steps and Staircases at Bedruthan

Enjoy glorious coastal views and see two sets of Iron Age remains

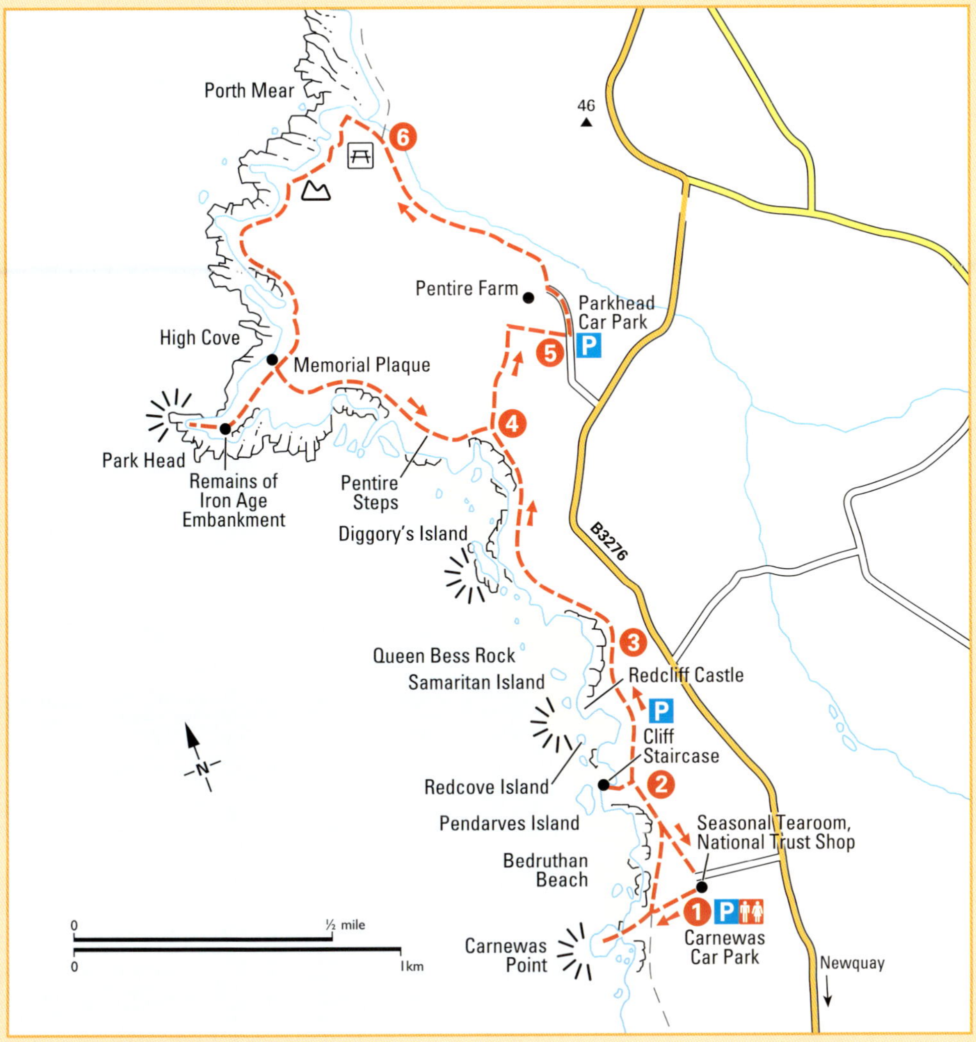

Distance 4.5 miles (7.2km)

Minimum Time 2hrs 30min

Ascent/Gradient 131ft (40m) ▲▲▲

Level of Difficulty ●●●

Paths Coastal paths and field paths. Coast path very close to unguarded cliff edges in some places. Take care in windy weather and with children and dogs. 1 stile

Landscape Spectacular cliffs and dramatic sea stacks

Suggested Map OS Explorer 106 Newquay and Padstow

Start/Finish Grid reference: SW 850691

Dog Friendliness Dogs on lead through grazed areas

Parking National Trust car park at Carnewas. Or at the National Trust Parkhead car park, grid reference: SW 851706, from where the walk can also be started at Point 5

Public Toilets Carnewas car park

1 From Carnewas car park, go through a gap in the wall to the right of the National Trust shop, then, in a few paces, bear off to the left at a junction. Follow the path to a crossing of tracks and go straight across and down a grassy path to the dramatic view from Carnewas Point of Bedruthan Beach and the sea stacks. Return to the crossing and follow a path left along the cliff edge. (Take heed of warning notices.) At a junction with a cobbled path, go left and descend down to a dip at Pendarves Point.

2 At a junction in the dip, go down left to reach the top of the cliff staircase. On re-ascending the staircase, go back uphill to the junction with the coast path and turn left past a National Trust sign for 'Carnewas'. Follow the coast path alongside a wooden fence and below a parking area.

3 Pass Redcliff Castle, then, where the path forks by a signpost, follow either fork to where they rejoin. Keep to the right of a stone wall that has tamarisk trees sprouting from it, to reach a wooden kissing gate. Continue along the open cliff top to reach a set of wooden gates on the right.

4 Go right through the smaller gate, then follow a permissive footpath along field-edges. Just before the buildings at Pentire, go right through a gate and follow field-edges to Parkhead car park.

5 Turn left and go left down a surfaced lane. Just before the Pentire buildings go through a gate on the right, signposted 'Porthmear Beach and Park Head'. Bear left across the field to a stile and gateway. Bear right down the next field to a wooden kissing gate in its bottom corner. Go through the gate and follow a path through a wetland area to join the coast path above Porth Mear.

6 Go left and follow the coast path uphill and then round Park Head. Take care when close to the cliff edges. At a memorial plaque above High Cove, divert to the promontory of Park Head itself. Return to the plaque and follow the coast path south to Point 4. Retrace your steps to Point 2, in the dip above the start of the cliff staircase. Follow the cobbled walkway uphill and back to Carnewas car park.

3 Rollercoaster Cliff Path to Port Quin

This exhilarating hike between the villages of Port Isaac and Port Quin on the North Cornish coast leads along airy clifftop paths commanding wonderful views

Above: The walk is not unusually long, but there is plenty of up and down

Right: Low tide at Port Isaac

Below: This way Port Quin – Varley Head and glorious North Cornish coastline

The North Cornish coast between the sea inlets of Port Isaac and Port Quin is a marvellous chaos of tumbled cliffs and convoluted hills. The price of this, for the keen walker, is a strenuous passage along the coastal footpath between the two. You rise and fall like a dipping gull, but without the same effortlessness. The inland return, across fields, to Port Isaac, is undramatic but is not strenuous.

A Protected Inlet at Port Isaac

Port Isaac is one of the West Country's most popular visitor destinations. The village is enclosed between the steep slopes of a narrow valley that reaches the sea at a protected inlet, a natural haven for vessels. It is this orientation to the sea that has produced the densely compact nature of the village. The sea was the common highway here, long before the modern road became so; until the early 20th century, trading ships brought coal, limestone, timber and other commodities to Port Isaac and carried away fish, farm produce, mineral ore and building stone. It is worth taking a little time to explore the village before setting off uphill on the coastal footpath. The path leads around the smooth-browed Lobber Point, then traces a remarkable rollercoaster route along the folded coastline to Kellan Head and on to Port Quin.

The Former Glories of Port Quin

There is a slightly haunted air about Port Quin today. It is a remote, silent place, yet in 1841 nearly 100 people lived here in a village of more than 20 households. Now only a few cottages remain, not all of them occupied permanently.

Port Quin survived until the 19th century on pilchard fishing and on coastal trade that involved the import of coal and lime in exchange for slate and lead from small mining concerns. Legend claims that most of the men of Port Quin were lost at sea in a fishing or smuggling disaster and that the womenfolk and children moved away. There was certainly rapid depopulation, but it may simply have been through emigration when mining failed and pilchard fishing declined in the late 19th century. The route you follow through the fields back to bustling Port Isaac must once have been a local highway between two thriving communities.

3 Rollercoaster Cliff Path to Port Quin

Rise to the challenge of a demanding route along the coast from Port Isaac

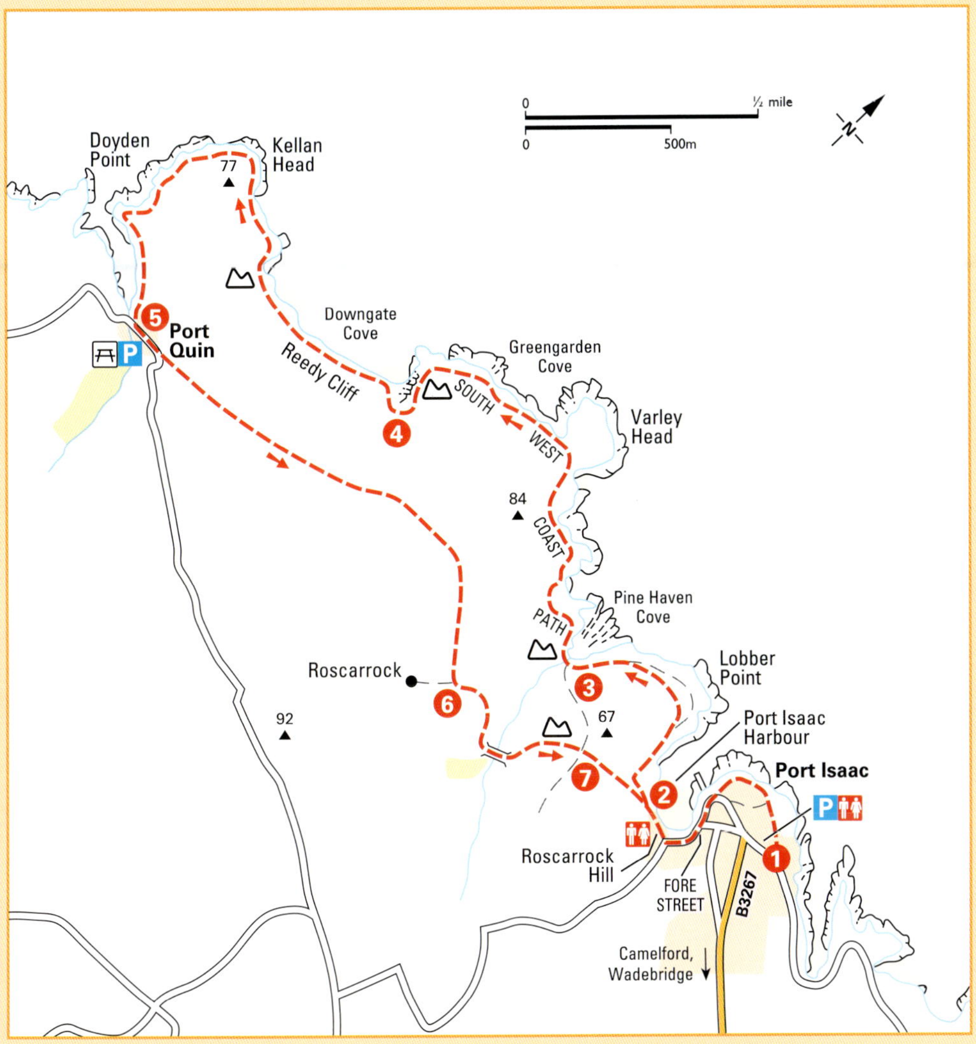

Distance 6 miles (9.7km)

Minimum Time 4hrs

Ascent/Gradient 984ft (300m) ▲▲▲

Level of Difficulty ●●●

Paths Good coastal and field paths, several sections of coast path run very close to unguarded cliff edges. May not be suitable for children and dogs, 14 stiles

Landscape Coastal scenery and inland fields, one wooded valley

Suggested Map OS Explorer 106 Newquay and Padstow

Start/Finish Grid reference: SW 999809

Dog Friendliness Dogs on lead in grazed areas

Parking Port Isaac, large car park on outskirts of village, can be busy in summer. Allowed on Port Isaac's stony beach, but this is tidal so you need to know tides. Small car park at Port Quin

Public Toilets Port Isaac car park and at start of Roscarrock Hill

1 Leave the Port Isaac main car park by the lower terrace and turn left along a track, keeping right where it branches, signposted 'Coast Path'. At the road, keep ahead and down Fore Street to reach the open space known as the Platt at the entry to the harbour. Just past Port Isaac Fishermen Ltd, turn right up Roscarrock Hill, signposted 'Coast Path'.

2 At the top of the lane, pass a public footpath sign on the left, then, in 30yds (27m), keep to the right of the gateway to a terrace of houses and bear right, signposted 'Coastal Footpath'. Follow the path round Lobber Point.

3 Descend to Pine Haven Cove and then cross over a wooden stile. (A wooden fence marches alongside the inside edge of the path from here on.) Climb steeply uphill and round the edge of an enormous gulf. Go over a stile at the end of the fenced section and cross Varley Head. The path ahead again runs close to the cliff edge and is fenced on the inside.

4 Just beyond a bench descend steep steps into Downgate Cove and Reedy Cliff. Follow the coast path up steep sections to reach the seaward edge of Kellan Head. Continue along the coast path to Port Quin.

5 Turn left at Port Quin and go up the road past the car park entrance. At a bend in the road bear off left, signposted 'Public Footpath to Port Isaac'. Go past cottages and keep up the slope to a gate with a stone stile. Dogs should be kept under control from here on. Follow the path along a hedge, then climb to a stile between two gates. Keep alongside the right-hand edge of the next fields.

6 Go over a stile beside an open gateway near Roscarrock, then turn left and follow the left field-edge to a wooden stile. Go left over the stile and down to the wooded valley bottom. Cross a wooden footbridge over a stream, then go over a stone stile. Keep ahead and climb very steeply through gorse to reach an open field slope. Keep ahead across the field (no apparent path), aiming to the left of a tall wooden pole that soon comes into view.

7 Cross a stone stile and follow the left field-edge downhill to a junction with the lane at Point 2. Turn right and retrace your steps to Port Isaac and the car park.

4 The Dramatic Geology of Crackington Haven

A fascinating coastal and inland ramble offers breathtaking views of the headlands, sea cliffs and rocks along this stretch of the North Cornish coast

Above left: Shoreline and village at Crackington Haven

Above: Crackington Haven beach and headland, looking towards Pencannow Point

Crackington Haven is famous for having given its name to a geological phenomenon, the Crackington Formation, a fractured shale that has been shaped into twisted and contorted forms. On the sheared-off cliff faces of the area, you can see the spectacular swirls and folds of this sedimentary rock that was 'metamorphosised' by volcanic heat and contorted by geological storms millions of years ago.

The name Crackington derives from the Cornish word for sandstone, *crak*. The very sound of the word hints at dangerous friability and dramatic decay. Written across the face of the vast cliffs seen on this walk are the anticlines (upward folds) and synclines (downward folds) that are characteristic of these great earth movements.

Grand Plans Unfulfilled

During the 18th and 19th centuries, Crackington Haven was a small port, landing coal and limestone and shipping out local agricultural produce and slate. Small coastal ships would anchor off the beach, or settle on the sands at low tide, in order to exchange cargoes.

Plans to expand Crackington into a major port were made in the early 19th century. The grandiose scheme aimed to build huge breakwaters to protect Crackington and the neighbouring Tremoutha Haven from the often huge Atlantic swells. Quays and docks were to be built inside the protected harbour. A rail link to Launceston was proposed and a new town planned for the Haven, which was to be renamed Port Victoria. As with many development plans of the time, the scheme did not materialise, otherwise the Crackington Haven might have been a dramatically different place.

A Geological Extravaganza

As you set out along the open cliff south from Crackington, the remarkable nature of the area's geology unfolds. Looking back from Bray's Point, you see the contortions in the high cliff face of Pencannow Point on the north side of Crackington.

Soon the path leads above Tremoutha Haven and up to the cliff edge beyond the domed headland of Cambeak. From here there is a breathtaking view of the folded strata and quartzite bands of Cambeak's cliffs. A short distance further on you arrive above Strangles Beach, where again you look back – this time on such fantastic features as Northern Door, a promontory of harder rock that is pierced by a natural arch created where softer shales have been eroded by the back and forth of the sea.

Heading inland, the second part of the walk descends into East Wood and the peaceful Trevigue Valley, itself part of a great geological extravaganza having once been a 'fjord' filled by the sea. Today much of the valley is a nature reserve and wandering down its leafy length is a splendid antidote to the coastal drama of the cliffs.

4 The Dramatic Geology of Crackington Haven

Read the story of the long-ago landscape written in the rocks

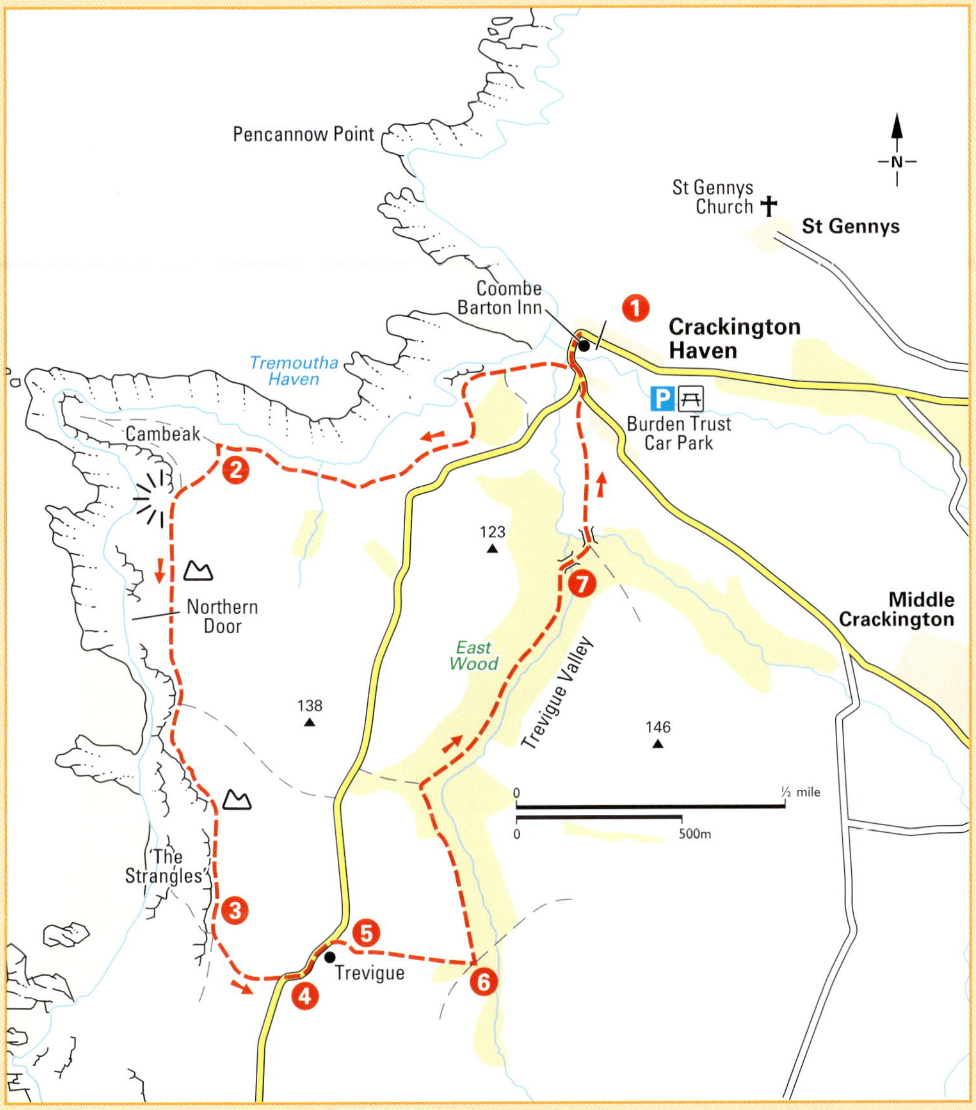

Distance 3.5 miles (5.7km)

Minimum Time 1hr 45min

Ascent/Gradient 270ft (82m) ▲▲▲

Level of Difficulty ●●●

Paths Good coastal footpath and woodland tracks. Can be very wet and muddy

Landscape Open coast and wooded valley

Suggested Map OS Explorer 111 Bude, Boscastle & Tintagel

Start/Finish Grid reference: SX 145969

Dog Friendliness Dogs on lead through grazed areas

Parking Crackington Haven car park. Can be busy in summer. Burden Trust car park and picnic area

Public Toilets Crackington Haven

1 From the Crackington Haven car park entrance go left across a bridge, then turn right at a telephone kiosk. Follow a broad track round to the left, between a signpost and an old wooden seat, then go through a kissing gate on to the coast path.

2 Eventually a stile leads to a steep, stepped descent to footbridges below Cambeak and a path junction. Keep left and follow a path up a sheltered valley on the inland side of the steep hill, then continue on the cliff path.

3 At the start of a stretch of low inland cliff, continue past a coast path post marked 'Trevigue'. Turn left at the next path and walk on until you reach a road by a National Trust sign for 'Strangles'.

4 Go left, past the farm entrance to Trevigue, then, in a few paces, turn right down a drive by the Trevigue sign. Afterwards bear off to the left across the grass to go through a gate with a yellow arrow.

5 Go directly down across the field, keeping to the left of a telegraph pole, and carry on until you reach a stile. Continue downhill as far as a second stile situated at the edge of a wood. Go down a pleasant tree-shaded path to a clear junction of paths in a shady dell by the river.

6 Turn sharp left at this junction, following the signpost towards Haven, and continue on the obvious path down the length of the wooded river valley.

7 Cross a footbridge, then turn left at a junction with a track. Cross another footbridge and continue to a gate by some houses. Follow a track and then a surfaced lane to the main road, then turn left to the car park.

5 Lee Bay and a North Devon Coast Classic

This simply beautiful excursion is one of lovely contrasts, from the seclusion and quiet beauty of Lee Bay to the craggy headland of Morte Point

Below: Wild flowers growing from a stone wall on Morte Point

Right: Along the cliff path towards Morte Point

Main picture: Lee Bay – a beautiful, sheltered spot

This part of the North Devon coast is very popular with holidaymakers, but you can escape pretty quickly from the crowds. After just a few minutes' walk from the car park at Mortehoe you will see tremendous views of the coast opening up to the left – on a clear day you can even see the Gower Peninsula in South Wales – and within half an hour you've left civilisation behind entirely.

This is a wonderfully varied route. You pass the ancient farmstead at Damage Barton to cross a lovely area of unimproved meadowland and penetrate deep down into the wooded Borough Valley to discover the secluded cove at Lee Bay. This is followed by a walk, with some tough sections along the coast path to the jagged headland of Morte Point, off which the white horses of the strong tidal race rage. It's a walk that shouldn't be rushed – you're advised to take it gently, and revel in the peace and solitude.

Flowers Galore in Lee Bay

Lee Bay is a very special place. The small village, with many cottages dating from the 16th and 17th centuries, lies along a narrow, winding lane running down to an attractive rocky cove. It's one of those places that many people never discover. Its sheltered position has encouraged a wealth of flowers, including hedges of naturalised fuchsia bushes, earning it the name 'Fuchsia Valley'.

If the tide's out when you reach Lee Bay, there's a fine alternative to the route given at Point 5. When you reach the cove, walk across the beach left, near the cliff, and along a deep gully through the rocks – with wonderful rockpools – to reach Sandy Cove. You rejoin the main route by climbing up a steep flight of wooden steps to the coast path.

5 Lee Bay and a North Devon Coast Classic

In one walk compare the atmospheres of inland valley, secluded cove and windy headland

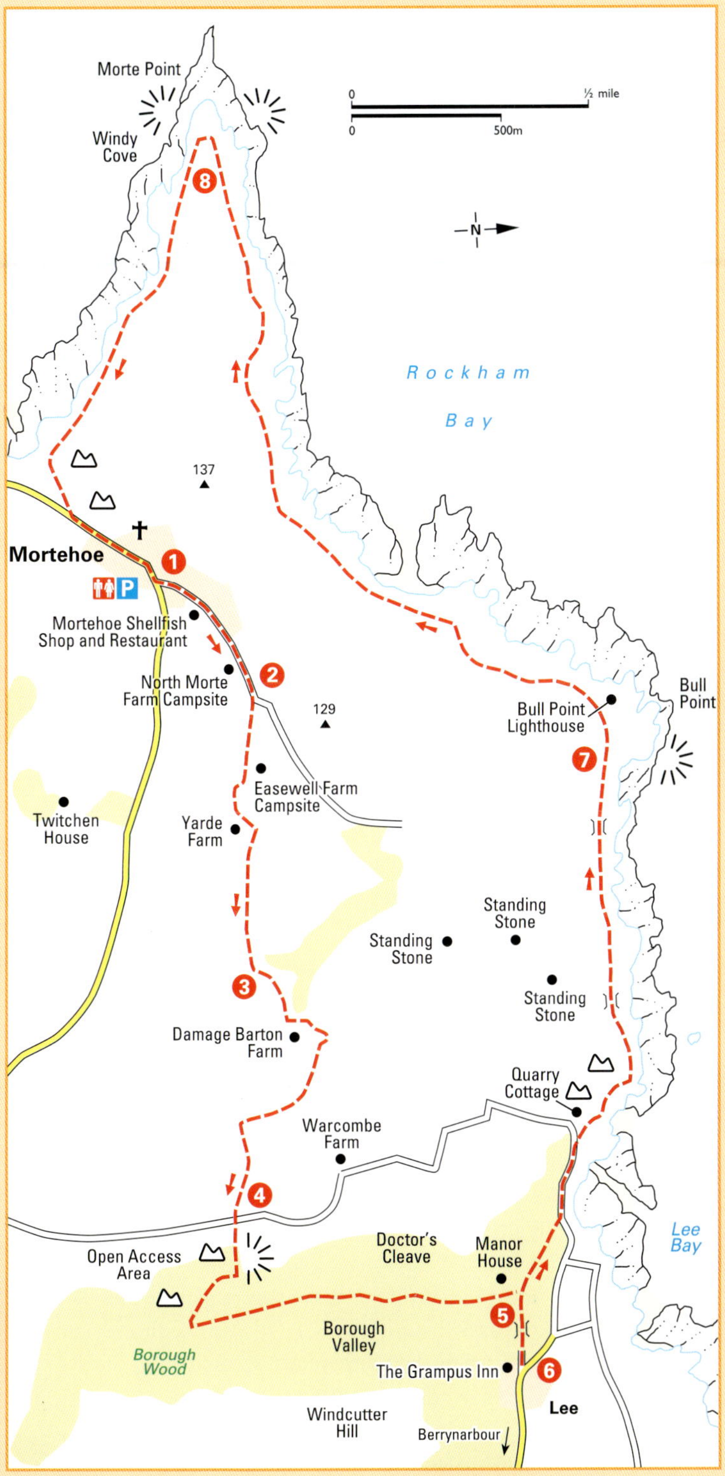

Distance 7 miles (11.3km)

Minimum Time 4hrs

Ascent/Gradient 426ft (130m) ▲▲▲

Level of Difficulty ●●●

Paths Fields, tracks and coast path, 15 stiles

Landscape Coastal farmland, wooded valleys and cliff tops

Suggested Map OS Explorer 139 Bideford, Ilfracombe & Barnstaple

Start/Finish Grid reference: SS 457452

Dog Friendliness Dogs under control at all times; some difficult stiles

Parking Car park at Mortehoe

Public Toilets Lee Bay and car park at Mortehoe

1 Take the lane opposite the car park at Morthoe, following the signs to 'Lighthouse & Lee'. Continue past North Morte Farm Campsite until you reach the end of the lane, where you find the private road to Bull Point lighthouse.

2 Follow footpath signs across Easewell Farm campsite and through the complex on the path to Lee. Leave over a stile with a pond right, and cross the field to Yarde Farm. Turn left uphill to a gate/stile into a field. Keeping the hedge on the left, go through a gate/stile, along the left edge of the next field, and through a gate/stile on to a tarmac drive.

3 Turn left through Damage Barton Farm, bearing right at the end of the buildings. Follow a footpath sign on a building to left, then a sign right, then left through a gate. Walk uphill to reach a footpath post. Go right towards another post, fork right up a track, then follow posts through a gate. Follow footpath signs to the next signpost atop a small hill. Turn left through a gate, then bear half right to a lane via a stile.

4 Cross the lane into an 'Open Access area'. Follow signs to Lee across a meadow. Go downhill into Borough Valley. At the bottom turn left.

5 Cross a stile and follow the valley down to emerge from the woods and turn right over a bridge and stile. Cross the field then a stile and turn right up the lane to The Grampus Inn.

6 Retrace your steps down the path to Lee Bay. Turn left uphill and join the coast path through a gate. Follow coast path signs to reach a stile/footbridge in a deep combe, then climb into another combe and rocky cove. Cross the footbridge/stile and walk up above Bull Point.

7 Follow coast path signs towards Morte Point. Go into a combe and up the other side. Cross Windy Lag and a stile to Rockham Bay; steps lead to the beach. Cross two stiles and go on towards Morte Point.

8 Follow the coast path signs past Windy Cove. Go through a gate, past Grunta Beach, then follow signs left, uphill, to join the road just below Mortehoe via a gate. Proceed uphill, bearing right to the start.

6 The Spectacular Heddon Valley on Exmoor

Past hanging oakwoods and a busy river, this delightful outing leads through a peaceful valley before visiting some of the highest sea cliffs in England

Within the Exmoor National Park, the deeply wooded Heddon Valley, leading to the stark cleft in the coastline at Heddon's Mouth, is a spectacular sight. There is no obvious main route into the valley, which you reach by turning off the A39 between Blackmoor Gate and Lynton, and then winding your way down miles of narrow lanes. While you're in the area take a look around the pretty village of Parracombe. Stop for a while to have a look at Parracombe Old Church, where nothing has been changed since the late 18th century when a new church was built nearer the village, then follow the course of the Heddon river as it descends through beautiful oak woodland to reach the sea at Heddon's Mouth.

Below: Rushing water and an abundance of green in Heddon Valley

Bottom: Heddon's Mouth, where the river meets the sea

Although only one-third of the Exmoor National Park is in Devon, around two-thirds of the National Park coastline lies within the county, and the stretch seen on this walk is the most awe-inspiring section. This walk is not recommended for anyone who suffers from vertigo, and dogs should be kept under control on the coast path where sheep often graze.

National Trust and English Nature

The National Trust owns 2,000 acres (810ha) of land here, much of which is designated a Site of Special Scientific Interest. The extensive oak woodlands, deep combes, coastal heath and tall cliffs combine to produce one of the most magnificent landscape areas in Devon. The National Trust information centre in the Heddon Valley is open from two weeks before Easter to the end of October.

The land immediately to the west and east of Heddon's Mouth Cleave rises very steeply up scree-covered slopes to a staggering 820ft (250m). Great Hangman, the highest coastal hill in southern England at over 1,000ft (305m), lies just beyond Holdstone Down to the west.

Exmoor, unlike Dartmoor, runs right to the coast, and the cliff scenery towards Combe Martin is quite superb. There is no access to the sea between Heddon's Mouth and Combe Martin, 5 miles (8km) to the west. There is a huge amount of wildlife interest here. The West Exmoor coastline holds one of two colonies of razorbills, guillemots and kittiwakes in North Devon. In the western oakwoods – unique to the west of Britain – you may find green and lesser spotted woodpeckers, pied flycatchers, wood warblers and nuthatches. The Heddon Valley is managed by English Nature to encourage the right plants for butterflies, in particular the rare high brown fritillary, and dark green and silver washed fritillaries.

6 The Spectacular Heddon Valley on Exmoor

Watch out for rare butterflies in the valley, then drink in views from towering sea cliffs

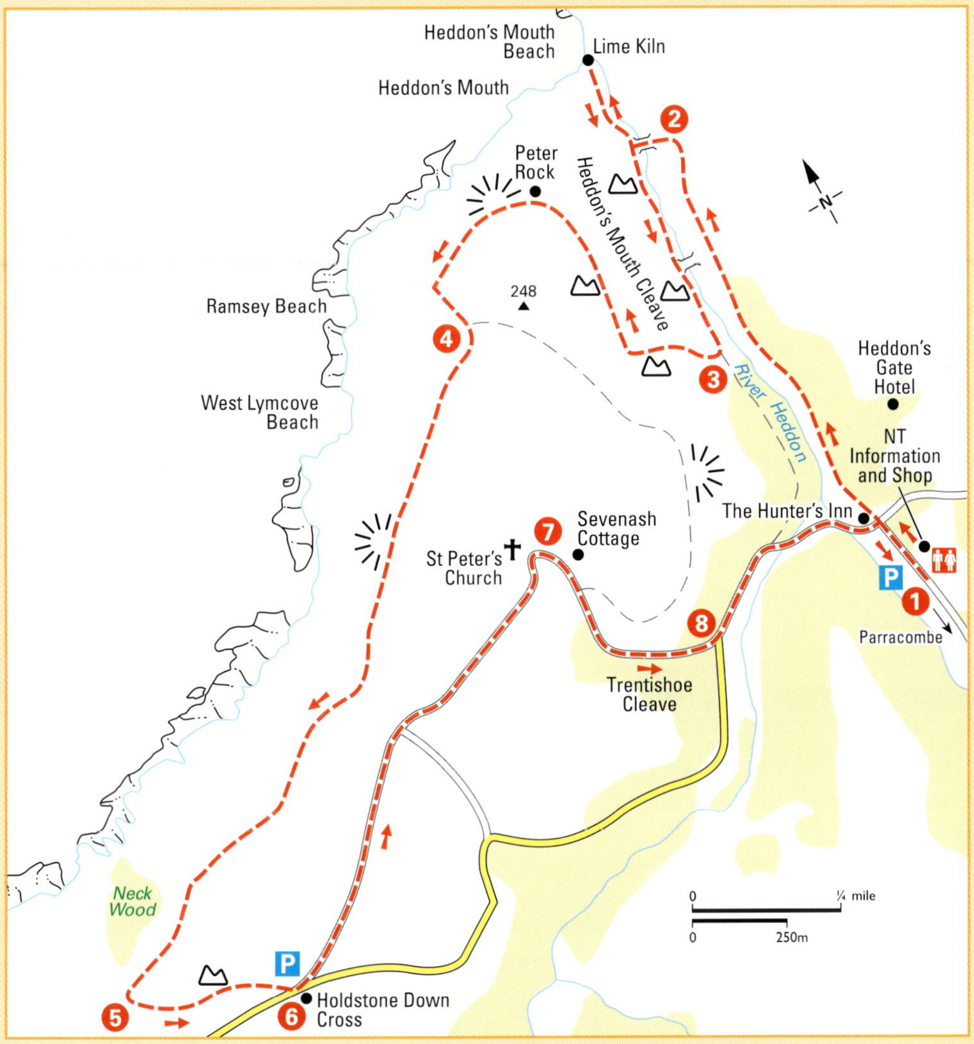

Distance 5 miles (8km)

Minimum Time 3hrs

Ascent/Gradient 787ft (240m) ▲▲▲

Level of Difficulty ●●●

Paths Wooded tracks, exposed coast path and quiet lanes

Landscape Deep, wooded river valleys and very high cliffs

Suggested Map OS Explorer OL9 Exmoor

Start/Finish Grid reference: SS 655481

Dog Friendliness Dogs to be kept under control at all times

Parking National Trust car park at Heddon Gate

Public Toilets Opposite car park

1 Walk towards The Hunter's Inn. Bear right past the building to walk along a wooded track signed 'Heddon's Mouth'. At the junction keep left, signed 'Heddon's Mouth only'. Where the path splits keep left, close to the river. Pass a stone bridge over the river and keep ahead.

2 Turn left over a wooden footbridge, then turn right and walk towards the coast to reach the 19th-century lime kiln above the rocky beach. Retrace your steps inland but stay on the west bank (river left) to pick up the coast path to Combe Martin. Pass through a gate, and keep ahead until a sign to Combe Martin directs you right, sharply uphill.

3 A steep zig-zag climb is rewarded with amazing views across the valley and inland. Keep going along the narrow path, which runs parallel to the valley to reach the coast above Heddon's Mouth, then turns left to run towards Peter Rock. The cliffs are more than 650ft (200m) high, and the path is narrow and exposed – take care. Continue along the path, which runs inland to meet a wall.

4 Turn right. Follow the coast path westwards for about 0.75 mile (1.2km), then follow signs through a gate, turn right, then through another gate to rejoin the cliff edge. Go through a gate above Neck Wood, cross the next field and pass through a gate on to open access land.

5 Immediately turn left uphill on a narrow path through bracken, then left again on a wider path. Head uphill, with the bank to the left, to reach the rough parking area and lane at Holdstone Down Cross, on the edge of Trentishoe Down.

6 Turn immediately left along the narrow lane, following signs for Trentishoe Church (the signpost here misleadingly points back the way you have come). Walk down the lane until you see the church above you on the left – this is a good place for a break.

7 Continue downhill below Sevenash Cottage to pass the point where there is an 'Access to coast path' sign pointing left. Walk straight on down Trentishoe Hill (this lane is unsuitable for vehicles) which runs through wooded Trentishoe Cleave.

8 Turn left at the valley bottom by two pretty white cottages. Walk along the lane past a footpath sign to the Heddon Valley on the left, cross over a small river, and then over the Heddon river just before The Hunter's Inn. Turn right to find your car.

7 Up through Hawk Combe onto Porlock Hill

A walk in a beautiful corner of coastal Exmoor mounts through ancient woodland onto open heath where you may encounter deer and wild ponies

Above: In their element – Exmoor ponies on Porlock Hill

Below: Beautiful contrasts on the Exmoor coast – flowering heather overlooking Porlock Bay

A wood used to be something that just happened: trees grew on a patch of ground too steep for the plough or in a place too far from the village to be cut for firewood. Sometimes a patch of trees in a field corner turns out to have been there since the ancient wildwood covered the land at the end of the Ice Age. This is shown by the number and variety of its plant species, in particular its lichens; and by certain sorts of tree, such as the small-leaved lime. The Exmoor coast is rich in such woodland and in Hawk Combe the woods are among the oldest in Somerset.

Ancient Oaks

On the sandstone soils and under the warm rainfall of the Exmoor combes the natural cover is an oak wood, specifically sessile oak. The more familiar common oak has its acorns on stalks, while on the sessile oak acorns grow straight on the twig; in addition, the sessile oak's leaves are longer and less rounded than those of the common oak.

Under the oaks grow native shrubs such as hazel and whitebeam. Our many sorts of native woodlice, leaf aphids and tree creepers flourish best on our native trees: they don't like nasty 'foreign' food like the horse chestnut. Dormice live in the hazel thickets, and the pied flycatcher darts through the green gloom. This bird prefers the western woods – some naturalists say that this is because the sessile oak, being lower and more spreading, gives better flight paths; others think it is just because these woods are allowed more creative neglect: rotten branches drop off, leaving handy nest holes.

Steep Demands on Porlock Hill

If the climb through the woods of Hawk Combe is a steep one for those on foot, the ascent along the A39 is an equally demanding one for those with wheels. The road climbs 800ft in a mile (24m in 1.6km), with the steepest part at the bottom. At one time extra horses were stationed at Porlock for attaching to the coaches here. Two-thirds of the way up the hill, until recently, stood a traditional AA phone box in black, retained as a memory of the days when steam would jet from your radiator and the helpful AA man would come on his motorbike with a can of water.

Modern cars can manage the ascent, although drivers unfortunate enough to stall their engines may have trouble with a hill start on a 1 in 4 gradient. Coming down, though, there's potential energy to be got rid of at roughly the rate of a one-bar electric fire. Those who neglect to engage low gear will end up with very hot brake discs – in Porlock car park you may catch the burnt-toast aroma of a car recently arrived from the west.

7 Up through Hawk Combe onto Porlock Hill

Take a steep climb through the wildwood for a sudden sea view

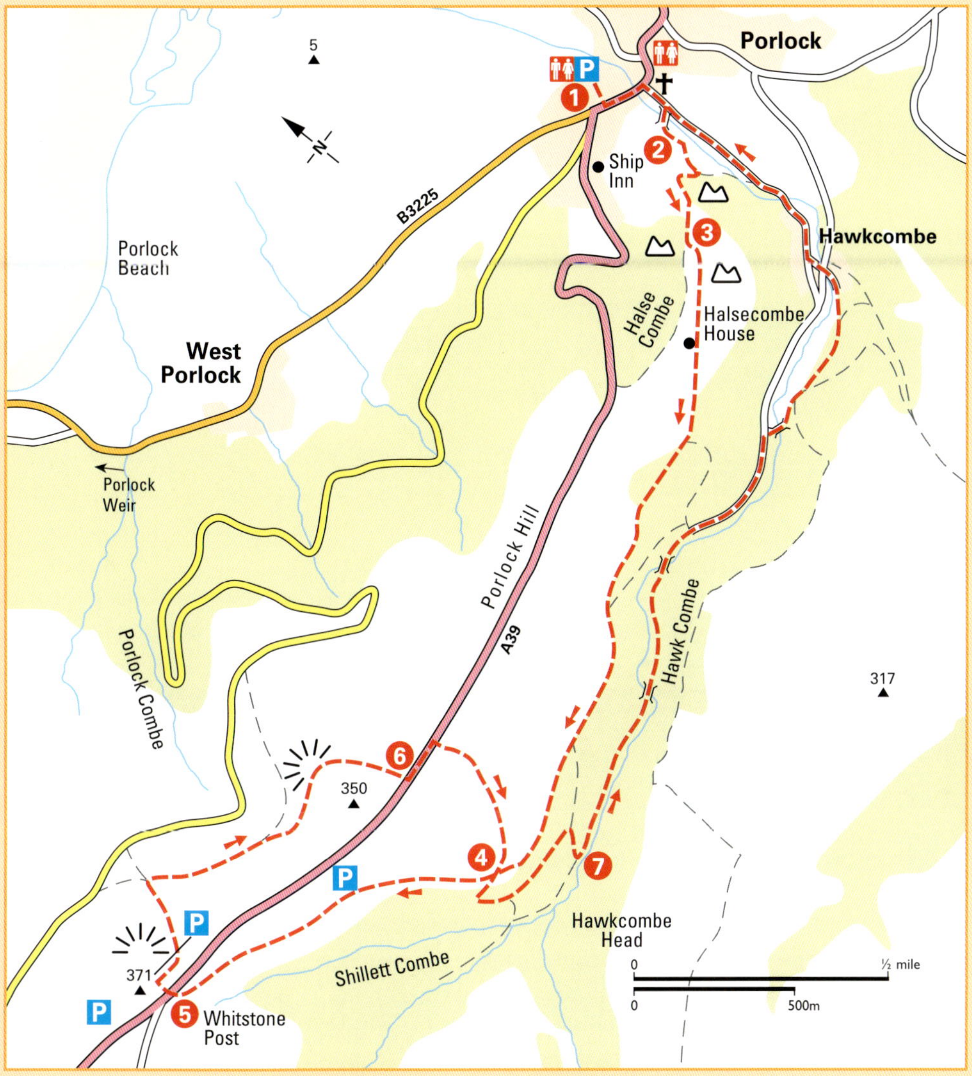

Distance 6 miles (9.7km)

Minimum Time 3hrs 15min

Ascent/Gradient 1,200ft (366m) ▲▲▲

Level of Difficulty ●●●

Paths Initial stiff climb then smooth, well-marked paths, no stiles

Landscape Steep woodland, leading on to open heath

Suggested Map OS Explorer OL 9 Exmoor

Start/Finish Grid reference: SS 885468

Dog Friendliness Deer and wild ponies so dogs must be under control

Parking Pay-and-display at Porlock Central Car Park; free parking at Whitstone Post, Point 5

Public Toilets At car park

1 Leave the car park at its top end, then turn left. Just before the church, turn right into Parsons Street. At a small parking area a bridleway sign for 'Hawkcombe' points upstream to a footbridge.

2 The path climbs through bamboo and laurel, to join another bridleway. This zig-zags steeply up through the wood, to pass below a wall with a small inset bench. At the top of this low wall, the paths then divide.

3 Turn left, still climbing, and at once bear left, signposted 'Hawkcombe', into a sunken path. Emerging at a white house, called Halsecombe, keep ahead to a field gate marked with a blue spot. Follow the left edge of a field, to the right-hand of two gates; the next gate leads back into woodland. Take the bridleway track ahead, gently descending. It becomes a terraced path, running near the top edge of the wood for a mile (1.6km) to reach a track.

4 Turn left down the track for just a few paces, and then turn right up a path between gorse bushes; the path then runs through bracken and heather, with views into the head of Hawk Combe. As the path enters a thicket of hawthorns, bear right to reach the road signpost at Whitstone Post.

5 Cross the A39 into a parking area, and then turn right down a heather path running parallel to the road. After roughly 110yds (100m), turn left down a broad track. Where it turns left, turn right on to a smaller track. This contours through gorse and heather, then rejoins the A39 at a cattle grid.

6 Turn left, then right on a track signposted to Hawkcombe. Cross two cattle grids to reach Point 4 of the outward route. Keep walking along the track for another 125yds (114m), then turn left into a small, terraced path. This runs gently downhill for 0.25 mile (400m), to meet a wider path. Turn sharp right down to the stream.

7 A broad path runs downstream. On reaching some houses, this path becomes a tarred lane and descends through a wood. At a high wall on the right a footpath sign points to a footbridge. Over this, the path ascends gently through the woods for 220yds (201m). Bear left on a crossing path and gently descend to reach a street. Turn left to cross over the stream, then turn right into Parsons Street and Porlock.

8 Straight to the Parrett's Mouth

Rather than offering cliffpaths and views of crashing waves, here is a coastal walk in Somerset that heightens your appreciation of flatlands reclaimed from the sea

Above left: An idyllic autumn scene on the Somerset Levels near Highbridge

Above: River Parrett near Huntspill

The starting point for this walk was once several miles out to sea, for at one time the shoreline was at the foot of the Polden Hills. Since the last Ice Age the tidal flow up and down the Bristol Channel has created the bank of clay mud on which you stand in the course of this walk.

Huntspill Church and the nearby houses are built on Plymor Hill. At just 2ft (60cm) high, this must be the lowest hill in the country; even so, during the floods of 1981, the people who live here were glad of the extra altitude.

Humans have drained the land behind this mud ridge to form the Somerset Levels and moors. The watercourses that drain all that fertile 'summer land' – the Kings Sedgemoor Drain, the Parrett itself – would also let the sea back in at every high tide, and so they must be closed off. You will pass the barrier that closes the River Brue in the course of the walk. On the left you see a concrete pillbox, a coastal defence from the Second World War; on the other side, across the River Brue, you see a defence built against an enemy even more dangerous than the Germans – the sea itself.

The Environment Agency, currently responsible for keeping the sea out of Britain, is coming to realise that such Canute-like ways of fighting the ocean will become less and less effective as global warming brings a rise in the sea, more autumn storms and higher rainfall to swell the rivers behind. In November 2000 the then deputy prime minister, John Prescott, was impressed by a Dutch system of overflow areas: allowing floodwaters into certain areas for pumping out afterwards. 'Britain needs such a system,' he declared – but in the Somerset Levels, Britain already has it.

Hinkley Point – and its Nature Reserve

On the other side of the estuary stands what is either a noble and striking focus for the rather flat landscape, or a sinister horror – which of the two you see depends largely on which newspaper you believe. Is the nuclear power station at Hinkley Point an environmental nightmare, spreading radioactive pollutants and threatening us all with cancer and worse? Or is it part of the only medium-term solution to carbon dioxide emissions and global warming?

There is a certain irony in the fact that within its fence the Hinkley Point power station harbours a small but valuable nature reserve protecting the home of 29 types of butterfly and the rare bee orchid, and is a haven for the nightingale as well.

8 Straight to the Parrett's Mouth

Walk where humans won a war with the sea

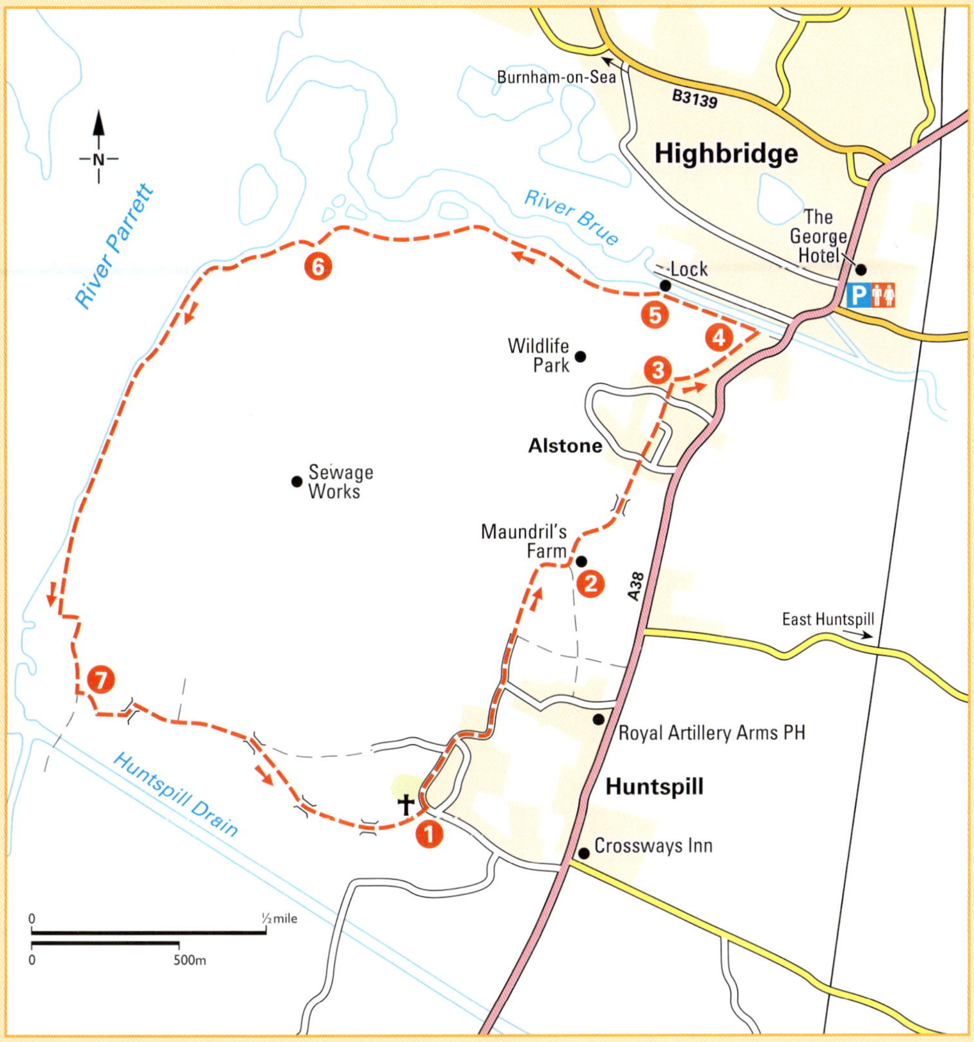

Distance 4.5 miles (7.2km)

Minimum Time 1hr 45min

Ascent/Gradient Negligible ▲▲▲

Level of Difficulty ●●●

Paths Town paths, wide, surfaced track and fields, 16 stiles

Landscape Level ground, mudflats and sea

Suggested Map OS Explorer 153 Weston-Super-Mare

Start/Finish Grid reference: ST 305455

Dog Friendliness Good, since half of walk is along open shoreline

Parking Street parking at Huntspill Church

Public Toilets Just off-route in Highbridge

1 Head away from the church, keeping the houses on your right and trees on your left (with the sea behind them). The street, Church Road, bends right then back to the left: at the next bend keep ahead in Longlands Lane, which becomes a hedged path between ditches. Join a concrete track that bends right to Maundril's Farm.

2 Turn left on a waymarked footpath between huge sheds. Cross a track to an overgrown path ending at a stile, and turn half right to cross a field to a footbridge. A fenced path leads to a street and continues beyond it. It passes along the end of a second street, to reach a third.

3 Again a tarred path continues opposite, to emerge into a field. A fenced-off way runs round the edge of the field to an overgrown path ending at a stile. Continue along the right-hand edge of the field to its corner.

4 Here a walled way leads out to the right. Take this if you wish to cross the bridge to visit Highbridge. Opposite the burnt-out Highbridge Inn is a memento of the former seaport: a handsome Victorian warehouse in brick and stone. (Toilets are found across the roundabout in a car park on the right.) The main walk continues from Point 4 along the field-edge near the River Brue, with its banks of brown mud, to reach the sea lock.

5 Bear left for roughly 30yds (27m) until you reach a stile, and then follow a path on the flood bank alongside the tidal river. As the banking reaches the sea, a stile and gate on the right lead on to the concrete top of further sea defences.

6 Follow what is in effect a concrete track along the shoreline for 1 mile (1.6km). Here the limestone blocks, broken up by the sea, have fairly easy-to-find fragments of large ammonites. Where the concrete disappears under grass bear left to a gate, and cross the earth barrier to reach a tarred lane. After 150yds (137m) this bends inland to a lay-by, with a stile on the left just beyond.

7 Cross a stile and head towards Huntspill Church on a path with a hedge and ditch on your left. Cross a footbridge on the left – field boundaries are water sometimes backed by a hedge. Turn right along the hedge to join a track. After 300yds (274m), watch out for a footbridge on the right. Turn left until blocked by a ditch, then right to a footbridge. Head straight for the church, over stiles and a bridge: enter the churchyard through a kissing gate.

9 The Serpentine Route to Cadgwith

This engaging ramble takes a wandering route between coast and countryside through the serpentine rock landscape of Cornwall's beautiful Lizard Peninsula

Above: The Devil's Frying Pan

Below: Looking down from the cliffs on Cadgwith harbour

Below right: Colour swirl – serpentine rock at Cadgwith

The serpentine rock of the Lizard Peninsula is fascinating – by name and by nature. Its geological label, serpentinite, fails to slither quite so easily off the tongue as does its popular usage 'serpentine'. The name derives from the sinuous veins of green, red, yellow and white that wriggle across the dark-green or brownish-red surface of the rock. The best-quality serpentine is highly desirable because it can be easily carved and shaped and can be polished to a beautiful sheen.

Height of 19th-century Fashion

In the 19th century serpentine furnishings were the height of fashion and the material was used for shop fronts and fireplaces. The industry declined in the 1890s, however, partly due to the vagaries of fashion but also because it turned out that the colourful stone of the Lizard decayed quickly in polluted urban atmospheres. Serpentine became less popular as cheaper, more resilient marble from Italy and Spain began to dominate the market. Today serpentine craftsmen still operate in small workshops on the Lizard and you can buy serpentine souvenirs at Lizard Village. Throughout this walk there are stiles built of serpentine; their surfaces are mirror-smooth and slippery from use. Admire, but take care when they are wet.

The walk first takes a suitably wandering route inland to the sleepy village of Ruan Minor, from where a narrow lane leads down to the Poltesco Valley. At the mouth of the valley is Carleon Cove, once the site of water wheels, steam engines, machine shops, storehouses and a factory in which serpentine was processed. Only a few ruins remain. A narrow harbour pool, almost stagnant now, is dammed on the seaward side by a deep shingle bank where once there was an outlet to the sea. From here, during the heyday of Carleon's serpentine industry, barges loaded with finished pieces were towed out during spells of fine weather to cargo ships awaiting offshore.

Thatched Cottages at Cadgwith

From Carleon Cove the walk follows the coast path to Cadgwith, an archetypal Cornish fishing village. Cadgwith has a number of thatched cottages, a rare sight in windy Cornwall, although a covering of wire-mesh is a wise precaution against storm damage. Cadgwith still supports a fleet of fishing boats and is given an enduring identity because of it. Beyond the village the coast path leads to the Devil's Frying Pan, a vast gulf in the cliffs caused by the collapse of a section of coast that had been undermined by the sea. From here the path leads along the edge of the cliffs before the route turns inland to the Church of the Holy Cross at Grade. Beyond the church you find the ancient St Ruan's Well and the road back to the start.

9 The Serpentine Route to Cadgwith

Visit a still-working Cornish fishing village – and see 'the Devil's Frying Pan'

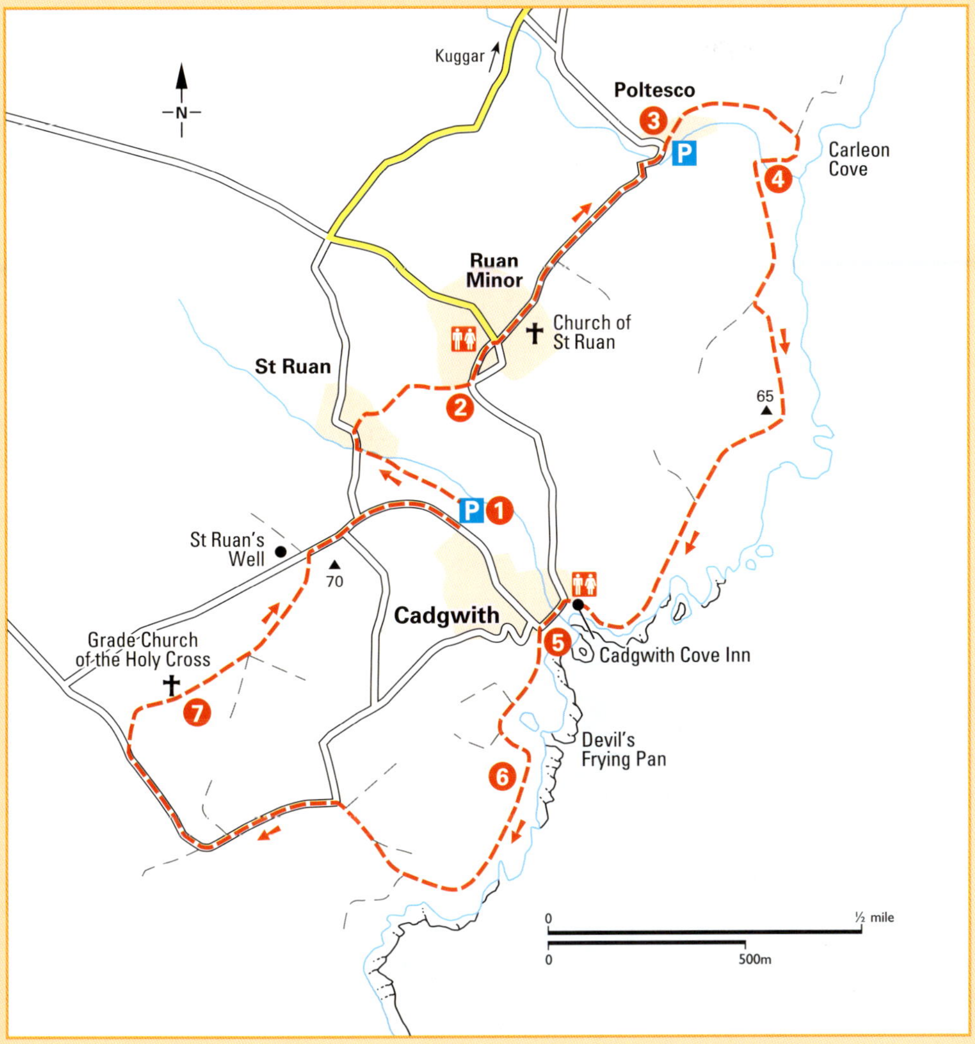

Distance 4.5 miles (7.2km)

Minimum Time 3hrs

Ascent/Gradient 230ft (70m) ▲▲▲

Level of Difficulty ●●●

Paths Very good, occasionally rocky in places, rock can be slippery when wet

Landscape Landlocked lanes and woodland tracks, coastal footpaths high above the sea

Suggested Map OS Explorer 103 The Lizard

Start/Finish Grid reference: SW 720146

Dog Friendliness Can let dogs off lead on coastal paths, but please keep under strict control on field paths

Parking Cadgwith car park. About 350yds (320m) from Cadgwith. Busy in summer

Public Toilets Ruan Minor and Cadgwith

1 Go left along a grassy ride below the car park, to a stile. Continue through a gate and into woodland. Turn right at a lane, then on the corner go up a track and continue to the main road at Ruan Minor.

2 Go left and, just beyond the shop, turn left down a surfaced path. Rejoin the main road by a thatched cottage. (You may want to take advantage of the fact that there are toilets just before the road). Cross diagonally to the right, then go down a lane past the Church of St Ruan.

3 In roughly 0.3 mile (500m), just past an old mill and a bridge, turn right at a T-junction to reach the car park at Poltesco. Go across the car park and from its far end follow a trackway, signposted to 'Carleon Cove'. On the track go right at a junction.

4 Go over a wooden bridge above the cove, then turn left at a T-junction and again turn left in roughly 0.25 mile (400m), where the path branches. Go through a kissing gate and continue along the cliff-edge path to Cadgwith. At the road, turn left.

5 Follow a narrow path, signposted 'Coast Path'. By a house gateway, go left up a surfaced path, signposted 'Devil's Frying Pan'. At an open area turn left, pass Townplace Cottage, then cross a meadow to reach the Devil's Frying Pan itself.

6 Keep on the coast path and at a junction, just past a chalet studio, follow a path inland to a T-junction with a rough track. Turn left and then, at a public lane, go left again and after roughly 0.5 mile (800m) turn right along a track to Grade Church.

7 Follow the left-hand field-edge behind the church, then go over a stile into the next field to reach a lane. St Ruan's Well is opposite diagonally left. Turn right for 200yds (183m), then branch off right between stone pillars to return to the car park.

10 A Glimpse of Old Cornwall at Polruan

This magical walk seems to lead back in time as it takes you from Polruan through the ancient parish of Lanteglos, with views of the Fowey estuary and Lantic Bay

Below: Looking from Fowey across the busy waters of the estuary at Polruan

Main picture: Greenery above dramatic Lantic Bay, and a beach doubtless once used by smugglers

There are parts of Cornwall so encompassed by the sea that they seem genuinely out of this modern world. The village of Polruan on the estuary of the River Fowey is one such place: the green headland on which it stands has the sea on its southern shore and is bounded to the north by the calm, tree-lined tidal creek of Pont Pill. The village can be reached by land only along fairly minor roads that detour at some length from Cornwall's main spinal highways. Yet Polruan lies just across the estuary from the bustling town of Fowey and a regular passenger ferry runs between the two.

Old Cornwall

Polruan and its surrounding parish of Lanteglos are redolent of old Cornwall. Prehistoric settlers found a natural refuge on the narrow headland on which it stands. Christian 'saints' and medieval worshippers set up chantries and chapels in the sheltered hollows; merchants prospered from the lucrative sea trade into Fowey's natural harbour. During the wars of the 14th and 15th centuries, Fowey ships harried foreign vessels, and because of their outstanding seamanship, earned themselves the admiring sobriquet of 'Fowey Gallants'.

The entrance to the estuary was protected from attack by a chain barrier that could be winched across the river's mouth from blockhouses on either bank. In peacetime the Gallants continued to raid shipping of all types until Edward IV responded to complaints from foreign merchants, and several English ones, by confiscating ships and by having the protective chain removed. Resilient as always, the seamen of Fowey and Polruan turned their hands to fishing and smuggling instead.

The peaceful countryside near Polruan was once owned by wealthy medieval families whose members played a major part in organising the freebooting activities of Polruan seamen. Fortunes made through piracy were turned to legitimate trade and to farming and land management, and the delightful landscape is the product of long-term land ownership and rural trade. The second part of the walk leads back to the sea, to the steep headland of Pencarrow and to the dramatic amphitheatre of Lantic Bay with its splendid beach, an old smugglers domain if ever there was one. From here, the coastal footpath leads airily back to Polruan and to the rattle and hum of an estuary that has never ceased to be alive with seagoing.

10 A Glimpse of Old Cornwall at Polruan

Gaze down on waters once dominated by the 'Fowey Gallants'

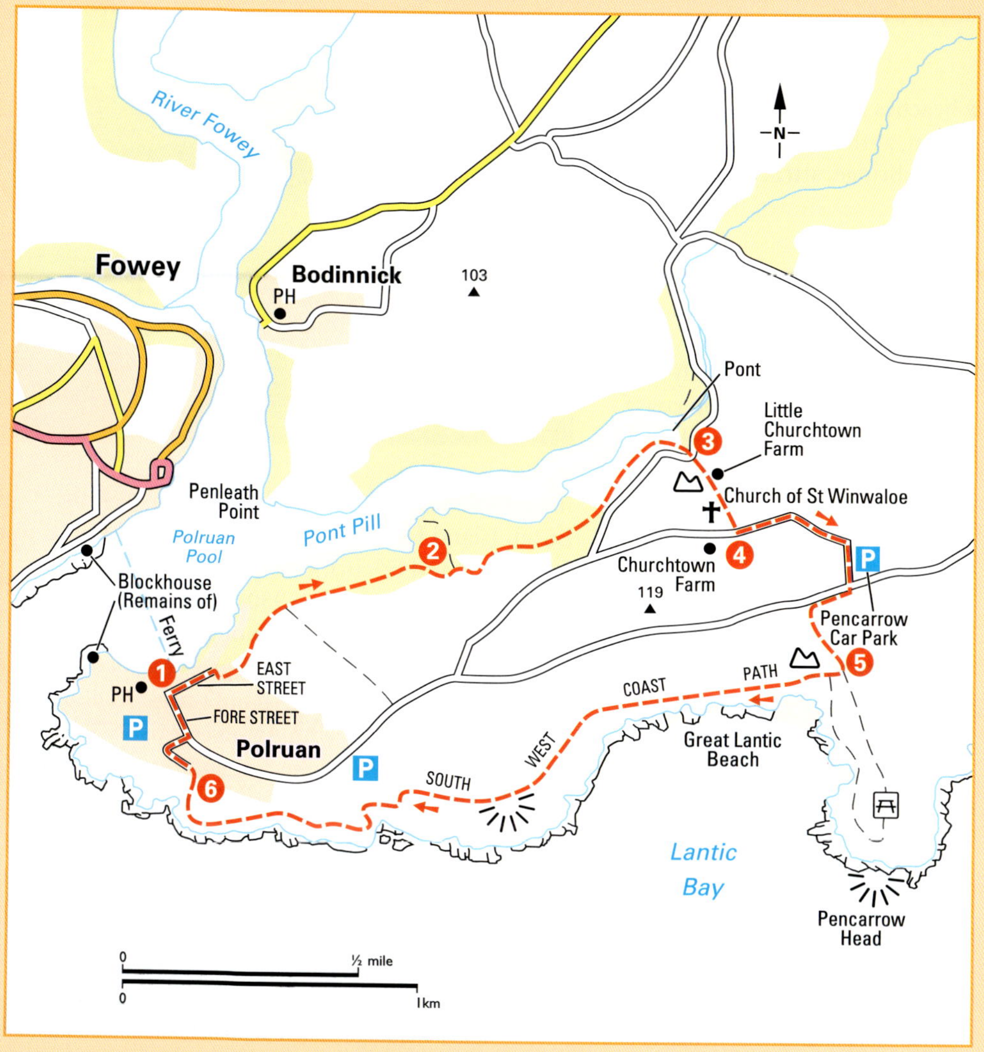

Distance 4 miles (6.4km)

Minimum Time 3hrs 30min

Ascent/Gradient 754ft (230m) ▲▲▲

Level of Difficulty ●●●

Paths Good throughout, can be very muddy in woodland areas during wet weather

Landscape Deep woodland alongside tidal creek, open coastal cliffs

Suggested Map OS Explorer 107 St Austell & Liskeard

Start/Finish Grid reference: SX 126511

Dog Friendliness Notices indicate dogs on lead through grazed areas

Parking Polruan. An alternative start to the walk can be made from the National Trust Pencarrow car park (Point 4 SX 149513). You can also park at Fowey's Central Car Park, then catch the ferry to Polruan

Public Toilets Polruan

1 Walk up from the Quay at Polruan, then turn left along East Street, by a telephone box and a seat. Go right, up steps, signposted 'To the Hills' and 'Hall Walk'. Go left at the next junction, then keep along the path ahead. Keep right at a junction and pass a National Trust sign, 'North Downs'.

2 Turn right at a T-junction with a track, then in just a few paces, bear off left along a path signposted 'Pont and Bodinnick'. Reach a wooden gate giving on to a lane. Don't go through the gate, but instead bear left and go through a footgate. Follow a path established by the National Trust and eventually descend some steep wooden steps.

3 At a T-junction with a track, turn right and climb uphill. It's worth diverting left at the T-junction to visit Pont. On this route, reach a lane. Go left for a few paces then, on a bend by Little Churchtown Farm, bear off right through a gate signed 'Footpath to Church'. Climb steadily to reach the Church of St Winwaloe.

4 Turn left outside the church and follow a narrow lane. At a T-junction just beyond Pencarrow car park, cross the road and go through a gate, then turn right along the field-edge to go through another gate. Turn left along the field-edge.

5 At the field corner, turn right on to the coast path and descend very steeply. (To continue to Pencarrow Head go left over the stile and follow the path on to the headland. From here the coast path can be rejoined and access made to Great Lantic Beach.) Follow the coast path for about 1.25 miles (2km), keeping to the cliff edge ignoring any junctions.

6 Where the cliff path ends, go through a gate to a road junction. Cross the road then go down School Lane. Turn right at 'Speakers Corner', then turn left down Fore Street to reach the Quay at Polruan.

12 Dartmouth and a Spectacular Castle

An easy round along the beautiful Devon cliffs passes above a succession of coves on its way to Blackstone Point and historic Dartmouth Castle

Above: Deadman's Cove with the mouth of the Dart in the distance

Right: In beautiful Devon countryside, historic Dartmouth and Kingswear occupy opposite banks of the river Dart

Dartmouth seems to have everything. Occupying a commanding position on the banks of the River Dart, the town has a rich and illustrious history. With its sheltered, deep-water harbour it developed as a thriving port and shipbuilding town from the 12th century. By the 14th century it enjoyed a flourishing wine trade, and thereafter benefited from the profits of piracy for generations. In 1620 the Pilgrim Fathers set sail for North America from Dartmouth in the *Mayflower* and the *Speedwell* before being forced back then departing once more from Plymouth. A plaque on the quay commemorates the sailing of the ships. Thomas Newcomen, who produced the first industrial steam engine, was born here in 1663.

Haven for Pleasure Craft

Today pleasure craft and the tourist industry have taken over in a big way – the annual Royal Regatta has been a major event since 1822 – but Dartmouth has lost none of its charm. One of its attractions is that there are many ways of getting there: by bus, using the town's park-and-ride scheme; by river, on a steamer from Totnes; by sea, on a coastal trip from Torbay; by steam train, from Paignton; or on foot along the coast path.

The 15th-century Dartmouth Castle enjoys an exceptionally beautiful position at the mouth of the Dart. Replacing the 1388 fortalice of John Hawley, it was one of the most advanced fortresses of the day and, with Kingswear Castle opposite (of which only the tower remains) was built to protect the homes and warehouses of the town's wealthy merchants. A chain was slung across the river mouth between the two fortifications, and guns fired from ports in the castle walls. Visitors can experience a representation of life in the later Victorian gun battery that was established.

A record of 1192 infers that there was a monastic foundation on the site, leading to the establishment of St Petrock's Church, rebuilt in Gothic style within the castle precincts in 1641–42. Earlier, a single-storey artillery fort had been built at Bayard's Cove before 1534 to protect the harbour. You can still see the gunports and the remains of a stairway leading to a walled walk above.

12 Dartmouth and a Spectacular Castle

View the sea approach to Dartmouth and the fortress that guarded the mouth of the River Dart

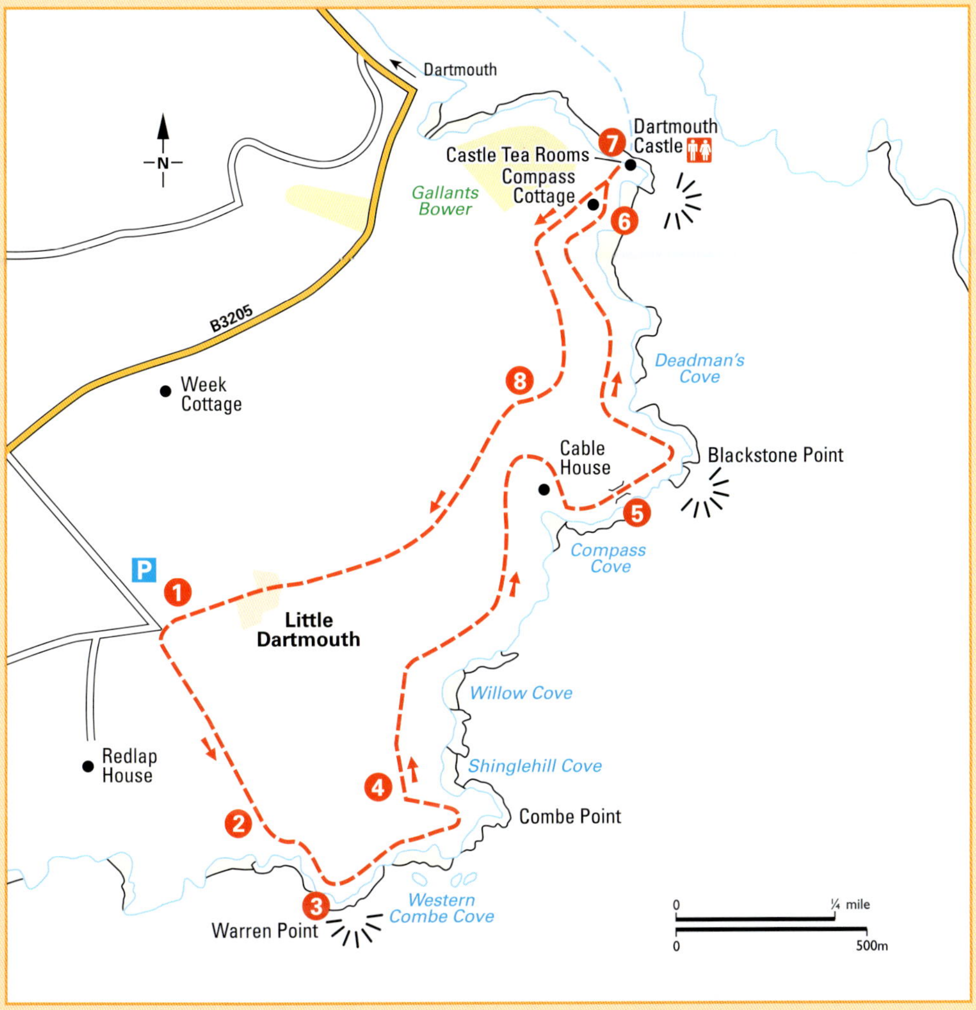

Distance 3.5 miles (5.7km)

Minimum Time 2hrs

Ascent/Gradient 115ft (35m) ▲▲▲

Level of Difficulty ●●●

Paths Easy coastal footpath and green lanes, 1 stile

Landscape Farmland, cliff tops and river estuary

Suggested Map OS Explorer OL20 South Devon

Start/Finish Grid reference: SX 874491

Dog Friendliness Livestock in some fields; on lead at Little Dartmouth

Parking National Trust car parks at Little Dartmouth

Public Toilets Dartmouth Castle

1 The car parks at Little Dartmouth are signposted off the B3205 (from the A379 Dartmouth-to-Stoke Fleming road). Go through the right-hand car park, following the signs 'Coast Path Dartmouth'. Go through a kissing gate, keeping the hedge to your right. Walk through the next field, then through a gate and another kissing gate to join the coast path.

2 Turn left. There are lovely views west to Start Point and east to the Day Beacon above Kingswear. The coast path runs inland from the cliff edge, but you can always walk out on to Warren Point. (A plaque reveals that the Devon Federation of Women's Institutes gave this land to the National Trust in 1970.)

3 From Warren Point follow the coast to pass above Western Combe Cove (with steps down to the sea) and then Combe Point. Take care – it's a long drop to the sea from here.

4 Rejoin the coast path through an open gateway in a wall and follow it above Shinglehill Cove. The path turns inland, passes a pond and follows a track, then bears right along the back of Willow Cove. It passes above woods (with a field left) and then climbs to pass through a gate. Follow the yellow arrow ahead to reach a footpath post, then turn sharp right down the valley, bearing right at the bottom to a stile as signed. Follow the path on, and through a gate near Compass Cove.

5 Take the coast path left over a footbridge, and continue towards Blackstone Point. The path turns inland to run along the side of the estuary through deciduous woodland.

6 The path meets a surfaced lane opposite Compass Cottage; keep ahead on to the lane and immediately right again steeply downhill. Follow coast path signs right to zig-zag steeply down then up steps to reach a turning space, then go right down steps to reach the castle and café.

7 Retrace your route up the steps, then turn left up the lane to Point 6. Turn left to pass Compass Cottage, and go straight up the lane (signposted 'Little Dartmouth') and through a kissing gate on to National Trust land.

8 The path runs along the top of a field and through a five-bar gate on to a green lane. Go through a gate and the farmyard at Little Dartmouth and carry on ahead on a tarmac lane to the car park.

13 Birds, Flowers and Jurassic Cliffs

Combining serene river meadows with an easy stretch of coastal paths, this is an ideal family walk and leads over red sandstone cliffs with a long history

Above: The yellow horned poppy (*Glaucium flavum*) growing on the banks of the River Otter

Right: The walk heads coastwards

Peaceful, tranquil, lush, idyllic – these are all words that could easily be applied to the first part of this walk, a stroll along the banks of the River Otter. Then after the river wends its way to meet the sea just east of Budleigh Salterton, the walk continues along the top of the red sandstone cliffs typical of this area – but the coast path here is not in any way heart-thumpingly strenuous.

Otter Estuary Nature Reserve

The estuary was much more extensive in the past, and 500 years ago cargo ships could travel upriver as far as Otterton. Today the estuary provides a haven for all kinds of birdlife, best seen between October and March. The Otter Estuary Nature Reserve, south of White Bridge, is a Site of Special Scientific Interest (SSSI) and a nationally important wildlife habitat. Oystercatchers, dunlins and other wading birds come to feed here; large flocks of waders and ducks, such as wigeons and teal, attract peregrine falcons, sparrowhawks and mink. To catch the action, about 0.25 mile (400m) from the start of the main walk take a small path right towards the river to a birding hide. Stop for a while and watch the activity on the waters below – there's always something happening.

On the Cliffs

The coastal section of the walk runs along part of the 95-mile (153km) Jurassic Coast, England's first natural UNESCO World Heritage Site, designated in 2001. Quartzite pebbles on the beach at Budleigh Salterton date from Triassic times.

The mid-section of the walk brings us within sight of Otterton, a pleasant village with many traditional cob and thatch buildings. St Michael and All Angels Church is most impressive. There was a Saxon church here before the Norman Conquest, rebuilt by Benedictine monks when they established a priory in the 12th century. The main monastery building lay on the north side of the church, and part of it – probably the guests' hall – remains today. After Henry VIII's Dissolution of the Monasteries, in 1539, the church gradually fell into disrepair until it was, eventually, totally rebuilt in the 1870s to a design by Benjamin Ferrey.

The church today is very grand, with superb blue marble columns along the nave. The west tower is Old Red Sandstone, seen in the cliffs earlier in the walk.

13 Birds, Flowers and Jurassic Cliffs

Take in a little birdspotting and enjoy a wide vista from an ancient stretch of coastline

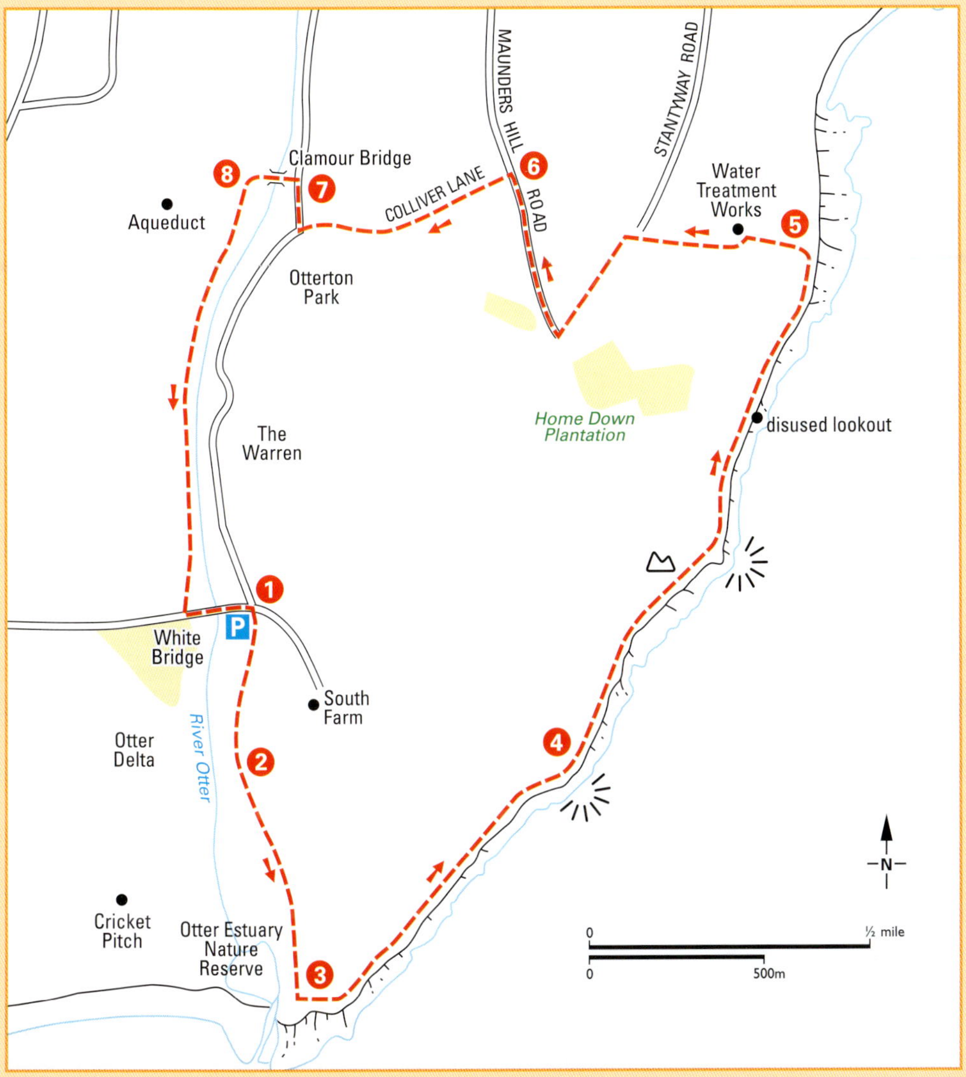

Distance 4.25 miles (6.8km)

Minimum Time 2hrs

Ascent/Gradient 164ft (50m) ▲▲▲

Level of Difficulty ●●●

Paths Good level paths, coastal section and lanes, 1 stile

Landscape River meadow, cliffs and undulating farmland

Suggested Map OS Explorer 115 Exeter & Sidmouth

Start/Finish Grid reference: SX 076831

Dog Friendliness Keep on lead near livestock

Parking By side of broad, quiet lane near entrance to South Farm

Public Toilets None en route

1 Walk through the kissing gate to the right of the gate to South Farm. Turn right, following signs for 'Coast Path Ladram Bay'. The narrow, sandy path runs along the field-edge, with lovely views right over the saltmarshes of the Otter Estuary Nature Reserve and the River Otter.

2 At the end of that field a shallow flight of wooden steps leads to a walkway and a footbridge, and up into the next field. There are good views downriver to the shingle bank at Budleigh Salterton and across the river to the cricket pitch.

3 The path continues downhill until it turns left following the line of the coast. Just before you turn east there are panoramic views right over the Otter delta, and along the beach.

4 After just over a mile (1.6km) the path rises and a view of Lyme Bay opens up ahead, including High Peak (564ft/157m) – one of the highest points on the South Devon coast. Follow the coast path: the red sandstone cliffs are extremely friable and 'chunks' frequently tumble seawards, but rest assured that the path is safe. Pass through a small gate by the disused outlook building (covered bench), and continue downhill.

5 Turn left to leave the coast path on the 'Permissive path to Otterton'. This grassy path goes through a kissing gate; turn left and follow the path right around the water treatment works, and up the gravelly lane to meet Stantyway Road. Turn left up the track, which soon bears right signed to the 'River Otter', and gives way to a tarmac lane.

6 After 400yds (366m) Clamour Bridge is signed to the left. Turn left here and follow a narrow, wooded green lane, which ends at a gate. Go through that, then almost immediately another, and follow the signs along the edge of the next field, which you leave over a stile on to a track.

7 Turn left between two big ornamental pillars, and then right under a very large oak tree. Descend a short flight of steps and cross over the River Otter on Clamour Bridge.

8 Turn left and follow the river south; go over a small leat (look out for the aqueduct coming across the meadows on your right), through a kissing gate and continue to White Bridge, where you go through a kissing gate, turn left and find your car.

14 The Cliffs of East Devon

This delightful outing along the coast from Weston to the village of Branscombe offers superb sea and coastal views – and a chance to watch paragliders in action

Above: Picturesque Branscombe

Main image: Sea spray – looking along Branscombe's pebbly beach towards Beer Head

Inset: Jurassic cliffs and uninterrupted sea views

At Branscombe three deep, wooded valleys converge. It is one of the most secluded villages in this unspoiled corner within the East Devon Area of Outstanding Natural Beauty. Pretty, flower-decked cottages sit either side of a long narrow lane that runs gradually down the valley from Street, giving rise to the claim that Branscombe is one of the longest villages in the county.

Riding the Wind

This walk takes you to the village along the coast path from Weston. There are extensive views all along the path, and on a clear day the promontory of Portland Bill can be seen to the east. The sloping grassy area on the cliff above Littlecombe Shoot is a popular spot for paragliders. If the weather conditions are favourable you can spend hours sitting on the clifftop watching them. At the footpath marker post here a sign leading right appears to direct you straight over the edge of the cliff. This steep, narrow, zig-zag path will take you on to the pebbly beach below. A number of private wooden chalets dot about the cliff: it's a wonderfully romantic spot.

St Winifred's Church, dedicated to an obscure Welsh saint, nestles halfway down the valley from Street, and is one of Branscombe's treasures. The squat tower dates from Norman times. Inside, there are remnants of the medieval paintings that once adorned the walls and an Elizabethan gallery. It also has an unusual three-decker pulpit dating to the 18th century. Near the village centre, by the village hall, many buildings are owned by the National Trust: The Old Bakery (the last traditional working bakery in Devon until 1987 – now a tea room), Manor Mill (a restored water-powered mill), and The Forge, complete with working blacksmith.

Branscombe Mouth beach is busy in summer, although it is pebbly and the seabed shelves away quickly to make for deep water. This is the halfway point of the walk and you can always wander a little way to east or west to escape the crowds.

14 The Cliffs of East Devon

Tramp along the coast near Branscombe, reckoned to be one of Devon's longest villages

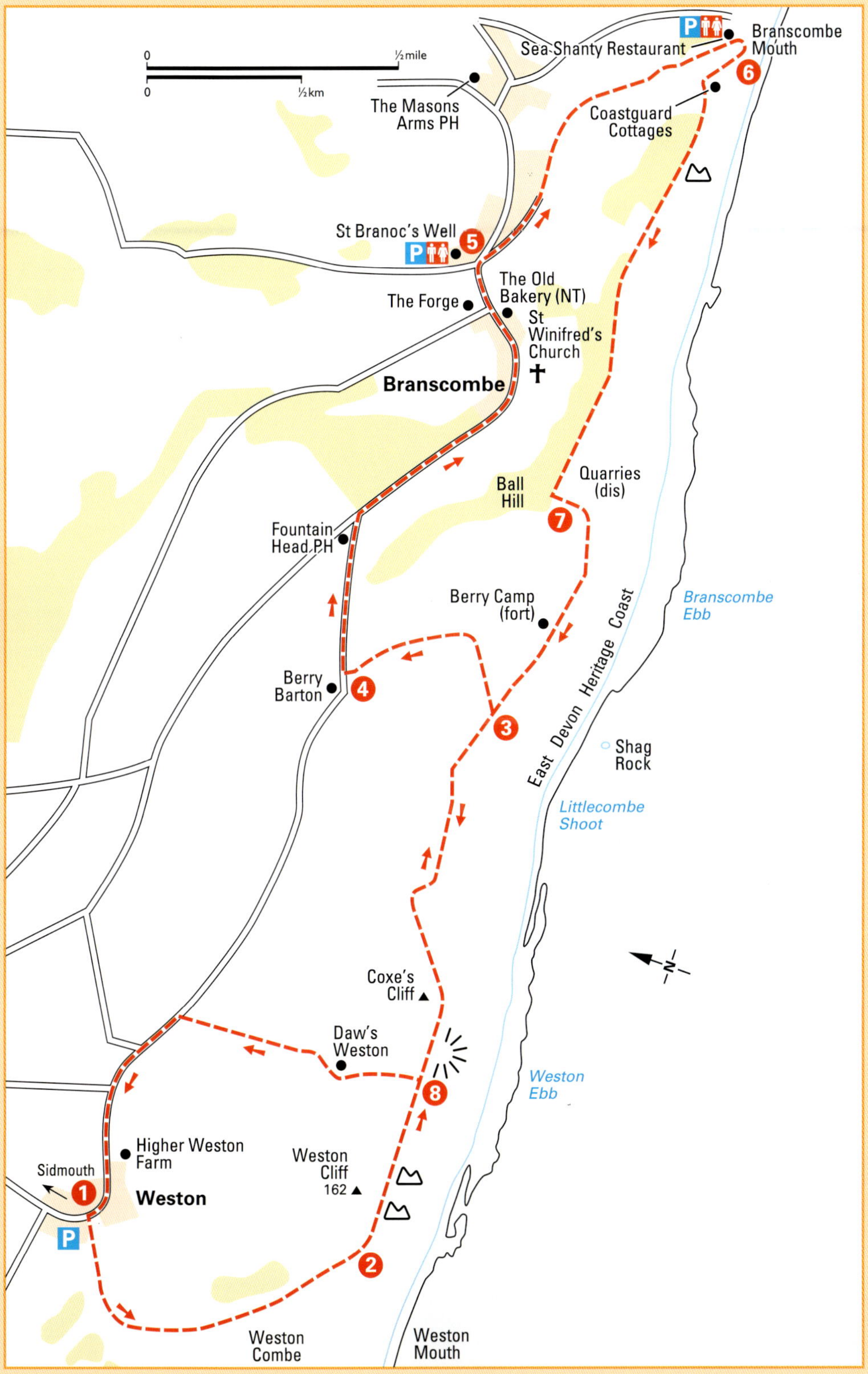

Distance 6.25 miles (10.1km)

Minimum Time 3hrs 30min

Ascent/Gradient 492ft (150m) ▲▲▲

Level of Difficulty ●●●

Paths Coast path (one steep ascent), country lanes, 3 stiles

Landscape Undulating cliffs, farmland and woodland

Suggested Map OS Explorer 115 Exeter & Sidmouth

Start/Finish Grid reference: SY 166889

Dog Friendliness Can be off lead but livestock in some fields

Parking Unsurfaced car park at Weston

Public Toilets Behind Branscombe village hall, also in car park at Branscombe Mouth

1 From the car park go over a stile on the path to Weston Mouth. The track descends, and bear left under trees to the coast path.

2 Turn left on the coast path. After Weston Cliff go through two kissing gates on Coxe's Cliff, then inland to a kissing gate in the top left of a field. In the next field keep right and go through a kissing gate on to grassland.

3 At the signpost turn half-left, signed 'Berry Barton'. Aim for a gap in the bank, bear left to the top corner of the next field, then left down to the lane at Berry Barton.

4 Turn right down the lane to the Fountain Head pub, right again down the valley, past St Winifred's Church to St Branoc's Well.

5 Turn right opposite Bucknall Close signed 'Branscombe Mouth'. In 200yds (183m) keep ahead through a gate on to a footbridge. Follow the path down the valley to the beach.

6 Turn right through a kissing gate uphill beneath the coastguard cottages. Through a gateway go left uphill to a kissing gate. Keep left up steps, go straight until a sign points left.

7 Follow the coastal footpath signs to rejoin the cliff edge, going through three kissing gates to Littlecombe Shoot. Retrace your steps through fields and gates to regain Weston Cliff.

8 Turn right through a kissing gate into a meadow. Pass the cottage and outbuildings over two stiles on to a track then a tarmac lane. Go left to return to Weston.

15 Golden Cap in Trust

Past a ruined chapel and a few National Trust cottages that remain from an abandoned fishing village, this exhilarating walk commands dramatic coast views

Golden Cap is the rather obvious name for a high, flat-topped hill of deep orange sandstone on the cliffs between Charmouth and Bridport in Dorset. It represents the tail end of a vein of warm-coloured sandstone. The Cap is the highest point on the south coast, at 627ft (191m), with views along the shore to the tip of Portland Bill in one direction and to Start Point in the other. Inland, you can see Pilsdon Pen.

Important Habitat

Climbing towards the top, you pass from neat fields through a line of wind-scoured oak trees into an area of high heathland, walking up through bracken, heather, bilberry and blackberry, alive with songbirds. The loose undercliff on the seaward side creates a different habitat. In botanical and wildlife terms, Golden Cap is one of the richest properties in the National Trust's portfolio. Today most people associate the National Trust with grand estates and historic houses. However, its first acquisition, in 1896, was a stretch of coast in Wales.

Earl of Antrim

On the top of Golden Cap itself is a memorial to the Earl of Antrim, chairman of the Trust in the 1960s and 1970s. He spearheaded its 1965 appeal campaign, 'Enterprise Neptune', to buy sections of coastline before the developers moved in. Golden Cap was part of this; over the years the Trust has continued to buy up land all around, with the aim of preserving the traditional field pattern that exists in the area between Eype and Lyme Regis.

The Trust's acquisition includes the ruined Chapel of St Gabriel's (little more than a low shell, with a porch to one side) and the neighbouring row of thatched cottages that have been smartly refurbished and are let out as visitor accommodation. These are all that remain of the fishing village of Stanton St Gabriel, sheltering in the valley behind the cliffs, which was largely abandoned after the coast road was rerouted inland in 1824; the chapel was derelict long before this.

Tranquil Lanes in Morcombelake

If you continue inland you reach Morcombelake. Seen from the speedy A35 coast road, this is an unexciting ribbon development. But when you explore it on foot, you discover a network of narrow, winding lanes on the slopes of Langdon Hill that takes you into a tranquil world.

Right: Glorious views of high heathland, cliff, beaches and sea

Below: Our walk starts from Seatown, near the Anchor Inn

15 Golden Cap in Trust

Climb the highest point on the south coast of England

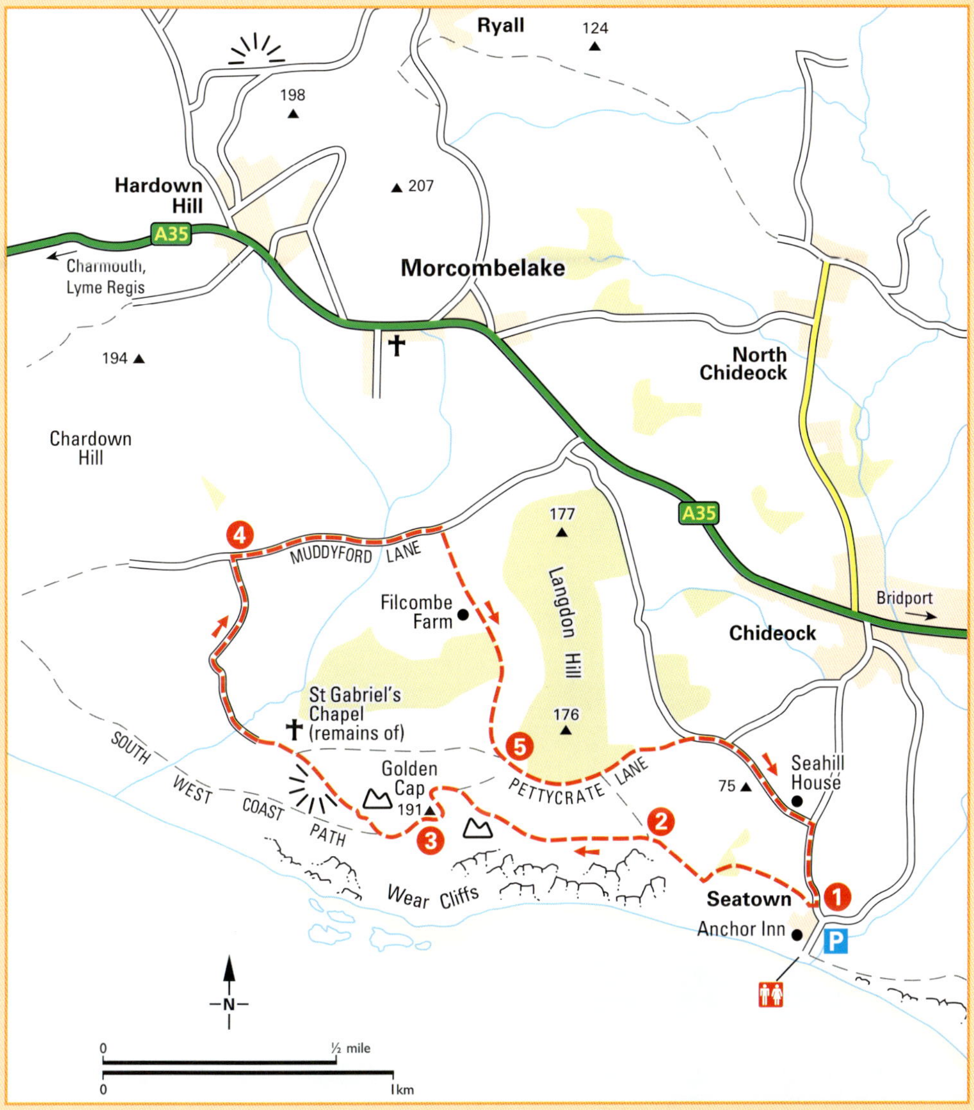

Distance 4 miles (6.4km)

Minimum Time 2hrs 30min

Ascent/Gradient 1,007ft (307m) ▲▲▲

Level of Difficulty ●●●

Paths Field tracks, country lanes, steep zig-zag gravel path, 5 stiles

Landscape Windswept coastline of lumps and bumps

Suggested Map OS Explorer 116 Lyme Regis & Bridport

Start/Finish Grid reference: SY 420917

Dog Friendliness Some road walking; all the stiles have dog gates

Parking Car park (charge) above gravel beach in Seatown; beware, can flood in stormy weather

Public Toilets At end of road, Seatown

1 Walk back up through Seatown. Cross a stile on the left, on to the footpath, signposted 'Coast Path Diversion'. Cross a stile at the end, carry on across the field to cross a stile and footbridge into woodland. Go over a stile at the other side and bear right up the hill, signposted 'Golden Cap'.

2 Where the track forks by a bench, keep left. Go through some trees and then over a stile. Bear left, straight across the open hillside, with Golden Cap ahead of you. Pass through a line of trees and walk up alongside the fence. Go up some steps, cross a stile and continue ahead. At the fingerpost, go left through a gate to follow the path of shallow steps up through bracken, heather, bilberry and bramble to the top of Golden Cap.

3 Pass the trig point and turn right along the top. Pass the stone memorial to the Earl of Antrim. At a marker stone, turn right and follow the zig-zag path downhill. Go through a gate and bear right over the field towards the ruined St Gabriel's Chapel. In the bottom corner, turn down through a gate, passing the ruins on your right, then go through a second gate. Go down the track, with cottages on the left, and right up the farm road, signed 'Morcombelake'. Follow this between high banks and hedges. Go through a gateway.

4 At the road junction, turn right down Muddyford Lane, signed 'Langdon Hill'. Pass the gate of Shedbush Farm and continue straight up the hill. Turn right up a concreted lane towards Filcombe Farm. Follow blue markers through the farmyard, bearing left through two gates. Walk up the track, go along the right edge of the first field and across the next field. Head left over the top of the green saddle between Langdon Hill and Golden Cap.

5 Go left through a gate in the corner and down a track beside the woods, signed 'Seatown'. Ignore a footpath over a stile to the right. At a junction of tracks keep right, downhill. Pass Seahill House on the left and turn right, on to a road. Continue down the road into Seatown village to return to your car.

16 Lulworth to Durdle Door

Along the beautiful and very ancient Jurassic Coast south of Lulworth Cove, this delightful walk leads past the remarkable natural stone archway of Durdle Door

Above left: The natural limestone arch of Durdle Door

Above: The circular bay at Lulworth Cove

Left: Looking along the coast from Durdle Door to Bat's Head

Lulworth Cove is an almost perfectly circular bay in the rolling line of cliffs that form Dorset's southern coast. It is part of the ancient Jurassic Coast, which runs from Swanage in Dorset to Exmouth in Devon, and earned World Heritage status in 2001. The cove provides secure anchorage for small fishing boats and pleasure craft, and a suntrap of safe water for summer bathers.

The cliffs around the eastern side of the bay are crumbly soft and brightly coloured in some places, while around the opposite arm the rock appears to have been folded and shoved aside by an unseen hand. The geology is intriguing.

Portland Stone, Purbeck Marble

The oldest layer is the gleaming white Portland stone, which was much employed by Christopher Wren in his rebuilding of London. It is a fine-grained oolite, 140 million years old, and consists of compressed fossilised shells – the flat-coiled ones are ammonites. Occasional giant ammonites, called titanites, may be seen incorporated into house walls across Purbeck. Like the rock of Bat's Head, it may contain speckled bands of flinty chert. Above this is a layer of Purbeck marble, a limestone rich in the fossils of vertebrates, where dinosaur, fish and reptile fossils are usually found. The soft layer above this consists of Wealden beds, a belt of colourful clays, silts and sands, that are unstable and prone to landslips when exposed.

Crumbly, white chalk overlays the Wealden beds. The chalk consists of the remains of microscopic sea creatures and shells deposited when a deep sea covered much of Dorset, some 75 million years ago. This is the chalk that underlies Dorset's famous downland and is seen in the exposed soft eroded cliffs at White Nothe. Hard nodules and bands of flint appear in the chalk – it's a purer type of chert – and in its gravel beach form it protects long stretches of this fragile coast.

The laying down of chalk marks the end of the Cretaceous period. After this the blanket of chalk was uplifted, folded and subjected to erosion by the slow movement of tectonic plates. The Dorset coast was exposed to extreme pressure between 24 and 1.5 million years ago, resulting in folding, crumpling or overturning of strata. You can see this on rocks around Durdle Door and Stair Hole.

16 Lulworth to Durdle Door

Brace yourself for a few steep up-and-downs on a captivating walk past ancient rocks

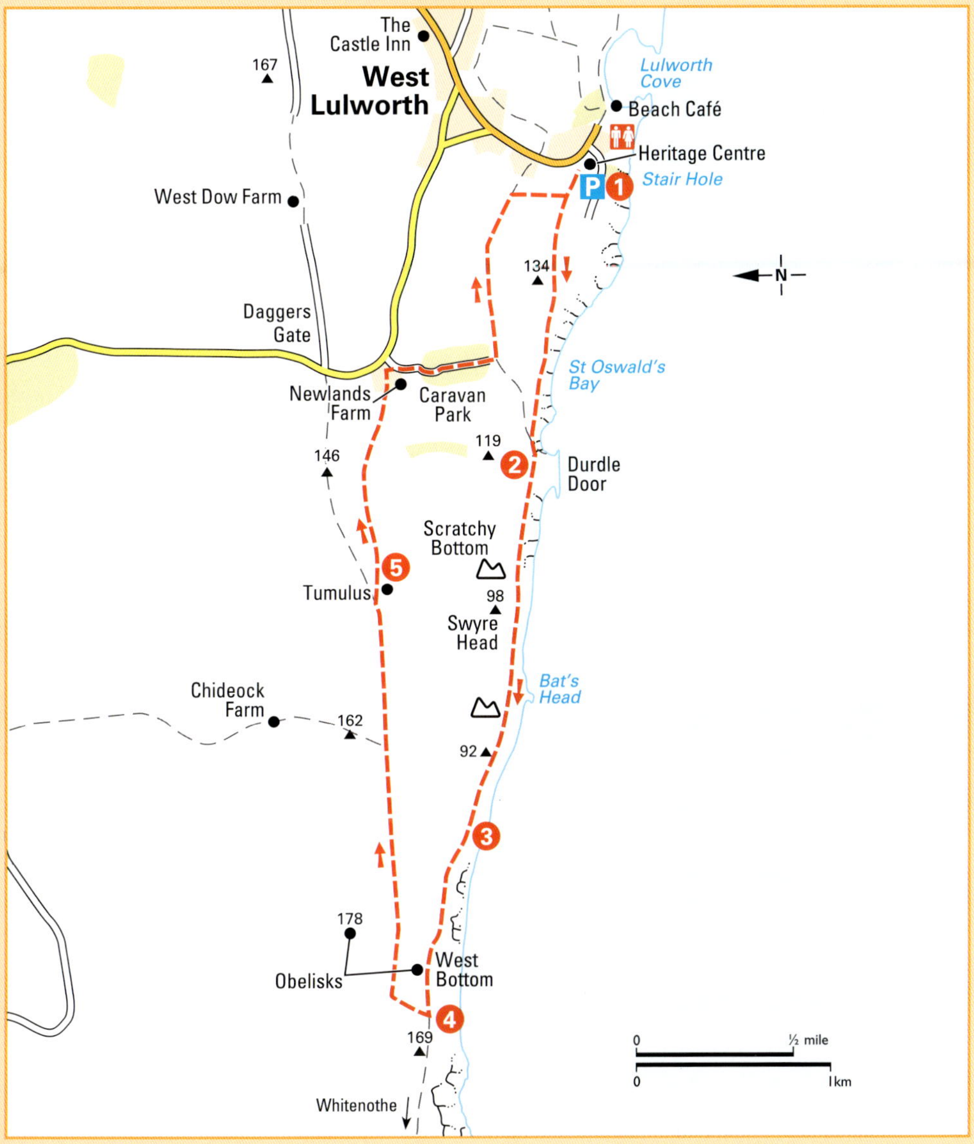

Distance 6.75 miles (10.9km)

Minimum Time 3hrs

Ascent/Gradient 1,247ft (380m) ▲▲▲

Level of Difficulty ●●●

Paths Stone path, grassy tracks, tarmac, muddy field path, 4 stiles

Landscape Steeply rolling cliffs beside sea, green inland

Suggested Map OS Explorer OL15 Purbeck & South Dorset

Start/Finish Grid reference: SY 821800

Dog Friendliness Excitable dogs need strict control near cliff edge

Parking Pay-and-display car park (busy), signed at Lulworth Cove

Public Toilets Beside Heritage Centre; also just above Lulworth Cove

1 Find the gate at the back of the car park. Pass through this to take the broad, paved footpath that leads up some shallow steps to the top of the first hill. Continue along the brow, and down the other side. Pass below a caravan park and through a gate.

2 Reach the cove of Durdle Door. A flight of steps leads down to the sea here, but carry on straight ahead on the coast path and the natural stone arch of the Door itself is revealed in a second cove below you. Walk down to the bottom then climb back up to Swyre Head. The path leads steeply down again on the other side, to a short stretch overlooking Bat's Head. Climb the next steep hill. Continue behind the cliffs, where the land tilts away from the sea.

3 The path climbs more gently up the next hill. Pass a navigation obelisk on the right, and follow the path as it curves round the contour above West Bottom.

4 At a marker stone that indicates Whitenothe ahead turn right, through a gate, and follow a fence inland. The path curves so you're walking parallel to the coast. Pass three stone embrasures with shell sculptures inside, and a second obelisk. Go through a gate. Keep straight along the top of the field and across a crossing of paths, signed to 'Daggers Gate'. Go through a gateway and straight on. The path starts to descend and becomes more of a track. Bear right to pass close by a tumulus and reach a gate.

5 Cross this gate and walk along the top of the field, above Scratchy Bottom. Cross a stile into a green lane leading to Newlands Farm. Follow it round to the right, and turn right into the caravan park. Go straight ahead on the road through here. At the far side go through a gate and turn left, signed to West Lulworth. Stay along the field-edge and walk above a farm lane, around the end of the hill. Keep straight on at the fingerpost and reach the gate above the car park. Turn left and retrace your route.

17 Kimmeridge and 'Ghostly' Tyneham

A fascinating coastal excursion leads along cliffs above three Dorset bays, and beside army ranges to a ghostly but not-quite-deserted village with a 1940s feel

There's a certain bleakness about Kimmeridge Bay, which the high energy of the surfers and the cheerful picture of families on the beach, eyes down as they potter in the rock pools, can't quite dispel. Giant slabs of black rock shelving out to sea, with crumbling cliffs topped by clumps of wild cabbage, create something of this mood. The slow, steadily nodding donkey-head of the oil well visible above a little terrace of unmistakably industrial cottages reinforces the feeling.

Below: Clavell Tower above Kimmeridge Bay is a folly and lookout, complete with Tuscan colonnade, built by Rev John Richards Clavell in 1830

Kimmeridge Coal and Oil

The story of the bay is intriguing. Iron Age tribes spotted the potential of the band of bituminous shale that runs through Kimmeridge, polishing it up into blackstone arm rings and ornaments, and later into chair and table legs. People have been trying to exploit it ever since.

The shale, permeated with crude oil, is also known as Kimmeridge coal, but successive attempts to work it on an industrial scale seemed doomed to failure. These included alum extraction (for dyeing) in the 16th century; use of the coal to fuel a glassworks in the 17th century – it was smelly and inefficient; and use for a variety of chemical distillations, including paraffin wax and varnish, in the 19th century. Then for one brief period the street lights of Paris were lit by gas extracted from the shale oil. However, nothing lasted very long.

Since 1959 BP has drilled down 1,716ft (520m) below the sea, and its beam engine sucks out some 80 barrels (2,800 gallons/12,720 litres) of crude oil a day. Transported to the Wytch Farm collection point (near Corfe Castle), the oil is then pumped to Hamble, to be shipped around the world.

Mrs Miniver in Tyneham

Just over the hill from Kimmeridge lies Tyneham, at first sight a cosy farming village clustered around a church in a glorious valley. As you get up close, however, you realise that something's wrong. The village is uncannily neat, like a film set from the 1940s – Greer Garson's *Mrs Miniver* (from the film of 1942) could appear at any moment. There's a spreading oak tree by the church gate; a quaint old phone box; even a village pump. The gravestones all look freshly scrubbed – no lichen here. The farmyard is clean and empty. The stone cottages are newly repointed, but roofless. And the church, as you enter on a chill mid-winter day, is warm!

Inside is an exhibition to explain all. The villagers were asked to give up their homes in December 1943 for the 'war effort', and Tyneham became absorbed into the vast Lulworth Ranges, as part of the live firing range. It's a touching memorial, although perhaps nothing can make up for the fact that the villagers were never allowed back to their homes. Emerging again from the church, you half expect to see soldiers popping out of the windows, but relax – you are in no danger, for you can only visit when the ranges are closed.

17 Kimmeridge and 'Ghostly' Tyneham

Enjoy wonderful coastal views and visit the 'lost village' of Tyneham

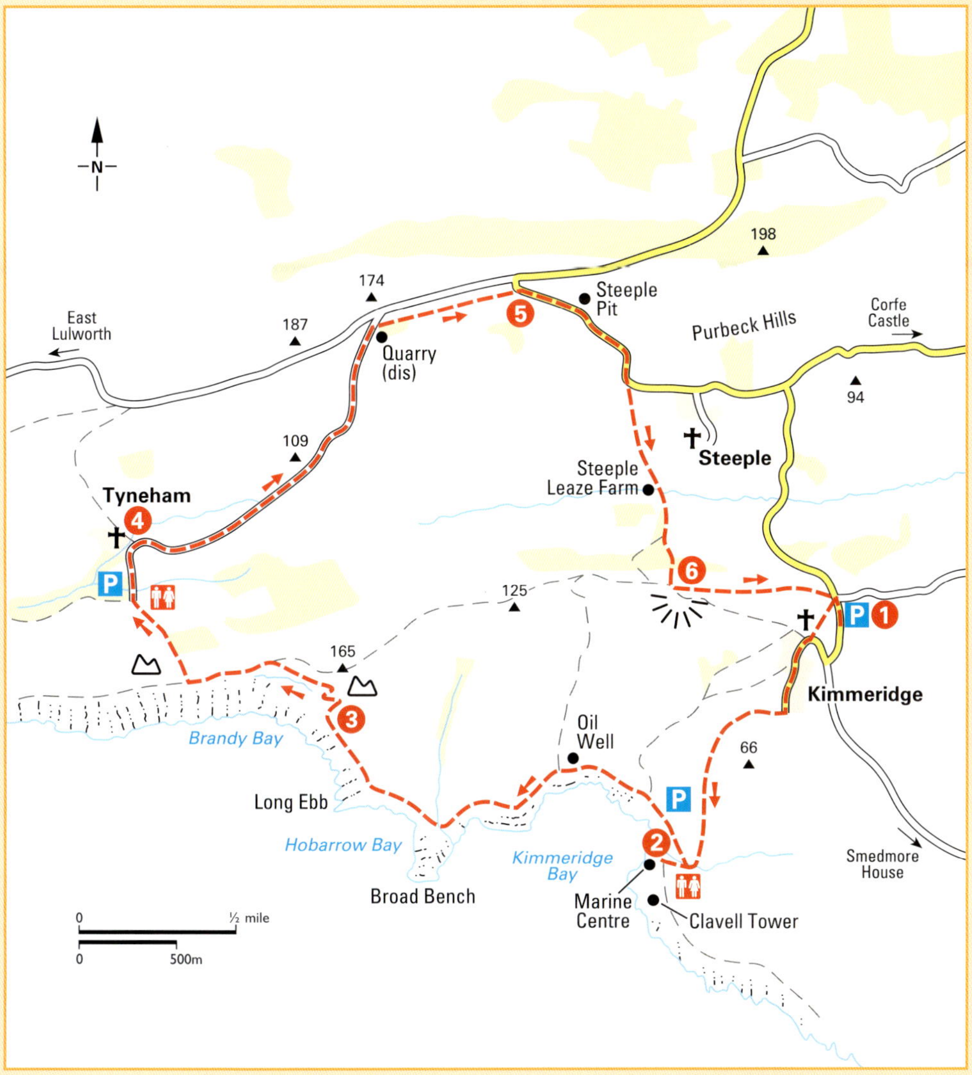

Distance 7.5 miles (12.1km)

Minimum Time 3hrs 30min

Ascent/Gradient 1,165ft (355m) ▲▲▲

Level of Difficulty ●●●

Paths Grassy tracks and bridlepaths, some road walking, 12 stiles

Landscape Folded hills and valleys around Kimmeridge Bay

Suggested Map OS Explorer OL15 Purbeck & South Dorset

Start/Finish Grid reference: SY 918800

Dog Friendliness Notices request dogs on leads in some sections; some road walking

Parking Car park (free) in old quarry north of Kimmeridge village

Public Toilets Near Marine Centre at Kimmeridge Bay and Tyneham

Note Range walks open most weekends throughout year and during main holiday periods; call 01929 462 721, ext 4819 for further information. Keep strictly to paths, between yellow-marked posts

1 Turn right up the road and soon left over a stile, signposted 'Kimmeridge' – enjoy the sweeping views as you descend. Go through a gate by the church, then another at the bottom. Turn right past some houses, go through a gateway and bear left. Go over a stile below a coppice and bear immediately left along the hedge, following it round to a pair of stiles. Go straight ahead to the next stile and turn right to follow the path along the hedge towards the sea. Turn left on to the road and turn right, across a car park after approximately 0.5 mile (800m).

2 Bear left to visit the marine centre (closed in winter), otherwise turn right on the coastal path to continue. Descend some steps, cross a bridge and bear right, signposted 'Range Walks'. Pass some cottages, on the right, and the oil well. Go through the gate on to the range walk and continue around the coast on a track between yellow posts, crossing several cattle grids. The cliffs of Brandy Bay stagger away to the west.

3 After 1 mile (1.6km) cross a stile and follow the path as it zig-zags sharply uphill. Continue around the top of Brandy Bay on the cliff path. When you reach a stile and marker stone, turn down to the right, signposted 'Tyneham'. Soon you come to a stile on the left: cross this and follow the track down into Tyneham village.

4 After exploring the village, take the exit road up the hill. At the top, by a gate, turn right over a stile and go along a path that runs parallel with the road.

5 Emerge at a gate and turn right down the road, to go past Steeple Pit. Where the road turns sharp left, go straight ahead down the gravel drive through Steeple Leaze Farm and take the gravel track ahead, leading straight up the hill. Go through a gate and keep left up a muddy path that winds through gorse and scrub, up the hill. Cross a stile at the top and continue straight ahead, with superb views over Kimmeridge.

6 Turn left across a stile and go along the edge of the field, following the ridge of the hill for 0.5 mile (800m), with views to Smedmore House and Corfe Castle. Go through the gate and turn right back to the start.

18 Studland's Sand and Heath

Easy walking on a charming coastal ramble leads through a significant nature reserve over heathland and through dunes to a beach rich in shells

The glorious sands in Studland Bay are justly famous, attracting over one million visitors a year, so you'll need to get up early to have the beach to yourself. You're unlikely to be alone for long and local horseriders are often the first to arrive. As you progress up the beach, getting warmer, you can shed your clothes with impunity, for the upper stretch is the less familiar form of nature reserve, opening its arms to naturists. Even on a winter's morning you'll spot brave souls sunbathing naked in the shelter of the marram-covered dunes.

Offshore you'll see big motor boats – of the 'gin palace' variety – letting rip as they emerge from Poole Harbour. Watch out, too, for the orange and blue of the Poole lifeboat on manoeuvres, and the yellow and black pilot boat nipping out to lead in the tankers. Jet-skiers zip around the more sedate sailing yachts, all dodging the small fishing boats.

Right: The walk provides views of Agglestone Rock, a 400-tonne sandstone block on nearby Godlingston Heath

Below: Beautiful light over sea, sands and dunes at Knoll Beach

Wealth of Shells

Studland's sand is pale gold and fine-ground, trodden by thousands of feet, piled into hundreds of satisfying sand castles and smoothed daily by the sea. The shells underfoot become more numerous as you approach the tip of the sand bar. It's a wonderful opportunity for some shell-spotting.

Look for the flattish conical mother-of-pearl whorls of topshells, the curious pinky-brown pockets of slipper limpets and the flat reddish-brown sun-rays of scallops. The deeply ridged fans of common cockles and the vivid blue flash of mussels are a common sight. More challenging is to identify the uneven ellipse of sand gapers or the delicate finger-nail pink of the thin tellin.

On the Heath

Behind the beach lies rugged heath, part of the same nature reserve, which is in the care of Natural England and the National Trust. These two bodies are currently working together on restoration. They are reclaiming heath that had become farmland, clearing scrub and maintaining controlled grazing to prevent it all reverting to woodland. You might spot a rare Dartford warbler, with its pinky-brown colouring and long tail. All six of Britain's reptiles – common lizard, sand lizard, smooth snake, adder, grass snake and slow-worm – live on the heath.

Trapped between the dunes and the heath is a freshwater lake known as the Little Sea. Hides allow you to watch the dizzying variety of coastal and freshwater birds which congregate here.

18 Studland's Sand and Heath

Keep your eyes peeled – for birds, adders, lizards, grass snakes and rare shells

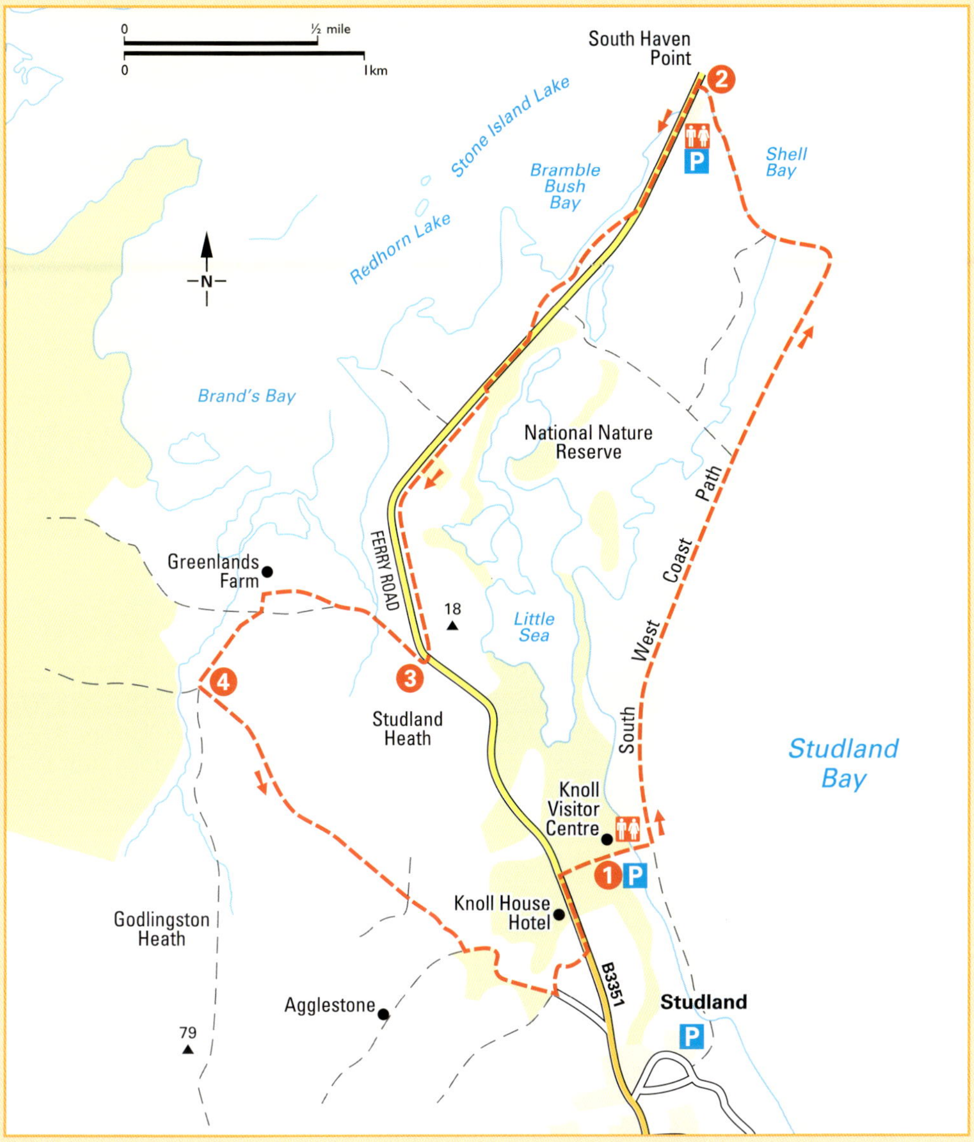

Distance 7 miles (11.3km)

Minimum Time 3hrs 30min

Ascent/Gradient 132ft (40m) ▲▲▲

Level of Difficulty ●●●

Paths Sandy beach, muddy heathland tracks, verges

Landscape Sandy Studland Bay, heath and views over Poole Harbour

Suggested Map OS Explorer OL15 Purbeck & South Dorset

Start/Finish Grid reference: SZ 033835

Dog Friendliness Not allowed on beach June to September, check locally for precise dates

Parking Knoll car park (fee), by visitor centre, just off B3351

Public Toilets By visitor centre and near ferry toll station

1 From the car park go past the visitor centre to the sea. Turn left and walk up the beach for about 2 miles (3.2km). Marram-covered dunes hide the edge of the heath on your left, but you have views to Tennyson Down on the Isle of Wight, and the golden cliffs of Bournemouth curve away ahead. Continue round the tip of the sand bar into Shell Bay. Poole opens out ahead – the spit of Sandbanks, with the white Haven Hotel facing you across the harbour mouth. There are good views of the nature reserve Brownsea Island.

2 Turn inland at South Haven Point, joining the road by the phone box. Pass the boatyard and toll booth, then bear right at a gate on to a bridleway leading down to some houseboats. Turn left along the inner shore of Poole Harbour and past Bramble Bush Bay. Choose any of the tracks up to the road. Cross and then follow the verge until you reach the end of some woods on your left, when you can pick up the broad muddy track on the heath. After 0.5 mile (800m) this track bends round to the left. Where the track bends sharply right to meet the road, stay ahead on the footpath for roughly another 220yds (200m).

3 Cross over the road by a bus stop and then head down the track, indicated by a fingerpost. Go past the marshy end of Studland Heath and up to reach a junction by Greenlands Farm. Bear left and, just round the next corner, turn left through a gate on to the heath. Walk straight along an old hedge-line, pass a barn on the left, and reach a fingerpost.

4 Turn left across the heath (not shown on the fingerpost), aiming for the distant lump of the Agglestone. Go through a gate by another fingerpost and continue along the muddy track over the top, passing the Agglestone away to your right. Go down into some woods, turn right over a footbridge and pass through a gate into a lane. Pass several houses then, where blue markers indicate a public bridleway, turn left into a field. Head diagonally right into a green lane and go through a gate at the bottom. Turn left along the verge, pass the Knoll House Hotel and turn right at the signpost to return to the car park.

19 Heights and Huts of Hengistbury Head

A walk past colourful beach huts and through a nature reserve at Hengistbury Head contains treats for naturalists and those interested in ancient history

The multi-coloured beach huts of Mudeford's sandy peninsula are a cheerful throwback to nostalgic bucket-and-spade holidays of the early 20th century. In fact, they hark back to the last days of the century before that, when bathers would undress in modest little huts on wheels, which could be horse-hauled down into the shallows in order to minimise any embarrassing exposure to public view. The carriages' successors, the huts, are still there and the desire for one's own bit of space right on the beach remains undiminished.

In the fashion of the day, candy-striped paintwork has given way to bold, plain colours, but the urge to individualise remains strong, with decks, weathervanes and windmilling, semaphoring sailors. While the huts' outer form remains much the same – central door, symmetrical windows, shallow, peaked roof – the insides are a Nosy Parker's dream. Some make the most of one light, airy space reflecting sparkling sea and sky, others may be divided into rooms, with perhaps a sleeping platform squeezed up under the roof. Each is customised with its owner's particular beach 'necessities' – minimalist fridge and drinks cabinet in one, kitchen sink and home comforts in another.

Below: First light on boulders at Hengistbury Head

Below right: Seaside colours – beach huts at Mudeford

Barn Field

The windswept peninsula of Hengistbury Head has an archaeological record dating back 12,500 years, when Stone Age hunter-gatherers left the remains of a camp site on its outer, seaward edge. Some 10,500 years later Iron Age folk settled here and built up a trading port on the more sheltered inner shore, where Barn Field stands today. The great Double Dikes date from this later period, built to shelter timber-framed dwellings.

Barn Field itself has remained untouched by farming improvements since the Romans left around AD410 – a rare status that is jealously protected by conservationists, especially on this crowded south coast, where land is at a premium. Its vegetation is low, acidic grassland that grips on to thin soil over gravel and sand, maintained down the centuries by salt-laden winds and the sharp teeth of the rabbit population. Decimation of the rabbits in the 1950s by myxomatosis allowed gorse and bramble to gain a hold, but a recent programme of scrub clearance and controlled grazing by cattle, managed by Natural England, has done much to restore the original balance. Today Barn Field is an important site for ground-nesting birds such as the skylark and meadow pipit, and adorned with the flowers of heath bedstraw, autumn hawkbit and harebell.

19 Heights and Huts of Hengistbury Head

Follow an easy coastal loop over land with a long history of human settlement

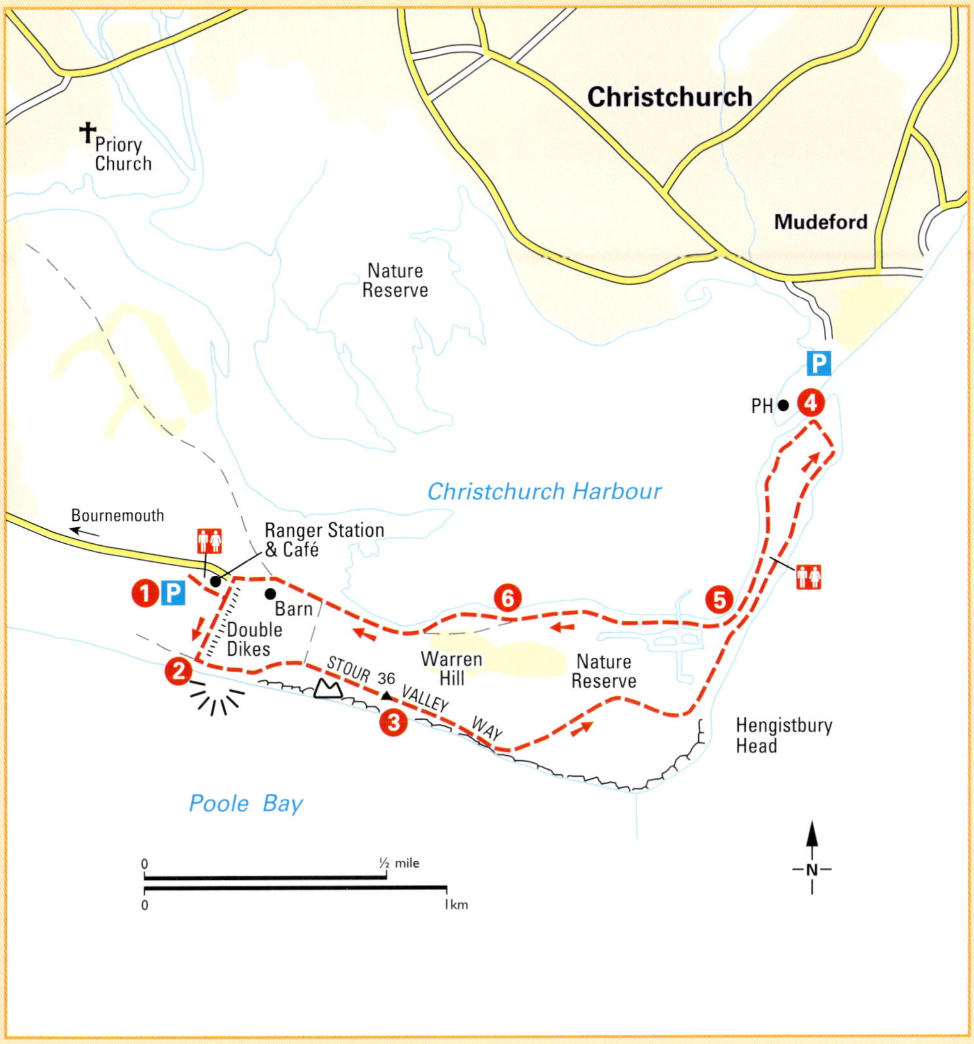

Distance 3.25 miles (5.3km)

Minimum Time 1hr 45min

Ascent/Gradient 109ft (33m) ▲▲▲

Level of Difficulty ●●●

Paths Grass, tarmac road, soft sand, woodland track, some steps

Landscape Heathland, sand cliffs, sand spit, mixed woodland

Suggested Map OS Explorer OL22 New Forest

Start/Finish Grid reference: SZ 163912

Dog Friendliness Keep to paths to avoid destroying habitat and disturbing ground-nesting birds

Parking Car park (fee) at end of road, signed 'Hengistbury Head' from B3059

Public Toilets Beside car park; also amid beach huts

1 From the car park take the gravel path towards the sea, with the fenced-off lines of the Double Dikes to your left. At the sea-edge you can see for miles each way: to the towers of Bournemouth, the chalky Foreland and Durlston Head to the west, Christchurch Bay and the Isle of Wight to the east.

2 Turn left and follow the road along the cliffs. The Priory Church in Christchurch dominates the view inland across the harbour, with St Catherine's Hill behind. Follow the road up the hill. Pause to admire the boggy pond on your right, home to the rare natterjack toad. The road narrows; climb up some steps, passing a numbered post marking the Stour Valley Way. As you climb the steep path, the views back along the coast are fabulous, and there are views across Christchurch Harbour, usually buzzing with windsurfers and dinghies.

3 On the heathy top of Warren Hill a viewing platform tells you that you're 75 miles (120km) from Cherbourg and 105 miles (168km) from Jersey. Keep right along the path, passing a deserted coastguard station and following the top of the cliffs. Descend into a deep hollow, where the sea appears to be breaking through. Keep straight on, following the curve of the head. At the end the path turns down through some trees; descend the steps. Walk along the sparkling, white sand on the sea side of the beach huts to the point. Stone groynes form little bays.

4 At the end of the spit you're only a stone's throw from the opposite shore (a ferry runs across to the pub from the end of a pier, passed further on). Turn round the end of the point, passing the old Black House, and walk up the side of the spit, overlooking the harbour.

5 If you've had enough beach, you can catch the land train back to the car park from here (times vary seasonally). Otherwise, join the metalled road which curves round to the right past the freshwater marsh and lagoon.

6 At a post marked '19' turn right on to the dirt path and follow it briefly through the woods, crossing a small ditch, to emerge back on the road. Turn right, passing extensive reedbeds on the right and a bird sanctuary on the left. Continue past the thatched barn and follow the road to the café, ranger station building and car park.

Southeast England

Southeast England

Southeast England is undoubtedly a busy, sometimes overcrowded place – with Greater London and its outlying areas, a bustling travel network and long stretches of the south coast built up. But within easy reach of all this activity are pieces of idyllic coastline and places immensely rich in history.

There are historic ports and shipyards, smugglers' havens, Roman forts, Saxon remains and ancient battlegrounds, as well as several areas of great natural beauty. The region boasts one of England's best known landmarks, the White Cliffs of Dover in Kent (see Walk 32). For many years these were the first sighting of England for waterborne travellers arriving across the English Channel from the European mainland and they became icons of England, associated with the country the world over.

To the east and almost equally celebrated are the majestic Seven Sisters cliffs (Walk 28) and nearby Beachy Head (Walk 29), where the beautiful rolling downland of the Sussex Downs Area of Natural Beauty ends in a vertiginous drop to the waves. On this towering headland stands the old *Belle Tout* lighthouse, built in 1831 by colourful local landowner 'Mad Jack' Fuller, and now a private home. The tides and currents near Beachy Head were so treacherous that Venetian sailors called the spot the 'Devil's Cape'. Situated at such a great height Fuller's lighthouse was, however, often lost in swirling sea mist and unable to help shipping; a second lighthouse was built around 540ft (165m) out to sea from the base of the cliffs and – an impressive and distinctive sight, with its hooped red-and-white colouring – it is still working today.

The *Belle Tout* is not the only historic lighthouse visited on the walks in this section. On the Isle of Wight, Walk 22 leads to Britain's only surviving medieval lighthouse, built in the 14th century by Walter de Godeton. Octagonal in shape, and known locally as 'the Pepperpot', it stands on St Catherine's Hill overlooking Chale Bay and the treacherous waters near Atherfield Ledge dubbed 'the Bay of Death', where – tradition has it – 14 ships once floundered in a single night.

Land and Sea

The waters may be extremely treacherous in places but the Southeast coast has nevertheless been associated with pleasure boating for centuries – at least since King Charles II kept a yacht in the natural harbour at Chichester in the 17th century. Today places including Chichester Harbour (Walk 25) and the Hamble estuary are busy centres of boating. All along this coast, from the time of the first settlers onwards, people have had an intense relationship with the sea. In some places

Opening pages: Some 500ft (152m) tall, Beachy Head is the country's highest chalk cliff

Previous page, main image: On the Solent foreshore this pier, now ruined, was used to embark troops on D-Day in1944

Previous page, bottom left: The remains of Britain's only medieval lighthouse, on St Catherine's Hill, Isle of Wight

Below: Remains of Second World War fortifications in the Rye Harbour Nature Reserve, Sussex

Below right: Woodland gardens at Exbury House, Hampshire

Top right: Rottingdean, Sussex

the sea invaded the land, forcing the inhabitants of coastal towns to move and establish a new settlement, while at others the sea retreated leaving a settlement high and dry. At Winchelsea, Sussex, both these things happened. The existing Winchelsea was established after the original town was overwhelmed in a storm in 1287. The New Winchelsea was planned by King Edward I and became a thriving port but then the sea receded and the town was left more than 1 mile (1.6 km) from the coast.

Winchelsea was once a significant town, one of the Cinque Ports – a confederation of medieval coastal towns granted privileges in return for contributing to the king's fleet at a time before the Royal Navy had been established. It came under frequent attack in the medieval period; much of its church was destroyed in a raid of 1449 but the tomb of England's first admiral, Gervase Alard, survives (see Walk 30). Walk 33 visits Sandwich in Kent, another of the Cinque Ports, and like Winchelsea once a notable port, often raided by enemy ships, but a place whose importance declined following the sea's retreat.

Illicit Trade, Church History

Sandwich is one of many places in this section where smugglers were once active. Another is the cove of Cuckmere Haven, Sussex, where it is still easy to imagine these reprobates unloading their forbidden cargoes of lace or brandy amid surf crashing on the sands and against a backdrop of towering chalk cliffs (see Walk 28); and on the Isle of Wight the pretty village of Brighstone (see Walk 21) was once a notorious centre for smuggling and 'wrecking' (salvaging cargoes from ships smashed by waves against the shore).

On the Dengie Peninsula in Essex, between the estuaries of the River Blackwater and the River Crouch (see Walk 36), smugglers landed and stored their illicit goods in the seventh-century Chapel of St Peter on the Wall. This building, founded in AD 654, is today celebrated less for its smugglers' links than its status as the oldest church in England that is still in use – and pilgrims from far and wide come in summer to worship in the chapel. St Peter on the Wall is also the only surviving building raised by Celtic Christians in Essex.

Those interested in the history of the Christian Church will certainly be keen to see the Church of Holy Trinity in Bosham, Sussex (see Walk 25), which has a Saxon tower base, and the 13th-century chapel at Climping in Sussex (see Walk 26); meanwhile Brighstone, the village on the Isle of Wight notorious for its smuggling (see Walk 21), is notable also for its rectors including Thomas Ken, author of the hymn 'Glory to Thee My God This Night', rector in the 17th century, and Samuel Wilberforce, son of the anti-slavery campaigner William; Samuel was rector at Brighstone in 1830-40 and, as Bishop of Winchester, was later a noted opponent of Charles Darwin's Theory of Evolution and took part in a celebrated public debate on the subject in 1860, at the Oxford University Museum against biologist T. H. Huxley.

King Harold and Earlier

While inspecting the Church of Holy Trinity at Bosham (Walk 25), you will be well placed to visit the spot from which King Harold, the last Anglo-Saxon King of England, sailed to Normandy in 1064. Bosham is just one of many sites of historic interest along the coast, sites dating back to Saxon, Roman and even Neolithic times: on Brighstone

Down, Isle of Wight (Walk 21), there are remains of Bronze Age and Neolithic burial mounds, while close to Bosham is the site of the Roman fort at Fishbourne; the Church of St Peter on the Wall on the Dengie Peninsula near Bradwell-on-Sea in Essex (Walk 36) was built on and using materials from the third-century Roman fort of Othona.

Then at Maldon, also in Essex, Walk 35 visits another former port made famous by battle – this time in AD 991 between Saxons led by Byrhtnoth, an Essex Ealdorman (royal official), and Viking invaders who had sailed up the estuary of the River Blackwater. The two-day conflict, in which Byrhtnoth was killed, ended in a Viking victory but the heroism of the Saxon warriors was celebrated in the Old English poem 'The Battle of Maldon'. A bronze statue of Byrhtnoth designed by artist John Doubleday was erected on Maldon Promenade Walk opposite the battleground, in 2006.

Best of the Rest

Hamble Estuary and Bursledon

Today one of England's principal centres for yachting, the shores of the Hamble estuary at Bursledon in Hampshire have a long history as a base for boatbuilding. At Bursledon local shipbuilder George Parsons built the 74-gun HMS *Elephant*, which in 1801 was Nelson's flagship at the Battle of Copenhagen. Walk 24 explores charming Hamble and Old Bursledon, and provides fine views of the estuary and the many yachts and pleasure boats on its waters.

West Wight

In a tranquil and beautiful corner of the Isle of Wight with glorious sea views, Walk 20 crosses Tennyson Down, the downland named in honour of the Victorian poet Alfred, Lord Tennyson, author of 'Idylls of the King' and 'The Charge of the Light Brigade', who lived in Farringford House (now a hotel) nearby. You can pay your respects at the Tennyson Monument, a tall granite cross at the top of the Down and at the grave of the poet's wife, Emily, in the churchyard of All Saints Church, Freshwater. The walk also follows a nature trail across Afton Marshes Nature Reserve, where in season you should look out for small tortoiseshell, red admiral and other butterflies.

Exbury House and Gardens

On the east bank of the River Beaulieu in Hampshire, Exbury House stands in 200 acres (81 hectares) of grounds including an area established as one of the world's most notable rhododendron gardens by British banker and Conservative politician Lionel de Rothschild (1882–1942). After buying the estate in 1919, Rothschild – a scion of the celebrated and immensely wealthy banking family of that name – redeveloped the house in a neo-Georgian style and created the largest rock garden in England; he sent expeditions as far as the Himalayas to bring back plants and seeds for his garden, in the process creating more then 1,200 new hybrids of rhododendrons and azaleas. Walk 23 visits Exbury Gardens, but also takes in nearby Lepe Country Park, which commands beautiful views of the Solent and the Isle of Wight – and along one of the most tranquil and beautiful regions of the Hampshire coast.

Rottingdean

East of Brighton in Sussex, Rottingdean is one of no less than seven originally Saxon settlements on this part of the coast that all end in 'dean' – derived from a word meaning 'hollow' in the downland landscape. They are collectively known as 'the Deans', and together with Roedean (home to the renowned girls' public school) Rottingdean is probably the best known. Walk 27 visits the village, which was home to Victorian author Rudyard Kipling in 1897–1902, at the time when he was writing the *Just So* stories and the novel *Kim*; other notable residents included PreRaphaelite painter Sir Edward Burne Jones and novelist and playwright Enid Bagnold, author of the 1955 play *The Chalk Garden*, which was inspired by the garden of her Rottingdean house. The village church contains stained-glass windows designed by Burne-Jones.

Rye and the Rye Harbour Local Nature Reserve

With views of the beautiful dunes and beach at Camber Sands and of the impressive remains of Camber Castle (built by King Henry VIII in 1539–44), Walk 31 passes through part of a designated Site of Special Scientific Interest alongside the Ternery Pool and other flooded gravel pits with the chance to see cormorants, grebes, reed warblers and other birdlife. There is also an opportunity to inspect the Martello Tower, a powerful fortification erected to defend against a feared French invasion at the time of the Napoleonic Wars in the early 19th century.

Paglesham

A walk between Paglesham Eastend and Paglesham Churchend on the east coast of Essex near Southend-on-Sea (see Walk 34) is through land once frequented by smugglers and other colourful characters. Daniel Defoe, author of Robinson Crusoe, described Paglesham in his *A Tour Through the Whole Island of Great Britain* (1724–26) as a place where polygamy was rife – some men he met claimed to have fifteen or more wives. The area was a major centre for oyster-farming in the 19th century, and an Oyster Festival is still held locally once a year.

20 Tennyson's Freshwater

From lofty downland with magnificent coastal views to tranquil estuary scenes, this exhilarating ramble explores the landscape the Romantic poet loved so well

West Wight is a quiet area of great natural beauty, offering open countryside, rugged cliffs, wonderful views and a fascinating wildlife. This walk encapsulates the contrasting landscapes of the area, from the wildlife-rich tidal estuary of the River Yar to magnificent chalk headlands and hills with their breathtaking views.

The 'Most Beautiful View in England'

Of the many literary greats who sought seclusion and inspiration on the island during the 19th century, the poet Alfred, Lord Tennyson was probably the foremost. He chose to reside in West Wight, where he and his wife Emily came to Farringford House, a castellated late-Georgian house (now a hotel) set in parkland beneath Tennyson Down, in 1853. From the drawing room he could look out across Freshwater Bay and the slopes of Afton Down, a view he believed to be the most beautiful in England – 'Mediterranean in its richness and charm'.

Almost daily he would take long solitary walks across the chalk downland, enjoying the bracing air, which he declared to be 'worth sixpence a pint'. The island inspired some of his greatest poems. 'The Charge of the Light Brigade' was written on the Down that now bears his name, and 'Maud', 'Enoch Arden' and the 'Idylls of the King' at Farringford.

A Cultural Centre

Tennyson's poetry was so popular that he soon became one of the richest poets in the country. He soon changed the face of West Wight, as tiny Freshwater became the cultural centre of England, attracting the most eminent Victorians of his age – Charles Kingsley, Garibaldi, Lewis Carroll, Charles Darwin, Prince Albert, to name but a few.

Farringford was the perfect place to entertain friends and celebrities, despite or perhaps because of its remoteness, but it was the time spent alone wandering the Downs or with his wife Emily in their fine garden that made Farringford so special to Tennyson. Eventually he and Emily bought a house on the mainland and returned to Farringford only for the winter, when they would be undisturbed.

Memories and Memorials

Alfred died in 1892 and Emily in 1896. Memories of the poet and his family are dotted along this walk. On Tennyson Down, you will find the granite monument erected in his honour in 1897. You can take lunch or afternoon tea at Farringford Hotel. In Freshwater, step inside All Saints Church to view the memorials to the family, while in the peaceful churchyard you will find Emily's grave and a lovely view across the serene estuary of the River Yar.

Below: Looking across Freshwater Bay to the poet's former home, now a hotel, and Tennyson Down beyond

20 Tennyson's Freshwater

Tread in the poet's footsteps as you cross Tennyson Down and enjoy wonderful sea views

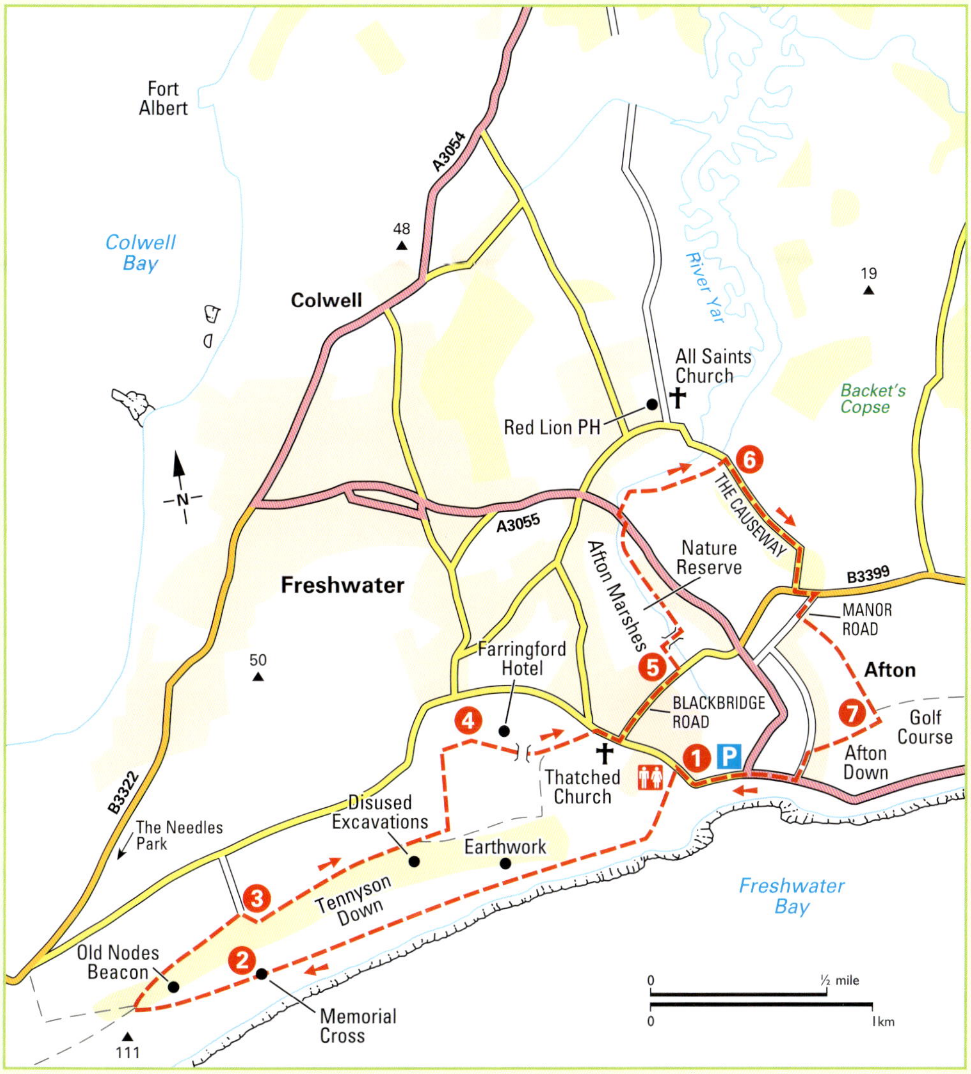

Distance 5.75 miles (9.2km)

Minimum Time 3hrs

Ascent/Gradient 623ft (190m) ▲▲▲

Level of Difficulty ●●●

Paths Downland, field and woodland paths, some road walking and stretch of disused railway, 4 stiles

Landscape Downland, farmland, freshwater marsh and salt marsh

Suggested Map OS Explorer OL29 Isle of Wight

Start/Finish Grid reference: SZ 346857

Dog Friendliness Let off lead on Tennyson Down and along old railway

Parking Pay-and-display car park at Freshwater Bay

Public Toilets Freshwater Bay and Yarmouth

1 From the car park, turn right along the road, then left before the bus shelter along a metalled track, signed 'Coastal Path'. After 50yds (46m) bear right through a gate and follow the well-walked path through a gateway and up to the memorial cross at the summit of Tennyson Down.

2 Continue down the wide grassy swathe, which narrows between gorse bushes, to reach the replica of the Old Nodes Beacon. Here, turn very sharp right down a chalk track. At a junction (car park right) keep straight on up the narrow path.

3 The path widens, then descends to a gate into woodland. Proceed close to the woodland fringe before emerging into more open countryside. Just beyond a disused pit on your right, fork left at a waymark post down a narrower path. Cross a stile, then follow the enclosed path as it turns sharp left to a stile. Cross the next field to a stile and turn right along the field-edge to a stile.

4 Cross a farm track, go through a gate and walk along the track beside Farringford Hotel. Pass beneath a wooden footbridge and continue downhill to a gate and the road. Turn left if you wish to visit the hotel, otherwise turn right then, opposite the thatched church, turn left down Blackbridge Road. Just before Black Bridge, turn left into Afton Marshes Nature Reserve.

5 Join the nature trail, following it across a footbridge and beside the stream to the A3055 – this can be very wet in winter. Turn left and almost immediately cross over to join the bridleway along the course of the old railway. In 0.5 mile (800m) you reach the Causeway. Turn left here to visit Freshwater church and the Red Lion.

6 Turn right and continue to the B3399, then left and shortly cross on to unmetalled Manor Road. In a few paces, bear left, signed 'Freshwater Way', and from this point ascend across grassland towards Afton Down.

7 Keep ahead at a junction of paths beside the golf course, soon to follow the gravel track right to the clubhouse. Go through a gate, pass in front of the building to reach the access track, keeping left to the A3055. Turn right downhill into Freshwater Bay.

21 Downlands to Brighstone

The beautiful country near Brighstone is perfect for walking, and this relaxing excursion takes in sand and coastal rocks as well as downs rich in ancient remains

The heart of old Brighstone is one of the prettiest village scenes on the Isle of Wight, full of old-world charm with thatched golden-stone cottages, tea gardens and a fine Norman church. It lies tucked away under the downland ridge in the centre of the south-west coastal shelf, less than a mile (1.6km) from the coast.

Smugglers and Wreckers

A sense of history pervades Brighstone. In the tiny village museum you will discover its notorious past. From the 13th century to the late 1800s, Brighstone was a noted smuggling village, with many of the locals involved in wrecking and contraband. Good money could be earned salvaging cargoes and timbers from ships wrecked along the coast, and it was common for local children to seek credit from the Brighstone shopkeeper by promising 'Mother will pay next shipwreck'.

It was not until the 1860s that the first lifeboats were launched from Brighstone and Brook. Reverend McCall aroused residents' consciences to Christian compassion for shipwrecked mariners, local benefactor Charles Seeley provided the finance and reformed smuggler James Buckett, having served five years compulsory service in the navy as punishment for his crimes, became the first coxwain of the Brighstone boat.

Notable Churchmen

Three of Brighstone's rectors were later appointed bishops. Thomas Ken, rector in 1667, wrote the hymn 'Glory to thee, my God this night' before becoming Bishop of Bath and Wells. Samuel Wilberforce, son of the anti-slavery campaigner William Wilberforce, was rector here for ten years (1830–40), founding the library and school, before being appointed Bishop of Winchester. In 1866, George Moberly arrived in the village, leaving three years later to become Bishop of Salisbury.

Above: Looking southwest on Brighstone Down

Right: Beyond the land, the sea – and glorious cliffs

21 Downlands to Brighstone

Tramp across downland above Brighstone to the wild and beautiful shore

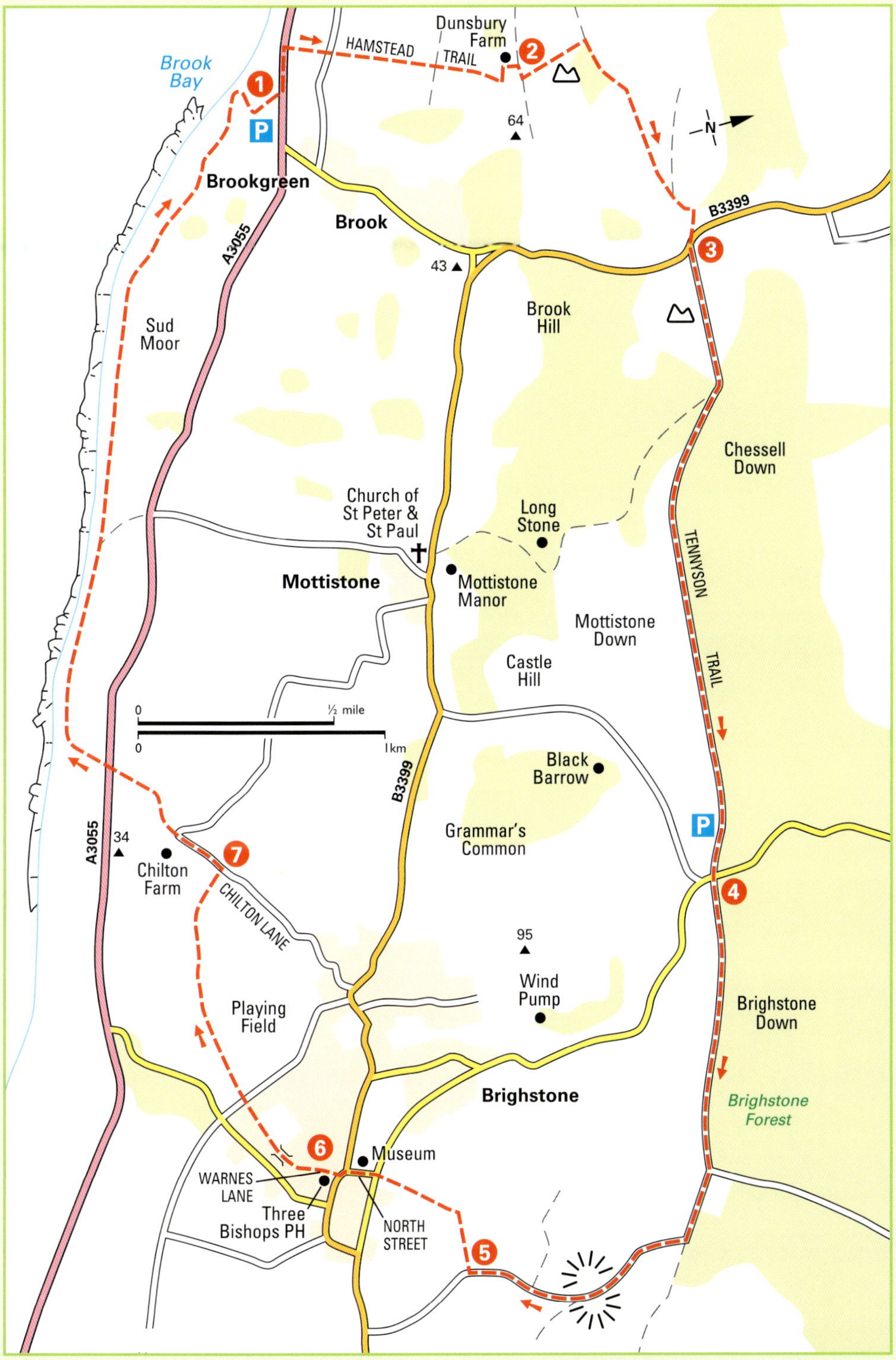

Distance 8.25 miles (13.3km)

Minimum Time 4hrs

Ascent/Gradient 941ft (287m) ▲▲▲

Level of Difficulty ●●●

Paths Field and clifftop paths, woodland tracks, 9 stiles

Landscape Farmland, chalk downland, woodland and coastal scenery

Suggested Map OS Explorer OL29 Isle of Wight

Start/Finish Grid reference: SZ 385835

Dog Friendliness Off lead on Mottistone Down, otherwise keep under control

Parking National Trust car park at Brook Chine

Public Toilets Brighstone

1 From the car park, turn left along the A3055 to a stile on the right, waymarked Hamstead Trail, and walk across the field to a track. Keep ahead beside cottages and when you reach a crossing of tracks, heading uphill on a metalled track. Bear left, then right around Dunsbury Farm to a T-junction.

2 Turn right, left through a gate and up between trees to a gate. Merge with a track at a junction and bear right. Go through a gate and climb, then bear right on the track down beside electricity poles. Keep right at a chalk track, through a gate and cross the B3399 to a bridleway, signed to 'Carisbrooke'.

3 Climb along the main Tennyson Trail to a gate on the top of Mottistone Down. Go down to the car park and right along the lane. In a few paces turn left along a stony track.

4 Follow the Tennyson Trail uphill. At the second junction of paths, take the bridleway right across Limerstone Down. Just beyond a stile, turn right for Brighstone.

5 Head downhill and join a sandy path to Brighstone. Cross the lane, walk along North Street to the B3399. Turn left, then right beside the Three Bishops pub into Warnes Lane.

6 Keep left of the car park to a road. Turn right, then left and cross a footbridge, go along the field's edge, to the rear of gardens to a lane. Cross and take the path to Chilton Lane.

7 Turn left and keep ahead at the bend to the A3055. Pass through the car park and take the path to the coast. Turn right on the coast path and over a stile. Keep to the path, go over four stiles to reach Brookgreen. Bear right and turn left to a stile and the car park.

22 The Peeping Pepperpot

A satisfying walk around the southern part of the Isle of Wight includes spectacular views and an introduction to Britain's only medieval lighthouse

Above: 'The Pepperpot' – also known as St Catherine's Oratory – was completed in 1328

Right: Changeable weather over St Catherine's hill. 'The Pepperpot' is visible to the right of the rainbow

The viewpoint car park high above Blackgang Chine is the ideal starting point for this intriguing ramble around the island's most southerly point, an area steeped in tales about shipwrecks, smuggling and three lighthouses. Before you lies the broad sweep of Chale Bay and high upon St Catherine's Hill to your right is a curious octagonal tower, known locally as 'the Pepperpot'. For centuries Chale Bay, in particular the treacherous rocks around Atherfield Ledge, was notorious for shipwrecks and the subsequent looting of desirable cargoes. Violent storms and huge seas drove fully rigged sailing ships crashing against the cliffs. Once as many as 14 floundered in the 'Bay of Death' on one single night.

Medieval Lighthouse

Your walk begins with a long, steady climb up St Catherine's Hill to 'the Pepperpot' and it is only here that you really realise its significance. It's all that remains of a medieval lighthouse or beacon and is, equally, a monument to the folly of Walter de Godeton. Its story begins with the wreck in 1313 of merchant ship, the *Ship of the Blessed Mary,* at Atherfield Ledge while bound for England with a consignment of wine. The sailors escaped and sold the 174 casks of wine to the islanders – one of whom, Walter de Godeton, took 53 casks. Because the wine belonged to a religious community in Normandy, taking possession of it in this way was considered an offence. Following a long trial, de Godeton was fined heavily and as an act of penance was ordered to build a pharos and oratory on the site of an earlier hermitage, so that a priest could tend the light and say prayers for those lost at sea.

The oratory has long since disappeared, but the lighthouse, operational until 1638, survives as Britain's only medieval lighthouse. Close by is another partially built lighthouse known as 'the Mustard Pot'. Begun in 1785 to rekindle the St Catherine's light, the project was abandoned due to cost and the realisation that its warning light would rarely be visible due to fog. It was not until the tragic loss of the *Clarendon* in 1836 that the present lighthouse at St Catherine's Point was built.

At the end of the St Catherine's Down stands Hoy's Monument, a 72ft (22m)-high column marking the visit of a Russian tzar in 1814. After taking in wonderful views, the walk ends above the dramatic undercliff of St Catherine's Point.

22 The Peeping Pepperpot

Gaze down on treacherous seas where luckless sailors met their end

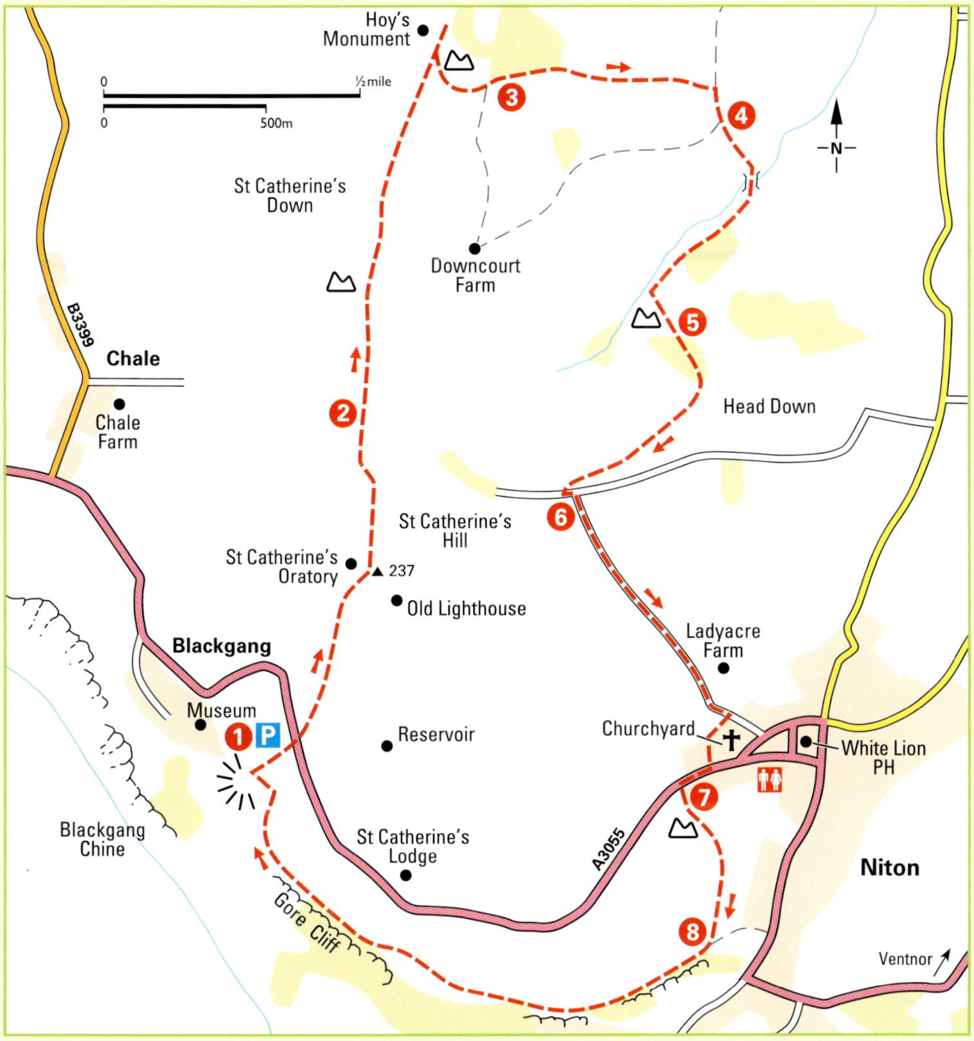

Distance 5.5 miles (8.8km)

Minimum Time 2hrs

Ascent/Gradient 745ft (227m) ▲▲▲

Level of Difficulty ●●●

Paths Field paths, downland tracks, coast path, 8 stiles

Landscape Rolling downland and farmland, breezy cliff top

Suggested Map OS Explorer OL 29 Isle of Wight

Start/Finish Grid reference: SZ 490767

Dog Friendliness Keep dogs under control at all times

Parking Free parking in viewpoint car park above Blackgang Chine

Public Toilets Niton

1 From the car park, cross the road and climb steps to a gate. Bear left, signposted 'St Catherine's Oratory'. Pass a broken stile and climb up the grassy downland to a stile. Walk up to the old lighthouse, known locally as 'the Pepperpot'. Ignore the stile by the trig point just beyond; then, keeping the fence on your right, continue downhill and bear left to a gate.

2 Go through the gate and proceed ahead on the broad grassy swathe to Hoy's Monument. Return for 80yds (73m) and take the bridleway left. Descend steeply through trees and bear left with the main path downhill to a gate. Follow the bridleway left, then bear right along the driveway.

3 Proceed ahead at a crossing of tracks (Downcourt Farm drive is to the right), heading downhill to a gate by a house. Walk along the right-hand field-edge to a gate and head downhill on a hedged path. At a T-junction, turn right and go through a gate, the path soon emerging into a field.

4 Keep to the left-hand field-edge, beside an overgrown gully, and cross the first stile on the left. In a few paces, turn right, then take the path left just before another gate. Head through the trees, cross a concrete bridge and keep right. Gradually ascend a stony path, which is very wet in winter, and which bears left then steepens to reach a stile.

5 Walk ahead, following the defined path uphill beside a hedge to two stiles in the field corner. Cross the right-hand stile and immediately turn right, down on to a path that heads diagonally uphill across the face of Head Down to a stile. Turn left to a stile and track.

6 Turn left, then almost immediately right along a hedged bridleway. Head downhill, the path becoming metalled as it enters Niton. Just before the lane, bear right into the churchyard. (Turn left, then first right, for the White Lion.) Keep left, exit the churchyard by a small gate and turn right alongside the A3055.

7 Take the footpath beside the last house on the left and climb up steeply through trees to a stile. Walk ahead across grassland to a stile and follow the left-hand field-edge to a kissing gate.

8 Turn right along the coastal path, through two kissing gates and soon emerge on to open cliff top. Remain on this narrow path close to the cliff edge for nearly a mile (1.6km) back to the car park.

23 Hampshire's Great Garden at Exbury

This delightful walk combines a stroll along the Solent foreshore with a visit to an estate village with woodland gardens on the banks of the Beaulieu River

With its shingle beaches, wild natural habitats and clumps of pine trees, Lepe Country Park is a perfect place to begin exploring one of the more remote and beautiful stretches of the Hampshire coast. The park commands superb views across the Solent to the Isle of Wight, and provides an excellent vantage point from which to watch passing yachts and ships – in particular huge tankers making their way to the oil refinery at nearby Fawley. To the west lie silent and eerie mudflats and marshland expanses at the mouth of the Beaulieu River and the fine gardens at Exbury, which form the focus of our walk.

Outstanding Gardens

Exbury is a rare surviving example of an estate village and enjoys an enviable position, situated on the edge of the New Forest and just 1 mile (1.6km) from the Solent coast. Pride of place in the village goes to Exbury House and its 200 acres (81ha) of landscaped woodland gardens, which lie on the sheltered east bank of the beautiful Beaulieu River.

The gardens were the life's work of Lionel de Rothschild, a member of the celebrated banking family, who bought the estate in 1919. Having extended the early 19th-century house, he set to work in establishing one of the most outstanding rhododendron gardens in the world. The acid-rich soil already supported fine specimens of oak, great cedars and Wellingtonias, which provided the perfect backdrop for the rhododendrons and other acid-loving plants, including azaleas, camellias and magnolias. Today, nearly 80 years on, the gardens are internationally famous for rhododendrons and azaleas and more than 1,200 hybrids have been created. A network of tracks enables you to explore the countless plantings, the cascades and ponds, a rose garden, heather garden and iris garden, daffodil meadow and a delightful walk along the banks of the river with views of Bucklers Hard.

Exbury provides a feast of visual delights all year round and you should allow at least two hours for a visit, especially in the spring and autumn. Stroll through the gardens in late spring and the vibrant colours of the rhododendrons and azaleas will be mesmerising. On a warm June day, head for the rose garden to experience the amazing range and the intoxicating scent of hundreds of blooms, while high summer is the perfect time to relax in the shade of the great trees – including the ancient, awe-inspiring yews – while admiring the peace and beauty of Exbury. Come here in the autumn and the beautiful specimen trees will reward you with a magnificent display of mellow colours.

Below: Glorious autumn colours at Exbury

23 Hampshire's Great Garden at Exbury

Take your pleasure in woodland gardens that delight in any season

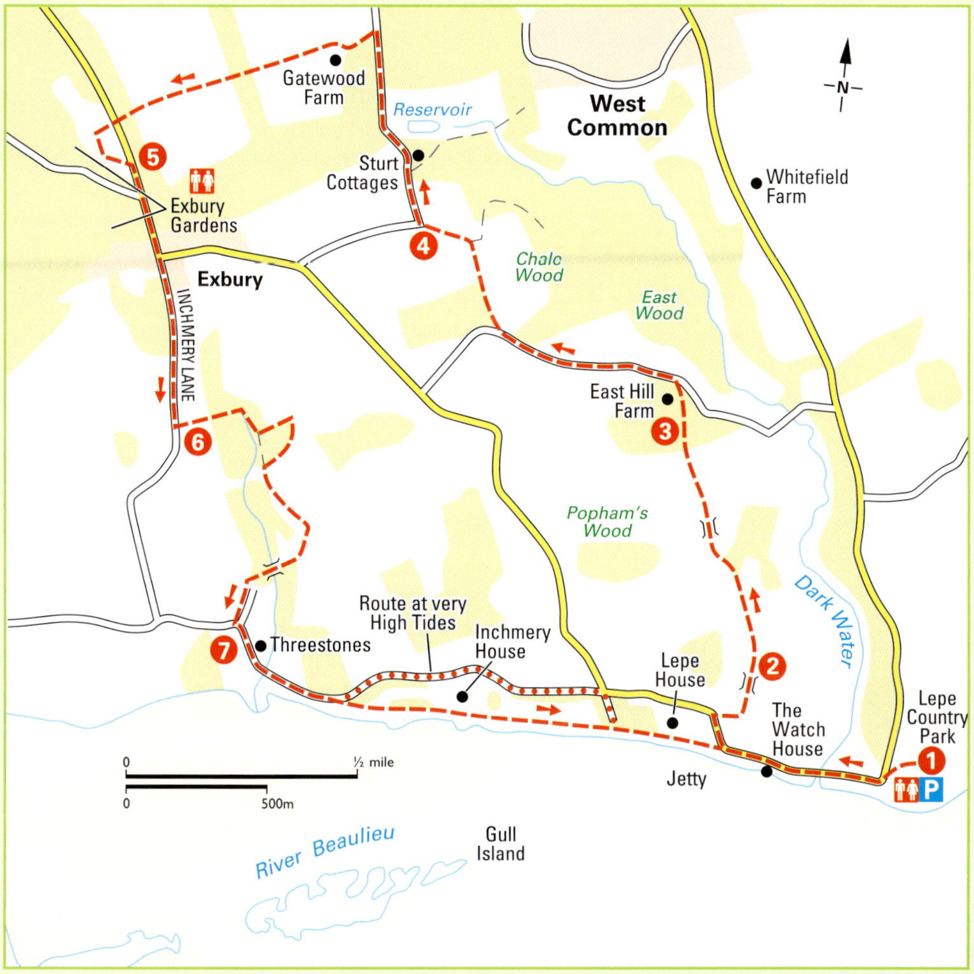

Distance 6.5 miles (10.4km)

Minimum Time 3hrs

Ascent/Gradient 114ft (35m) ▲▲▲

Level of Difficulty ●●●

Paths Fields, woodland and foreshore paths, some roads, 4 stiles

Landscape Coastline and farmland dotted with woodland

Suggested Map OS Explorer OL 22 New Forest

Start/Finish Grid reference: SZ 455985

Dog Friendliness Keep dogs under control at all times

Parking Pay-and-display car parks at Lepe Country Park

Public Toilets Lepe Country Park and Exbury Gardens

1 Walk west from the shore car park along the road. Keep left along the path above the foreshore, and pass the distinctive black-and-white painted Watch House. Then, at a small lighthouse, turn right to meet the lane. Turn left, then (as the road curves left) cross the stile on the right. Walk along the field-edge, then bear left over a bridge.

2 Keep alongside the fence to a stile and proceed straight across the field. Briefly pass beside some woodland and follow the path to a gap in the hedge near a telegraph pole. Follow the path across the next field and into the woodland ahead. Continue through the trees, bearing right beyond a footbridge, then right with waymarker post to join a fenced bridleway arrowed to the left.

3 Pass East Hill Farm, and walk along the gravelled farm track until it curves sharp left. Turn right through a gate. Follow the wide path ahead, bear right on entering a field and follow the field-edge to T-junction. Turn left to a stile and lane.

4 Turn right, continue through a gate beside a cattle grid and take the footpath left through a gate (by another cattle grid) to join a track to Gatewood Farm. Bear right at the fork, walk around the farm complex, and remain on the track for 0.75 mile (1.2km) to a gate and lane. Go straight across for Exbury Gardens (where there's a tea room).

5 On leaving Exbury Gardens, turn right along the road; where the road bends left, keep ahead, signed 'Inchmery Lane'. Continue to a waymarked path and stile on the left.

6 Cross the stile and walk straight across grassland into woodland, following the path right, through the trees. At a crossing of paths, turn left over a plank bridge. On leaving the trees, turn right along the field-edge to a gap in the hedge near a three-way signpost. Keep the woodland edge on your right until the path bears right over a footbridge into the woods. Two more footbridges lead out through a kissing gate to a lane.

7 Turn left and follow the lane to the shore. Proceed along the foreshore close to the high tide line and continue below Inchmery House. Pass Lepe House and rejoin your outward route past the Watch House back to Lepe Country Park. The final stretch along the foreshore may be impassable at high tide, so keep to the lane around Inchmery House, then, just before the road junction, turn right beside a barrier down to the foreshore to pick up the path past Lepe House.

24 Bursledon and Boatbuilding

A treat for boat-lovers, this walk offers stirring views of vessels bobbing on the estuary as well as visits to sites of profound importance in naval history

Hamble estuary between Bursledon and Southampton Water is one of the longest and busiest in Britain. The river's history of human activity extends from the time of the first Saxon settlers, who used it as a route to the fertile areas inland, to its current status as Britain's premier yachting centre. Today, this stretch of river is filled with yachts and pleasure craft, but between the 14th and early 19th centuries both Hamble-le-Rice (its formal name) and Bursledon were major centres for naval shipbuilding.

Right: Boats moored on the water at Hamble

Below: Looking across Hacketts Marsh to a marina

Nelson's Flagship

The valley provided a rich supply of timber for the warships, the ironworks at nearby Hungerford Bottom supplied essential fastenings and the bend in the river at Bursledon offered the necessary shelter: the Hamble was ideal for shipbuilding. At its peak during the Napoleonic Wars, the Elephant Yard – next to the Jolly Sailor pub – built the 74-gun HMS *Elephant*, Nelson's flagship at the Battle of Copenhagen. Two great local shipbuilders were George Parsons, who built the *Elephant*, and Philemon Ewer, who died in 1750 and whose epitaph states 'during the late war with France and Spain built seven large ships of war'. It was at Hamble Common in 1545 that Henry VIII watched in horror as his flagship, the *Mary Rose*, sank with the loss of 700 men just off the coast.

Historic Cottages and Beautiful Vistas

The six tiny Victory Cottages you pass in Lower Swanwick, just a stone's throw from the present-day Moody's Yard, were built in the late 18th century to house shipyard workers during the Napoleonic Wars. The bustling marinas and yacht moorings at Bursledon, best viewed from the terrace of the Jolly Sailor, have only appeared in the last 70 years.

Today, Hamble and Old Bursledon are a delight to explore. Hamble has a twisting main street, lined with pretty Georgian buildings, leading down to the Quay with lovely river views. Old Bursledon has a High Street but no shops, just peaceful lanes dotted with a range of interesting buildings, in particular the timber-framed Dolphin, a former pub. You'll find it a pleasure to stroll through, especially if you pause at the Hacketts Marsh viewpoint where a well placed bench affords the chance to admire the view.

24 Bursledon and Boatbuilding

Step out along both sides of the yacht-filled Hamble estuary

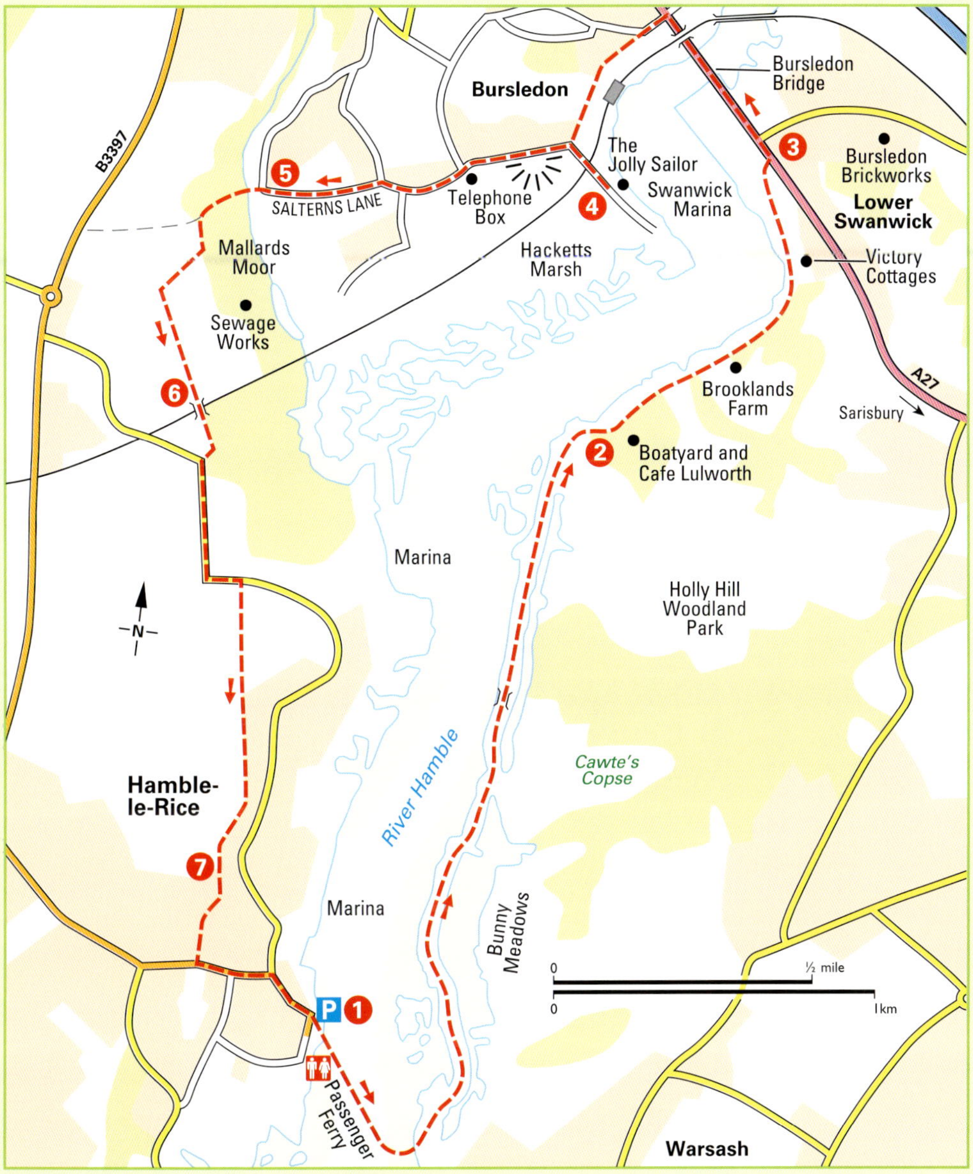

Distance 5.5 miles (8.8km)

Minimum Time 3hrs

Ascent/Gradient 164ft (50m) ▲▲▲

Level of Difficulty ●●●

Paths Riverside, field and woodland paths, some stretches of road

Landscape River estuary, farmland dotted with patches of woodland

Suggested Map OS Explorer OL 22 New Forest

Start/Finish Grid reference: SU 485067

Dog Friendliness Keep dogs on lead

Parking Pay-and-display car park by the quay in Hamble

Public Toilets Hamble

1 From the quayside car park, walk to the pontoon and take the passenger ferry across the estuary to Warsash (weather permitting; for details, visit www.hamble-warsashferry.co.uk). Turn left along the raised gravel path beside the estuary and mudflats. Cross a footbridge and continue to a gravelled parking area. During exceptionally high tides the path may flood, so walk through the car park and rejoin it by the marina.

2 Follow the path through a boatyard, pass in front of Cafe Lulworth, and rejoin the riverside path. Keep ahead at a lane, pass the row of Victory Cottages on your right, and continue to the A27.

3 Turn left, pass Swanwick Marina, and cross Bursledon Bridge. Pass beneath the railway, left into Church Lane, then fork left. Turn left into Station Road, then left into the station car park. Climb a path to the road. Turn left at the junction, left again to the pub.

4 Return along the lane and fork left into Old Bursledon. After the viewpoint at Hacketts Marsh, bear left at the telephone box. Pass the Vine Inn and Salterns Lane, then at a right bend, bear off left along a footpath.

5 Join a metalled lane beside the drive to the Coach House then, as the lane curves right, keep ahead beside a house called Woodlands, following the bridleway to a stream. Proceed uphill through woodland. At a junction of paths on the woodland fringe, bear left with the bridleway, then at a concrete road bear right, then left to join a fenced bridleway.

6 Cross a railway bridge and pass a barrier to a road. Keep left round a bend. Look out for a waymarked footpath (right) and follow behind houses for 0.5mile (800m).

7 Join a metalled path and keep ahead past modern housing to a road. Follow out to Hamble Lane and turn left on the High Street. At the roundabout, bear right down Lower High Street back to the quay and car park.

25 West Itchenor – Harbour Sails and Trails

Chichester Harbour's plentiful plant and animal life and its colourful yachting activity form the backdrop to a fascinating waterside walk

Weekend sailors flock to Chichester's vast natural harbour, making it one of the most popular attractions on the south coast. The harbour has about 50 miles (81km) of shoreline and 17 miles (28km) of navigable channel, although there is almost no commercial traffic. The Romans cast an approving eye over this impressive stretch of water and established a military base and harbour at nearby Fishbourne after the invasion of Britain in AD 43 under Emperor Claudius. King Charles II had a fondness for the area, too, and kept a yacht here.

Situated at the confluence of the Bosham and Chichester channels of the estuary is the sailing village of Itchenor, with its main street running down to the waterfront. Originally named Icenor, this small settlement started life as a remote, sparsely populated community, but by the 18th century it had begun to play a vital role in the shipbuilding industry. Small warships were built here by the merchants of Chichester, although in later years shipbuilding ceased altogether and any trace of its previous prosperity disappeared beneath the houses and the harbour mud. However, the modern age of leisure and recreation has seen a revival in boat-building and yachting, and today Itchenor once again contains boatyards, sailors and chandlers.

Tidal Habitat, Harbour Village

But there is much more to Chichester Harbour than sailing. With its intertidal habitats, the harbour is a haven for plant life and wildlife. Curlew, redshank, dunlin and terns may be spotted. Plants include sea lavender and glasswort.

Stand on the harbour at West Itchenor and you can look across the water towards neighbouring Bosham, pronounced 'Bozzum'. Better still, take the ferry across to explore the delights of this picturesque harbour village. It was from here that King Harold left for Normandy before the Norman Conquest of 1066. 'The sea creek, the green field, the grey church,' wrote Tennyson and this sums up perfectly the charm of this unspoilt spot. Take a little time to have a look at the Church of the Holy Trinity and its Saxon tower base while you're here.

Top: A variety of sailing boats on the foreshore at Itchenor

Above: Boats in Chichester Harbour

25 West Itchenor – Harbour Sails and Trails

Make a tour of Itchenor – and consider a trip across the water to historic Bosham

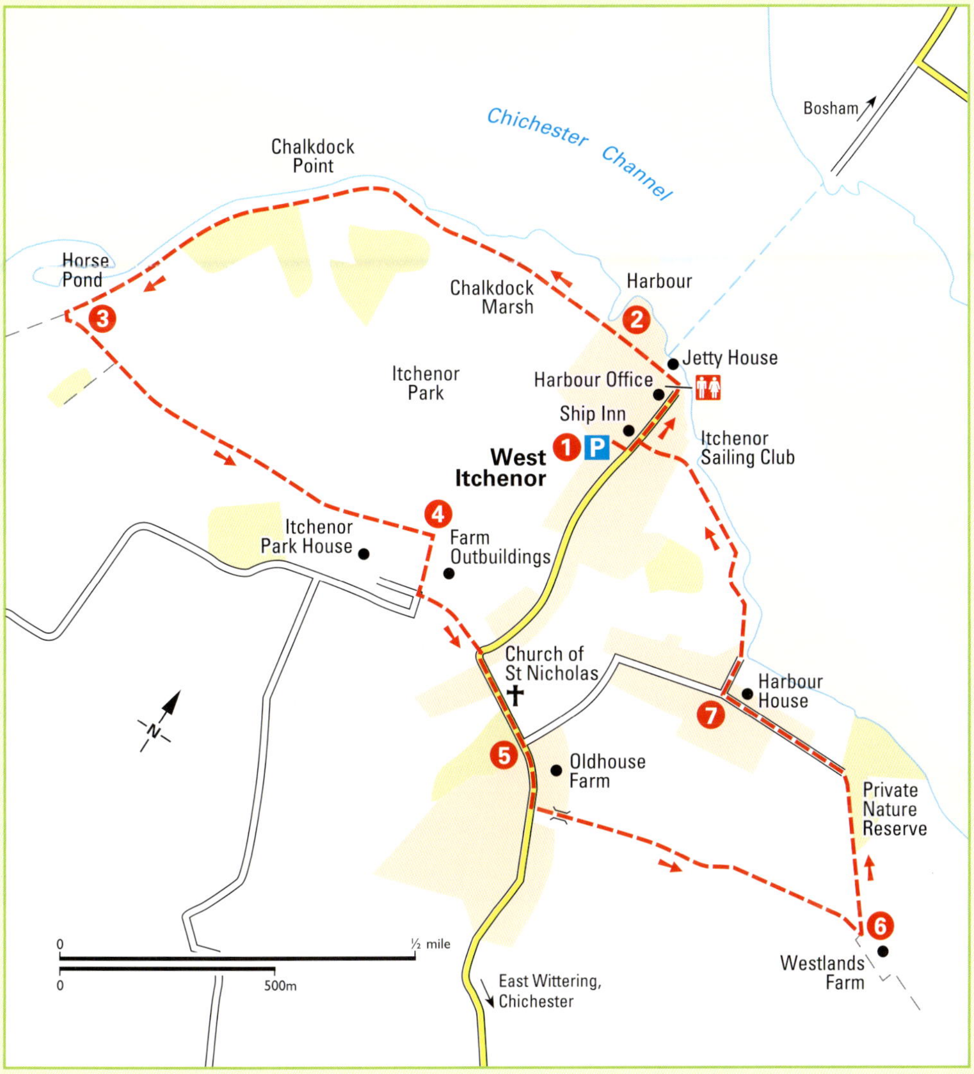

Distance 3.5 miles (5.7km)

Minimum Time 1hr 30min

Ascent/Gradient Negligible ▲▲▲

Level of Difficulty ●●●

Paths Shoreline, field tracks and paths, 1 stile

Landscape Open farmland and coastal scenery

Suggested Map OS Explorer 120 Chichester, South Harting & Selsey

Start/Finish Grid reference: SU 797013

Dog Friendliness Waterside paths are ideal for dogs but keep under control on stretches of open farmland and on short section of road. Dogs permitted on harbour water tour

Parking Large pay-and-display car park in West Itchenor

Public Toilets West Itchenor

1 From the car park walk along to the road and bear left, heading towards the harbour front. Pass the Ship Inn and make your way down to the water's edge. Look for the harbour office and the toilets and follow the footpath to the left of Jetty House.

2 Cut between hedging and fencing to reach a boat yard and then continue ahead on the clear country path. Keep left at the next junction and shortly the path breaks cover to run by the harbour and its expanses of mudflats. Cross Chalkdock Marsh and continue on the waterside path.

3 Keep going until you reach a footpath sign. Turn left here by a sturdy old oak tree and follow the path away from the harbour edge, keeping to the right-hand boundary of the field. Cross a stile to join a track on a bend and continue ahead, still maintaining the same direction. Pass Itchenor Park House on the right and approach some farm outbuildings.

4 Turn right by a brick-and-flint farm outbuilding and follow the path, soon merging with a concrete track. Walk ahead to reach the next junction and turn left by a white gate, down to the road. Bear right here, pass the speed restriction sign and soon you reach the little 13th-century Church of St Nicholas.

5 Follow the road beyond Oldhouse Farm and turn left at the footpath sign to cross a footbridge. Keep to the right of barns and follow the path straight across the field. Pass a line of trees and keep alongside a ditch on the right into the next field. The path follows the hedge line, making for the field corner. Ahead are the buildings of Westlands Farm.

6 Turn sharp left by the footpath sign and follow the path across the field. Skirt the woodland, part of a private nature reserve, and veer left at the entrance to the Spinney. Follow the residential drive to Harbour House.

7 Turn right just beyond it and follow the path along the edge of the harbour. Keep going along here until you reach Itchenor Sailing Club. Bear left and walk up the drive to the road. Opposite you should be the Ship Inn. Turn left to return to the car park.

26 Climping – Where Countryside Meets Coast

The last surviving stretch of undeveloped coast between Bognor Regis and Brighton forms is the setting for a gentle and engaging walk by the Sussex sea

Main picture: Climping Beach

Inset: Dunes at West Beach

Above: A gull bides his time on a groyne at Climping

The Sussex coast has evolved since early photographers captured classic seaside scenes at Worthing, Hove and Littlehampton, and now a chain of urban development extends almost continuously from Bognor to Brighton. Here and there, are still hints of the coastline as it used to be before the builders moved in, but Climping Beach, where this walk begins, is an altogether different place. There is a welcome feeling of space and distance here, rarely experienced on the Sussex coast. One of Climping's main attractions is its remoteness. It is approached along a country lane that terminates at the beach car park.

Lost to the Waves

A glance at a map of this area might cause some confusion. The village of Climping, which has a 13th-century church, lies a mile (1.6km) or so inland and the nearest settlement to Climping Beach is Atherington. The medieval church and various dwellings of this old parish now lie beneath the sea, which has steadily encroached upon the land, and all that is now left of low-lying Atherington are several houses and a hotel.

Shingle Banks and Dunes

Climping Beach, together with neighbouring West Beach, is popular with holidaymakers as well as locals. The National Trust protects more than 2 miles (3.2km) of coastline here. The low-water, sandy beach is backed by shingle banks that support vegetation in places, a rare habitat in Britain. In addition, there are active sand dunes, which are another rare and fragile feature of the coastline. Only six areas of active sand dunes survive on the south coast between Cornwall and Kent and three of them are in Sussex.

After crossing a broad expanse of flat farmland, the walk reaches the River Arun, opposite Littlehampton. From here it's a pleasant amble to West Beach, finishing with a stroll by the sea back to Climping Beach. There is much to divert the attention, but it is the lonely stretch of coastline that makes the greatest impression – a reminder of how the entire West Sussex coast once looked.

26 Climping – Where Countryside Meets Coast

Explore the coast near rare shingle and dune habitats

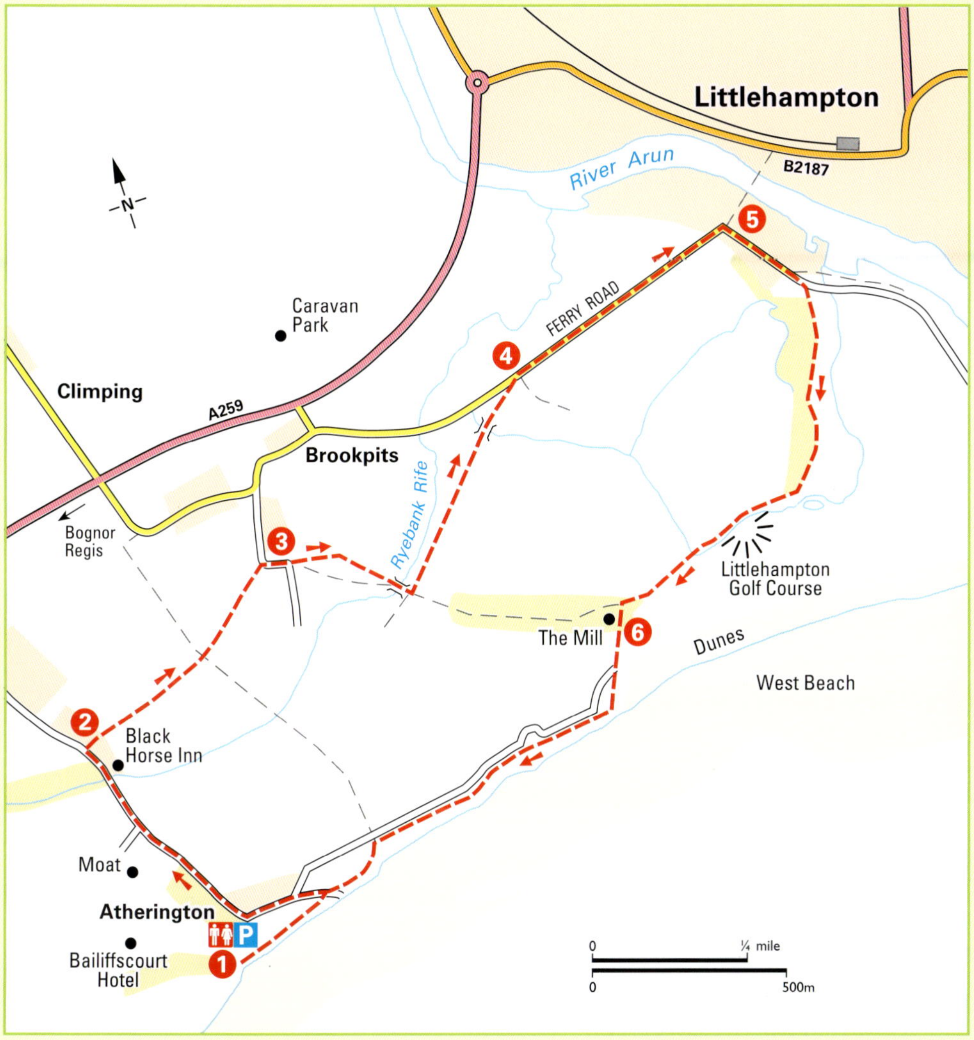

Distance 4 miles (6.4km)

Minimum Time 2hrs

Ascent/Gradient Negligible ▲▲▲

Level of Difficulty ●●●

Paths Field paths, roads and stretches of beach, 1 stile

Landscape Sandy beaches, open farmland and riverside development

Suggested Map OS Explorer 121 Arundel & Pulborough

Start/Finish Grid reference: TQ 005007

Dog Friendliness Off lead on enclosed paths and beach area. Under control near the Arun and on road at Climping Beach

Parking Car park at Climping Beach

Public Toilets Climping Beach

1 From the beach car park take the road leading away from the sea, passing the entrance to Bailiffscourt Hotel on the left-hand side. Continue walking along the road until you reach the Black Horse Inn and take the next footpath on the right, by thatched cottages.

2 When the track swings left, continue ahead across the field to a signpost, in line with a distant blue building, at a junction with a byway. Go straight over and follow the path through the fields.

3 By some derelict outbuildings, join a track on a bend and turn right. As it swings right, take the signposted path and begin by following the boundary hedge. Stride out across the field, cross the concrete footbridge and bear left at the footpath sign to follow a deep ditch known as the Ryebank Rife. When the path veers away from the ditch, cross the field to a line of trees, aiming towards a distant blue storage tower. There is a stile to cross here, followed by a footbridge.

4 Turn right and walk along the road to a turning on the right for Littlehampton Golf Club. The walk follows this road, but before taking it, continue ahead for a few steps to have a look at the footbridge crossing the Arun. The buildings of Littlehampton can be seen on the far side and you may like to extend the walk by visiting the town.

5 Continuing the main walk, follow the road towards West Beach and the golf club, veering right at a car park sign to follow an enclosed path to a kissing gate and briefly cross the golf course to enter a wood. The path runs along a raised bank and later emerges into the open with good views over this unspoilt coastal plain. Keep to the path and at the end of the golf course you reach a house known as The Mill. Avoid the path on the right here and keep left.

6 Continue walking along the footpath and soon it reaches West Beach. Look for the interpretation board which explains how this open stretch of coastline has been shaped and influenced by climatic conditions and the sea over the centuries. Follow the footpath sign towards Climping, skirting the edge of the beach and avoiding a byway on the right as you approach the beach car park.

27 From the Sea to the Deans

This exhilarating tramp across coastal downland provides an opportunity to visit a picturesque village celebrated for its artistic and literary associations

Rottingdean, to the east of Brighton, is a picturesque village with a green and several flint houses. Despite expanding development over the years, the village still retains the feel of an independent community. But there's a lot more to Rottingdean than historic buildings and landmarks. Start the walk by following the scenic Undercliff, with its close-up view of the sea, then look for a comprehensive information board at the junction of the High Street and the A259, which helps you to identify who lived where as you explore the village streets. The Black Horse was said to have been a meeting place for smugglers, while Whipping Post House was the home of Captain Dunk, local butcher and bootlegger.

Indian-born British author Rudyard Kipling lived at The Elms in Rottingdean until driven away by inquisitive fans and autograph hunters. He wrote the novel *Kim* (1901) and the *Just So Stories for Little Children* (1902) here – among other works. Kipling loved the South Downs and he found these hills a great source of inspiration. 'Our blunt, bow-headed, whale-backed Downs', he wrote in his famous poem 'Sussex'.

Statesman and Artist

Some of Kipling's relatives had local associations and it was in the village that his cousin Stanley Baldwin met and married Lucy Ridsdale, whose family lived at The Dene. Baldwin was a Conservative statesman who, as prime minister, secured three terms in office during the 1920s and 30s. The flint church at Rottingdean is noted for its stained-glass windows designed by the Pre-Raphaelite artist Sir Edward Burne-Jones, who lived at North End House on the west side of the green. Enid Bagnold who wrote the novel *National Velvet* (1935), was also a local resident. From the green, the walk climbs up above Rottingdean. The views are breathtaking as you make your way down to Ovingdean church and back towards Roedean.

Above: A plaque commemorates Rottingdean's most famous literary resident

Right: The Rottingdean war memorial on the village green

Far right: The windmill near the village was built in 1802

Bottom right: The 11th-century St Wulfran's Church in Ovingdean

27 From the Sea to the Deans

Investigate the village on the downs that inspired Kipling

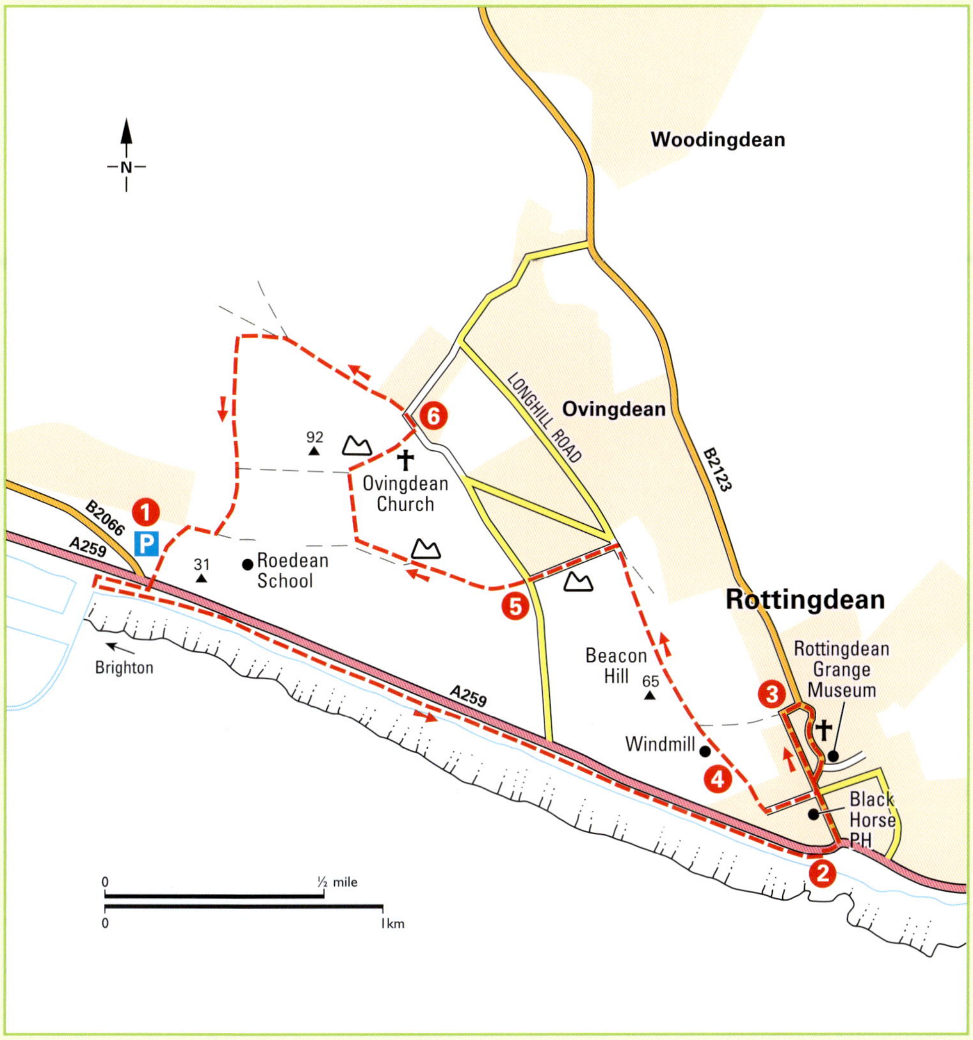

Distance 5 miles (8km)

Minimum Time 2hrs

Ascent/Gradient 305ft (92m) ▲▲▲

Level of Difficulty ●●●

Paths Busy village streets, downland paths and tracks, 6 stiles

Landscape Rolling downland extending to the sea

Suggested Map OS Explorer 122 Brighton & Hove

Start/Finish Grid reference: TQ 347032

Dog Friendliness On lead in Rottingdean. Under careful control in places

Parking Free car park at Roedean Bottom, at junction of A259 and B2066

Public Toilets Rottingdean village and the Undercliff

1 From the car park cross the A259 and turn right towards Brighton, following the path parallel to the road. Look for the path on the left and follow it down to the Undercliff. Head east towards Rottingdean, passing a café. Continue on the path until you reach a slope and a sign for historic Rottingdean on the left.

2 Make for the village and pass the White Horse pub on the left. Cross the A259 into Rottingdean High Street. Pass the Black Horse, Nevill Road and Steyning Road and continue along the street. As you approach The Green, look for The Dene on the right.

3 Follow the road round to the right and make for the junction. Keep right and head back into Rottingdean village. Pass the war memorial and the village pond and look for the church on the left. Pass The Plough Inn and walk back down to the High Street. Turn left, then right into Nevill Road. Climb quite steeply and bear right into Sheep Walk. Look right here for a good view of the village and its church.

4 Keep the windmill on your left and follow the bridleway over the Downs. Woodingdean can be glimpsed in the distance and the buildings of Ovingdean are seen in the foreground. The outline of Roedean School is visible on the horizon. Continue to Longhill Road, turn left and walk down to the junction.

5 Cross over to a stile and then head up the slope to a second stile in the right-hand boundary. Bear left and keep going up the hillside. Pass a private path to Roedean School and continue beside the wire fence to a stile in the field corner. Turn right and skirt the pasture to the next stile. Descend steeply towards Ovingdean Church, cutting off the field corner to reach a stile. Cross into the field and keep the churchyard wall hard by you on the right.

6 Cross a stile to the lychgate and walk down to the junction. Turn left and when the road bends right, go straight on along a wide concrete track, following the bridleway. Keep left at the fork, then immediately left again at the next fork, a few paces beyond it. When the track swings quite sharply to the left, go straight on along the path. Pass a path and stile, and the car park by the A259 looms into view. When you reach the road, by the entrance to Roedean School, cross the grass to the car park.

28 'Snake River' and the Seven Sisters

A peaceful walk along the banks of a snaking river passes behind the beauty spot of Cuckmere Haven, and delivers wonderful views of the Seven Sisters cliffs

Above: Easy does it – the meandering path of the River Cuckmere

Right: The high chalk cliffs of the Seven Sisters

One of the few remaining undeveloped river mouths in the Southeast is the cove known as Cuckmere Haven. It was used by smugglers in the 18th century to bring ashore their cargoes of brandy and lace, and the scene has changed very little in the intervening years with the eternal surge of waves breaking on the isolated shore.

The River Cuckmere joins the English Channel at this point, but not before it makes a series of extraordinarily wide loops through lush water meadows. It's hardly surprising that this characteristic has earned it the occasional epithet 'Snake River'. Winding ever closer to the sea, the Cuckmere emerges beside the famous white chalk cliffs known as the Seven Sisters. Extending east towards Birling Gap, there are, in fact, eight of these towering chalk faces, with the highest one, Haven Brow (253ft/77m), closest to the river mouth. On the other side of the estuary rise the cliffs of Seaford Head, a local authority nature reserve.

Seven Sisters Country Park

The focal point of the lower valley is the Seven Sisters Country Park, an attractive amenity area of 692 acres (280ha) developed by East Sussex County Council. There are artificial lakes and park trails, and an old Sussex barn nearby has been converted to provide a visitor centre that holds many interesting exhibits and displays. There is more to the park than just these attractions, as the wildlife provides naturalists with hours of pleasure and enjoyment. The flowers and insects found here are at their best in early to mid summer, while spring

and autumn are the time to bring your binoculars with you for a close-up view of migrant birds.

A Haven for Birds

Migrant wheatears are sometimes spotted near the river mouth from late February onwards, followed later in the season by martins, swallows, whinchats and warblers. Grey phalaropes have also been seen in the park, usually after severe autumn storms. These birds spend most of their lives far out to sea, usually off South America or western Africa.

As you explore the Cuckmere Valley, you might wonder why the river meanders the way it does. The meltwaters of the last Ice Age shaped this landscape, and over the centuries rising sea levels and a freshwater peat swamp influenced the river's route to the Channel. Around the start of the 19th century, the sea rose to today's level and a new straight cut with raised banks, devised in 1846, shortened the Cuckmere's journey to the sea. This unnatural waterway controls the river and helps prevent flooding in the valley.

28 'Snake River' and the Seven Sisters

Follow a breezy trail beside the Cuckmere River as it winds lazily towards the sea

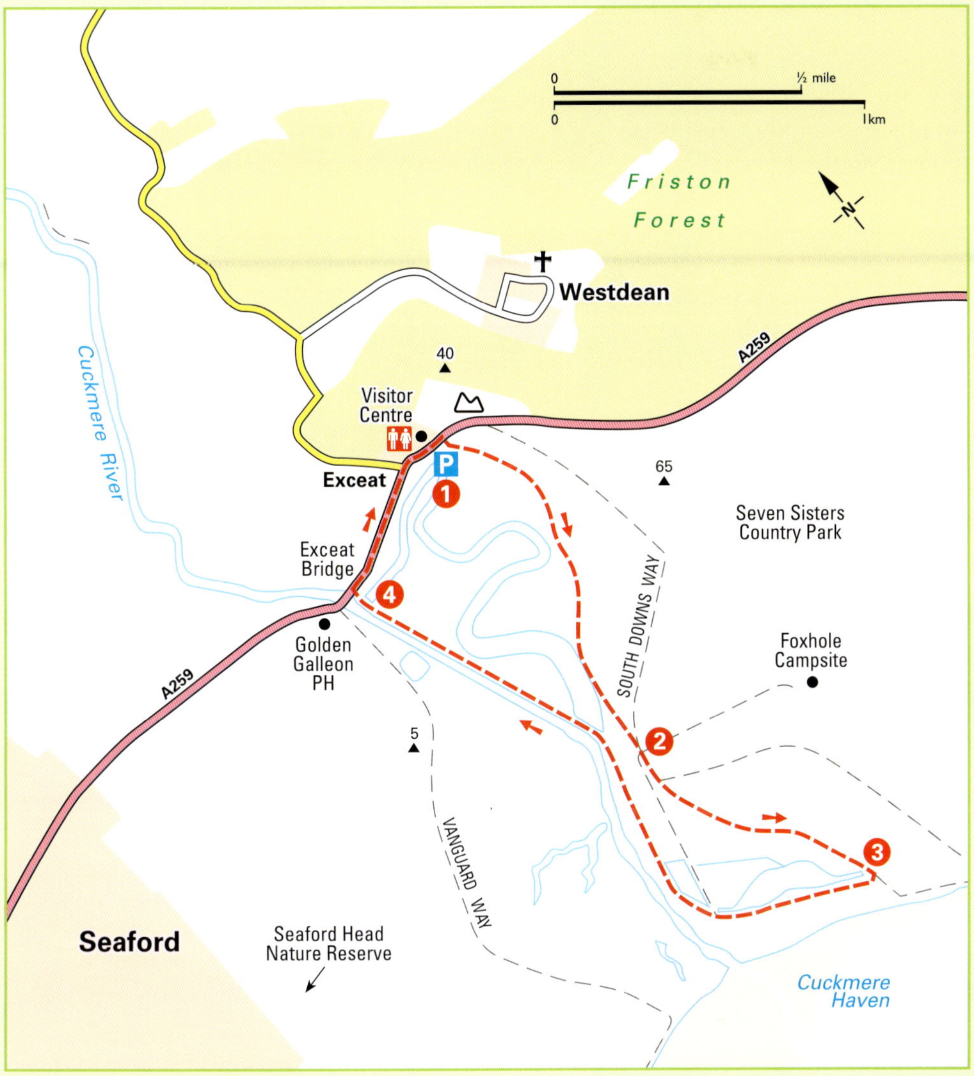

Distance 3 miles (4.8km)

Minimum Time 1hr 30min

Ascent/Gradient Negligible ▲▲▲

Level of Difficulty ●●●

Paths Grassy trails and well-used paths, mostly beside the Cuckmere or canalised branch of river

Landscape Exposed and isolated valley and river mouth

Suggested Map OS Explorer 123 Eastbourne & Beachy Head

Start/Finish Grid reference: TV 518995

Dog Friendliness Under close control within Seven Sisters Country Park. On lead during lambing season and near A259

Parking Fee-paying car park at Seven Sisters Country Park

Public Toilets Opposite car park, by visitor centre

1 Make for the gate situated near the entrance to the Seven Sisters Country Park and follow the wide, grassy path towards the beach. The path gradually curves to the right, running alongside a concrete track. The River Cuckmere meanders beside you, heading for the open sea. Continue ahead between the track and the river and make for a South Downs Way sign.

2 Avoid the long distance trail as it runs in from the left, pass it and the Foxhole campsite and keep ahead, through the gate towards the beach. Veer left at the beach and South Downs Way sign. On reaching the next gate, don't go through it: keep right and follow the beach sign. Pass a couple of wartime pillboxes on the left, an evocative reminder of less peaceful times, and go through a gate. Join a stony path and walk ahead to the beach, with the white wall of the Seven Sisters rearing up beside you.

3 Turn right and cross the shore, approaching a Cuckmere Haven Emergency Point sign. Branch off to the right to join another track here. Follow this for about 50yds (46m) until you come to a junction and keep left, following the Park Trail. Keep beside the Cuckmere; the landscape here is characterised by a network of meandering channels and waterways, all feeding into the river. Pass a turning for Foxhole campsite and follow the footpath as it veers left, in line with the Cuckmere. Make for a kissing gate and continue on the straight path by the side of the river.

4 Keep ahead to the road at Exceat Bridge and on the left is the Golden Galleon pub. Turn right and follow the A259 to return to the car park at the country park.

29 Birling Gap to Beachy Head

This delightful coastal ramble leads along a scenic stretch of the Sussex coast to the famous headland of Beachy Head, passing the old *Belle Tout* lighthouse.

The chalk cliffs of Beachy Head were formed from the shells of billions of minute creatures that fell to the bottom of a subtropical sea. Today, this stretch of coast is one of Britain's most famous landmarks. The treeless South Downs reach the sea in spectacular fashion and over 500ft (152m) below the towering cliffs, lies Beachy Head's distinctive red-and-white lighthouse, standing alone on a remote beach. This blend of natural and artificial features creates a magnificent picture.

The Waters of the 'Devil's Cape'

The present 142ft (43m) lighthouse, automated in 1983 and modernised in 1999, has been vital to the safety of mariners off this coast since it was completed in 1902. But even as far back as 1670 a beacon shone from this point, helping to guide ships away from the treacherous ledges below. Beachy Head has always been a navigational nightmare. Sailors have long feared it and the Venetians dubbed it the 'Devil's Cape'.

In 1831 eccentric Sussex landowner John Fuller, or 'Mad Jack', built the *Belle Tout* lighthouse high up on the headland to the west of Beachy Head. The lamp was first lit in 1834, but the lighthouse was never a great success. Its lofty position on the clifftop meant that it was often shrouded in mist and fog and therefore invisible to shipping in the English Channel. A decision was eventually taken to erect a lighthouse at sea level.

Right: The charming red-and-white lighthouse is dwarfed by the cliffs at Beachy Head

Below: The beautiful, treeless South Downs

'Beautiful Headland'

The name Beachy Head comes from the Norman French *Beau Chef* – meaning 'beautiful headland'. The description is certainly apt. This breezy, sprawling clifftop draws visitors and tourists from far and wide who come to marvel at the breathtaking sea views or saunter along the South Downs Way. The whole area is a designated Site of Special Scientific Interest (SSSI).

The walk begins at Birling Gap to the west of Beachy Head. Before long it heads inland, running across the slopes of the South Downs. Within sight of Eastbourne, it suddenly switches direction, following the South Downs Way to Beachy Head and back to Birling Gap. On the way it passes the old *Belle Tout* lighthouse, now a private home.

29 Birling Gap to Beachy Head

Enjoy sprawling countryside, tall skies and vast sea and cliff views

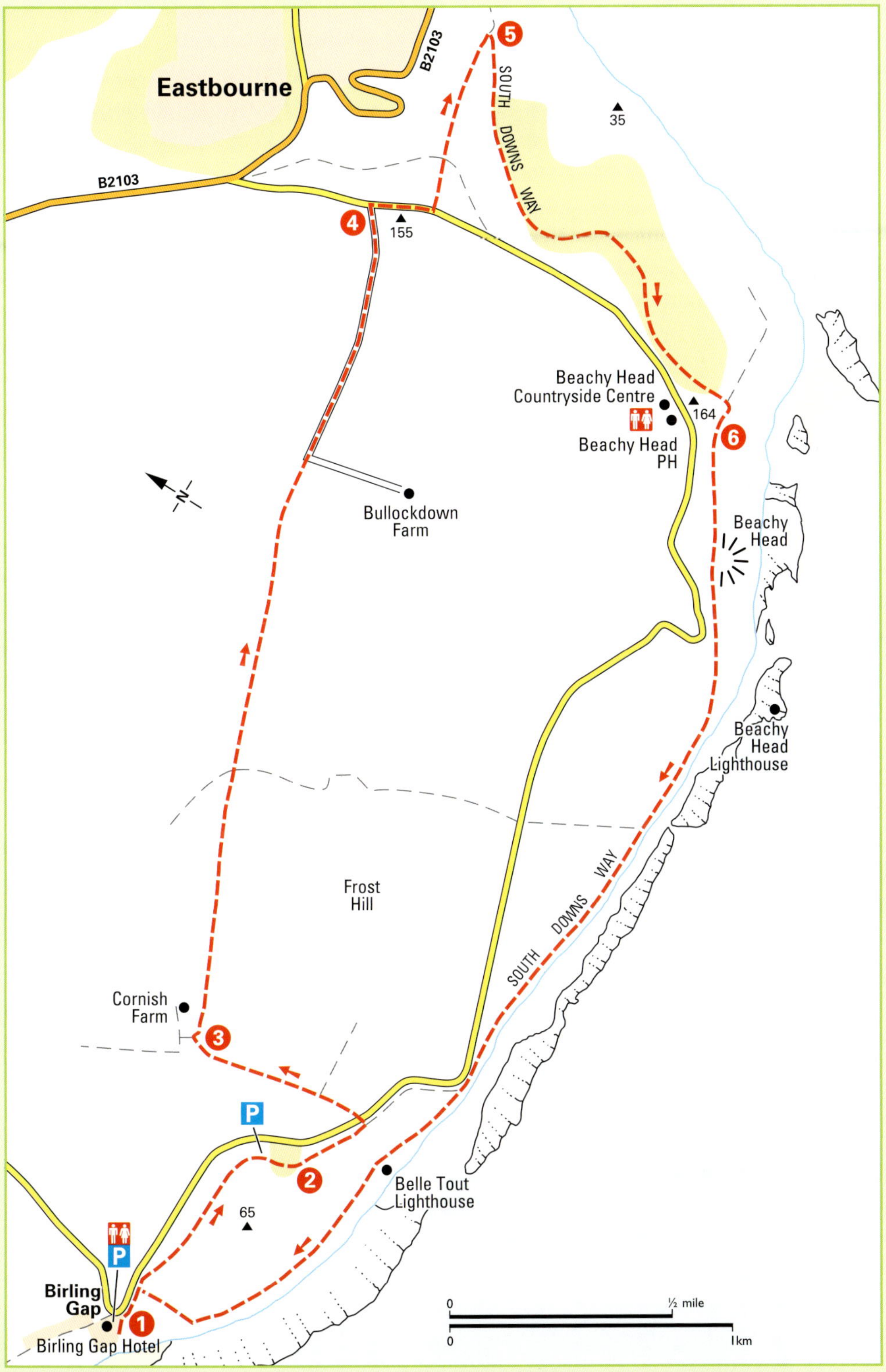

Distance 7 miles (11.2km)

Minimum Time 3hrs

Ascent/Gradient 536ft (163m) ▲▲▲

Level of Difficulty ●●●

Paths Downland paths and tracks, clifftop greensward, no stiles

Landscape Southern boundary of South Downs and headland

Suggested Map OS Explorer 123 Eastbourne & Beachy Head

Start/Finish Grid reference: TQ 554959

Dog Friendliness On lead by Cornish Farm and on South Downs Way

Parking Free car park at Birling Gap

Public Toilets Birling Gap and Beachy Head

1 Leaving the car park, keep the road on your left. Continue on a grassy path, right of a car park and go on between the trees.

2 Keep parallel to the road; at a junction with a concrete track, take the next left to meet it. Follow the bridleway to 'East Dean Down'. Pass a fingerpost and continue ahead.

3 Follow the concrete track as it bends right towards Cornish Farm, avoiding the bridleway going straight on. Look for a gate on the right and head east, keeping the fence on your right-hand side. Make for another gate and continue ahead. Pass alongside lines of bushes before reaching the next gate. Pass an access track to Bullockdown Farm.

4 Pass beside a barrier to the road and turn right. On reaching two gates on the right, cross the road and take the grassy path down to a waymarked junction. Follow the path towards Eastbourne, signposted 'seafront'; soon you meet the South Downs Way.

5 Bear sharp right and follow the trail as it climbs between bushes and vegetation. Keep right when another path comes in and make for a viewpoint. Cross the grass, up to the trig point.

6 Return to the South Downs Way and go west. Keep the Belle Tout lighthouse in your sights and follow the path up towards it. Keep to the right of the old lighthouse and the car park at Birling Gap edges into view. Bear right at the South Downs Way post and follow the path down and round to the left. Swing left just before the road and return to the car park.

30 Stranded Winchelsea – Abandoned by the Sea

A lovely Sussex village, once a thriving medieval port, is the start and end point for an intriguing walk across farm and marshland that once lay beneath the waves

Looking at the sleepy village of Winchelsea today, it is hard to believe that this was once one of the most important ports on the whole south coast of England. The story of Winchelsea is fascinating. This is an extraordinarily unlucky place – surely nowhere else in the country can have fallen victim to fate in quite the same way.

High and Dry

This delightful little town was one of the seven Cinque Ports, the confederation of coastal towns in medieval Sussex and Kent that were granted privileges in return for taking a role in the defence of the realm. Characterised by elegant houses and quiet, grid-pattern streets, this was a notable and prosperous place. But it became stranded when the sea receded, exposing a stretch of fertile marshland. Now it lies more than 1 mile (1.6km) inland.

Yet Winchelsea's run of bad luck did not begin and end with the vagaries of the ocean. The existing settlement is a new town, which replaced Old Winchelsea in the late 13th century when the old place was inundated by the sea and swept away by a great storm in 1287. The remains of the old town now lie beneath the waves of the English Channel, somewhere out in Rye Bay.

A Planner's Dream

The new town was conceived and sited personally by King Edward I, and with its regular grid pattern has long been acknowledged as perhaps the first example of medieval English town planning. Only a dozen of the proposed 39 grid squares were ever completed and the ambitious plans for the new Winchelsea were eventually abandoned. Three gates, part of the original fortification, still survive, including Strand Gate with its four round towers; however, many of the buildings you see in the town today date back only about 100 years.

In the Middle Ages Winchelsea came under constant attack from the French and suffered heavy damage. The church, much of which was destroyed during the last raid of 1449, includes the tomb of Gervase Alard, England's first admiral, as well as various monuments and a wall painting from the 14th century. Before starting the walk, take a leisurely tour round the town. It's well worth the effort and the views from breezy Strand Gate out towards the Channel are very impressive.

This is a walk of two extremes. From lofty vantage point of Winchelsea, you'll descend to a bare, rather featureless landscape, skirting a flat expanse of water-meadows known as Pett Level. The return leg is more undulating, and the higher ground delivers good views both of the coast and Winchelsea's unspoiled hilltop setting.

Below left: Looking out to sea from Pett Level

Below: The walk starts from close to the New Inn, Winchelsea

Bottom: Our route follows part of the 1066 Country Walk

30 Stranded Winchelsea – Abandoned by the Sea

Admire a Cinque Port with a remarkable record of bad luck

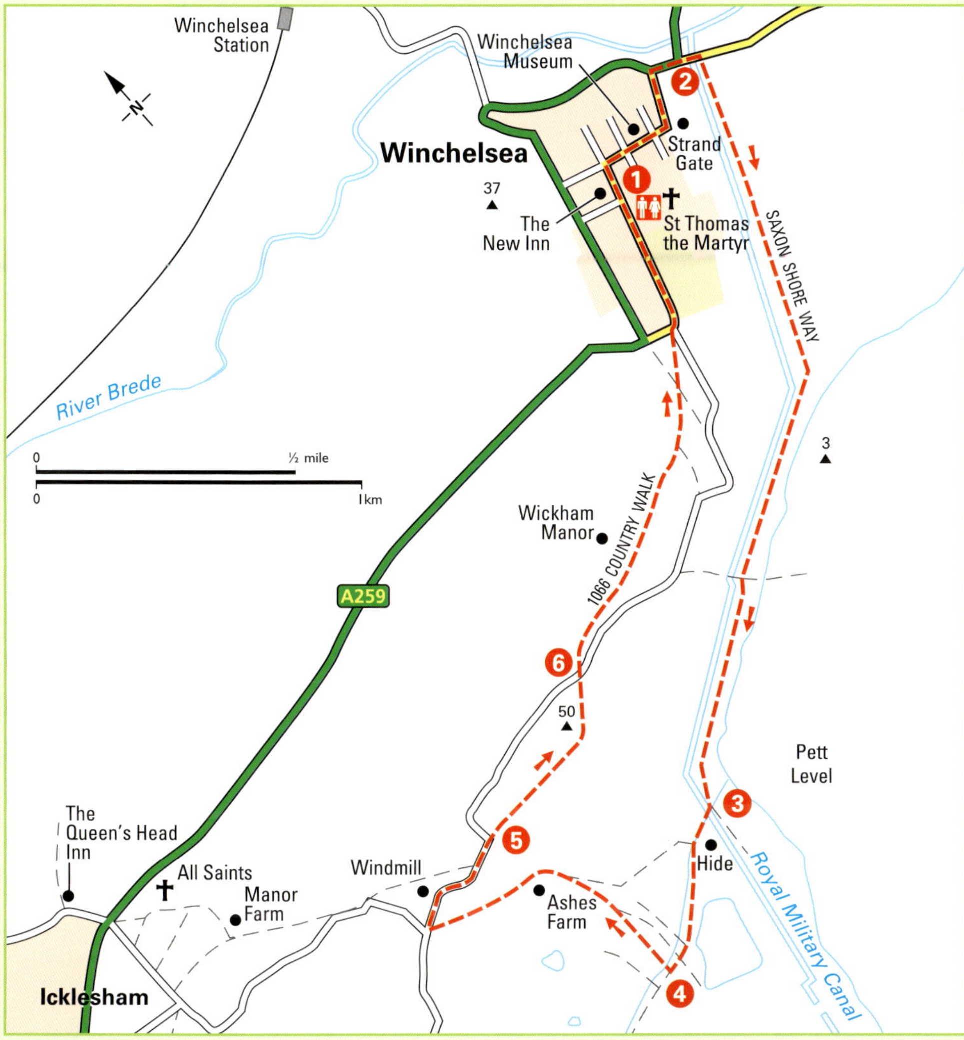

Distance 4.5 miles (7.2km)

Minimum Time 2hrs

Ascent/Gradient 197ft (60m) ▲▲▲

Level of Difficulty ●●●

Paths Field paths and pavements, 15 stiles

Landscape Mixture of marshland and undulating farmland

Suggested Map OS Explorer 124 Hastings & Bexhill or 125 Romney Marsh, Rye & Winchelsea

Start/Finish Grid reference: TQ 905173

Dog Friendliness On lead near birding hide and across farmland

Parking Roadside parking near St Thomas's Church at Winchelsea

Public Toilets Winchelsea

1 With The New Inn on your left and ruined St Thomas's Church on the right, follow the road round the right-hand bend. Head down to Strand Gate and then take the road to the junction with the A259. Turn right and follow the pavement along here.

2 When the road bends left, turn right at the sign for Winchelsea Beach. Cross the Royal Military Canal and bear immediately right. Follow the towpath across this empty landscape. Cross a stile and avoid a concrete footbridge. When the canal begins to curve left, look for a stile and galvanised gate.

3 Bear right for a few paces beyond it at the footbridge. Cross a second wooden footbridge over a ditch and make for a gate. Pass the birding hide and continue along the path, making for the next footbridge.

4 Turn right here, veer right and then follow the path as it curves left through the reedbeds. Head uphill, towards a house. Keep to the left of it and follow the path through the trees. Bear right at gates up some steps to a stile, turn left along the field-edge to another stile. Cross a drive, go through a gate and go straight across the field to a stile, then bear right for a few paces to two more stiles. Skirt the field to the next stile and exit to the road. Keep right here, signposted 'Winchelsea', and soon you pass below the hilltop windmill, avoiding the 1066 Country Walk, which meets the road at this point.

5 Go straight ahead over a stile when the lane bends left and cross the field. Look for a stile and keep alongside some trees to the next stile. Continue ahead, pass an old pill box and head down the gentle slope to the road.

6 Turn right for a few paces to a stile on the left. Bear right, on the 1066 Country Walk, and cross the next stile. Keep to the right of Wickham Manor and look for a stile in the far boundary. Cross the drive to a stile and keep ahead across the fields. Make for a stile and gate in the bottom left corner and follow the 1066 Country Walk waymarks. The path veers over to the right to two stiles. Bear left and begin a moderate ascent to a stone stile. Turn right at the road, follow it round to the left and return to the centre of Winchelsea.

31 Bombs, Birds and Flowers at Rye

A gentle tour past wartime defences and around a local nature reserve crosses shingle and skirts old gravel pits that are now a habitat for plants and birds

Above right: A black-headed gull (*Larus ridibundus*) approaches its nest

Below: Rye harbour with St Mary's church in the background

If you turned the clock back to the dark days of the Second World War you would find Rye Harbour a very different place. Blockhouses for machine guns littered the coast and barbed wire and landmines made it a 'No Go' area. During the hours of darkness great searchlights swept across the sky; they were particularly effective at detecting the dreaded flying bombs. Go there now and you can still identify some of these crumbling relics of war. It's a fascinating exercise to imagine what might have happened had enemy forces landed on the coast in this forgotten corner of England.

Napoleonic Threat

The Second World War was not the first time this area had been under threat. During the Napoleonic Wars, 150 years earlier, Rye Harbour was considered an obvious target for invasion and attack when the Martello Tower, seen by the car park at the start of the walk, became the first of 47 fortifications built in Sussex as a defence against the French. The tower would have been a tough deterrent. The walls are nearly 12ft (4m) thick at the base, and the middle floor would have been occupied by a garrison of one officer and 24 men.

Since then, the sea has built up over half a mile (800m) of land in front of it, with violent storms dumping huge deposits of shingle on the shore every winter. Today, the little community of Rye Harbour is peaceful – and yet, years after the shadows of war have passed, there remains a sense of bleak isolation.

Nature Reserve

Part of a designated Site of Special Scientific Interest (SSSI), Rye Harbour Local Nature Reserve lies at the mouth of the River Rother, which forms its eastern boundary. During its early stages, the walk follows the river and at first glance the shingle seems so bare and inhospitable that it is hard to imagine any plant could grow here. But in late May and June the beach is transformed by a colourful array of flowers. Delicate yellow horned poppies, sea kale, carpets of seaweed and countless other species of plants thrive in this habitat.

Salt marsh, vegetation along the river's edge, pools and grazing marsh add to the variety and the old gravel pits now represent an important site for nesting terns, gulls, ducks and waders. Rye Harbour is perhaps best known for its superb bird life; this spot is always popular with ornithologists.

The walk follows the coast for some time, passing the Ternery Pool, originally two separate gravel workings dug by hand early in the 20th century. The route continues along the coast, before heading inland to some more flooded gravel pits. Here you might easily spot gulls, grebes, cormorants, swallows and reed warblers. Turtle doves are often seen in the fields and sometimes perch in pairs on the overhead wires.

31 Bombs, Birds and Flowers at Rye

Gaze on wide skies beside Rye Bay

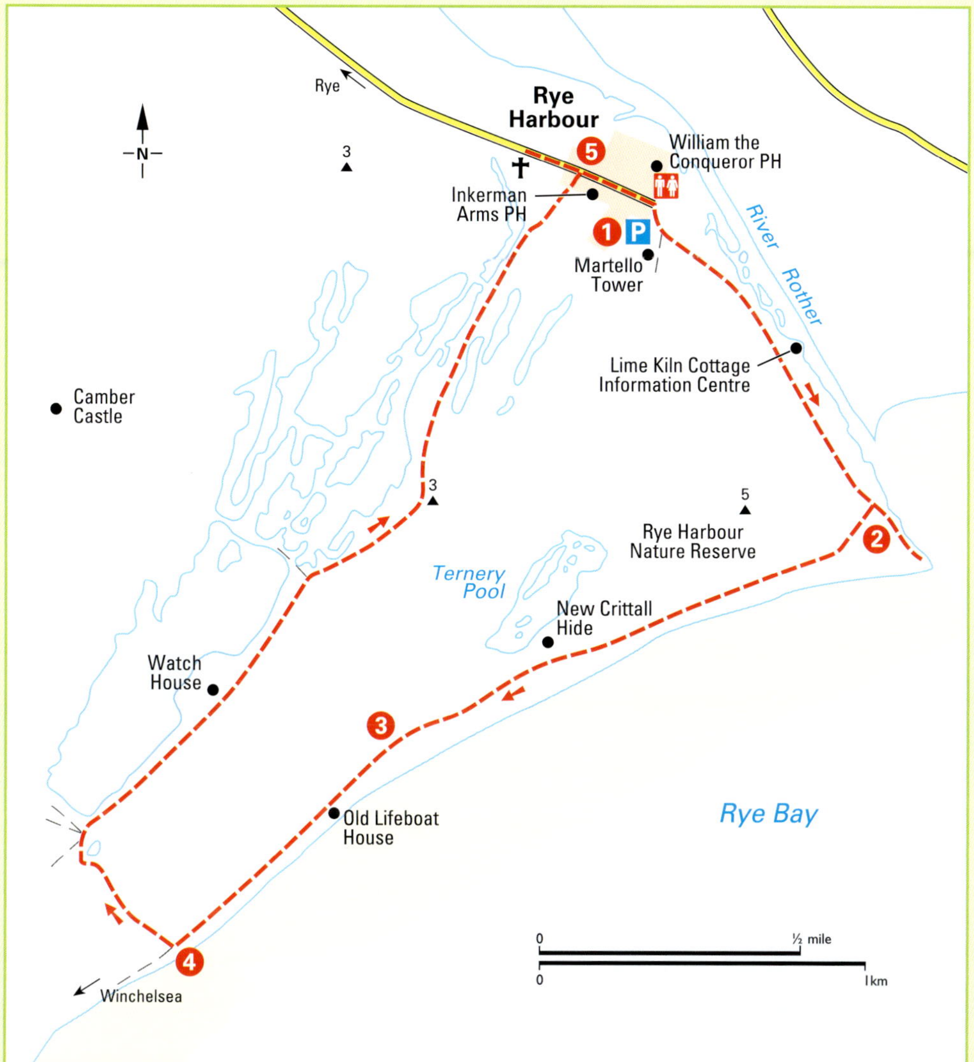

Distance 4.5 miles (7.2km)

Minimum Time 2hrs

Ascent/Gradient Negligible ▲▲▲

Level of Difficulty ●●●

Paths Level paths and good, clear tracks, no stiles

Landscape Mixture of shingle expanses and old gravel workings, now part of a local nature reserve

Suggested Map OS Explorer 125 Romney Marsh, Rye & Winchelsea

Start/Finish Grid reference: TQ 942189

Dog Friendliness Dogs on lead within Rye Harbour Local Nature Reserve

Parking Spacious free car park at Rye Harbour

Public Toilets Rye Harbour

1 Keep the Martello Tower and the entrance to the holiday village on your right and enter Rye Harbour Local Nature Reserve. The Rother can be seen on the left, running parallel to the path. Head for the Lime Kiln Cottage information centre and continue on the firm path, with the Rother still visible on the left. The sprawling expanse of Camber Sands, a popular holiday destination, nudges into view beyond the river mouth.

2 Follow the path to the beach, then retrace your steps to the point where a permissive path runs off to the left, cutting between wildlife sanctuary areas where access is not allowed. Pass the entrance to the New Crittall hide on the right. From here there are superb views over Ternery Pool. In the distance, Rye's jumble of houses can be seen sprawling over the hill. Continue west on the clear path and gradually it edges nearer the shore.

3 Ahead now is the outline of the old abandoned lifeboat house and, away to the right in the distance, the unmistakable profile of Camber Castle. Keep going on the clear path until you reach a waymarked footpath on the right, running towards a line of houses on the eastern edge of Winchelsea.

4 Take this footpath and head inland, passing a small pond on the right. Glancing back, the old lifeboat house can be seen standing out starkly against the sky. Turn right at the next junction, pass the Watch House and continue on the track as it runs alongside several lakes. Pass to the left of some dilapidated farm outbuildings and keep going along the track. The lakes are still seen on the left-hand side, dotted with trees, and the silent, motionless figures of fishermen can often be seen along here. Begin the approach to Rye Harbour and on the left is the spire of the church.

5 On reaching the road in the centre of Rye, turn left to visit the fascinating parish church before heading back along the main street. Pass the Inkerman Arms and return to the car park at the start of the walk.

32 Across the White Cliffs

Along part of the Saxon Shore Way, this unforgettable trail enables us to see the famous White Cliffs with new eyes – as a habitat for wild flowers and butterflies

Dover's white cliffs are a distinctive landmark, known the world over and seen as a symbol of England, associated forever with thoughts of Dame Vera Lynn singing 'There'll be bluebirds over the white cliffs of Dover.' Yet few people realise the cliffs are an important wildlife habitat – so important that they supports species rarely found elsewhere. The cliffs, made of chalk, are topped with a thin, porous soil that has been grazed by animals for hundreds of years, creating what is known as chalk downland. Grazing stops coarse grasses and scrub invading the land and creates the ideal environment for wild flowers to flourish. And while the early farmers didn't realise it, they were creating unique plant communities.

While you're walking, keep your eyes peeled for plants like horseshoe vetch, early spider orchid and yellow rattle, which gets its name from the seed pods that rattle in the wind. With wild flowers, of course, come butterflies – particularly those wonderful blue ones that you so rarely see these days. Look out for the silvery chalkhill blue and the gorgeous sapphire Adonis blue.

Adders and Grazing Ponies

Other wild creatures of the cliffs include adders (although you're unlikely to see one), slow worms (a legless lizard), common lizards and birds such as fulmars, peregrine falcons and skylarks – there are no bluebirds, however, because they are an American species not found in Britain.

Unfortunately, modern farming methods have led to a 98 per cent decline in chalk downland and with it, of course, a similar decline in the plants and animals it supports. In an attempt to halt this decline, the National Trust has introduced Exmoor ponies to the white cliffs. These hardy little ponies eat the coarse grasses that would otherwise invade the land, and so allow the wild flowers to grow.

Top: An Exmoor pony on the Saxon Shore Way. There are around 2,700 ponies globally; 350 mares live wild in their original home, Exmoor

Above: A haven for wild flowers. A thin layer of soil tops the White Cliffs, and grasses and scrub are kept at bay by grazing. The cliffs are up to 350ft (107m) tall

Right: The South Foreland lighthouse, built in the Victorian era, was the first powered by electricity. In use until 1988, it is now owned by the National Trust

32 Across the White Cliffs

Wander the iconic cliffs and visit a village that was once home to James Bond creator Ian Fleming

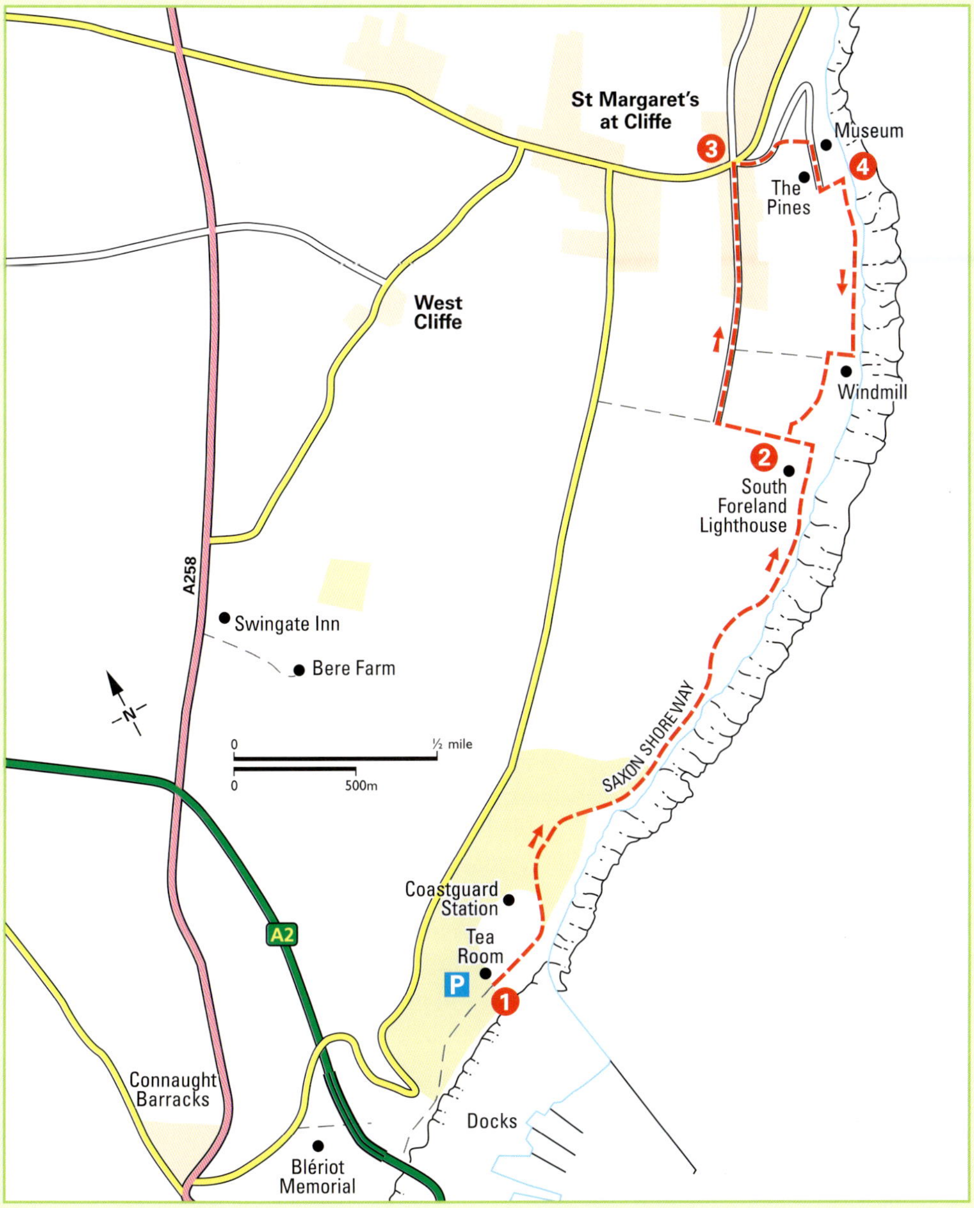

Distance 5.5 miles (8.8km)

Minimum Time 2hrs 30min

Ascent/Gradient 131ft (40m) ▲▲▲

Level of Difficulty ●●●

Paths Chalky cliff paths, short section of road

Landscape Grassy cliff tops with extensive sea views

Suggested Map OS Explorer 138 Dover, Folkestone & Hythe

Start/Finish Grid reference: TR 334421

Dog Friendliness Good, cliff top is popular with local dog walkers

Parking National Trust White Cliffs Visitor Centre car park

Public Toilets None en route; customers can use toilets in the National Trust tea room

1 From the car park and visitor centre walk away from Dover, following the Saxon Shore Way through a gate and up over the cliffs past the coastguard station. Drop down and follow the trail around the edge of Langdon Hole, the path continuing along the cliffs and up to the impressive South Foreland Lighthouse. Some of the tracks branch off and lead very close to the cliff edge – but there is a real danger of cliff falls so you are well advised to keep to the main route. You may see some Exmoor ponies. They've been introduced to the cliffs to graze the rare chalk downland and help preserve the habitat.

2 With the lighthouse on your left-hand side, take the metalled track ahead and keep straight on along a narrow tarmac path where the track curves right in a few paces. At the end, turn right and follow another metalled track, passing houses to reach the road at St Margaret's at Cliffe.

3 Turn right, keep ahead at the junction down Bay Hill, soon to take the path right, signed 'Steps to the Beach'. Steeply descend to a road and turn right, passing The Pines Garden and St Margaret's at Cliffe Museum. The village was an exclusive resort, and the museum celebrates two famous residents: James Bond novelist Ian Fleming (1908–64) and playwright Sir Noel Coward (1899–1973).

4 From the museum continue along the track, bearing sharp left before a cattle grid with the Saxon Shore Way sign. At the right-hand bend, go through the gate ahead and bear right along the grassy cliff path. Eventually reach another gate and turn left along the track, passing a windmill, to return to South Foreland Lighthouse. Retrace your steps along the cliff back to the car park – no hardship when you have these views.

33 A Taste of Sandwich

From the medieval port of Sandwich a walk full of historic interest leads further back in time to Richborough Fort, dug in the Roman invasion of Britain in AD 43

Above: Today the only waterborne vessels in the former port of Sandwich are pleasure boats on the River Stour

Below: The inner defences of Richborough Fort – the fort was a supply base for the invading Roman army under Aulus Plautius

As you walk around Sandwich, you can't help but be struck by the town's picturesque appearance. With its half-timbered houses and historic churches, it has a quiet English charm. It's hard to imagine these narrow streets echoing to the footsteps of raiders, smugglers and pirates. Yet Sandwich was once the most important port in England – the Dover of its day – and was one of the original Cinque Ports.

England's Defenders

The Cinque Ports (pronounced 'sink') was the name given to the confederation of five (later seven) important ports on the south-east coast that guarded England in the days before there was an official navy. Hastings, New Romney, Dover, Hythe and Sandwich, together with Rye and Winchelsea, were important fishing and trading centres. This meant they had plenty of men and ships that the king could press into service, whether his family wanted free transport to Europe or a force to repel invaders. It was convenient for the monarch – and in those days no one would argue.

By the 13th century, the towns had become so important to England that they were formally granted rights and privileges. These included freedom from taxes and customs duties, some trading concessions, and even their own courts. In return, each town had to supply a quota of men and ships whenever these were required.

This was a pretty good deal and provided considerable opportunities for merchants to make money. The Cinque Ports became some of the richest and most powerful centres in Europe.

Merchants, Smugglers and Pirates

The quay at Sandwich, now so quiet, would have bustled in those days as fighting men embarked for Europe, and ships laden with valuable cargoes of silks, spices and wine were unloaded. It would have been intimidating, too, for smugglers and pirates operated from here, attracted by the rich pickings on offer. All the ports had a violent reputation.

However, their power and influence was not to last. A terrible storm in 1287 permanently altered the coastline. The sea began to retreat and the harbour at Sandwich, and other ports, eventually became so choked with silt they could no longer be used. After a permanent navy was established the privileges of the Cinque Ports were revoked and Sandwich sank back into relative obscurity.

33 A Taste of Sandwich

Follow a gentle trail around this picturesque town

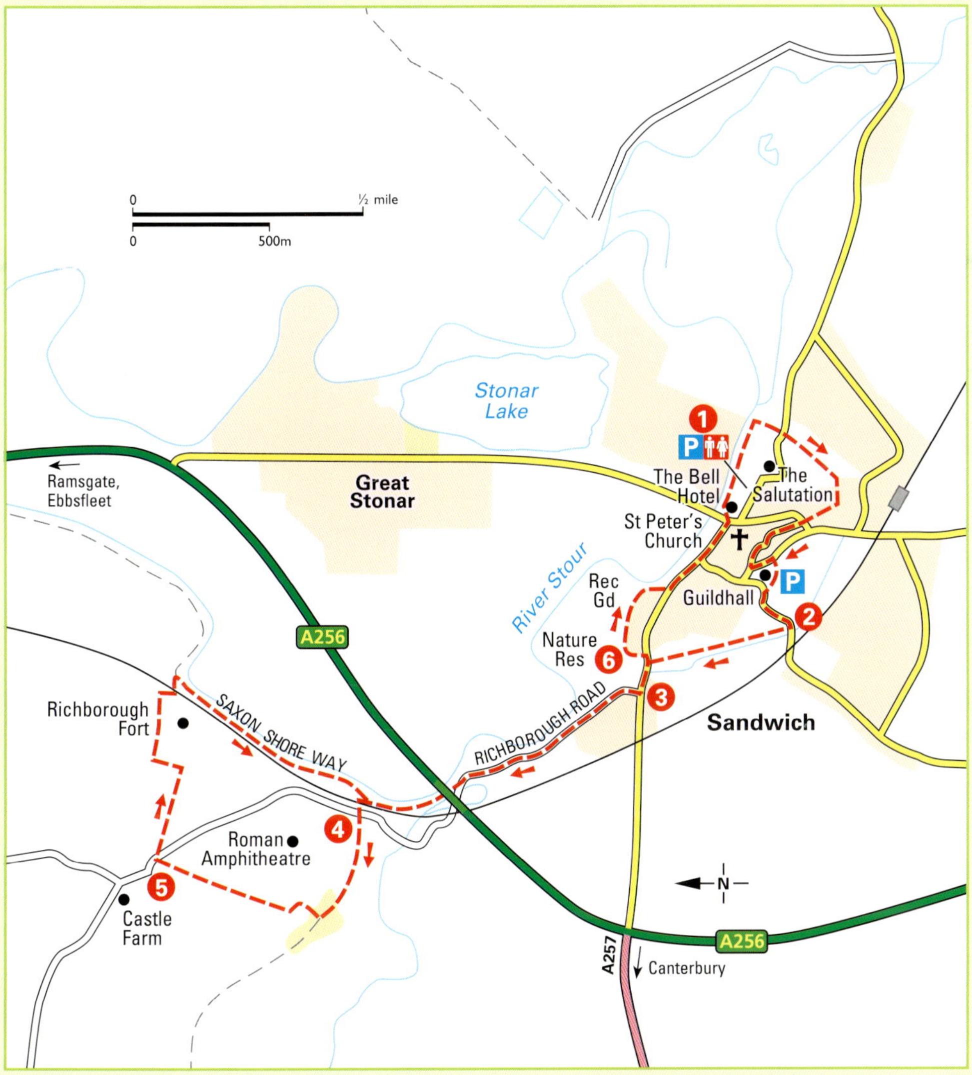

Distance 3 miles (4.8km)

Minimum Time 1hr 30min

Ascent/Gradient 98ft (30m) ▲▲▲

Level of Difficulty ●●●

Paths Easy town streets and field tracks, 9 stiles

Landscape Townscape, salt flats, golf course and beach

Suggested Map OS Explorer 150 Canterbury & The Isle of Thanet

Start/Finish Grid reference: TR 332582

Dog Friendliness Pretty good, can run free in some sections

Parking Car park (fee) at Sandwich Quay

Public Toilets New Street and Sandwich Quay and Sandwich Bay

1 Walk along the river bank away from the town, following the line of the old wall. At a bend in the river, turn right along a tarmac path to the road. Turn right, then left and continue along the path, passing the bowling green. Next turn right down steps into Mill Wall Place. When you reach the crossroads, go straight ahead along King Street, passing St Peter's Church, and then turn left along the intriguingly titled No Name Street. Afterwards cross New Street to the Guildhall, then walk though the car park and up to the Rope Walk, where rope makers used this long, straight area to lay out their ropes.

2 Turn right and when you reach the road, cross over and walk down The Butts. At the main road turn left, cross over and turn right up Richborough Road.

3 Walk ahead, past a scrapyard, and through a gate to join a footpath on the right. Follow the track round, under the main road and turn left to cross the railway line via stiles.

4 Cross the road, go through a kissing gate, then walk across the field to the trees, heading for the third telegraph pole. The path now goes into the trees: where it splits, fork right to a stile. Now follow the fence line and turn right at the marker beyond a ditch to reach a gate. Walk up the left-hand field-edge, cross a stile, go through a gate and cross a further stile to the road.

5 Cross over and walk up the track ahead. Richborough Fort is ahead. The track runs around the fort with expansive views over this seemingly endless landscape. At the bottom of the track turn right along the end of a garden. Cross the stile and back over the railway, leaving it by another stile. The path now goes immediately right, over a bridge and back beside the river. You will eventually rejoin the road, and retrace your steps to the end of Richborough Road where you turn left.

6 Go left through a kissing gate, pass the Nature Reserve and go round the edge of a recreation ground. Bear right through trees and pass a car park to reach Strand Street and turn left. Go left in front of the Bell Hotel, and right past the Barbican and return to the car park.

34 Paddling up Paglesham Creek

A stroll along the sea wall leads from Paglesham Eastend to Paglesham Churchend, in the footsteps of Saxons, smugglers and oyster fishermen

Paglesham, just a few miles from Southend-on-Sea, is bordered to the north by the River Crouch and to the south by the River Roach. It was founded in Saxon times and its population survived mainly by rearing sheep that grazed on the flat marshlands. But its remote position on Essex's east coast, and its proximity to waterways, attracted smugglers who would sail up the river bringing in their ill-gotten gains to pass on at a profit to anyone who was happy to make some easy money.

Smuggling was big business in Paglesham. In the 18th century one of the most notorious of the town's smugglers was William Blyth – also known as 'Hard-Apple Blyth'. He started out as the village grocer, progressed to churchwarden and was reputed to have torn up church records to use as wrapping for his butter and bacon. His party piece was spending evenings at the Punch Bowl pub drinking kegs of brandy and crunching wine glasses. This unusual diet and lifestyle clearly did him no harm – he died in 1830, aged 74.

Right: Oysters are still farmed locally and an annual oyster festival brings a flurry of foodies to the local pubs

Below: View across the River Roach near Paglesham

Below right: Our walk starts from the Plough and Sail Inn at Paglesham Eastend

Wife- and Oyster-farming

'Wife-farming' seems to have been another pastime. Daniel Defoe, in his travels around Paglesham, noted that some men boasted that they had fifteen or more wives. Stories circulated that the women who couldn't stand the rigorous lifestyle and bad weather here either died from the cold or abandoned their husbands for a more comfortable existence in the uplands from where they originally came. The men simply chose a replacement.

When the villagers weren't smuggling or 'wife-farming' they were engaged in oyster farming, a lucrative business that peaked in the mid-19th century when scores of fishermen would sail out along the estuaries of the Crouch and Roach and return to have their oysters processed by one of the big companies, such as the Roach River Company, now long gone. On this walk you will see sheep grazing along the grassy sea wall, just as they have done for centuries, but you'll have to look hard for smugglers in the creeks and estuaries.

34 Paddling up Paglesham Creek

Try out a former hotbed of smuggling, where oysters are today's main attraction

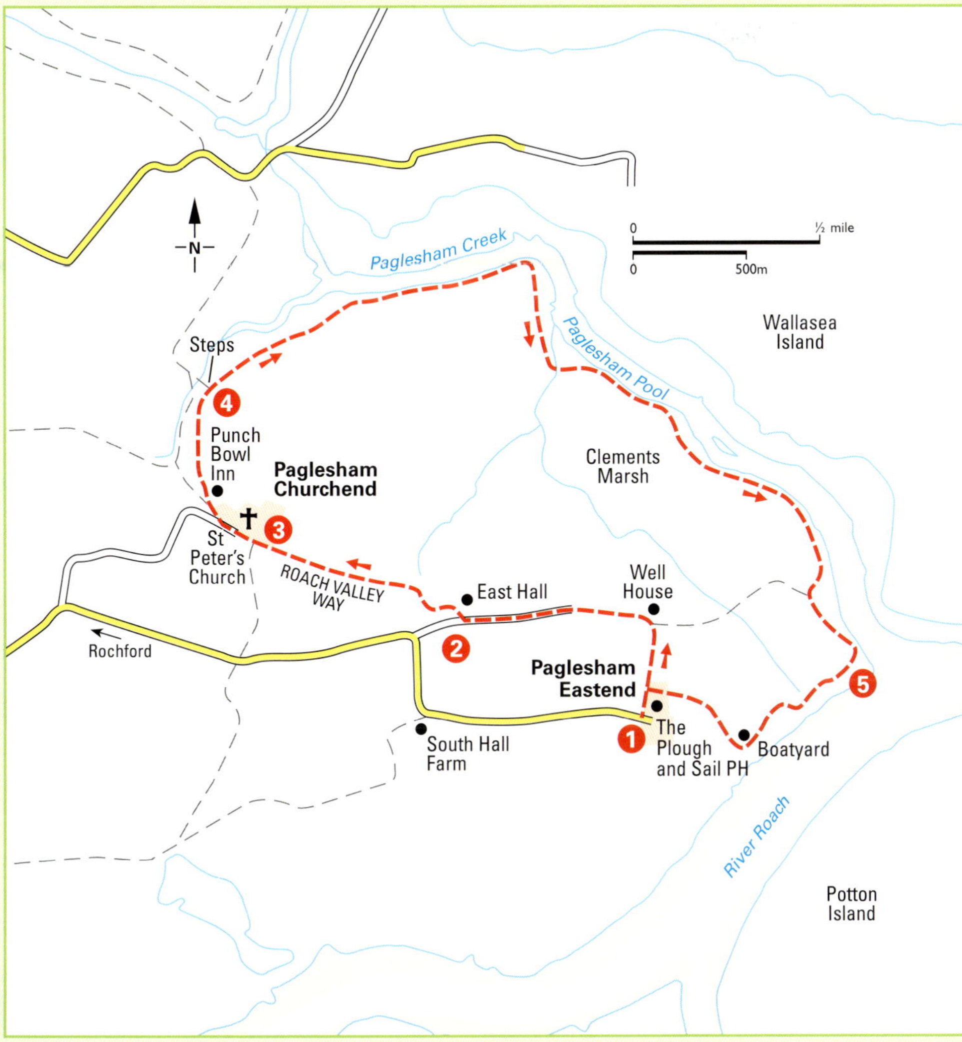

Distance 6.25 miles (10.1km)

Minimum Time 2hrs 45min

Ascent/Gradient Negligible ▲▲▲

Level of Difficulty ●●●

Paths Grassy sea wall, field-edge, unmade tracks, 3 stiles

Landscape River estuary, salt marsh, mudflats, grazing and arable farmland

Suggested Map OS Explorer 176 Blackwater Estuary, Maldon

Start/Finish Grid reference: TQ 943922

Dog Friendliness Lots of water, but keep on lead along sea wall, where sheep are grazing; enclosures often divided by stiles and low-voltage electric fencing might cause problems for larger dogs

Parking On-street parking at Paglesham Eastend beside the Plough and Sail Inn

Public Toilets None en route

1 Walk to the left of The Plough and Sail Inn along a track, and after 100yds (91m) follow the fingerpost ahead to the left of the house called Cobblers Row. Maintain direction along a field-edge path, with arable fields either side, until you reach a red brick wall on your left. Go along the lawn of Well House and follow the tarmac lane as it curves left.

2 At the corrugated barn of East Hall, follow the Roach Valley waymark, right and then left, and maintain direction along the grassy field-edge. Walk by paddock fencing, Church Hall on your right and the pond on your left, to St Peter's Church at Paglesham Churchend.

3 Keeping the church on your right, continue along Churchend High Street to the Punch Bowl Inn. Maintain direction for 50yds (46m), take the concrete path to your right soon after the two houses and after a few paces continue along the Roach Valley Way. Follow the public footpath sign, left, which soon becomes a grassy field-edge path running parallel with a waterway on your left.

4 Take a short clamber up the embankment and, leaving the Roach Valley Way, turn right on to the sea wall of Paglesham Creek. Keep to the path by Paglesham Creek, which widens as you approach the River Roach. To your left the salt marshes stretch towards the River Crouch where you have views of the marinas of Burnham-on-Crouch and the warehouses and timber yards of Wallasea Island. Much of the landward side of the embankment is given over to sheep grazing, which makes this walk somewhat difficult for larger dogs as enclosures are often divided by wooden stiles and low-voltage electric fencing.

5 As the path bears right, with the river on your left, maintain direction past oyster beds until you reach the boatyard. Go down the steps from the sea wall and pick your way through boats and machinery to the gate. Pass beside the gate and follow the unmade track until you pass a row of cottages on your left, followed by Cobblers Row and the fingerpost on your right that was the direction for the outward journey. Turn left and return to The Plough and Sail Inn at Paglesham Eastend.

35 A Meander Through Salty Maldon

This gentle excursion explores the former port of Maldon, site of a 10th-century battle, leading between ancient hedgerows and past a 12th-century abbey

Top television chefs swear by the healthy attributes of sea salt and keen cooks will notice that they often refer to Maldon Sea Salt in their culinary creations. On this charming walk you'll not only discover picturesque pathways, historic buildings and estuarine bird life, and see the town that gives its name to a celebrated battle and the Old English poem that described it, but also pass the factory that has been the home of salt manufacturing in this corner of Essex since 1882.

A Viking Battle

Salt aside, it is hard to imagine that the rural riverside town of Maldon, perched on a hill above the River Chelmer, was once the scene of that bloody battle. But one morning, back in AD 991, the Saxon inhabitants awoke to witness 93 Viking longboats sailing up the estuary of the River Blackwater. The invaders were forced to camp at Northey Island because a receding tide left their ships stranded. Word had spread that Sandwich and Ipswich had been plundered, and under the leadership of Byrhtnoth, Maldon's leader, a two-day battle on the marshes opposite Northey Island ended in a Saxon victory.

Byrhtnoth, however, died on the battlefield, his head carried off as a trophy. These heroic events were described in an Old English poem that was probably passed down for generations orally but survives today in a stirring 11th-century fragment generally known as 'The Battle of Maldon'.

Admiralty Town

Between the 17th and early 19th centuries, Maldon thrived as a port town and centre of Admiralty jurisdiction due to its position at the head of the Blackwater Estuary. In 1797 the Chelmer and Blackwater Navigation linked the town with Chelmsford. Although Maldon lost out on port dues and maritime trade declined, the town retained its prominence, due to its thriving oyster industry and the barge trade.

Maldon was second in importance only to Colchester, and had already established its own abbey, grammar school and Moot Hall, which later served as a police station, a court and a jail house. Thanks to the popularity of salt-water bathing in the 18th century and the growing barge trade from London, Maldon flourished. By 1847 the town was linked to London by rail and a promenade park attracted wealthy citizens. Ships still come up on the tide, bringing grain from Holland to the flour mill on the banks of the River Chelmer and you can also see the traditional Thames sailing barges, identified by their red sails. Many are now given over to pleasure sailing, but in days gone by they plied their trade along the east coast to London.

Centre for Boating

Today this smart town, with its narrow streets and attractive timber-framed buildings, many with 18th- and 19th-century facades, welcomes the boating fraternity. Landlubbers, more interested in Maldon's social history, can explore the pathways along the River Chelmer or the tow paths of the Chelmer and Blackwater Navigation, which meet in a complex of waterways at Beeleigh Falls.

Below: Canada geese explore the River Chelmer

Bottom: Peaceful waters by Beeleigh Falls

35 A Meander Through Salty Maldon

See where the sea salt comes from

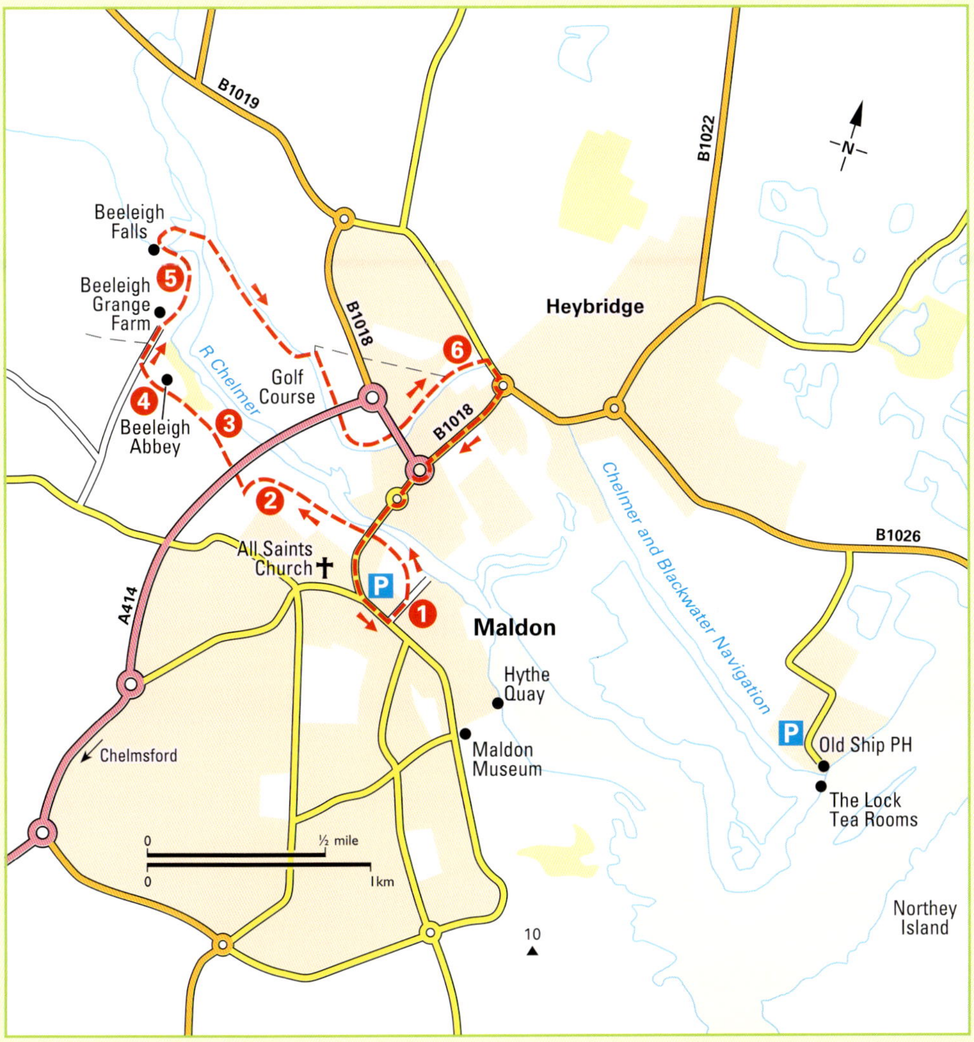

Distance 4.25 miles (6.8km)

Minimum Time 2hrs

Ascent/Gradient 115ft (35m) ▲▲▲

Level of Difficulty ●●●

Paths Mainly grassy paths, narrow in parts and prone to mud after rain, some roads

Landscape River estuary, some woodland, canal tow path, marshland and mudflats, some urban streets

Suggested Map OS Explorer 183 Chelmsford & The Rodings, Maldon & Witham

Start/Finish Grid reference: TL 853070

Dog Friendliness Lots of water but dogs shouldn't take a dip, they could get stuck in mud. Watch out for Shetland ponies, too

Parking Pay-and-display car park at Butt Lane

Public Toilets Butt Lane

1 From the car park turn left and walk along Downs Road. The footpath drops quite steeply and soon you have views of the River Chelmer and the salt works. Where the road curves right at the riverside turn left, cross Fullbridge with care, and follow the grassy embankment, keeping the river over on your right. Maintain direction and cross a stile. Follow the often muddy path, which meanders uphill through a sloping meadow usually occupied by horses.

2 Go through a kissing gate and over the adjacent stile and keep ahead, looking out for a stile on the right at the top of the hill. Turn right over this stile, then turn immediately right again along a downhill path through woodland and pass under the A414 Maldon bypass. Continue along the rising concrete path, and at the end turn right.

3 Maintain your direction along a canopied green lane bounded by ancient hedgerows, and cross the stile. Follow the yellow waymark along the grassy path keeping left to emerge on to the gravel path.

4 On your right is Beeleigh Abbey. Continue past the abbey and at the end of the road turn right. Ignore the footpath on the left and pass Beeleigh Grange Farm on your left, and Beeleigh Falls House, an impressive Victorian villa, on the right. Go through the kissing gate and soon you hear the sound of the rushing water of Beeleigh Falls.

5 Cross the timber bridge over the weir. At the end of the bridge turn right, keeping the river on your right. Stop at the second weir for good river views. Continue, keeping the river on your right, and at Beeleigh Lock turn right and walk, with the canal on your left, towards the red-brick bridge. Do not cross the bridge, instead turn right on to the concrete path and just before the club house, left on to the grassy path. Maintain your direction with the canal on your left and the golf course on your right. Cross the next bridge and turn right, keeping the canal on your right. Continue under two sections of the Maldon bypass and keep ahead on to the grassy bridleway running parallel with the canal.

6 At the next bridge take the set of steps up to Heybridge Street. At the top turn right and join the B1018 towards Maldon. Maintain your direction to cross the River Chelmer via Fullbridge, bear left into Market Hill, turn left into the High Street and return to the car park via Butt Lane on your left.

36 Bracing Bradwell-on-Sea

An atmospheric walk in coastal Essex takes you in the footsteps of smugglers to the isolated seventh-century chapel in which they used to store contraband

If you yearn for huge skies, bracing sea air and long yellow sands, with not an inflatable sunbed or a parasol in sight, then this walk is for you. The Dengie (sounds like 'Benjie') Peninsula, a vast area of pancake-flat marshes and arable farmland, really does seem in a world of its own, its haunting beauty attracting those seeking to escape the stresses of modern city life.

The Dengie Peninsula is bounded by the estuaries of the River Blackwater to the north and the River Crouch to the south. It is an isolated spot, jutting out into the dove-grey waters of the North Sea. In the third century AD, the Romans built a fort here. The walk starts on an isolated pathway leading to the Chapel of St Peter's-on-the-Wall, the oldest church still in use in England and certainly the sole monument to Celtic Christianity in Essex. Built by the missionary St Cedd in AD 654, it is almost entirely made from the debris of the Roman fort on which it stands.

In the 18th and 19th centuries the chapel took on a different role as a hiding place for bands of smugglers, who would use it to store crates of whisky and rum and other contraband. Meanwhile, notable Bradwell residents, such as Hezekiah Staines, played part-time policeman by day and criminal by night, and spread rumours that the chapel was haunted. Maybe it is. In 1920 the chapel took on its present name, and since 1948 has attracted pilgrims from all over the world. Each summer, services are held in the simple interior.

Modern Power House

Perhaps the most obvious landmark, as you continue along the sea wall to Bradwell Waterside, is the looming grey block of the former Bradwell Nuclear Power Station. It started life in 1962, but costs of continued operation outweighed its earning potential; it is now in the decommissioning phase of its lifecycle, following 40 years generation. You can take refreshment at The Green Man pub, a smugglers' haven in its day, before continuing to Bradwell-on-Sea, in truth a good way from the seaside. And to complete the contraband course, pause at the parish church where miscreants were incarcerated in a tiny square cell, the Cage, or punished at the whipping post.

Below: Smugglers' storehouse and ancient place of worship – the 7th-century Chapel of St Peter's-on-the-Wall

Inset: Our walk also passes the largely 14th-century St Thomas's Church, Bradwell-on-Sea

36 Bracing Bradwell-on-Sea

Skirt salt marshes and mudflats on which Romans, Celtic Christians and later smugglers all left their mark

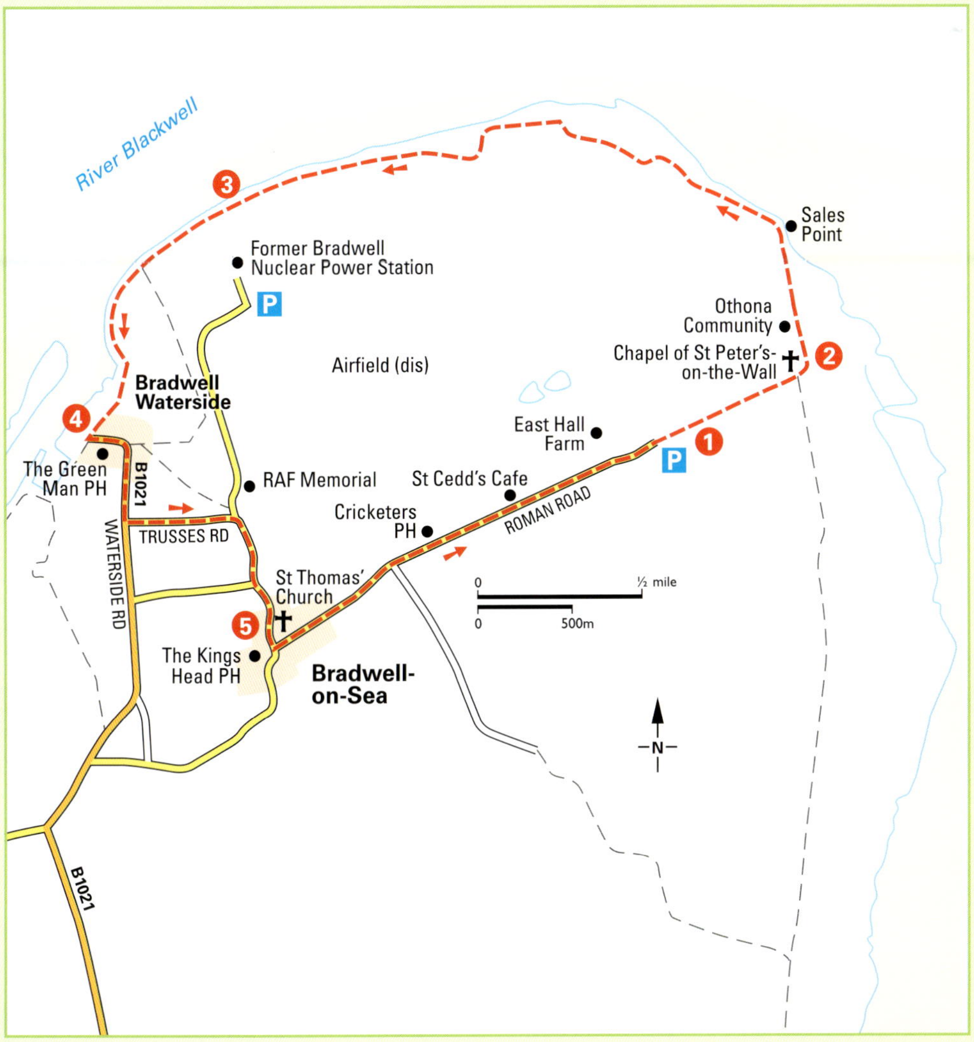

Distance 6 miles (9.7km)

Minimum Time 3hrs

Ascent/Gradient Negligible ▲▲▲

Level of Difficulty ●●●

Paths Stony and grassy paths with some road walking

Landscape Mudflats, salt marshes, beach, farmland, sea wall and former nuclear power station

Suggested Map OS Explorer 176 Blackwater Estuary, Maldon

Start/Finish Grid reference: TM 024078

Dog Friendliness A beach for a good romp and paddle

Parking Informal parking at entrance to footpath at East Hall Farm

Public Toilets None en route

1 Take the wide grassy path from the car park towards the sea and in 0.5 mile (800m) reach the ancient Chapel of St Peter's-on-the-Wall. Continue walking towards the sea for another 30yds (27m) and turn left at the T-junction. After 100yds (91m) climb the wooden steps to the sea defence wall.

2 Keep ahead, passing to the right of the religious community of Othona and walk along the wall with the sea on your right. For the next 2 miles (3.2km) your route remains on top of the sea wall, mainly a firm, grassy path punctuated with areas of concrete. On your left, and sometimes seemingly at a lower level than the sea, is private farmland. On your right, salt marsh gives way to white sand and shingle and extensive mudflats at low tide. The seashore makes a lovely detour but at high tide you have to remain on the concrete path. There are good views across the Blackwater estuary to Mersea Island. On the seaward side of the path there are concrete pill boxes, relics of the Second World War. Follow the path for 1 mile (1.6km) and you can see the framework of the beacon, a good place for spotting cormorants.

3 In 1.5 miles (2.4km) the bulk of Bradwell Nuclear Power Station is upon you. You may either continue on the route by the coast or make a detour to take in the nature trail around the station. Our route continues along the sea wall to Bradwell Waterside.

4 At the jetty, turn left on to Waterside Road keeping the yacht club and The Green Man pub on your right. Continue along Waterside Road with the marina on your right. Sean Connery, Bobby Moore and Roger Moore all had a hand in turning this marina into a business venture in the 1960s. Continue past the marina and turn left into Trusses Road. Where the road bends, turn right towards Bradwell village (a left turn here towards Bradwell Nuclear Power Station will take you to the RAF memorial at Bradwell Bay Airfield).

5 At Bradwell-on-Sea follow the High Street to its junction with East End Road where, on the corner, you will find St Thomas' Church opposite The Kings Head pub. Pass Caidge Cottages on your left, the village school on your right and continue for about a mile (1.6km) along the straight Roman Road, with maybe a stop at the Cricketers pub, before reaching the car park.

Eastern England

Best of the Rest

Aldeburgh
This Suffolk coastal town, a busy port in medieval times, is today known above all as the final home and burial place of Benjamin Britten, probably Britain's greatest 20th-century composer, and through the Aldeburgh Music Festival that Britten and his partner Peter Pears founded here in 1948. Born in Lowestoft, Britten was inspired by Aldeburgh poet George Crabbe to write one of his finest operas, *Peter Grimes* (1945). He later settled in Aldeburgh with his partner Peter Pears and is buried beside Pears in the churchyard at St Peter and St Paul's in the town. Walk 42 leads past a sculpture by artist Maggi Hambling on the shingle beach between Aldeburgh and Thorpeness, intended to celebrate Britten's life there and his achievements; it is in the shape of a giant scallop shell, 13ft (4m) tall made in stainless steel, and bears the words (from *Peter Grimes*), 'I hear those voices that will not be drowned.'

Brancaster
On the north Norfolk coast at Brancaster was the site of the Roman fort and settlement of Branodunum. Walk 50 leads past the remains of the fort, which now lie within a beautiful coastal reserve managed by the National Trust. Birdwatchers can expect to see greenshank, gannets, common terns (often known as 'sea-swallows') and Sandwich terns. In summer look out for the Arctic skua. The village of Brancaster Staithe is celebrated for its fine mussels.

Horsey Mere
Another ramble in a National Trust reserve, Walk 46 leads through reed beds and across water meadows beside Horsey Mere in Norfolk. Known in local legends as 'the Devil's Country', the area has a wild and even desolate air – according to tradition, on one day a year the calls and cries of drowned children rise eerily from the waters. Watch out for herons, and the restored four-storey Horsey Drainage Mill. The mill and others like it played a fascinating role in local smuggling – when a customs man was on the prowl the mill sails would be displayed as a St Andrew's cross (with its arms at the diagonal, as on the Scotland flag) and when it was all clear they would be moved into the shape of a St George's cross (with arms vertical and horizontal, as on the England flag). If the mill were working, it would be stopped in these shapes long enough to be sure that people at the next mill had seen the message and could pass it on.

Overstrand
At Overstrand in Norfolk Walk 47 leads through an area developed in Victorian times after journalist Clement Scott wrote a series of newspaper articles about the charms of the village and area, which he called 'Poppylands' on account of the wild poppies that grew – and still grow – locally. Architects including Edwin Lutyens built large houses for wealthy incomers, and a substantial hotel was built on the clifftop – although this, in an area of severe coastal erosion, collapsed into the sea in the 1950s.

Walton-on-the-Naze
This Essex resort stands partly on a headland called 'the Naze' and was a major holiday destination in the 19th century. It is the proud owner of a pier that is half a mile (800m) in length, making it the country's second longest (after Southend Pier). Walk 37 leads to the Naze Tower, built in 1720 as an aid to navigation then pressed into service in the early 19th century as a defensive structure against possible French invasion. Today town and tower are threatened by coastal erosion, which is progressing locally at the alarming rate of almost 7ft (2m) a year.

Felixstowe Ferry
Near Felixstowe in Suffolk, Walk 41 leads from the village of Felixstowe Ferry along the estuary of the River Deben and then beside the King's Fleet. This inlet, now no longer navigable, was in regular use in the 13th century and takes its name from the fact that King Edward III once assembled a fleet here prior to sailing to France.

extinguished as part of wartime measures at the start of the First World War. The town's history in fact goes back all the way to the time of St Edmund, who was shipwrecked on this part of the coast in AD 855 and raised a chapel in thanks for his deliverance from death; later King of the East Angles, he was killed by Vikings in AD 869, dying a martyr's death, and declared a saint (known from finds of 'St Edmund pennies') by AD 890.

Hunter of Witches in Essex

Up and down the East Coast many walks visit places of great historical interest. In Essex Walk 38 is in and near Manningtree, where in the mid-17th century lawyer Matthew Hopkins briefly maintained a reign of terror as a 'witch-finder' appointed by Parliament during the English Civil War to stamp out sorcery; a fictionalised version of his life was made in 1968 into what is now a cult British film, *Witchfinder General*, directed by Michael Reeves and starring Vincent Price. There are remains in Manningtree High Street of Elizabethan housing, and the walk also delivers interesting insights into the history of Manningtree and neighbouring Mistley as a thriving port and a centre for boatbuilding and the malting industry.

In Suffolk Walk 40 passes the impressive brick pile of Erwarton Hall, a Tudor country house with connections to Anne Boleyn, King Henry VIII's second wife and the mother of Queen Elizabeth I; Anne's uncle owned the house and, having spent happy times there in her childhood, she is said to have asked for her heart to be buried there – although there is no definitive evidence that this happened. Walk 40 also passes the intriguing HMS *Ganges*, which is not a ship but a naval training establishment that operated in 1905-76.

Those with an interest in naval history will take pleasure in Walk 39, which visits the Essex coastal town of Harwich, where naval pressgangs once roamed the alleys looking for boys to be carried off to sea. In Harwich, also, the hero of Trafalgar Horatio Nelson lived with Lady Hamilton. Walk 49 visits Nelson's boyhood haunts in the vicinity of Burnham Thorpe, Norfolk, where he was born, the son of Edmund Nelson, local rector, in 1758. The walk starts at a pub called The Hero in Burnham Overy Staithe, while in Burnham Thorpe itself there is a pub called The Lord Nelson. Nelson's parents are buried in the largely 13th-century All Saints' Church, and a plaque marks the spot of the rectory (now demolished) where Nelson was born.

Above: Colour-washed houses behind the shingle beach at Aldeburgh in Suffolk

Opposite left: Beach huts behind the sands at the Essex resort of Walton-on-the-Naze

Opposite right: On the pier at Harwich in Essex

37 Waltzing Around Walton-on-the-Naze

A gentle walk with wonderful beach views explores an Essex coast town whose pier, half a mile (800m) long, is the second longest in England, after Southend

Above: The Naze Tower is a Grade II listed building

Below: Seaside colour – beach huts on the promenade at Walton-on-the-Naze

In the early 19th century Walton-le-Soken, as Walton-on-the-Naze was then known, emerged as a notable seaside resort, attracting fashionable folk from London and county families from Essex, who used bathing machines to dip their toes in the waters. The first terraced houses brought genteel residents, a hotel provided visitors with accommodation and before long the area became as popular as Southend with a pier packed with pastimes. Although Walton's name has since changed, two neighbouring villages, Kirby-le-Soken and Thorpe-le-Soken, still retain the original suffix.

Nowadays visitors can enjoy amusement arcades, tenpin bowling, restaurants and sea fishing, and the holiday atmosphere is complete with kiss-me-quick hats, jellied eels and seaside rock. But if you wander north of the town and its wide sandy beaches, you'll discover a haven for bird life in the John Weston Nature Reserve, named after a local warden, and a multitude of sailing craft tucked in the creeks.

Under Threat from Erosion

Part of the town is situated on a headland called The Naze, hence its name. The word originates from the Anglo-Saxon *ness* or *naes* meaning 'a headland', while Walton may mean 'walled town' from the sea wall. Natural erosion has played a big part in the development of Walton-on-the-Naze. In 1798 Walton's second church was washed away, then in 1880 its first pier was destroyed by heavy seas; Second World War gun emplacements and pill boxes built on the Naze itself fell on to the beach and in the next few years, the Naze Tower,which is only just 100yds (91m) from the cliff's edge, will also be at some risk.

Conservationists predict that unless coastal erosion is stopped, or at least slowed down to managable levels, then the area known as the Walton backwaters – home to thousands of birds, seals and other wildlife – will disappear, along with a large part of Walton itself. It may come as no surprise that even the lifeboat here lacks a permanent mooring. In fact it is the only lifeboat in Britain to have a mooring in the open sea. It is near the end of the pier and, when the alarm is raised, the lifeboat crew cycle the length of the pier and use a small launch to reach it.

On a summer's day this is a relaxing ramble. You can walk along the beach or the promenade, depending on the tidal conditions. But all year round, Walton-on-the-Naze is a delight to explore – in winter you'll see waders and a range of wildfowl, including brent geese; in summer, you may be lucky to spot rare avocets, which breed here. They have unusual upturned bills that they sweep through the water to collect shrimps and worms.

37 Waltzing Around Walton-on-the-Naze

Wander along the seafront to the 18th-century Naze Tower

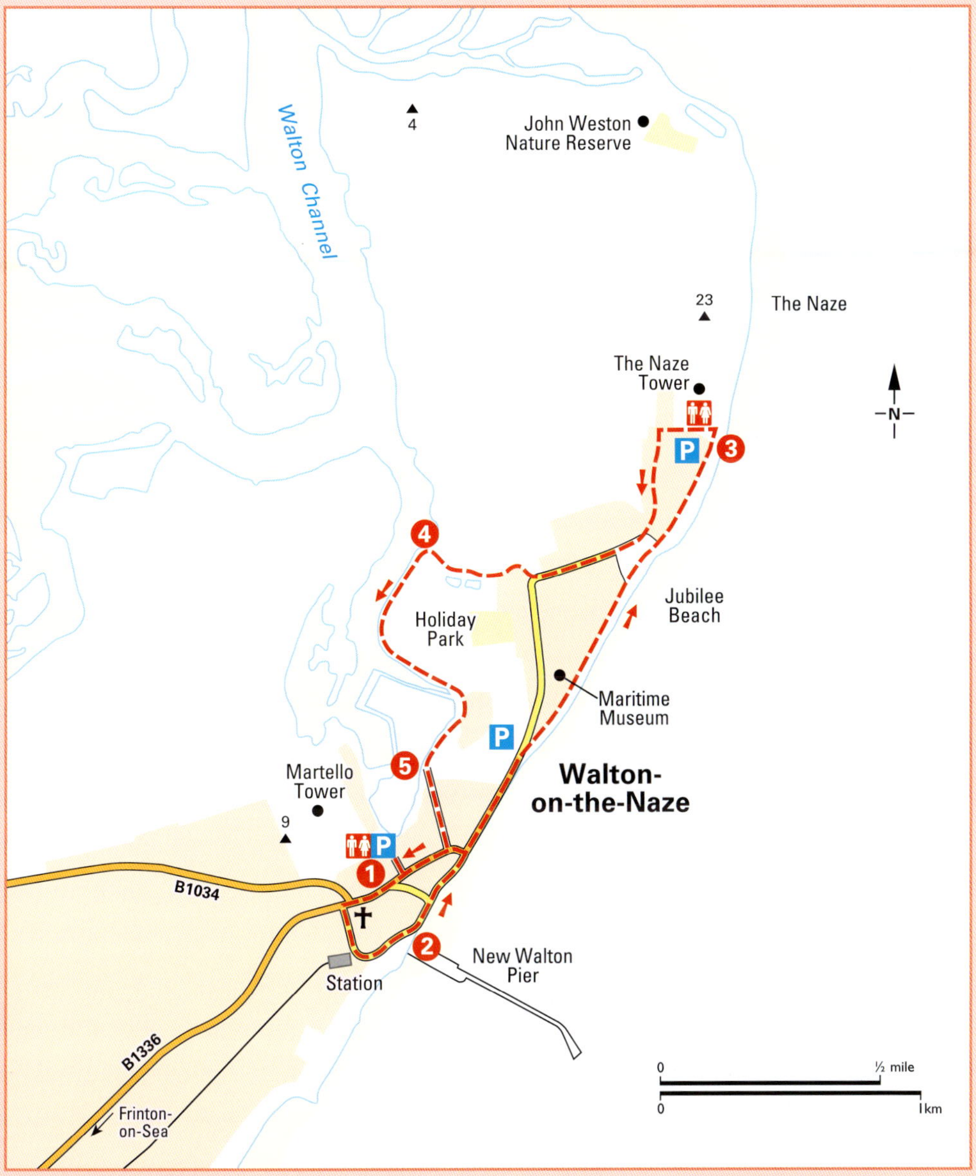

Distance 4.25 miles (6.8km)

Minimum Time 2hrs

Ascent/Gradient Negligible ▲▲▲

Level of Difficulty ●●●

Paths Grassy cliff paths, tidal salt marsh and some town streets

Landscape Cliffs, sandy beaches, creeks and marshes

Suggested Map OS Explorer 184 Colchester, Harwich & Clacton-on-Sea

Start/Finish Grid reference: TM 253218

Dog Friendliness Take care on narrow paths along cliffs

Parking Pay-and-display at Mill Lane and Naze Tower

Public Toilets Mill Lane and Naze Tower

1 From Mill Lane car park turn right into the High Street then left into Martello Road. Bear left along New Pier Street and go on to Pier Approach. To your right is the pier. From here there are good views of the beaches of Walton-on-the-Naze and Frinton.

2 Turn left and, with the sea on your right, walk along Princes Esplanade through East Terrace. Continue walking along Cliff Parade and the cliff tops to Naze Tower. Built in 1720 as a navigational aid, it was to join many Martello towers built along the east and south-east coasts to fend off Napoleonic invasion. Nowadays, the grassy area on which the tower stands is a good place to rest and recuperate.

3 From the car park café walk inland to Old Hall Lane, turn left and then right into Naze Park Road. At the end of Naze Park Road, where it bears sharp left, turn right on to the narrow path and left on to the field-edge path passing two small ponds filled with wildlife.

4 After 100yds (91m), turn left on to the cross path, go through the gate and on to the permissive path that follows the sea wall, keeping the caravan site on your left and Walton Channel on your right. This wide expanse of mudflats, islands, channels and small boats, ever changing with the tide, is a paradise for seabirds and a Site of Special Scientific Interest (SSSI). Skippers Island, an Essex Wildlife Trust nature reserve, is the habitat of rare seabirds and wildlife and full-time wardens are employed to protect them. Follow the sea wall for 0.75 mile (1.2km) then bear half left down the embankment and into a field used as an overflow car park.

5 With the school field on the left, follow railings for 70yds (64m) to a path between the school and terraced cottages and continue to Saville Street past old cottages on your right. Take the first right into North Street, continue to the High Street and turn right. Turn right again into Mill Lane to the car park.

38 Manningtree – England's Smallest Town

An outing rich in historic interest visits a former port and shipbuilding centre in which the notorious 'Witchfinder General' plied his trade in the 17th century

Above: Walk this way – footpath markers in Manningtree

Below: Look out for the Witchfinder's grave at the partly demolished Church of St Mary the Virgin in Mistley

Below right: Tide's out – the River Stour at Manningtree

On the banks of the River Stour, Manningtree and neighbouring Mistley have long been associated with mills, maltings and timber. In 1753, ships for the Napoleonic Wars were built at Mistley Quay, and Newcastle coal, Scandinavian timber, grain, bricks, chalk, flour and hay were brought downriver and transported by barge to London. But these tiny towns, separated by a few miles, are possessed of a darker side...witches!

The 'Witchfinder General'

In the mid-17th century Manningtree's best known resident was Matthew Hopkins – better known as the 'Witchfinder General'. In this period if you were female and happened to own a black cat, you risked being branded a witch and hunted down by Hopkins' band of distinctly unmerry men. Securing a conviction for witchcraft on the flimsiest of evidence was Hopkins' stock-in-trade, a profession made more unpalatable by the fact that Parliament paid him 20 shillings for each 'guilty' witch.

The fate of Hopkins himself is in dispute. Some believe he died a peaceful death at his home in Manningtree in 1647, while others say he was subjected to one of his own witchfinding tests, found guilty and sentenced to death. He is believed to be buried in St Mary's Church at Mistley.

This walk starts from Manningtree Station overlooking the River Stour, which separates Essex from Suffolk, and rises to 14th-century St Mary's Church at Lawford to join the Essex Way. It crosses undulating meadows and thick forest – perfect for fleeing witches. A green lane emerges at Mistley where the Swan Fountain is the last surviving example of landowner Richard Rigby's attempts to turn the area into a fashionable spa.

By the end of the 17th century, Mistley and Manningtree were busy ports. Malting, Mistley's oldest industry, took off, and you can see the chimneys of the English Diastatic Malt Extract Company (EDME) factory on this walk. If you follow the River Stour back to Manningtree you may spot a large colony of swans, attracted by the waste of the maltings, and other estuary birds including shelduck, teal and ringed plover.

At Manningtree, many of the roof beams of the delightful shops and houses in the High Street date back to Elizabethan times. The witches are long gone, and it's hard to believe that in 1644–46 up to 300 victims were rounded up. Hopkins sometimes held court at local inns, but most of his victims were sent for trial at the Chelmsford Assizes, and many were tried on the evidence of children. Those found guilty were either burnt at the stake or hanged, some here on Manningtree's tiny green.

38 Manningtree – England's Smallest Town

Admire Manningtree's Elizabethan houses and step back into the town's colourful past

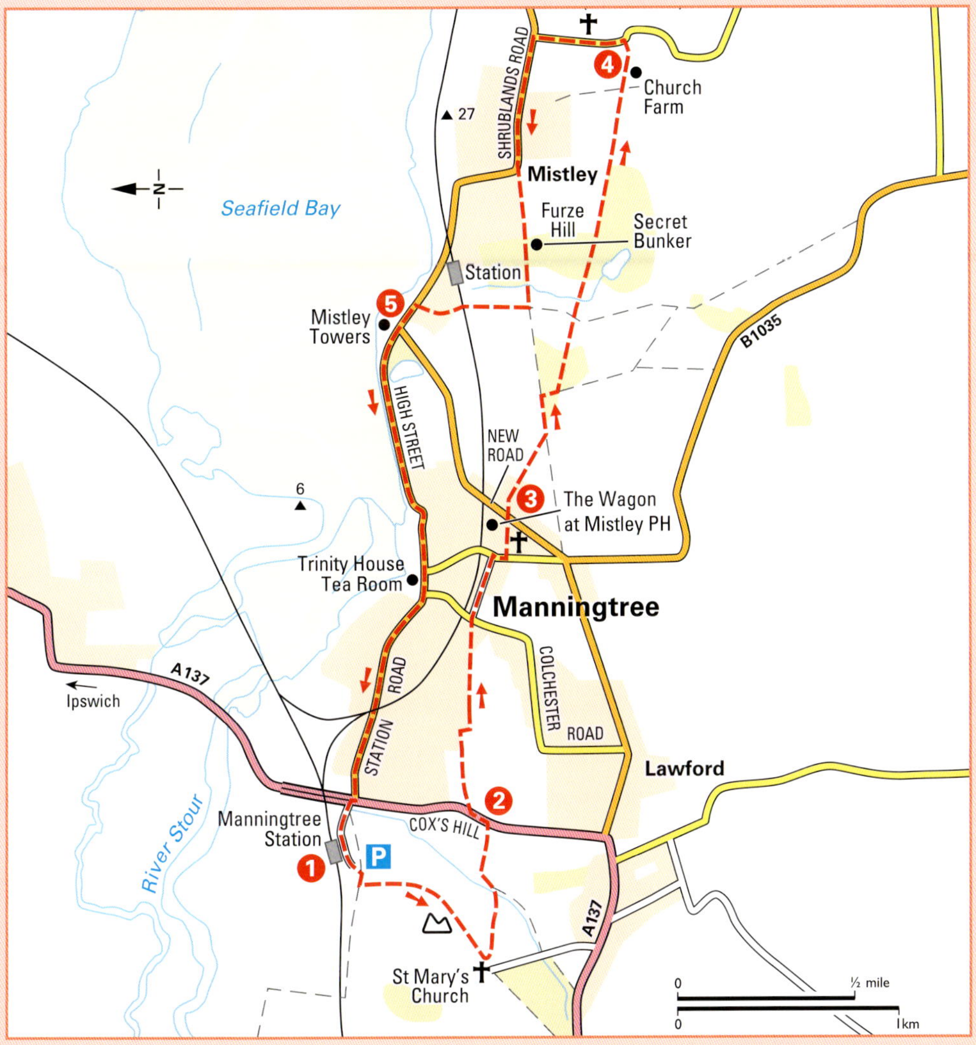

Distance 7 miles (11.3km)

Minimum Time 3hrs 30min

Ascent/Gradient 98ft (30m) ▲▲▲

Level of Difficulty ●●●

Paths Field paths, footpaths, tracks and sections of road, may be boggy, 4 stiles

Landscape River estuary, undulating farmland dotted with woodland and residential areas

Suggested Map OS Explorer 184 Colchester, Harwich & Clacton-on-Sea

Start/Finish Grid reference: TM 093322

Dog Friendliness Can romp free in woodland but must be on lead on farmland and in town

Parking Pay-and-display at Manningtree Station

Public Toilets Manningtree Station

1 With your back to the station building turn right at the public footpath sign to Flatford and after a few steps turn left along a steep, grassy path to St Mary's Church. Go through the black gate and, keeping the church on your right, cross the stile over the church wall. Turn left and, at the wooden post, follow the yellow waymark half-right across the meadow. Cross the earth bridge over Wignell Brook, then go left uphill. Keep the line of trees on your right and go through a kissing gate to join the Essex Way. Just before the house at the top of the hill, go through another kissing gate and bear left to Cox's Hill, on to the A137.

2 Cross Cox's Hill with care, turn left and after 40yds (37m), at a public footpath sign marking the Essex Way, turn right. Walk downhill, passing to the right of a pond, and cross the plank bridge over a stream. Bear right to join the gravel path through the Owl's Flight Dell Conservation Area and pass to the right of a housing estate. Ignoring the concrete path on the left, turn half-right on to the cross-field path towards playing fields and join a concrete path to the road. Cross Colchester Road, and at the T-junction turn right into Trinity Road, ignoring signs for the Essex Way. At the Evangelical church, turn left to New Road. The Wagon at Mistley pub is on the left.

3 Cross New Road and follow the yellow waymarked footpath between backs of houses. At the T-junction turn left on to the wide canopied bridleway. After 70yds (64m) follow the waymark half right and rejoin the Essex Way. Maintain direction, go through a kissing gate, cross an earth bridge over the brook followed by a stile and another kissing-gate. Keep ahead through the thickly wooded slopes of Furze Hill. As you emerge from the woods, go straight ahead, keeping to the field-edge path to Church Farm. Turn left here on to Heath Road.

4 Cross the road to the low wall to see the remains of St Mary's Church. Continue north and turn left on to the B1352 and into Shrublands Road which soon becomes a green lane. Cross the first stile on the right towards the English Diastatic Malt Extract Company (EDME) malt chimney and walk under the railway. Keep ahead into The Green.

5 Turn left into the High Street, past Mistley Towers, and continue beside the River Stour into Manningtree. Bear left along the High Street and continue for 1 mile (1.6km) along Station Road to the car park.

39 Harwich's Seafarers and Wanderers

A fascinating ramble uncovers the maritime past of this Essex coastal town in which 17th-century diarist Samuel Pepys was the local Member of Parliament

One of the main gateways to the Continent, Harwich is a must for aficionados of all things maritime. The town lies beside the North Sea on an isthmus between Dovercourt and Bathside bays, overlooking the Stour and Orwell estuaries. In the 12th century a storm caused the rivers to break their banks and form the promontory on which Harwich stands. Realising the promontory's strategic importance, the lord of the manor developed the site into a walled town. You can see the remains of the walls in St Nicholas' churchyard.

Below: The Low Lighthouse, one of the two built by General Rebow, is now the Maritime Museum in Harwich

Below right: Harwich harbour sees a large amount of commercial shipping including fishing and container traffic

The walk begins at the Ha'penny Pier, where you can spot ferries sailing to and from Europe. Keeping the sea to your left, you'll see traditional inns, such as the Globe, in Kings Quay Street. Such pubs were once stormed by rowdy pressgangs, whose members kidnapped boys for service in the Royal Navy. Trying to escape, hapless lads would scurry like rats into the labyrinthine passages linking the houses, but many were caught and never seen again.

The town has played host to famous faces, too. Sir Francis Drake dropped in on his way to Spain and Queen Elizabeth I stayed here, remarking that 'It is a pretty town that wants for nothing'. Diarist Samuel Pepys was the local MP and Lord Nelson sojourned here with Lady Hamilton. Home-grown boys include Christopher Jones, captain of the *Mayflower*, the ship in which the Pilgrim Fathers sailed from Plymouth to the Americas in 1620.

Twin Lighthouses

Wander at will and see the quirky, two-wheel man-operated treadwheel crane on Harwich Green or climb Redoubt Fort, built to fend off a threatened Napoleonic invasion, for great sea views. Along the seafront is a pair of 19th-century lighthouses. They were built by General Rebow, who charged each ship a penny per ton to come into port. When Rebow got wind that the sandbanks were shifting he craftily sold the lighthouses to Trinity House. As you round the breakwater there are fine beaches and another pair of lighthouses mounted on stilts, built to replace the earlier ones at Harwich. They, too, became redundant (in 1917), but serve as a reminder of Harwich's seafaring history.

39 Harwich's Seafarers and Wanderers

Explore a historic town and walk the first part of the Essex Way

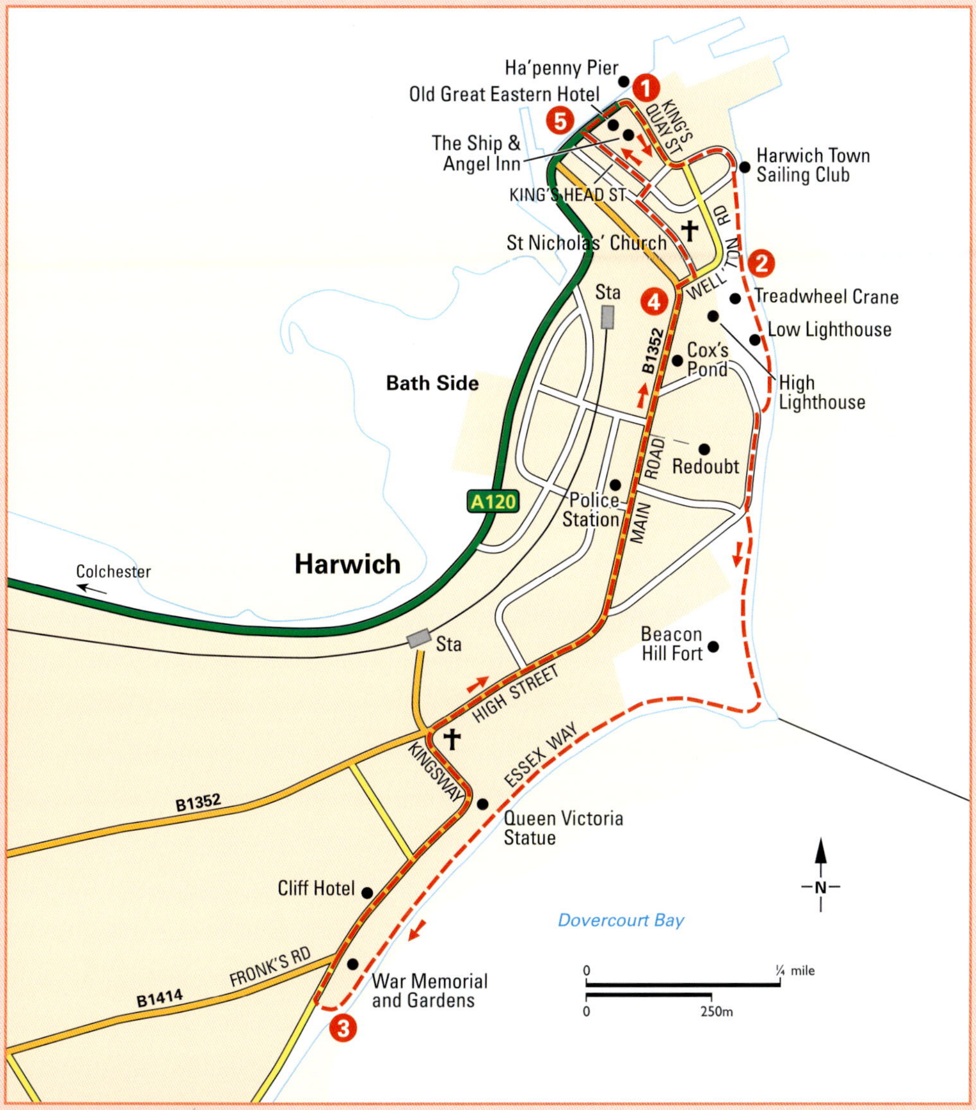

Distance 4 miles (6.4km)

Minimum Time 1hr 30min

Ascent/Gradient Negligible ▲▲▲

Level of Difficulty ●●●

Paths Town streets and promenade with gentle cliffs

Landscape Coast, beach, cliffs and town

Suggested Map OS Explorer 197 Ipswich, Felixstowe & Harwich or 184 Colchester, Harwich & Clacton-on-Sea

Start/Finish Grid reference: TM 259328

Dog Friendliness Between 1 May and 30 September dogs have to be on lead on promenade and cliff walks

Parking Pay-and-display car parks at Ha'penny Pier and informal street parking

Public Toilets Beside Quayside Court opposite Ha'penny Pier

1 With your back to Ha'penny Pier, turn left along The Quay and follow the road into King's Quay Street. Turn left just before the colourful mural (painted by the Harwich Society and Harwich School in 1982 and again in 1995) depicting local buildings and ships. Follow the road, with the sea on your left, until it turns inland. Take the path by the sea, which is the start of the Essex Way, a long-distance path of 81 miles (130km) connecting Harwich with Epping. Pass Harwich Town Sailing Club and maintain direction along the Esplanade, where at low tide you can walk along the shingle beach.

2 Pass the Treadwheel Crane on your right and continue along the seafront. Keep the raised, fenced area of Beacon Hill Fort and the gun emplacements from both world wars to your right. As you pass the breakwaters around the bay there are views of the holiday resort of Dovercourt. Ignore the steps to your right and continue along the Essex Way, walking parallel with the upper road of Marine Parade.

3 Turn right into Lower Marine Parade and pass the War Memorial and Gardens at the junction with Fronk's Road and Marine Parade. Maintain direction passing the Cliff Hotel on the left and then go left into Kingsway, opposite the statue of Queen Victoria. Turn right into the High Street and bear left into Main Road, passing the police station on your left. Walk for 250yds (229m) and turn right up the track to see Redoubt Fort, a Martello-style fort, part of the defences against Napoleonic invasion. Continue to pass Cox's Pond, once owned by local bankers of the same name.

4 Pass High Lighthouse on the right, turn right into Wellington Road and left into Church Street passing St Nicholas' Church. Turn right into Market Street and left into King's Head Street, pausing to admire the timber-framed houses including No 21, the home of Captain Christopher Jones of the Mayflower.

5 Turn right into The Quay, where Quayside Court faces the sea. Now apartments, Quayside Court was built as one of the Great Eastern hotels in the 19th century and catered for travellers from the Continent who would arrive by steamer at what is now Trinity Quay and continue their journey to London by rail.

40 Between Two Rivers

On a lonely spit between the Stour and Orwell estuaries, this walk offers views of Harwich and Felixstowe and passes a country house connected to Anne Boleyn

The rows of silent headstones in the sloping cemetery of St Mary's Church tell the story of HMS *Ganges*. Between 1905 and 1976, more than 150,000 recruits passed through the doors of this naval training establishment at Shotley. When they arrived, they were little more than boys – and some of them never came out. Among the graves of submariners killed in action and German prisoners of war are those of numerous boys aged between 15 and 17 years old, who died before they ever got the chance to serve their country.

Training Centre

A newer churchyard across the way contains the graves of those killed in the Second World War. Here are commanders, petty officers, ordinary seamen and 'a sailor of the 1939–45 war known unto God', the different ranks, named and unnamed, brought together in death. Here, too, are 16 crewmembers of HMS *Worcester* who lost their lives in February 1942, and from a later generation a 19-year-old seaman who drowned in Nova Scotia in 1968. The first HMS *Ganges* was built in 1782, a gift to the Royal Navy from the East India Company. A second ship of the same name was manufactured at the Bombay shipyards and eventually became a boys' training ship, arriving at Shotley in 1899. The ship left but the name HMS *Ganges* remained as that of a new shore-based training centre. Discipline was legendary. Edward, Prince of Wales, said in the 1930s that it made the French Foreign Legion seem like a Sunday school. This was a regime of cold showers and food rations, a system designed to turn boys into men.

Anne Boleyn

HMS *Ganges* will soon be developed for housing, though the 142ft (43m)-tall mast that stands in the parade ground will remain as a memorial to the building's naval past. At one time it was the custom for naval cadets to shin up the mast during training. In 1918, to celebrate the end of the First World War, the entire school of boys climbed the mast, resulting in several accidents.

Shotley is situated on a lonely peninsula where the rivers Stour and Orwell meet as they flow into the sea. To one side is the ferry port at Harwich, to the other Felixstowe Docks. The area has historical associations with Anne Boleyn (1501–36), the second wife of Henry VIII and mother of Elizabeth I, and whose uncle was the owner of Erwarton Hall. Before her execution, Anne is said to have requested that her heart be buried at Erwarton. There is no evidence that it happened, but in 1836 a lead casket in the shape of a heart was found in a wall of the church. It is now buried beneath the organ.

Below: A busy scene at Shotley marina

40 Between Two Rivers

Pass oyster beds and salt marshes as you follow the Suffolk Coast and Heath Path beside the Stour

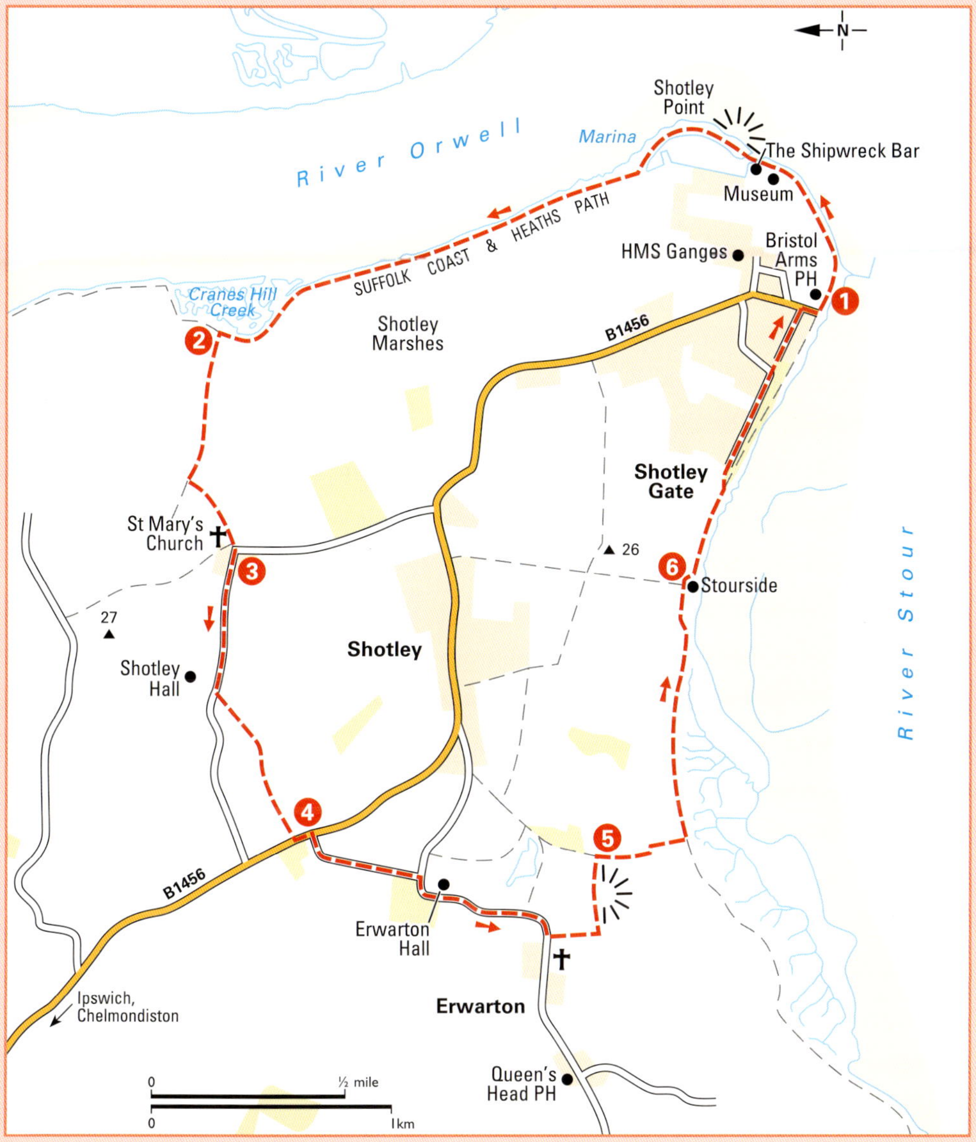

Distance 6 miles (9.7km)

Minimum Time 3hrs

Ascent/Gradient 262ft (80m) ▲▲▲

Level of Difficulty ●●●

Paths Field and riverside paths, country lanes, 2 stiles

Landscape Farmland between Stour and Orwell estuaries

Suggested Map OS Explorer 197 Ipswich, Felixstowe & Harwich

Start/Finish Grid reference: TM 246336

Dog Friendliness On lead on farmland, off lead on riverside path

Parking Opposite Bristol Arms at Shotley Gate

Public Toilets None en route

1 Start at the Bristol Arms, looking across to Harwich, and head left along the waterfront to Shotley Marina. Pass to the right of the HMS *Ganges* Museum (open on summer weekends) and keep right to walk across the lock gates to Shotley Point. A path follows the headland around the marina basin, with good views of Felixstowe Docks. Turn right to continue along the flood bank between marshes and mudflats. After 1 mile (1.6km) the path passes old oyster beds and swings left beside the salt marshes at Crane's Hill Creek.

2 Halfway around the creek, where you see a three-finger signpost, descend the bank to your left and then cross a stile to join a meadow-edge path. Cross another stile and bear left along a track to climb past vineyards until you reach St Mary's Church.

3 Walk straight ahead at the crossroads beyond the church, on a tarmac lane leading to Shotley Hall, then turn left on to a cross-field path opposite the drive. Follow this path diagonally across the field, then bear right at the far corner, following the line of telegraph poles towards a road where you turn left.

4 After 50yds (46m), turn right along a lane signposted 'Erwarton Walk'. At the end of this lane, turn right, passing the red-brick Tudor gatehouse of Erwarton Hall. Stay on this quiet country road as it bends towards Erwarton village. Just after a right-hand bend, turn left beside the churchyard on to a wide track. Pass to the right of a cottage and turn left along a field-edge path with views over the River Stour.

5 At the end of the field, turn right and follow the field-edge down to the Stour. Turn left and follow the Suffolk Coast and Heath Path beside the river, eventually passing cottages, and a property called Stourside.

6 Continue between fields and the river, and soon climb gently through trees to houses and a road. Follow the road and keep straight on along a tarmac path where the road curves left. Join another road and follow this to a T-junction. Turn right downhill back to The Bristol Arms on the left.

41 Fish and Ships by the Felixstowe Ferry

A pleasant walk along the Deben estuary and the King's Fleet stream reveals a different, more peaceful aspect to the bustling coastal resort of Felixstowe

Above: Shingle and water at Felixstowe Ferry

Felixstowe, whose name means 'happy place', is a large Edwardian seaside resort that embodies the carefree, kiss-me-quick atmosphere of an earlier age and continues to provide thousands of families with buckets of summer fun. Children ride bumper boats, go fishing for crabs and buy sticks of rock from kiosks on the pier, while pensioners stroll along the promenade and drink tea at seafront cafés. At the same time, Felixstowe has grown to become Britain's largest container port.

This walk begins well away from the arcades and the sandcastles, in the small hamlet of Felixstowe Ferry, with its boatyard, fishing huts and ferry across the river. The café here serves some of the freshest fish and chips you will find anywhere; if you prefer, you can buy fish straight off the fishing boat at the huts down by the quay. The walk leads along the estuary of the River Deben and beside the King's Fleet, a peaceful stream that takes its name from a fleet of ships assembled here by King Edward III ready to sail to France. The King's Fleet is no longer navigable but back in the 13th century it was regularly used by trading ships.

Right: Seen it all – gulls atop wooden posts in the river

Martello Towers

Returning to the sea, you pass two Martello towers, rare survivors of a chain of defensive outposts built between 1805 and 1812 to protect the English coastline against a threatened invasion by Napoleon of France. These round towers were 30ft (9m) tall and had walls up to 13ft (4m) thick in order to withstand incoming cannonballs. They were based on a tower at Mortella Point in Corsica, Napoleon's birthplace, which the British Navy had tried unsuccessfully to bombard. The towers were three storeys high and contained living quarters for one officer and 24 men, together with gunpowder stores, provisions and a rooftop gun tower.

By 1815 Napoleon had been defeated at the Battle of Waterloo and the Martello towers were redundant. Many of them have disappeared into the sea, but a few of the towers remain as a line of follies along the coast. One of the towers at Felixstowe was once used by the coastguard, and another at Felixstowe Ferry is now a private house. They stand above the beach as lonely reminders of the time when England faced the real threat of foreign invasion.

41 Fish and Ships by the Felixstowe Ferry

Escape the Felixstowe crowds along the Deben estuary – and try local fish and chips

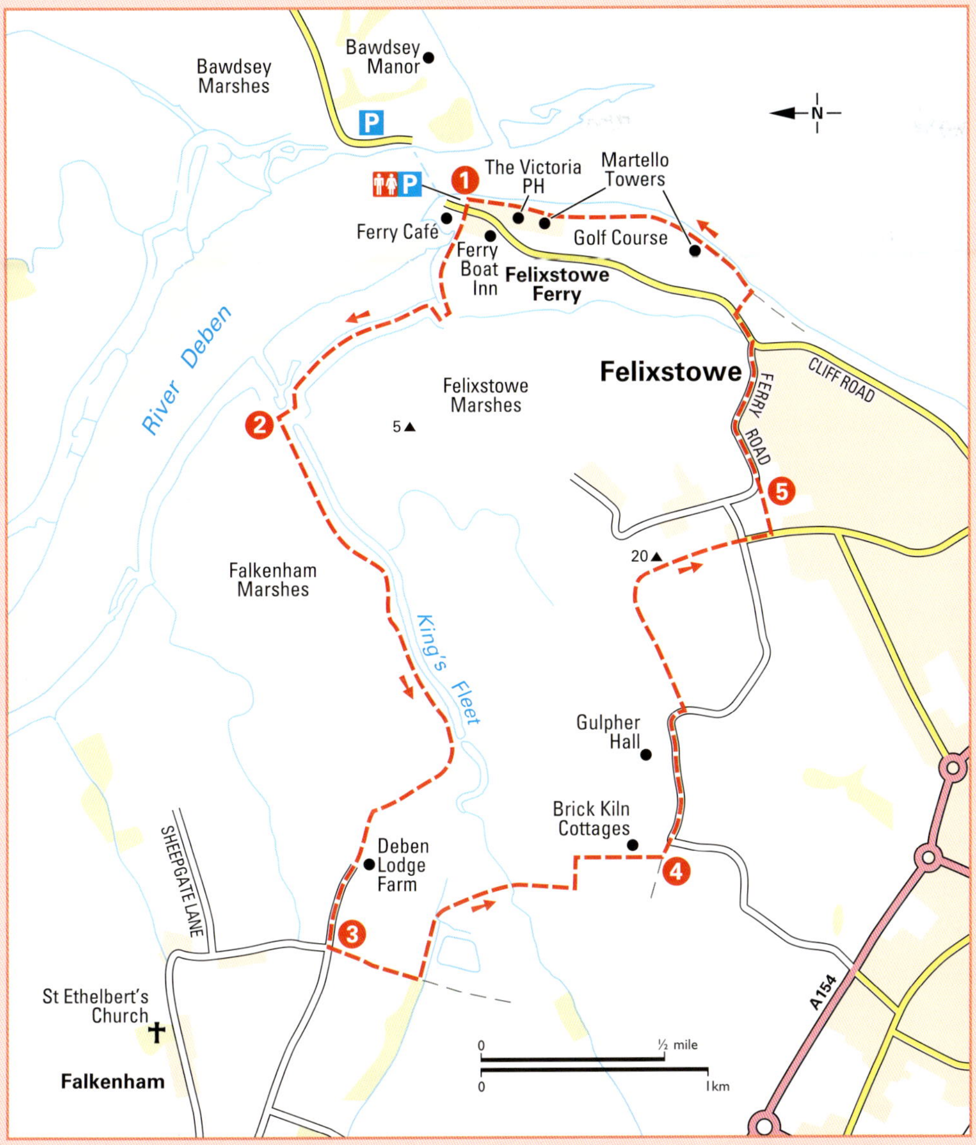

Distance 6.5 miles (10.4km)

Minimum Time 3hrs

Ascent/Gradient 164ft (50m) ▲▲▲

Level of Difficulty ●●●

Paths Field and riverside paths, country lanes, farm tracks, sea wall, 4 stiles

Landscape Farmland, estuary and coast

Suggested Map OS Explorer 197 Ipswich, Felixstowe & Harwich

Start/Finish Grid reference: TM 328376

Dog Friendliness Mostly off lead except across farmland

Parking Ferry Café car park (fee), Felixstowe Ferry

Public Toilets At Felixstowe Ferry

1 Take the tarmac path along an embankment behind the Ferry Café car park. The path passes the boatyard and follows the river wall as you look down on abandoned boats lying moored in muddy flats. Turn right through a squeeze stile to walk beside the Deben Estuary. After 0.5 mile (800m), the path swings left and then right across an inlet at the entrance to King's Fleet.

2 Turn left to descend the embankment and walk along a broad track. You pass an old wind pump and stay on this track as it winds its way between farmland and King's Fleet. After 1 mile (1.6km), the track bends right and climbs to a farm where it becomes a tarmac lane. Continue until you reach a T-junction.

3 Turn left across the field to climb to a ridge, then drop down through the next field to The Wilderness, a belt of trees beside Falkenham Brook. Turn left through the trees and follow this path alongside the stream, then bend right to cross a stile and a meadow. Make for the corner of a hedge opposite and bear right alongside a fence to cross a footbridge and take a grassy path between the fields. When you get to the end of a field, turn left and continue to the end of a hedge, then turn right to climb a track to Brick Kiln Cottages.

4 At the top of the track, turn left along a lane and stay on this lane past Gulpher Hall and its duck pond. As the road bends right, walk past the entrance to The Brook and turn left on a field-edge path. The path ascends, then turns right around a field and cuts straight across the field corner, unless it is diverted by crops. Pass through a gate and keep straight on along the lane, then turn left before houses in 150yds (137m) to join another path that runs between fields.

5 When you reach a pill box, turn right on to Ferry Road. Cross Cliff Road and turn left, walking past the clubhouse and turning half right across the golf course on a signposted path to reach the sea wall. Turn left and walk along the wall, passing two Martello towers and a row of beach huts. Continue to the mouth of the estuary and turn left just before the jetty to return to the Ferry Café.

42 Benjamin Britten's Beloved Aldeburgh

This engaging walk celebrates Britain's best-known 20th-century composer and explores the town in which he founded an internationally renowned music festival

In medieval times Aldeburgh was a busy port with fishing and shipbuilding industries, but its harbour silted up and it went into decline as the River Alde was diverted southwards by the shingle bank of Orford Ness. Today, however, Aldeburgh is buzzing; the cafés on the seafront are full of excited chatter as visitors come in their thousands to pay homage to the town's most famous resident, Benjamin Britten. The leading British composer of the 20th century, Britten (1913–76) introduced many people to classical music through works such as *The Young Person's Guide to the Orchestra* and his opera for children, *Noye's Fludde*. Born in Lowestoft, the son of a local dentist, he grew up with the sound of the sea and began composing at the age of five. During the Second World War, he moved to the United States as a conscientious objector, and it was here that he first read the work of George Crabbe (1754–1832), an Aldeburgh poet.

It was through Crabbe that Britten rediscovered his Suffolk roots. He returned to Snape to write *Peter Grimes*, an opera based on Crabbe's poems about the gritty lives of Aldeburgh fishermen. If ever a piece of music had a sense of place, this is it. You hear the waves breaking on the shingle beach, the seagulls calling and swooping over the coast, the wind roaring in the sky above the incoming tide. The leading role was created for Britten's lifelong partner and collaborator, the operatic tenor Peter Pears.

Aldeburgh Festival

Benjamin Britten's most lasting contribution to Aldeburgh was the foundation of the Aldeburgh Festival, which he achieved together with Pears and the librettist Eric Crozier in 1948. A number of Britten's best-known works were first performed at the festival, including *Noye's Fludde*, the 'church parable' *Curlew River* and the opera *A Midsummer Night's Dream*. At first the concerts took place in local churches and the Jubilee Hall, but eventually a larger venue was needed. In 1967, the festival was moved to a new concert hall at Snape Maltings, a 19th-century granary outside Aldeburgh.

Britten and Pears continued to live in Aldeburgh, initially in a seafront house on Crabbe Street and later in a large farmhouse on the edge of town. They are buried side by side in the churchyard of the parish church of St Peter and St Paul.

Above: The Aldeburgh Moot Hall is home to the local museum

Below: A scallop-shell sculpture on the shingle beach between Aldeburgh and Thorpeness celebrates Britten's life

42 Benjamin Britten's Beloved Aldeburgh

Take in the Suffolk coast and seascape views admired by Britten

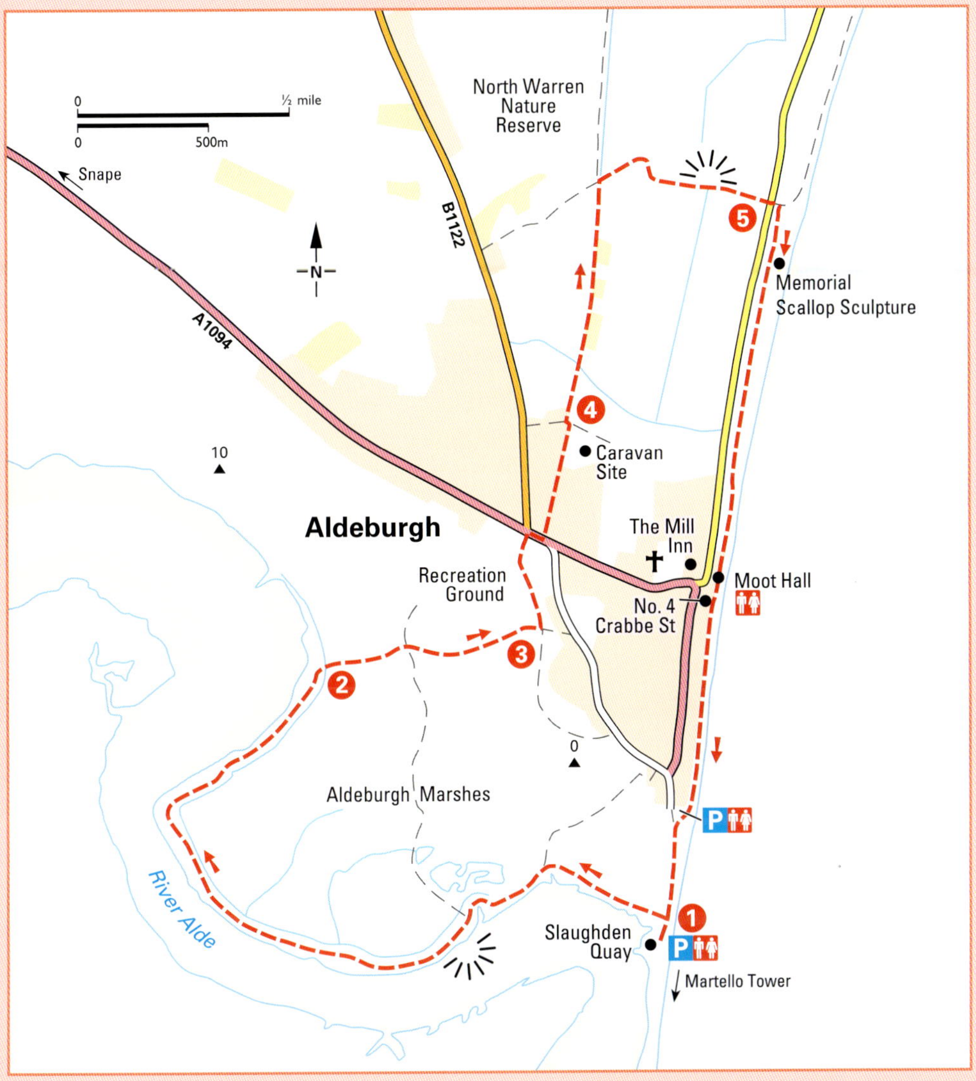

Distance 5.75 miles (9.2km)

Minimum Time 2hrs 30min

Ascent/Gradient Negligible ▲▲▲

Level of Difficulty ●●●

Paths River and sea wall, meadows, old railway track

Landscape Town, river, marshes and beach

Suggested Map OS Explorer 212 Woodbridge & Saxmundham

Start/Finish Grid reference: TM 463555

Dog Friendliness Off lead on river wall, on lead on permissive path – not allowed on beach between May and September

Parking Slaughden Quay free car park

Public Toilets Slaughden Quay, Fort Green, Moot Hall

1 Start at Slaughden Quay, once a thriving port, now a yacht club. Walk back briefly in the direction of Aldeburgh and turn left along the river wall on the north bank of the River Alde. There are good views to your left of the Martello tower that marks the northern end of Orford Ness. Stay on the river wall for 2 miles (3.2km) as the river swings to the right towards Aldeburgh.

2 When the river bends left, go down the wooden staircase to your right and keep straight ahead across a meadow, with a water tower visible ahead. Go through a gate and bear half-left across the next meadow to cross over a footbridge. Next, follow the waymarks, bearing half-right, then keep straight ahead across the next field to come to another footbridge. After crossing a fifth footbridge, the path runs alongside allotments and goes through a gate to reach a lane.

3 Turn left by a brick wall and cross the recreation ground. Continue past the fire station to reach a road. Turn right for 75yds (69m), then go left on a signposted footpath almost opposite the hospital entrance. Go between houses, cross a road and keep straight ahead with a caravan site on the right.

4 When you see a footpath on the right, leading to a track across the caravan park, turn left and immediately right on a permissive path that follows the trackbed of an old railway. Stay on this path for 0.5 mile (800m) as it climbs steadily between farmland to the left and woodland and marshes to the right. Turn right at a junction of paths to reach the open meadows. Stay on this path, crossing the North Warren Nature Reserve with views of Sizewell power station to your left.

5 Cross the road and turn right along a tarmac path that runs parallel to the beach. As you approach Aldeburgh, you pass a striking scallop sculpture on the shingle (erected in 2003 to celebrate Benjamin Britten's life in Aldeburgh), fishermen's huts and fishing boats that have been pulled up on to the shingle. Pass the timber-framed Moot Hall and continue along Crag Path, past a lifeboat station and a pair of 19th-century look-out towers. At the end of Crag Path, bear right across a car park and walk around the old mill to return to Slaughden Quay.

43 Sizewell A, B… and Sea

Against the futuristic backdrop of a controversial nuclear plant, this relaxing circuit delivers unexpected delights in woodland, heathland, marshes and coast

Top left, centre: Look out for bluebells in the nature reserve in spring

Above left: You may see a rare black redstart (*Phoenicurus ochruros*) at Sizewell

Above right: Sizewell B's unmistakeable 'golf-ball'reactor lies behind the seawashed sands

Taking a walk around a nuclear power station may seem like a strange idea, especially to those who come from that generation of students whose windows were plastered with stickers proclaiming 'Nuclear power? No thanks.' Yet this walk in the shadow of Sizewell B is a special one. It has wetland, woodland, heathland, farmland sections and runs for a while along unspoilt coast, with the surreal sight of the white dome of the power station as an ever-present backdrop.

Sizewell B power station is probably the most controversial building in Suffolk. The first gas-cooled reactor, Sizewell A, opened in 1966, but it was the appearance of the 'golf ball' at Sizewell B that prompted a wave of protests and one of Britain's longest public enquiries. Sizewell B is the only pressurised water reactor in Britain. It began operating in 1995, when memories of nuclear disasters at Chernobyl (in 1986 in Ukraine, then part of the Soviet Union) and Three Mile Island (in 1979 in Pennsylvania, United States) were still fresh. The hemispherical dome is 148ft (45m) in diameter and 213ft (65m) tall, protected by concrete walls designed to withstand a nuclear accident or an earthquake.

The land around the power stations, owned by British Energy, is managed as a nature reserve in conjunction with Suffolk Wildlife Trust, and there is a network of waymarked walks that you can follow across woodland and grazing marshes.

Orchids grow in the meadows in early summer, bluebells appear in the woods in spring and dragonflies and damselflies buzz around the marshes. Some of the few pairs of black redstart in Britain have even started to nest on the power station buildings – a treat for birdwatchers.

'Merrie England' at Thorpeness

An alternative walk takes you to Thorpeness, a fairy-tale village created by Glencairn Stuart Ogilvie after he purchased the Sizewell Estate in 1910 and transformed the fishing hamlet of Thorpe into a holiday resort. The chief attraction at Thorpeness is The Meare, an artificial boating lake with islands and play houses themed around the story of *Peter Pan*, created in 1902-04 by J.M. Barrie.

Ogilvie wanted to create a slice of 'Merrie England' – there is a golf course, a country club, mock-Tudor houses and numerous architectural follies including the delightful House in the Clouds. This cleverly designed water tower, built to supply the water pump across the road, was disguised as a timber-framed house and has become the dominant feature of the Thorpeness skyline, appearing, from a distance, to be lodged in the trees. It is now a charming holiday home.

43 Sizewell A, B… and Sea

Cross one nature reserve and enjoy views of another

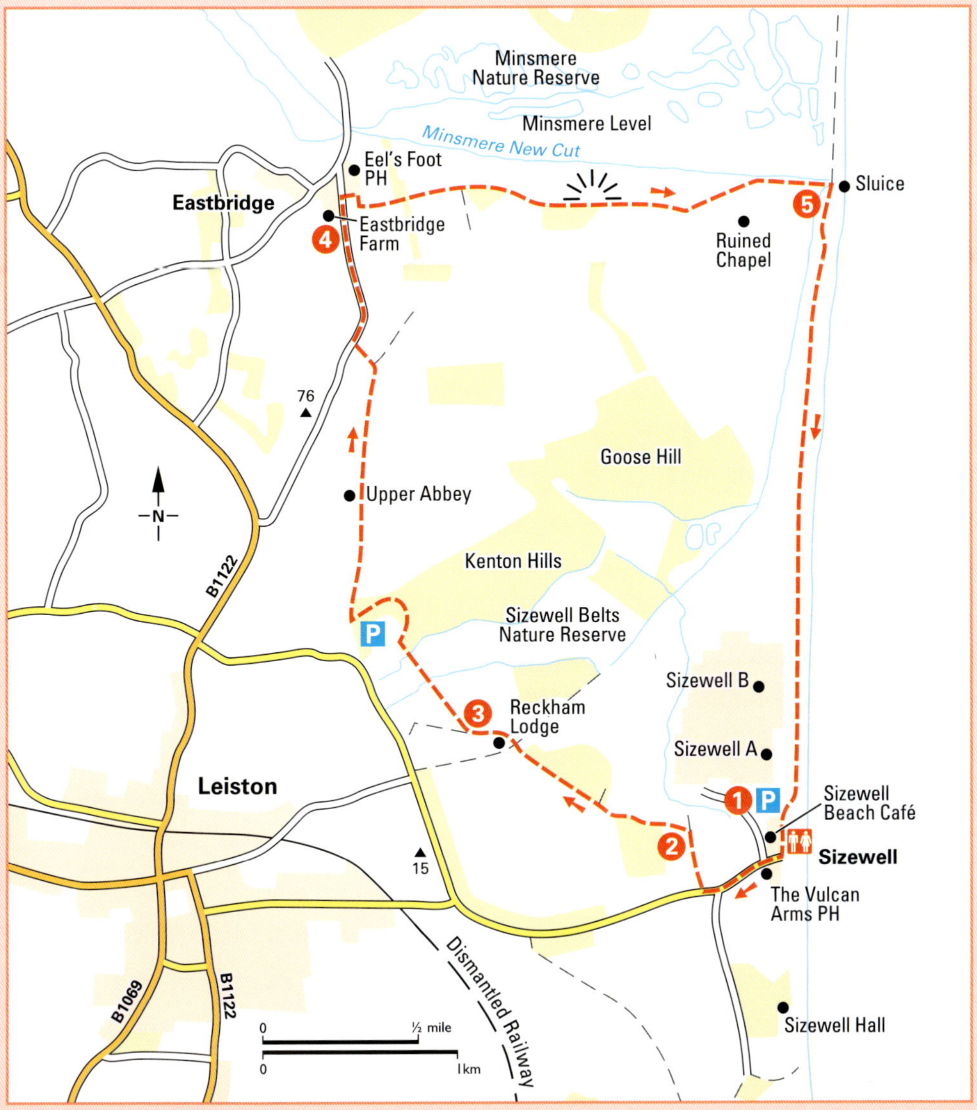

Distance 6.75 miles (10.9km)

Minimum Time 3hrs

Ascent/Gradient 164ft (50m) ▲▲▲

Level of Difficulty ●●●

Paths Footpaths, coast path, short stretches of road, 2 stiles

Landscape Sizewell power station and its surroundings

Suggested Map OS Explorer 212 Woodbridge & Saxmundham

Start/Finish Grid reference: TM 475629

Dog Friendliness Be aware of wildlife and nesting birds on beach; no dogs allowed in Sizewell Belts Nature Reserve

Parking Sizewell Beach car park (free in winter)

Public Toilets Sizewell Beach

1 Walk up the road away from the beach or cross the meadow behind the car park and cross a stile to reach the Vulcan Arms. Continue along the road past the entrance to the power stations. Turn right after 400yds (366m) on to a track and stay on this track for 300yds (274m).

2 Turn left just before a cottage and follow this path beneath the power lines and alongside a small wood on the left. Cross a stile beside a gate and continue across the open meadow with views of Sizewell B to your right. A path on the right leads into the Sizewell Belts Nature Reserve (no dogs). Keep straight ahead on a wide bridle path. Cross a stile, then where the path swings left, turn right and immediately left beside Reckham Lodge to cross an area of heathland.

3 At a meadow and fork of paths, bear half-right, then drop down through bracken to a footbridge before crossing a meadow to another footbridge. Cross duckboards and continue through trees to a track. Turn left, then left again to reach the car park for the permissive walks. Turn right on to a track and continue ahead for 0.75 mile (1.2km), following it left at a cottage to meet a road. Turn right to walk into Eastbridge.

4 After passing Eastbridge Farm on the left, look for a footpath on the right, signposted 'Minsmere Sluice'. After 50yds (46m), the path swings sharp right then turns left beside a hedge and continues alongside a field. Pass through a belt of trees and stay on this narrow footpath across the fields with views over the Minsmere Level to your left. Pass through two gates to cross to the far side of a ditch and continue on a grassy lane. The path swings left to run alongside the New Cut, with views of the Minsmere Nature Reserve to your left and the strange sight of Sizewell B juxtaposed behind a ruined chapel on your right-hand side.

5 Turn right at Minsmere Sluice to return to Sizewell along a wide track or scramble up to the top of the cliffs. Turn right just beyond the power stations to return to the car park.

44 The Ghosts of Dunwich

A thought-provoking walk near a medieval city lost to the sea takes in National Trust land on Dunwich Heath with plentiful opportunities for birdwatching

Medieval Dunwich was a splendid city and a major seaport, exporting wool and grain to Europe and importing cloth and wine. It had six churches as well as numerous chapels, convents, monasteries, hospitals, alehouses, farmhouses and mills. Now it is a small seaside village with a handful of houses and a pub. So where has it gone? The answer is that, like so much of the Suffolk coast, it has simply vanished into the sea.

The sea has been the making and breaking of Dunwich. The sea was the reason for its existence and supported its industries of shipbuilding and fishing. It was the sea that brought Dunwich's most famous figure, St Felix of Burgundy, a missionary invited by King Sigebert to preach Christianity to the pagans of East Anglia and rewarded with a bishopric and a cathedral at Dunwich in AD 630. It was the sea that silted up the harbour during a terrible storm in 1286, leading to the city's inevitable decline. And it is the sea, ever since, that has taken Dunwich back, a process that continues at the rate of around 1yd (1m) every year.

A scale model of the 12th-century city, housed in Dunwich Museum, reveals the full truth about its decline. The Roman town here extended 1 mile (1.6km) out to sea beyond the present coastline. Half of this had disappeared by the time of the Norman Conquest in 1066, but the worst was yet to come. The last church tumbled over the cliffs as recently as 1920 and the museum has a series of dramatic photographs showing it collapsing year by year. According to a local legend, you can still hear the bells of the sunken churches pealing beneath the sea on a stormy night.

Heathland Conservation Area

This walk also takes you to Dunwich Heath, where the National Trust manages some 215 acres (87ha) of sandy cliffs and a mile (1.6km) of beach as a conservation area. The area was once part of the extensive Sandlings Heaths and consists of miles of excellent walks and tracks through open heathland. It borders the RSPB's Minsmere Nature Reserve and the shady woods and expanses of heather attract a wealth of birdlife, including Dartford warblers and nightjars. Come, if you can, between June and September, when the heathland on the cliff top is carpeted with purple and pink heather.

Below: On Dunwich beach

Bottom: Summer glory – pink heather on Dunwich Heath

Main image: These waves conceal the remains of medieval Dunwich

44 The Ghosts of Dunwich

Conjure up visions of a lost city on a bracing coastal tramp

Distance 8 miles (12.9km)

Minimum Time 4hrs

Ascent/Gradient 262ft (80m) ▲▲▲

Level of Difficulty ●●●

Paths Farm tracks, heathland paths, quiet roads, shingle beach

Landscape Heathland, woodland, farmland, marshes and coast

Suggested map OS Explorers 212 Woodbridge & Saxmundham; 231 Southwold & Bungay

Start/Finish Grid reference: TM 479707 (on Explorer 231)

Dog Friendliness On lead on National Trust land and Dingle Marshes

Parking Dunwich Beach free car park

Public Toilets At car park

1 Walk up from the beach car park and keep left at the junction. When the road bends, turn left up through the woods. Turn left on the cliff top, go over steps and right through trees. At the end of the path, turn right on to a road.

2 Turn left off the road after 100yds (91m) on a track to the Dairy House. Go ahead on this path in Greyfriars Wood and to a road.

3 Turn left and walk along this road for 0.5 mile (800m). Enter National Trust land and turn left on a path marked with white arrows.

4 Walk around the National Trust's Coastguard Cottages and take the track beside Heath Barn field centre. Go right on a sandy path through the heather. Keep on this path, bearing left and right at a crossing track to follow the Sandlings Walk nightjar waymarks. When you reach a bridleway, keep straight ahead on a farm track passing Mount Pleasant Farm. Cross the road and keep straight ahead on a concrete lane until you reach Sandy Lane Farm.

5 Turn right for 0.5 mile (800m) on a shady path to emerge by St James's Church. For a short cut, go straight ahead here to Dunwich.

6 Turn left at the road and, in 100yds (91m), go right at Bridge Nurseries and Café. Keep to the right around farm buildings and stay on this track for 1.5 miles (2.4km) before turning seawards. Pass through a gate to enter a covert and fork right at a junction around Great Dingle Farm, then follow the path through the reed beds towards the sea.

7 Turn right at a junction when you see an old drainage mill to your left, and follow the flood bank across Dingle Marshes. Turn right to return to Dunwich along the beach or take the path behind the shingle bank.

45 The Crumbling Cliffs of Covehithe

This promenade along a beautiful and rapidly disappearing Suffolk clifftop reveals the startling – and dispiriting – effects of coastal erosion at first hand

Nowhere else in Suffolk do you feel the power of the sea so much as on this walk along the cliffs at Covehithe. Coastal erosion is threatening much of East Anglia, but here the sea is advancing at the rate of almost 10yds (9m) a year. The ground is being swallowed up from under your feet and the beach is littered with the debris of collapsed trees. This is not a walk for those with a fear of heights.

Coastal Erosion

Come here and walk along the coast soon because this landscape will probably not be here in 50 years' time. Right along the coast of north Suffolk the tides are eating away at the cliffs, depositing the shingle further south on Orford Ness. This is a process that has been going on for thousands of years, part of the natural realignment of the coastline that has already seen most of Dunwich disappear beneath the waves (see Walk 44). But rising sea levels caused by global warming and the extraction of sand and gravel from the seabed used in the construction of new homes and roads have accelerated the erosion to the point where Covehithe will soon be little more than a memory.

Thatched Church

The small village is dominated by St Andrew's Church, whose tall tower has long been a beacon to sailors. Built in the 15th century, when Covehithe was perhaps 2 miles (3.2km) from the shore, the church was always out of all proportion to the population of a village that never exceeded 300 people and is now down to fewer than 30. In 1672 the roof was dismantled and a smaller church was built within the ruins, using material stripped from the earlier structure. The thatched church now stands beneath the original tower, a beautiful sight but one whose days are numbered.

From the church, a tarmac road leads to the edge of the cliffs and then suddenly comes to an abrupt end, forcing you to wonder what once lay beyond. Stern notices warn you not to continue, but in fact there is a well-used concessionary path along the edge of the cliffs. Each year the path is pushed further inland as valuable farmland is lost to the encroaching tides and the few remaining houses edge closer to the sea.

Try to imagine, as you walk along the cliffs, that the path you are walking on will probably not be here next year. It's not a very comforting thought.

Above: Crumbling cliffs on the Suffolk coast

Right: St Andrew's at Covehithe – a small later church stands within the ruins of the original

45 The Crumbling Cliffs of Covehithe

Seize your chance to walk the Covehithe cliffs before they disappear into the sea

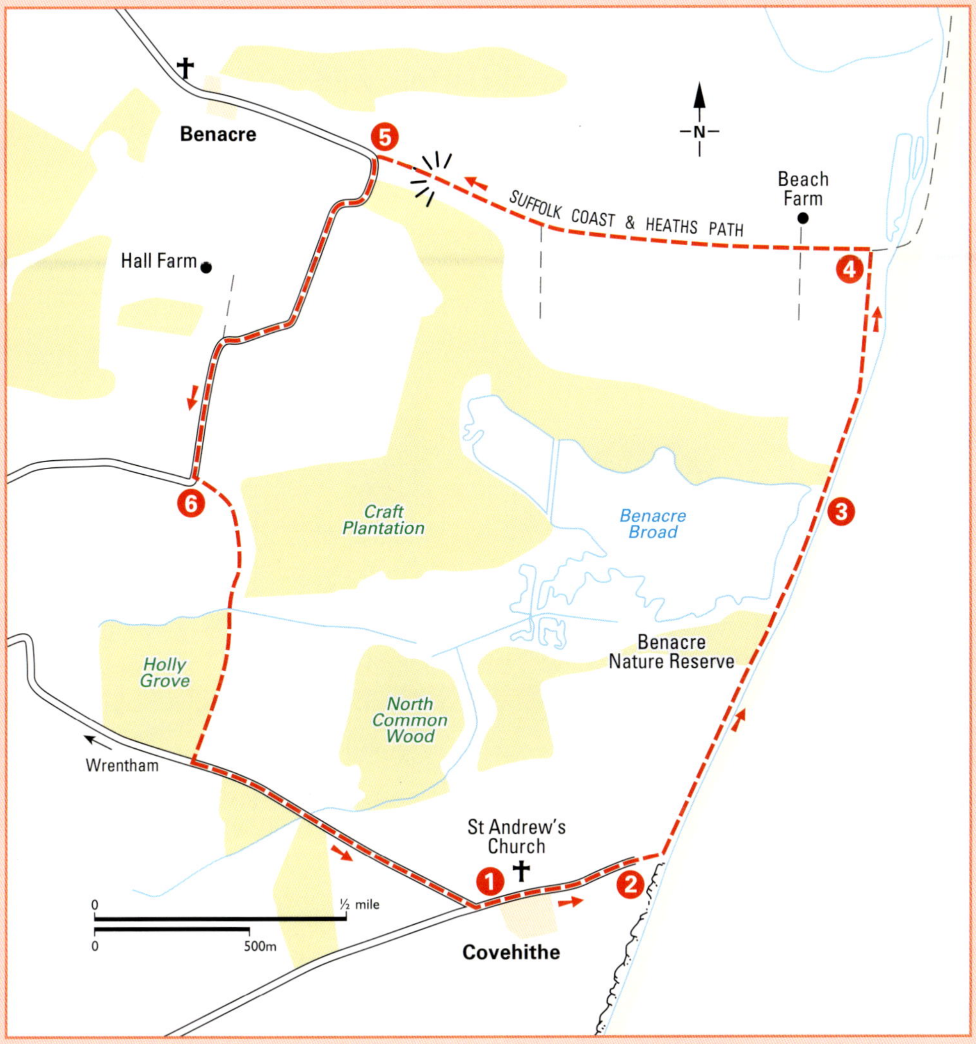

Distance 4.5 miles (7.2km)

Minimum Time 1hr 45min

Ascent/Gradient 131ft (40m) ▲▲▲

Level of Difficulty ●●●

Paths Cliff top, shingle beach, farm track and country lanes, 1 stile

Landscape Farmland, woodland, cliffs, sea, lagoon

Suggested Map OS Explorer 231 Southwold & Bungay

Start/Finish Grid reference: TM 522818

Dog Friendliness On lead across nature reserve and beach

Parking On street near Covehithe Church

Public Toilets None en route

1 Take the tarmac lane from the church down towards the sea. You reach a barrier with a 'Danger' notice and a sign warning that there is no public right of way. Although this is strictly true, this is a well established and popular path stretching north towards Kessingland Beach and you are likely to meet many other walkers. The warnings are serious, but it is quite safe to walk here so long as you keep away from the cliff edge.

2 Walk through the gap to the right of the road barrier and continue towards the cliffs, then turn left along a wide farm track with a pig farm to your left. The path follows the cliff top, then drops down towards the beach to enter the Benacre Nature Reserve. On the left is Benacre Broad, once an estuary, now a marshy lagoon. Like others on the Suffolk coast, the beach here attracts little terns in spring and summer and you should keep to the path to avoid disturbing their nesting sites.

3 Climb back on to a well worn path on the cliffs at the end of Benacre Broad. The route cuts through pine trees and bracken on a constantly changing path, before running alongside a field and swinging right to drop back down to beach level – where you should take the wide grass track on your left to make your way across the dunes.

4 When you reach a concrete track, with the tower of Kessingland Church visible in the distance, turn left following the waymarks of the Suffolk Coast and Heaths Path. Go through a kissing gate and keep straight ahead, passing Beach Farm on the right. Stay straight ahead for 1 mile (1.6km) on a wide track between the fields with views of Benacre Church up ahead.

5 Go through some steel gates and turn left on to a quiet country lane. Stay on this lane for 0.75 mile (1.2km) as it passes between hedges with arable farmland to either side and swings left at the entrance to Hall Farm.

6 When the road bends right, turn left past a gate. Stay on this path as it swings right around a meadow and continues into the woodland of Holly Grove. Pass through another gate and turn left along the road for the last 0.75 mile (1.2km) back into Covehithe. Turn left at the junction to return to the church.

46 Around the Mysterious Horsey Mere

This atmospheric walk leads through an area of Norfolk wilderness that remains vulnerable to the ravages of tides and coastal storms – and is rich in local legends

Above left: Reed beds on the banks of Horsey Mere

Above right: Horsey Drainage Mill has four storeys of brick and a weather-boarded cap in the shape of a boat

In 1938 a devastating combination of high tides and storms occurred around Horsey. The sea surged inland, flooding buildings and fields, and forcing people to evacuate their homes. It was four months before the water subsided and the villagers were able to resume normal life, although it took another five years before the damaging effects of salt water on the fields was finally overcome and crops could be grown again.

Horsey is barely 3ft (1m) above sea level and, as you walk around the reed-fringed mere and stroll along its many drainage channels, you will appreciate the unchanging wildness of this part of Norfolk and its vulnerability at the hands of the sea. Not for nothing was this area known as 'Devil's Country' in local legends.

Listing Brograve Mill

You will see part of the devil's handiwork when you pass Brograve Mill, between Horsey and Waxam. The story goes that one Thomas Brograve was determined to reclaim part of this wilderness for farming, and built a mill. The devil was furious and tried to blow it down. He did not succeed, but you will see a distinct list to the mill today, indicating that the battle was a close-run thing! Horsey has its own legend: it is said that on 13 June each year, the wailing voices of drowned children can be heard from the mere. The village and surrounding area is now in the care of the National Trust, so its picturesque tranquillity is unlikely to be spoiled. All Saints' Church dates from the 13th century, and has an attractive thatched nave. Go inside and look for the stained-glass window in the south chancel commemorating Catherine Ursula Rising, who died in 1890. She is shown painting in her drawing room at Horsey Hall. The hall is to the south, built in 1845 for the Risings, who bought the manor from the Brograves.

The village's most famous feature is the Horsey Drainage Mill, built to pump water from the surrounding farmland. It dates from the middle of the 19th century, but was rebuilt in 1897 and again in 1912. It was working in 1940 when it was struck by lightning, and was restored in 1961. Today it is owned by the National Trust and is open to visitors.

On the Broads

Away to the southwest is Horsey Mere, a part of the Broads. The mere is surrounded by reed beds, which are used for thatching many of Horsey's pretty houses. This peaceful stretch of water offers a haven for countless birds, particularly in winter, when it is filled by thousands of waterfowl.

46 Around the Mysterious Horsey Mere

Explore whispering reed beds and silent windmills and finish at a National Trust-owned pub

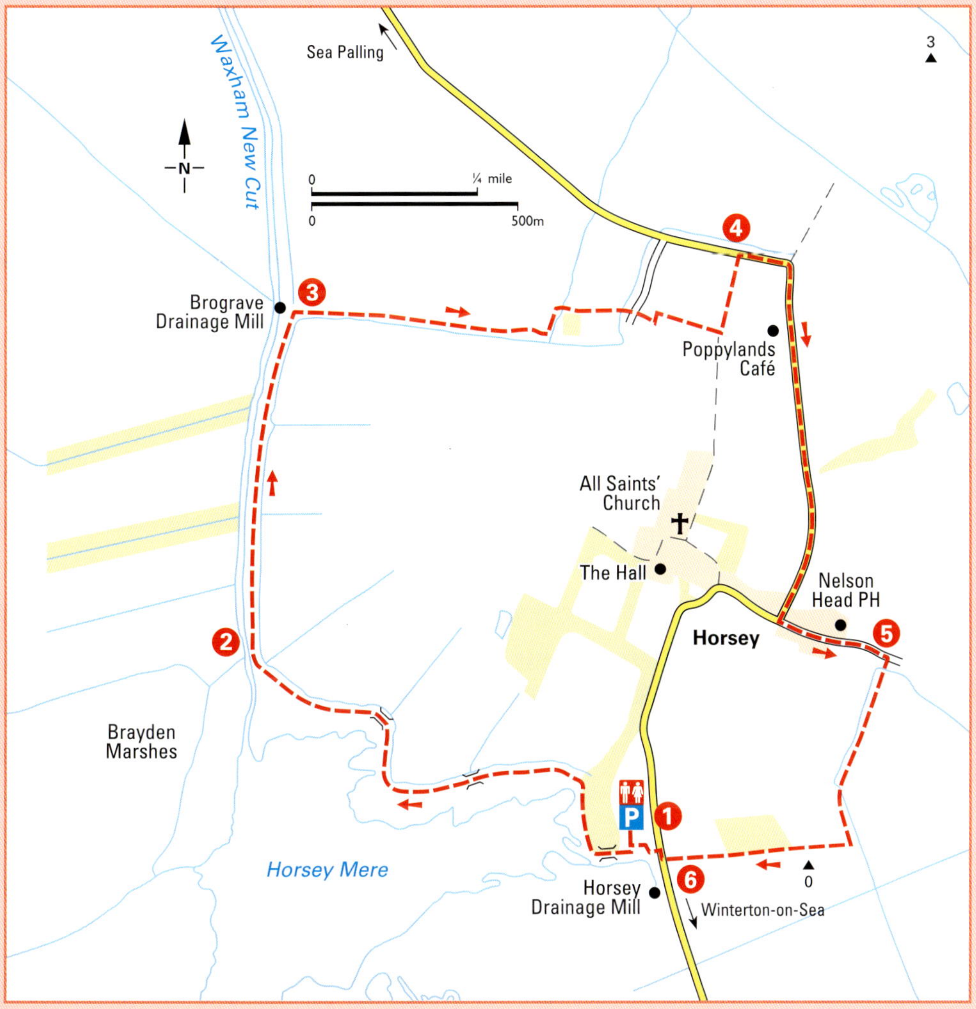

Distance 3.5 miles (5.7km)

Minimum Time 1hr 30min

Ascent/Gradient Negligible ▲▲▲

Level of Difficulty ●●●

Paths Marked trails along dykes (walk quietly to avoid disturbing nesting birds), 5 stiles

Landscape Reed-fringed drainage channels, marshy lake and water-meadows

Suggested Map OS Explorer OL40 The Broads

Start/Finish Grid reference: TG 456223

Dog Friendliness On lead over farmland (livestock breeding area), avoid areas used by nesting water birds

Parking National Trust pay-and-display at Horsey Drainage Mill

Public Toilets At car park

1 From the National Trust car park walk towards the toilets and then take the footpath to the right of them. This leads to a footbridge. After crossing the bridge, turn right and follow the path along the side of Horsey Mere through reeds and alder copses. Cross a wooden bridge across a dyke and go through a gate to enter a grassy water meadow. Look for the white disc across the field. Go through a second gate and over a bridge.

2 Turn right when the path meets a brown-watered dyke (Waxham New Cut). Eventually, you will see derelict Brograve Drainage Mill ahead. Herons and other birds often perch on its battered sails, so it's worth stopping to look.

3 Turn right immediately adjacent to the mill and walk along the edge of a field. Reed beds give way to water meadow. Cross another plank bridge and continue straight ahead. The path bends left, then right, then crosses a small lane and continues through the field opposite. At the end of the field, make a sharp left, eventually coming to another lane.

4 Go right at the lane, bearing right where it meets a track, and walk past Poppylands Café. When you reach a junction turn left, following the sign for the Nelson Head. Pass the pub on your left-hand side, then look for a well-defined footpath going off to your right.

5 Walk past the gate and continue along the wide sward ahead, with a narrow dyke on either side. When the sward divides, bear left and head for a stile at the end of the footpath. Climb this and turn right to walk along a spacious field. This area is used for grazing breeding stock and you should look for signs warning of the presence of bulls. Since this part of the walk is permissive, and not a public footpath, the National Trust is within its rights to put bulls here, so it is important to check for warning signs before you venture forth. These are always prominently displayed. If this is the case, you will have to walk back to the lane and turn left. This will take you back to the car park at the start of the walk.

6 Assuming there are no bulls to hinder your progress, climb the stile between the field and the road and cross the road. The car park where the walk began is ahead of you and slightly to your right. This is a good time to explore the delights of Horsey Drainage Mill, which you will find just to your left.

47 Overstrand to Northrepps

An invigorating ramble at Overstrand leads along farm tracks through pleasant countryside to the area charmingly dubbed 'Poppylands' by the Victorians

There is a constant battle raging between the sea and the land at Overstrand, and although the land is holding its own thanks to some serious sea defences, it looks as though the waves will be the eventual winners.

Land Reclaimed by Sea

The cliffs around Overstrand are crumbling, being reclaimed by the North Sea. Further east, the cliffs are so precarious that there is no access to them until you reach Mundesley. In the 14th century, the sea swept away the land on which the Church of St Martin stood, and the villagers were obliged to build another – the one you can see today.

The Beauty of 'Poppylands'

This walk has more to offer than eroded cliffs and tales of disappearing churches, however. It wanders through Poppylands, so called after the name was given to the area by poet Clement William Scott in late-Victorian times. Scott loved this part of Norfolk and wrote a series of newspaper articles about the unspoiled beauty of its fishing villages, rolling farmland with wild poppies and rugged coastline. His descriptions were so vivid that readers were inspired to visit and flocked in large numbers to the area. The humble fishing village developed to accommodate the rich and famous.

Houses were designed by celebrated architects such as Edwin Lutyens and Arthur William Bloomfield. The Pleasaunce was designed by Lutyens with gardens by Gertrude Jekyll for Gladstone's Chief Whip, Lord Battersea, and the splendid Overstrand Hall was built for the banker Lord Hillingdon in 1899. Even the Churchill family had a residence here. As the population grew to include an upper-class community, more facilities were needed to accommodate them. St Martin's Church had become unsafe in the 18th century and Christ Church was raised in 1867 to replace it. But the newcomers preferred the ancient simplicity of St Martin's and so it was rebuilt and restored in 1911–14. For those who preferred nonconformist worship, there was a handsome Methodist chapel, designed in 1898 by Lutyens. It is an odd building, with a brick lower floor and arched clerestory windows in the upper floor.

After strolling through the farmland south of Overstrand, you reach the village of Northrepps, which became famous when Verily Anderson wrote a book called *The Northrepps Grandchildren*, describing what life was like at Northrepps Hall.

Above right: The largely 15th-century Church of St Mary the Virgin in Northrepps

Right: Looking out from the sea wall at Overstrand

47 Overstrand to Northrepps

Take an energetic walk to Northrepps

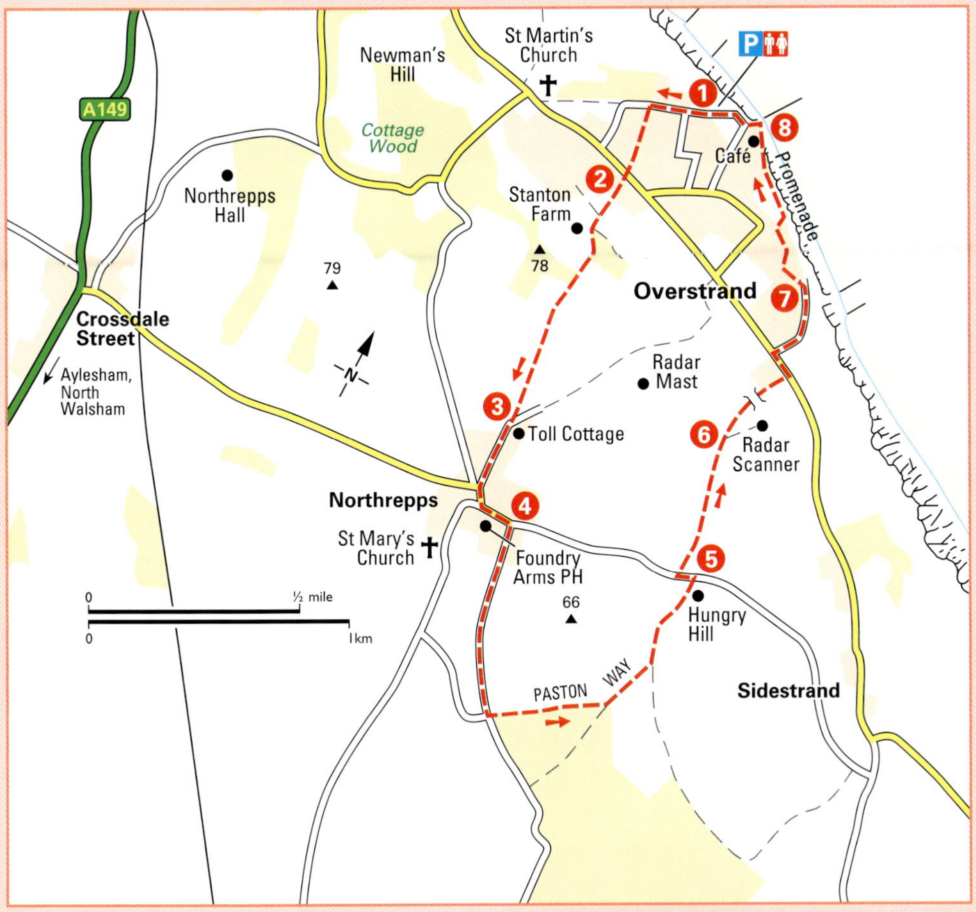

Distance 4 miles (6.4km)

Minimum Time 2hrs

Ascent/Gradient 295ft (90m) ▲▲▲

Level of Difficulty ●●●

Paths Farm tracks, footpaths, quiet lanes

Landscape Attractive rolling farmland

Suggested Map OS Explorer 252 Norfolk Coast East

Start/Finish Grid reference: TG 247410

Dog Friendliness Dogs not allowed on Promenade

Parking Pay-and-display car park on Coast Road in Overstrand

Public Toilets At car park

1 Turn right out of the car park and on to Paul's Lane. Pass the Old Rectory, then walk along the pavement on the left. Pass Arden Close, then look for the public footpath sign on your left-hand side. Follow this alley until you reach a road.

2 Cross the road, aiming for the sign 'Private Drive. Please Drive Slowly.' To the left of this is a footpath. Go up this track, then take the path to the left of the gate to Stanton Farm. Climb up the hill, taking the path to the right when the main track bears to the left. At the brow of the hill follow the path towards a line of trees. Then go downhill, eventually reaching Toll Cottage.

3 Take the lane ahead, passing Broadgate Close. At the Northrepps village sign and a T-junction, turn left on to Church Street, keeping to the left. After passing the Foundry Arms, look out for the phone box and bus stop, beyond which lies Craft Lane.

4 Turn right along Craft Lane, using the pavement until a sign marks this as a 'quiet lane' for walkers. After 700yds (640m) there is a Paston Way sign on your left. Take this through the woods, and bear left when it becomes a track to Hungry Hill Farm.

5 At the lane next to the farm, turn to the left. Then after a few paces go right, following signs marked 'Circular Walk Paston Way'. Follow this gravel track towards the radar scanner installation.

6 Keep left where the track bends towards the radar tower, following the footpath signs. The path descends through woods, passing under a disused railway bridge before meeting the main road. Cross this, then turn left to walk on the pavement for a few paces before turning right along Coast Road. When the road starts to bend, look out for signs to Overstrand Promenade.

7 Go down the steep ramp to your right to arrive at a concrete walkway. Up to your left you will see the remains of fallen houses in the crumbling cliffs. Follow the walkway (or you can walk on the sand, if you prefer) until you reach a slipway for boats. To the left of the slipway is a zig-zag pathway.

8 Follow this upwards to the top of the cliffs. The car park is just ahead of you.

48 Cliffs and Hungry Seas

A tramp along the Overstrand cliff path leads between golf course and sea to bustling Cromer, famous for its crabs, and then back along the beach

Top: The imposing seafront, sandy beach and pier at Cromer

Above: Cromer crabs can be bought in the town

Right: Cromer's memorial to Henry Blogg

In 1779 a bathing machine was advertised at Cromer, and soon the rich Norwich banking families of Gurney and Barclay and their Quaker relations began to take their holidays here, and to rent or buy houses. The resort developed further in the 19th century. The sandy beach was an attraction, and so (it was said) were the simple manners of the inhabitants, the fact that the sun could be seen both rising and setting in the sea, and the local dressed crab.

It was a place for gentlefolk. In her novel *Emma* (published 1815), Jane Austen has Mr Woodhouse declare to his daughter, 'You should have gone to Cromer, my dear, if you went anywhere. Perry was a week at Cromer once, and he holds it to be the best of all the sea-bathing places. A fine open sea, he says, and very pure air.'

There was opposition when the railway arrived at Cromer in 1877. Hotels and lodging houses now proliferated, after journalist Clement Scott publicised this stretch of coast as 'Poppyland' (see Walk 47), and a new pier and bandstand were built in the 1900s.

The earlier Cromer was a fishing village, which took the place of a still earlier one, called Shibden, which was consumed by the sea.

The impressive church of St Peter and St Paul, whose 160ft (49m) tower is Norfolk's tallest by far, was built in the 14th century. Nearby cottages have been turned into a museum of the area's history and natural history.

Cromer's Heroic Lifeboatman

The Royal National Lifeboat Institute's Henry Blogg was an old man when he died in 1954, but anyone reading about his exploits in plucking imperilled sailors from the treacherous sea will wonder how he managed to cheat death for so long. His bravery is legendary and he was awarded more medals and commendations than any other lifeboatman in the British Isles, and hundreds of sailors owed him their lives. You can learn more about the life of Blogg at the Henry Blogg Museum in Cromer.

Cromer crabs, said to be the best in the country, are caught on long lines from little clinker-built boats that chug out to sea regardless of the weather. Once the pots are out, the fishermen must collect them the following day, whether a gale is raging or not. Tractors haul the boats to and from the water's edge, and watching them makes for an interesting diversion.

48 Cliffs and Hungry Seas

Pay your respects to a hero before tasting a local delicacy

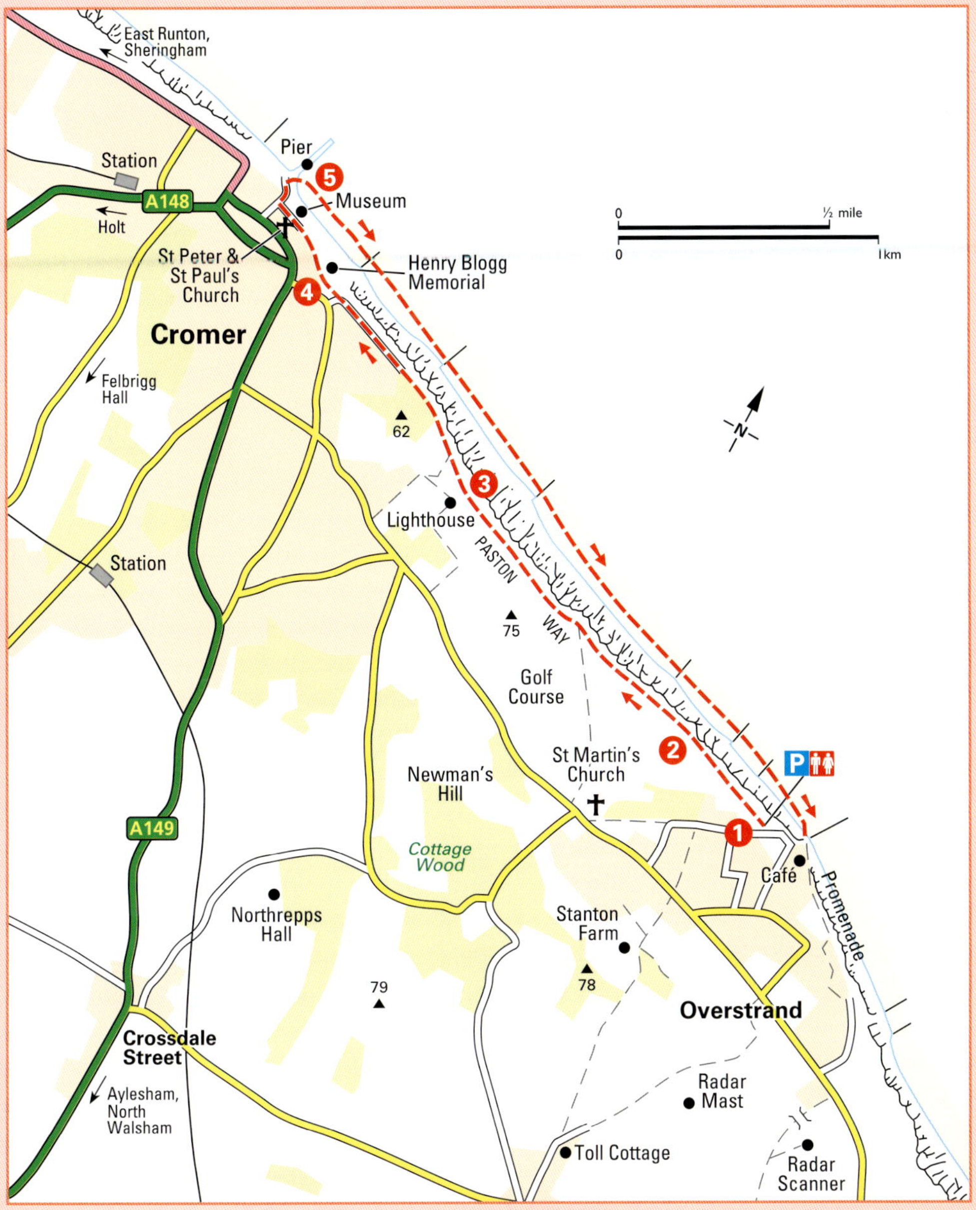

Distance 4 miles (6.4km)

Minimum Time 1hr 45min

Ascent/Gradient 295ft (90m) ▲▲▲

Level of Difficulty ●●●

Paths Farm tracks, footpaths, quiet lanes

Landscape Attractive rolling farmland and cliff scenery

Suggested Map OS Explorer 252 Norfolk Coast East

Start/Finish Grid reference: TG 247410

Dog Friendliness Dogs not allowed on Promenade

Parking Pay-and-display car park on Coast Road in Overstrand. Parking also in Cromer

Public Toilets At car parks

1 It's almost impossible to get lost on this walk. Start in the Overstrand car park and walk to the flagpole. To your left you will see the cliff path winding away through brambles. This is part of the Paston Way.

2 Follow this past the golf course, from where you will be able to see your destination – Cromer Pier. It is important to keep to the path at all times: too far to the right and you risk falling over the cliffs, too far to the left and you will be at risk from flying golf balls. Be prepared for a few climbs. The path goes up and down a fair amount.

3 When you reach the lighthouse, at the end of the golf course, the path drops down steeply. The path becomes paved and you reach the first houses. Follow signs to the seafront, passing the monument to Henry Blogg and a tiny garden.

4 When the footpath ends, cross the street and turn right on to Brunswick Terrace, a pathway with railings. Then go straight along East Cliff, passing St Peter and St Paul's Church (originally 15th century, but restored in 1862) on your left. Go right down Jetty Street to the pier, which was built in 1900 to replace one lost in 1895.

5 Walk down the ramp to the beach, turn right and walk for about 2 miles (3.2km) until you arrive back at Overstrand and the car park again. Alternatively, follow Walk 47, which starts here.

49 Blakeney Eye's Magical Marshes

Once a port, then a Victorian centre for shooting, Blakeney today hosts a reserve that makes a great place for a country walk – whether or not you're a birdwatcher

Blakeney was a prosperous port in medieval times, but went into decline when its sea channels began to silt up. However, although the merchants decried the slow accumulation of salt marsh and sand bars, birds began to flock here in their thousands. By Victorian times it had become such a favoured spot with feathered migrants that it became known as the place to go shooting and collecting. Some sportsmen just wanted to kill the many waterfowl, while others were more interested in trophy collecting – looking for species that were rare or little-known. The maxim 'what's hit is history; what's missed is mystery' was very characteristic of the Victorians' attitude to biological science. Many of these hapless birds ended up stuffed in museums or private collections.

After many years of bloody slaughter the National Trust arrived in 1912 and purchased the area from Cley Beach to the tip of the sand and shingle peninsula of Blakeney Point. It became one of the first nature reserves to be safeguarded in Britain. Today it offers delights in all seasons. A bright summer day will show you glittering streams, salt-scented grasses waving gently in the breeze and pretty-sailed yachts bobbing in the distance. By contrast, a wet and windy day in winter will reveal the place's stark beauty, with white-capped waves pounding the beach, rain-drenched vegetation and a menacing low-hung sky filled with scudding clouds. A walk here is always invigorating.

Winged Visitors

Although these days we regard the Victorians' wholesale slaughter with distaste, they did leave behind them a legacy of information. It was 19th-century trophy hunters who saw the Pallas' warbler and the yellow-breasted bunting in Britain for the first time – and they were seen at Blakeney. A little later, when the Cley Bird Observatory operated here between 1949 and 1963, the first subalpine warbler in Norfolk was captured and ringed.

The Victorians' records tell us that a good many red-spotted bluethroats appeared in September and October, and any collector who happened to visit then was almost certain to bag one. In the 1950s the observatory discovered that these were becoming rare at this time of year. Today, bluethroats are regular spring visitors but are seldom seen in the autumn. It is thought that this change over time is related to different weather patterns and indicates how climate change, even on this small scale, can dramatically affect the behaviour of birds.

Below: Blakeney may no longer be a port but it is an idyllic setting for sailing

49 Blakeney Eye's Magical Marshes

Walk along the sea defences to one of the finest bird reserves in the country

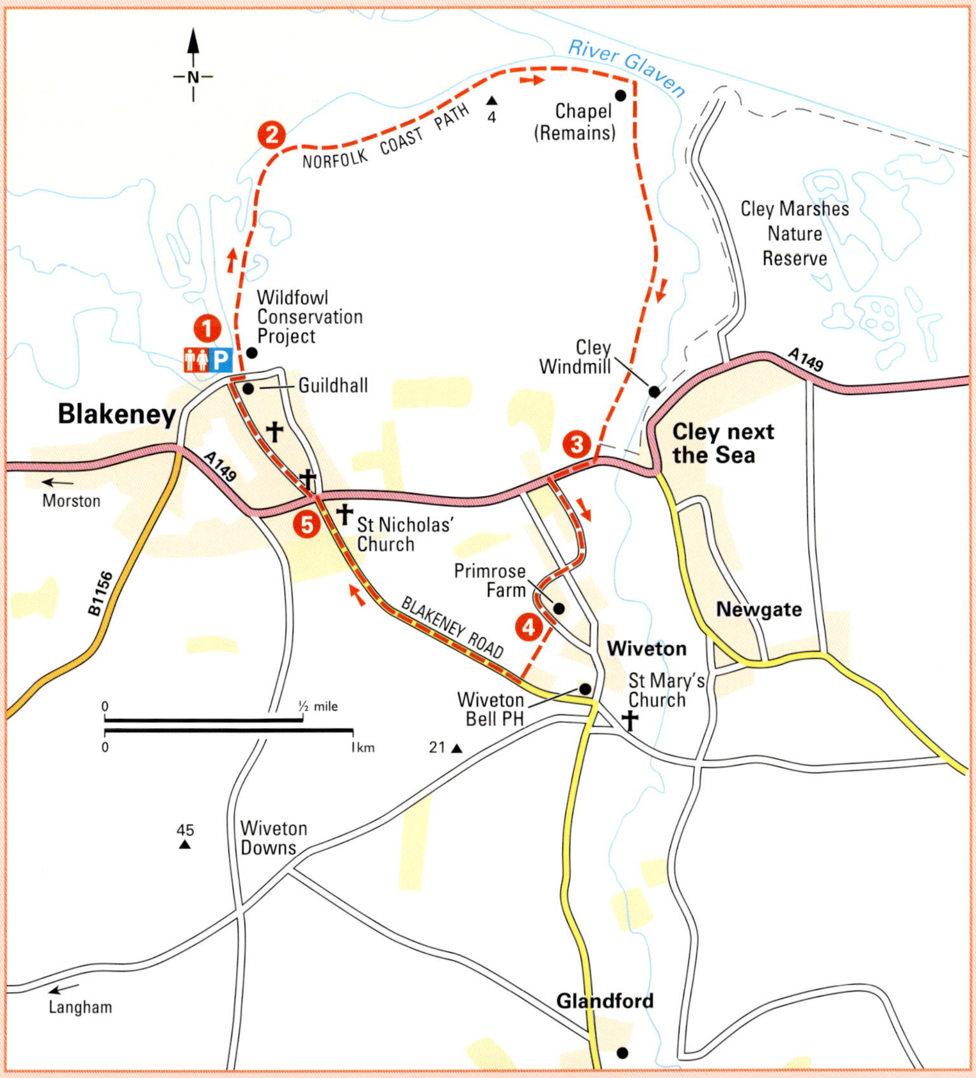

Distance 4.5 miles (7.2km)

Minimum Time 2hrs

Ascent/Gradient 98ft (30m) ▲▲▲

Level of Difficulty ●●●

Paths Footpaths with some paved lanes, can flood in winter

Landscape Salt marshes, scrubby meadows and farmland

Suggested Map OS Explorer 251 Norfolk Coast Central

Start/Finish Grid reference: TG 028442

Dog Friendliness Under control as these are important refuges for birds

Parking Carnser (pay) car park, on seafront opposite Blakeney Guildhall and Manor Hotel

Public Toilets Across road from Carnser car park

1 From the car park head for the wildfowl conservation project, a fenced-off area teeming with ducks, geese and widgeon. A species list has been mounted on one side, so see how many you can spot. Take the path marked Norfolk Coast Path out towards the marshes. This raised bank is part of the sea defences, and is managed by the Environment Agency. Eventually, you have salt marshes on both sides.

2 At the turning, head east. Carmelite friars once lived around here, although there is little to see of their chapel, the remains of which are located just after you turn by the wooden staithe (landing stage) to head south again. This part of the walk is excellent for spotting kittiwakes and terns in late summer. Also, look for Sabine's gull, manx and sooty shearwaters, godwits, turnstones and curlews. The path leads you past Cley Windmill, built in 1810 and which last operated in 1919. It is open to visitors and you can climb to the top to enjoy the view across the marshes. Follow the signs for the Norfolk Coast Path until you reach the A149.

3 Cross the A149 to the pavement opposite, then turn right. Take the first left after crossing the little creek. Eventually you reach the cobblestone houses of Wiveton and a crossroads; go straight ahead.

4 Take the grassy track opposite Primrose Farm to a T-junction. This is Blakeney Road; turn right along it. However, if you want refreshments before the homeward stretch, turn left and walk a short way to the Wiveton Bell. The lane is wide and ahead you will see St Nicholas' Church nestling among trees. This dates from the 13th century, but was extended in the 14th. Its two towers served as navigation beacons for sailors, and the east, narrower one is floodlit at night.

5 At the A149 there are two lanes opposite you. Take the High Street fork on the left to walk through the centre of Blakeney village. Many cottages are owned by the Blakeney Neighbourhood Housing Society, which rents homes to those locals unable to buy their own. Don't miss the 14th-century Guildhall undercroft at the bottom of Mariner's Hill. After exploring the area, continue to the car park.

51 From Brancaster to Branodunum

The air is rich with the scent of the sea on this breathtakingly beautiful walk from Brancaster past the remains of its Roman fort and through a nature reserve

Above: Tidal marshes on the foreshore

Right: Sea and sand dunes at Brancaster

Some time around AD 240–250 the Romans came to Brancaster and built a fort. It was square, with a tower at each corner; between the towers was a curtain wall about 10ft (3m) thick, and there was a gate halfway along each of the four walls. In addition to this, they added a wide ditch, so that any attackers would have to climb down it and up the other side – all the while bombarded with arrows and stones from the defenders above. They reinforced the walls by adding a rampart inside.

Waterside Fortifications

The fort was quite large – about 6.5 acres (2.6ha), and was probably built over a site that had been levelled by previous occupants. Although it lies in a field that is about a mile (1.6km) from the sea today, when the Romans built it, it was right on the estuary. It was a fabulous location, because not only did it provide good access to the sea, but it was near the Peddars Way, an important line of communication in Roman times.

By the fourth century AD, the civilian population that relied on the fort's protection had moved away from Branodunum. The military settlement survived for a while, as the most northerly of the Saxon Shore fort systems designed to protect the Dalmatian cavalry against Anglo-Saxon raids, but eventually it was abandoned. You will not see much of the fort, except for some earthworks covered in vegetation, but walking around the field will give you an idea of its size.

Birds in the Marshes

The fort is now in the care of the National Trust, which owns around 2,000 acres (810ha) of the coast, of which Branodunum is a part, comprising 4 miles (6.4km) of tidal foreshore. The entire region, with its salt marshes, mudflats and sand dunes, is a haven for wildlife and you might expect to see redshank, greenshank, sharp-eyed gannets with their dazzling white plumage, and the delicate common and Sandwich terns. Watching and waiting patiently for a chance to grab a sick, weak or careless bird is the Arctic skua, a fierce scavenger-predator, which is a summer visitor.

When you are out in the marshes take the opportunity to stop, close your eyes and listen – to the hiss of wind in long grass, the muted roar of distant waves and the piping whistles of birds. The countryside is never completely silent and it is always a restful and reviving experience to hear the many sounds of nature.

51 From Brancaster to Branodunum

Look out for fields of poppies – and listen for nightingales

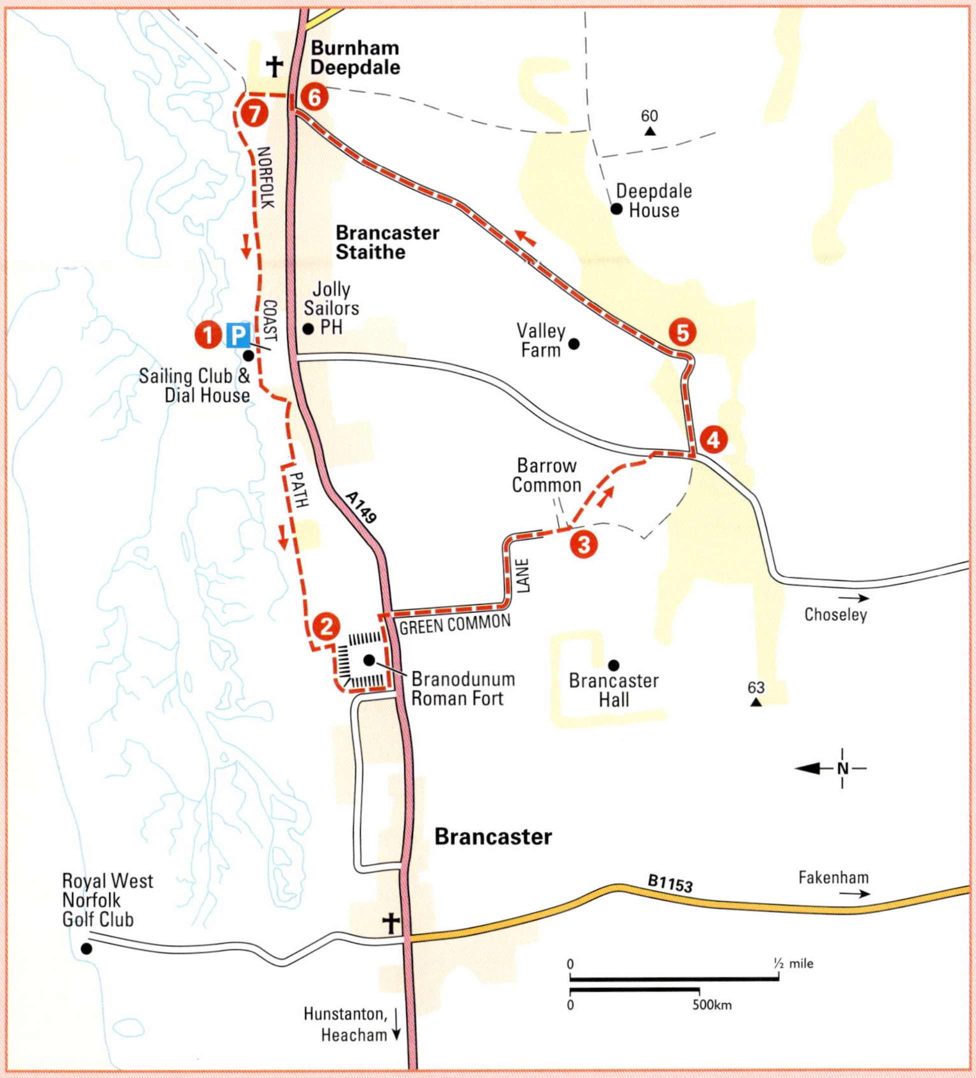

Distance 4.5 miles (7.2km)

Minimum Time 2hrs 15min

Ascent/Gradient 148ft (45m) ▲▲▲

Level of Difficulty ●●●

Paths Winding paths and tracks, with some paved lanes, 3 stiles

Landscape Salt marshes, mudflats, farmland and common

Suggested Map OS Explorer 250 Norfolk Coast West

Start/Finish Grid reference: TF 793443

Dog Friendliness On lead in nature reserves and farmland. Note also dog-free areas on beaches

Parking Near National Trust's Dial House or in lay-by on A149 on the edge of Brancaster Staithe

Public Toilets None en route

1 Walk into the area owned by the Sailing Club and, just before the slipway, you will see the National Trail marker on your left. Go through the kissing gate and stroll along the boardwalk edging the marshes. Continue ahead until you pass a brick and flint house.

2 Turn left and leave the coastal path, going through a kissing gate to enter a large field. This is Rack Hill, the area that houses the Roman fort. Follow the left-hand side of the field until you reach another kissing gate. Cross the lane through another kissing gate. Keep to the right side of the field, following around the top of the field until you reach yet another kissing gate in the corner of the field. Cross the A149 on to Green Common Lane. Walk past the felled tree stumps blocking vehicular access and start to go uphill. The track bends twice, but follow it until it comes to a gate and footpath junction to your left. Go straight along the grassy track between the hedges.

3 Here you enter Barrow Common Nature Reserve. At the seat you have the choice of three paths. Take the middle one. You will eventually exit on to a peaceful, paved lane. Turn right, and follow the lane as it descends a fairly steep hill.

4 Turn left at the junction. Across from here, during the early summer, are fields of beautiful poppies. Continue until you reach a wood, where it is worth pausing in case you can hear the lilting song of nightingales.

5 The road bends sharply left, eventually ending at the A149.

6 Cross the A149 with care and turn right. After a few paces take the first left down The Drove, opposite the garage and post office. At the end of the lane is a sign for the coast path. Follow it down a narrow, tree-lined track until it emerges on to marshes and the main Norfolk Coast Path.

7 Turn left and walk along the path until you see the yacht masts of the Sailing Club. First you reach a small boatyard then follow the trail through wooden huts. The next buildings are home to the Sailing Club itself and the car park.

52 Old Hunstanton's Dunes

A restorative coastal ramble leads along over beach and dunes before heading through a nature reserve grazed by traditional hill sheep

Old Hunstanton is steeped in history and legend. It is said that St Edmund was shipwrecked here in AD 855, and was so grateful for being spared a watery death in the Wash that he built a chapel as an act of thanksgiving. The 13th-century ruins still stand today, looking out across grey, stormy seas from near the old lighthouse. Edmund left Hunstanton soon after and went on to become King of the East Angles. Between 869 and 870 Vikings invaded his kingdom and after a number of battles he was either killed in battle or, according to the traditional account, captured and tortured when he refused to renounce his Christian faith. In this version, he died an unpleasant death, after being shot with countless arrows.

Some years later, Edmund's grave was dug up and his body was found to be uncorrupted. It was declared a miracle and his remains were moved around the country for many years in an attempt to keep them safe from Vikings. They were eventually kept in Bury St Edmunds, although records are vague about what happened to them later. Some say they were taken to France, while others claim he was reinterred at Bury after the Reformation. Regardless of the fate of the relics, Hunstanton is proud of its claim to a piece of this saint's history.

Owners of the Wash

Edmund is not the only remarkable historical figure to be associated with the village. Members of the Le Strange family have been squires and landlords here for more than 800 years. They laid claim to the beach and, according to one charter, all that is in the sea for as far as a horseman can hurl a spear at low tide. The family still holds the title of Lord High Admiral of the Wash. There is a popular local story that tells of a famous German lady swimmer called Mercedes Gleitze performing the impressive feat of swimming the Wash from Lincolnshire to Norfolk in the 1930s and the admiral promptly stepping forward to claim her as his rightful property!

Unlit Lighthouse

The lighthouse that has become a symbol of this attractive town dates from 1830. When the First World War broke out in 1914, the light was extinguished and was never lit again. The lighthouse is now in private hands. Because of its strategic position on the coast, Hunstanton was the site of some very clandestine happenings in that war. Hippesley Hut, a bungalow, was used to house a secret listening post to monitor the activities of German Zeppelins and some of its secrets remain hidden even today.

Before you leave the village, spare a thought for poor William Green, a Light Dragoon officer, who was shot here in 1784 by smugglers while helping the King's customs men. The killers were never brought to justice, although the villagers, as members of a small community, must have known their identities. The association of the village with contraband can be seen in the name Smugglers' Lane, along which you will walk.

Below: The famous Hunstanton lighthouse occupies an imposing clifftop position

52 Old Hunstanton's Dunes

Tramp over sand and beautiful countryside, through an area rich in history

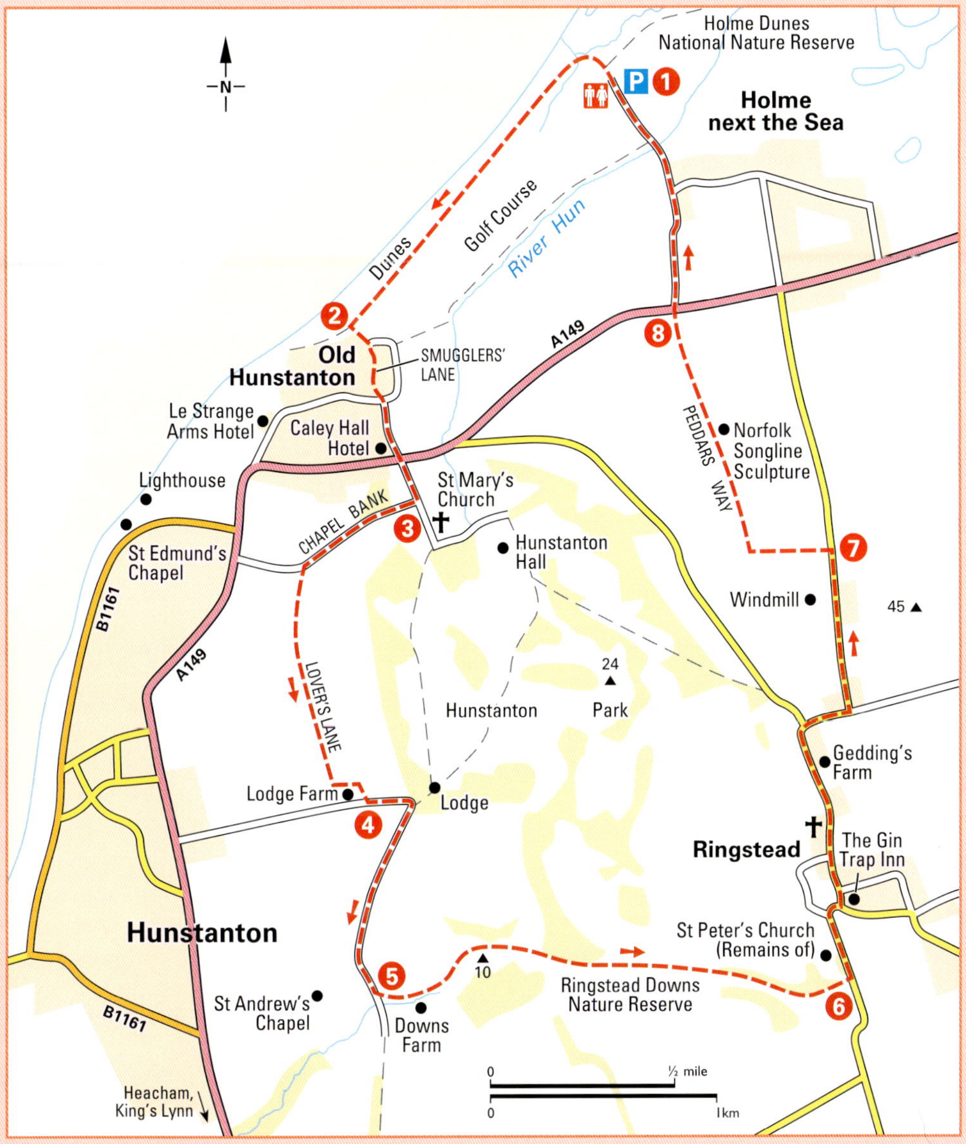

Distance 8 miles (12.9km)

Minimum Time 3hrs 30min

Ascent/Gradient 164ft (50m) ▲▲▲

Level of Difficulty ●●●

Paths Country tracks, lanes, muddy paths and sand dunes, 1 stile

Landscape Sandy beaches, rolling chalk valleys and farmland

Suggested Map OS Explorer 250 Norfolk Coast West

Start/Finish Grid reference: TF 697438

Dog Friendliness On lead in nature reserves and on farmland

Parking Beach car park at Holme next the Sea (pay at kiosk)

Public Toilets By beach car park

1 From the car park at Holme next the Sea, walk towards the sea and turn left to head across the dunes. This is Norfolk at its best, with miles of sandy beaches and dunes, and the lighthouse at Old Hunstanton visible on a cliff. Keep close to the golf course and after about a mile (1.6km) you will arrive at a colourful row of beach huts.

2 When you see a gap in the fence to your left, take the path across the golf course and continue straight ahead into Smugglers' Lane. Emerging at a junction, take the lane opposite, past the post box to reach Caley Hall Hotel. Cross the A149 and aim for the road signed 'To St Mary's Church', where you can see the grave of William Green.

3 Turn right up Chapel Bank, through a tunnel of shade before reaching open farmland. After 700yds (640m), turn left on a grassy track, Lovers Lane, a permissive path. When you reach Lodge Farm, follow the track around farm buildings to a lane.

4 Turn left along the route marked Norfolk County Council Ringstead Rides. When you see the lodge of Hunstanton Park ahead, follow the lane to the right along an avenue of trees.

5 Bear left at Downs Farm and head for the gate to enter Ringstead Downs Nature Reserve. Follow the path right through the reserve until you reach a lane.

6 Turn left into Ringstead, where the tower of St Peter's Church still stands. Stay on this road as it bends right and left through the village, passing The Gin Trap Inn. Continue to follow the road as it climbs gently out of the village, forking right and left along Peddars Way, towards a sail-less windmill.

7 At the last house, look for the waymarked path to the left. This cuts across a field, then turns right into a lovely tunnel of hedges. Note the Norfolk Songline sculpture half-way along the path.

8 Cross the A149 road and walk through Holme village, with its long green, to reach the car park and the start of the walk.

53 It All Comes Out in the Wilds of the Wash

A walk across part of England's largest national nature reserve provides many opportunities for birdwatching – or for admiring offshore RAF bombing practice

Above: The endless views of Lincolnshire make a peaceful setting for walking

It has to be said that the Wash is a peculiar place. On the Norfolk side is Hunstanton, England's only east coast resort where you can watch the sun setting across the water – since it faces west. The rivers Welland, Witham, Nene and Great Ouse all issue out into this vast, shallow lagoon covering 300 square miles (776sq km), which is sometimes covered by water but more often than not by endless tidal mudflats. These have built up over a long period as the four rivers have deposited huge quantities of clay and silt. The burrowing and surface invertebrates here have attracted a healthy bird population. The Wash supports more birds than any other estuary in Britain, plus one of Europe's largest concentrations of common seals.

Much of the walking around the edge of the Wash is along high embankments, which mark more than 300 years of reclaiming farmland from the sea. This route around Gedney Drove End follows the old and the current sea bank, which as you will see has allowed the rich agricultural belt to be extended right up to the sea wall. Dykes and drainage channels, controlled by sluices and pumping stations continue to keep the salt water at bay and maintain this artificially fertile land.

Making a Splash

Military airfields dot the Lincolnshire coast, and planes from nearby RAF Holbeach in particular use a range off the Gedney coast for bombing practice: small but brightly coloured targets are scattered offshore across the salt marsh. Red flags fly all along the shore when bombing is taking place (weekdays between 9am and 5pm), but it is safe and legal to walk along the sea bank and watch the proceedings (as indeed many people do), so long as you obey official signs and don't venture beyond the sea wall or pick up any unusual-looking souvenirs.

53 It All Comes Out in the Wilds of The Wash

Explore sea walls and tidal mudflats on the South Lincolnshire coast

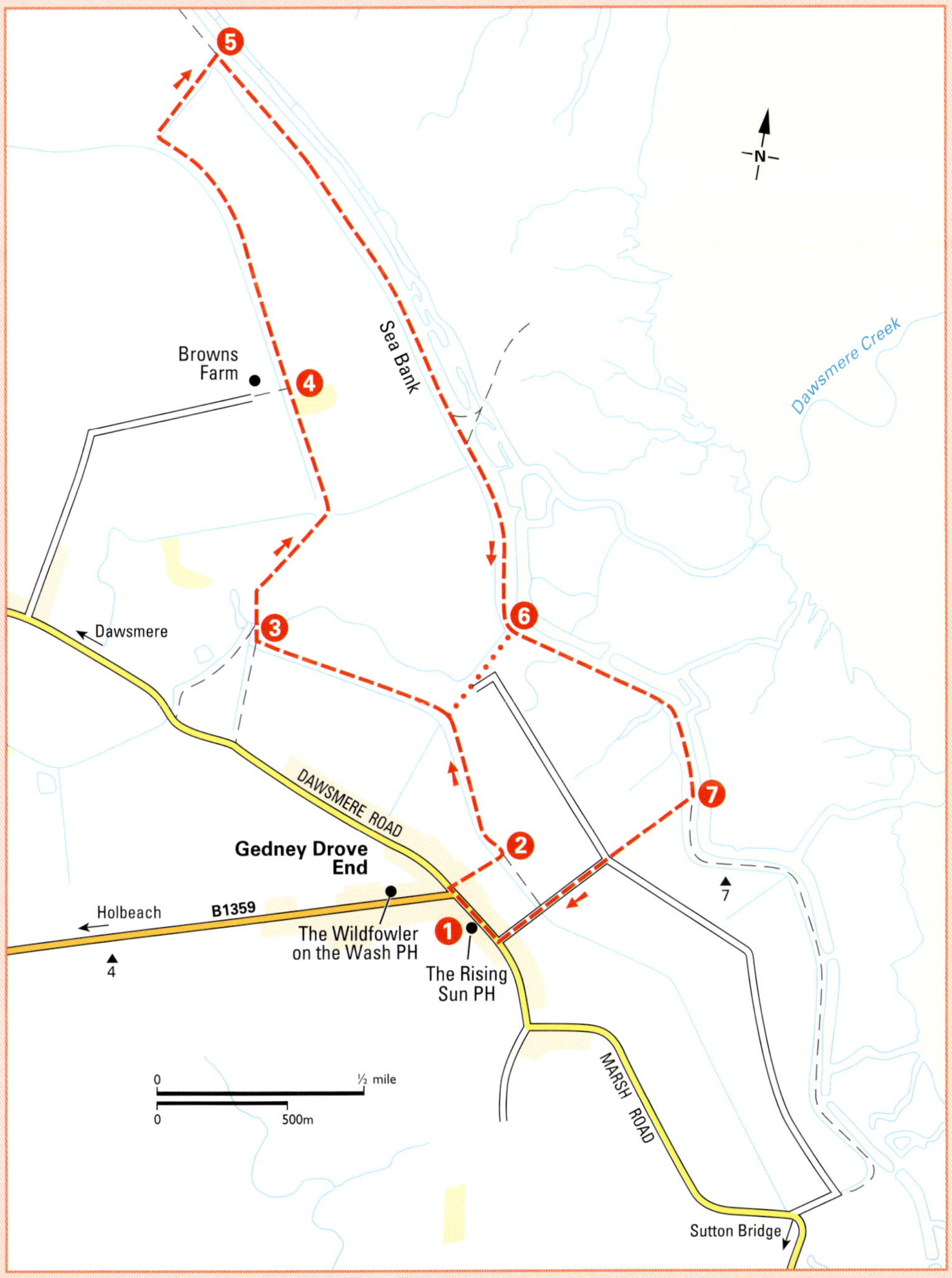

Distance 5.75 miles (9.2km)

Minimum Time 2hrs 30min

Ascent/Gradient Negligible ▲▲▲

Level of Difficulty ●●●

Paths Field, 1 stile

Landscape Open arable fields and bare marsh and mudflats

Suggested Map OS Explorer 249 Spalding & Holbeach

Start/Finish Grid reference: TF 463292

Dog Friendliness Overhead military planes on weekdays can be very loud

Parking Roadside parking in centre of Gedney Drove End (off A17 east of Holbeach)

Public Toilets None en route

1 With your back to The Rising Sun pub, turn left and walk along Dawsmere Road past the junction and take the signposted public footpath on the right, between bungalows. At the far side of the field go across a small footbridge and up some steps in order to turn left into a wide field.

2 For 1 mile (1.6km) walk along the edge of this field, which is in fact the line of the former sea wall, keeping more or less parallel with the present and much higher sea bank over to your right. As a sign indicates, continue straight ahead at the point where the old sea bank veers invitingly away to the right.

3 When the field ends turn right for 50yds (46m) then, faced with a small thicket, drop down to the farm track on your left. Turn right, and follow the main route (ignore the lower track) alongside a narrow shelter-belt of woodland. This wide, gravel track heads out towards the sea bank then bends left and continues past Browns Farm.

4 Stay on the main track for about 0.75 mile (1.2km) beyond the farm, then go right by an old wartime pill box for a short path over to the sea wall.

5 Turn right and follow either the grassy top of the sea bank (a public right of way) or the surfaced lane just below it past a succession of military observation towers. The bombing range is spread out before you, with the low Norfolk coast over to your right and the Lincolnshire seaboard towards Boston and Skegness leftwards.

6 After the third tower ignore the gated road that heads off inland (a short cut back to Gedney), but instead continue along the sea bank past one final watchtower until you reach a stile. Cross the stile and continue ahead for another 400yds (366m).

7 Turn right at a public footpath sign, down some steps, for a direct path along a field-edge to the junction of an open lane. Here continue straight ahead into Gedney, turning right at the end back on to Dawsmere Road.

54 On Saltfleet's Dunes

A fascinating nature ramble along the dunes and beside the salt marshes of Lincolnshire offers the chance to see rare plants, seabirds and seals

Above: Hunting bird – a kestrel hovers above Saltfleet

Below: Part of our walk leads gently along Saltfleet Haven

A cross-section of Lincolnshire from west to east reveals a highly contrasting county – from the agricultural flatlands around Lincoln and Gainsborough to the pleasantly undulating Wolds. However, it's the long North Sea coastline that perhaps holds the most surprises. If you thought there was little more to this coast than funfairs and holiday camps, try this engaging nature walk for size. It's centred on the Saltfleetby–Theddlethorpe Dunes National Nature Reserve (and try saying that with a mouthful of crisps), an extensive strip of unspoilt beach and marshland that is also a valuable natural habitat for wildlife.

Carpets of Orchids

To get a flavour of this peculiar landscape, set aside a few minutes either before or after your walk to explore the short (930yds/850m) Easy Access Trail just to the south of the car park. Information panels explain such fascinating phenomena as 13th-century sand dunes and identify plants such as wild asparagus and bee orchids. Several different habitats make up this nature reserve. The early summer highlight of the bog and freshwater marshes landward of the dunes are carpets of deep pink and purple marsh orchids, and when the temperature rises sufficiently dragonflies and damselflies will take to the wing.

The vast rolling dunes are partly covered by clumps of wiry grass and bushes of spiky sea buckthorn, which in autumn are covered by bright orange berries. Meanwhile plants such as sea lavender and sea purslane thrive on the salty fringes of the beach, while oystercatchers, with their distinctive black and white plumage and long orange beaks, are busy probing the mud for worms or prising open shellfish.

Poor Man's Asparagus

The marshes off Saltfleet are famous, in particular, for vast beds of samphire. Also known as glasswort, this small herbaceous annual with thick green stems was once burnt to provide ash for use in the glass-making industry. It used to be called 'Poor Man's Asparagus', and is still eaten as a starter for a meal. First, you wash and soak it in cold water to remove the saltiness, then boil it for a few minutes in a small amount of water and serve it with lemon juice and a generous knob of butter. Alternatively, a Lincolnshire variation has it pickled and eaten with chine or boiled bacon.

It's also worth pointing out that this part of the coast is sometimes used by the RAF for pilot training, and in particular to practise bombing offshore targets. When this is happening a large red flag will be flying at the end of Sea Lane at Saltfleet, and there will also be red beacons and buoys to cordon off the precise area in which the bombing practice will take place. It doesn't affect the walk at all, and in fact the event often becomes something of an attraction in its own right, but don't expect to see many birds on those days.

54 On Saltfleet's Dunes

Wander the wildlife-rich salt marshes of North Lincolnshire

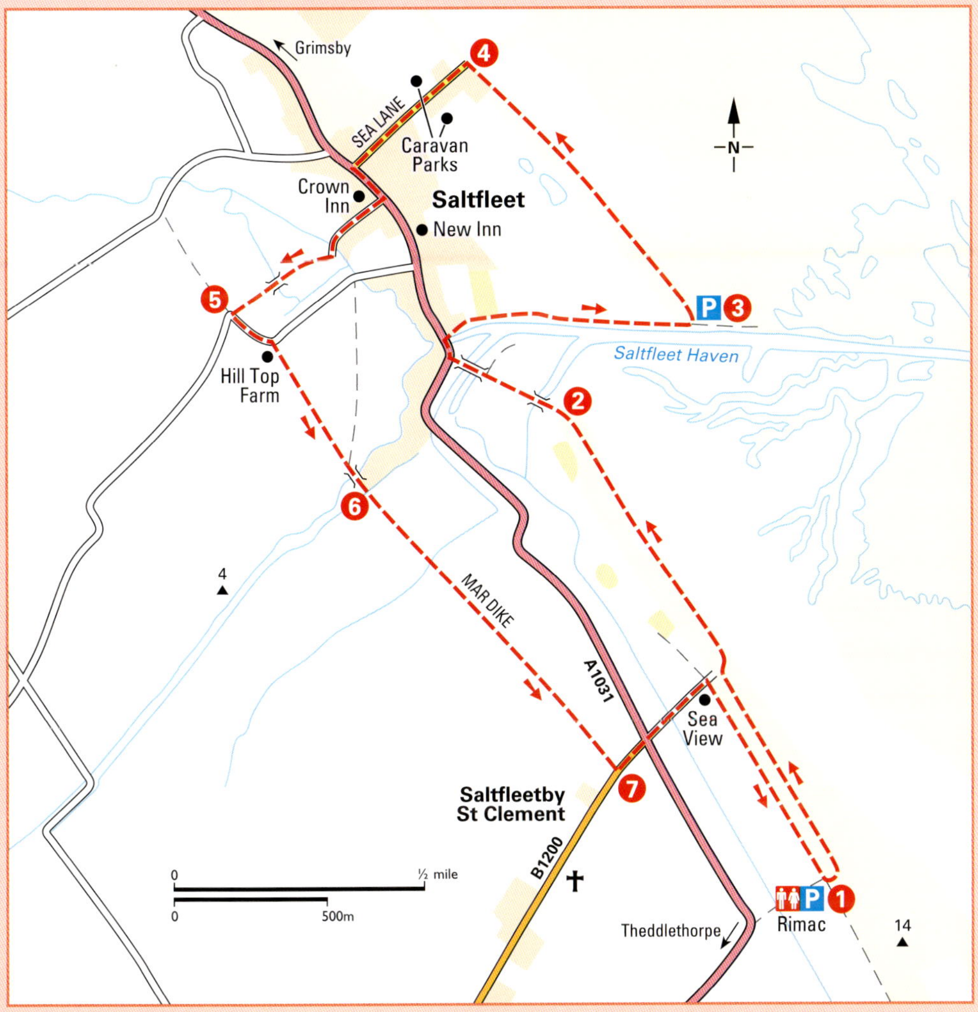

Distance 4.75 miles (7.7km)

Minimum Time 2hrs 30min

Ascent/Gradient Negligible ▲▲▲

Level of Difficulty ●●●

Paths Coastal tracks and field paths, some steps, 3 stiles

Landscape Rolling dunes, open marshland and cultivated fields

Suggested Map OS Explorer 283 Louth & Mablethorpe

Start/Finish Grid reference: TF 467917

Dog Friendliness On lead on dunes and marsh between March and August, because of nesting birds

Parking Nature reserve car park at Rimac, off corner of A1031

Public Toilets At car park and in Saltfleet

1 Walk out of the seaward end of the car park and immediately turn left through a gate, then climb the steps to stroll along the top of the dunes with the sea away to your right. Go past Sea View Farm and a small parking area and continue beyond a white barred gate, forking right to reach the marshes. Go left and follow the clear track along the edge of the marshes.

2 At the far end of the dunes, join a rough lane that crosses two successive bridges, then turn right on to the pavement of the coast road. After 100yds (91m) cross another small bridge and turn right on to a wide, bumpy lane with signs for 'Saltfleet Haven'. Walk along this all the way to the small car park that you'll find among the dunes – and a bit further if you want to view the sandy bay and river mouth (tide permitting) where seabirds and sometimes seals can be spotted.

3 At the back of the small car park, and with your back to the Haven, go up the steps and take one of several feint paths through the dunes in order to pick up the wide track that runs just seawards of the vegetation-topped dunes (not along the actual water's edge). The strip of marshes is spread out to your right.

4 In just under 0.5 mile (800m), turn left up a concrete ramp by some trees and walk down Sea Lane past the caravan parks. Turn left at the end, then right after the Crown Inn into Pump Lane. At the far end follow the unmade track as it curves left between houses and, at the gap in the hedge, take the footbridge on the right for a path across fields.

5 Crossing another footbridge to emerge on the bend of Louth Road, turn left and, just after Hill Top Farm, right, across another footbridge, for a field-edge public footpath.

6 At the junction of tracks at the far side go straight on, over a small stone bridge across a ditch near a house. Go over the first of three wooden footbridges and continue alongside Mar Dike until you switch banks nearing the far end to reach the road.

7 Turn left and walk down to the crossroads. Go straight over and along the drive opposite as far as Sea View Farm. Turn right on the waymarked public footpath through the farmyard and field beyond, and continue on the clear path along the landward edge of the dunes to return to the car park.

Northern England

WALK

Northern England

The coasts of northern England, washed by the North Sea to the east and the Irish Sea to the west, run through spectacular, often rugged landscapes. Rich in sites of historical interest, the region contains several areas of great natural beauty and scientific interest that provide natural habitats for rare animals and plants.

Preceding pages: Clifftop towers – the romantic ruin of Dunstanburgh Castle near Craster, Northumberland

Opposite: Across Northumberland sands at Bamburgh

Below: Beach habitat in the Arnside-Silverdale Area of Outstanding Natural Beauty in Lancashire

At Formby Point in Lancashire, on the northwest coast between Liverpool and Stockport, is one of the country's largest areas of dunes (see Walk 63), where you may find endangered species such as the Natterjack toad and the Northern Dune tiger beetle. Nearby are shady pine woods that are a haven for the rare red squirrel, fields which used to grow asparagus celebrated around the world and once served to well-heeled passengers on luxury liners sailing from Liverpool, and beaches on which erosion has uncovered animal and human footprints from the Neolithic and Bronze Ages up to 7,000 years ago.

Further north, near Arnside on the northeastern part of Morecambe Bay, the 29 square-mile (75 sq-km) Arnside–Silverdale Area of Outstanding Natural Beauty (AONB) contains highly varied landscapes, including heath, salt marsh, wetlands, beaches, ancient woodland and stretches of limestone cliffs; it is home to a great variety of native flowering plants as well as dragonflies and many migrating and wintering birds. Rare and endangered species found in this area include the Lancastrian whitebeam, the Marsh harrier and the High Brown Fritillary butterfly. Designated an AONB in 1972, the area straddles the border between Cumbria and Lancashire and, although relatively small, contains no fewer than 15 Sites of Special Scientific Interest (see Walk 65).

Industrial Heritage

Walk 65 through Arnside-Silverdale leads past the remains of a 200-year-old copper smelting mill, one of several reminders of the area's fascinating industrial past found in the walks of this section. Elsewhere near Knott End-on-Sea in Lancashire,

Walk 64 visits the former brine fields in which 19th-century industrialists extracted salt by pumping out deep bore holes.

Meanwhile on the east coast in Northumberland, Hauxley Nature Reserve and Druridge Bay Country Park (see Walk 58) were created from the craters left behind by open-cast mining for coal, situated just inland from a seven-mile stretch of unspoiled beaches and sand dunes. Both reserves provide great opportunities for birdwatchers, with chances to see resident swans and rare birds such as the Golden Eye Snipe, as well as migrating waders in spring and autumn. The area contains remains of pillboxes, anti-tank blocks and other defences raised in the Second World War, when officials feared that Druridge Bay might be selected by the Germans as an invasion point.

Ancient Remains

At Hauxley there is evidence of a Bronze Age burial, one of several ancient remains around the coasts of Northern England. At Birkrigg Common in Cumbria (see Walk 67) a Bronze Age standing circle known as the Druid's Circle overlooks the waters of Morecambe Bay. The circle consists of two circuits – an inner one, with a diameter of around 28 feet (8.5 metres) containing 12 limestone pillars, and an outer one, diameter about 79 feet (24 metres), containing 20 irregularly placed stones; some of the stones are covered in turf.

Near Muston and Gristhorpe in North Yorkshire, Walk 55 leads through landscape associated with a Bronze Age warrior-chieftain named 'Gristhorpe Man' after his remains were unearthed from a burial mound on the cliffs in 1834 by labourers working for a Gristhorpe landowner. The skeleton of Gristhorpe Man, who was buried in a hollowed tree trunk probably in *c.*1600–1400BC, are stored together with his burial goods including a bronze dagger with a whalebone handle, a wicker basket containing food remnants and a flint knife, in the Rotunda Museum, Scarborough. The skeleton is that of a man 6ft (1.8m) tall – a remarkable height for that era – who died at the relatively advanced age of about 40 and with a full set of well preserved teeth; these facts, together with his burial in a prominent cliff-top position commanding wide views up and down the coast and inland, have persuaded archaeologists and scientists that he was an individual of very high status.

Near the coastal village of Ravenglass in Cumbria, a ramble over Muncaster Fell (Walk 69) leads past the remains of a Roman fort. All that can be seen now is the bathhouse because other remains were destroyed when a railway was laid across the land in 1850; nonetheless, the bathhouse – also known as Walls Castle – is one of the largest Roman remains in England, measuring 40 by 90ft (12 by 27m) and 12ft (3.6m) tall. At Ravenglass,

which they called Glannaventa, the Romans developed a notable port with a garrison of 500 soldiers; they also built mile forts and watchtowers right around the Cumbrian coast in a defence system that linked with Hadrian's Wall.

In addition to the chance to see ancient remains, Walk 69 leads past Muncaster Castle, home to the Pennington family since 1208, and expanded over the years from a pele tower on Roman foundations. In its current form the castle dates mainly from 1862 when it was rebuilt by Victorian architect Anthony Salvin for the 4th Lord Muncaster. It stands in 77 acres (31 hectares) of woodland gardens, renowned for their rhododendrons and a Terrace Walk described by Victorian aesthete and writer John Ruskin as 'the Gateway to Paradise'.

In an area that was certainly no stranger to armed conflict, Muncaster Castle is only one of several fortified ancient homes, and among others visited in this section is the romantic ruin of Dunstanburgh Castle on the beautiful Northumberland coastline. The present castle was begun by Thomas, Earl of Lancaster, in 1313 (see Walk 59). It was a massive and important fortress, improved by John of Gaunt, Duke of Lancaster, but was badly damaged in 1462-64 during the Wars of the Roses and never afterwards repaired.

The fortress fell into its present dilapidated state, which inspired Romantic artist J. M. W. Turner in the 19th century, and also made it an atmospheric setting for Italian film director Franco Zefferelli's 1991 movie version of William Shakespeare's play *Hamlet*, starring Glenn Close and Alan Bates. Walk 59 from the village of Craster provides several stirring views of the Northumberland coast and the castle perched on its craggy clifftop.

Below: In the sand dunes at Formby Point, Lancashire, there is evidence of animal and human activity 4,000 years ago

Opposite left: Robin Hood's Bay, North Yorkshire, looking across to Ravenscar headland

Opposite right: Vast sands at Filey Brigg, North Yorkshire

Best of the Rest

Robin Hood's Bay

On the beautiful North Yorkshire coast south of Whitby, Robin Hood's Bay (see Walk 56) is a picturesque fishing village whose white-walled, pantiled cottages cling to the cliff side amid a cluster of vertiginously steep steps and streets. The village is known for its history of smuggling, particularly in the 18th century, when gin, tea, brandy and rum were shipped into Yorkshire from France and Holland; in 1779 there was even a pitched battle between smugglers and revenue men at the dock. Among many colourful traditions seeking to explain how the village got its name, one tells that the outlaw Robin Hood (whom some claim as a Yorkshireman) outwitted French pirates at sea and redistributed their wealth among the villagers on this stretch of coast.

Marsden Bay

A ramble along the South Tyneside coast near South Shields (see Walk 57) commands a breathtaking vista of cliffs, beaches and rugged, wave-washed stacks that are home to colonies of seabirds. The walk leads past the Marsden Grotto – a public house established at the foot of the Marsden Bay cliffs, and once a favoured haunt of smugglers – to the world's first electric lighthouse, the Souter Lighthouse designed in 1871 by James Douglass; decommissioned in 1988, it is now owned by the National Trust and operated as a tourist attraction. It stands north of a coastal park created from the Whitburn colliery, which was operational in 1873–1968.

Berwick-upon-Tweed

Walk 61 tours the English border town of Berwick and explores the town walls and fortifications rebuilt by Queen Elizabeth I in the 16th century. On the east coast at the mouth of the River Tweed, the town was once part of Scotland and the country's most prosperous port, exporting salmon, wool and grain. The walk leads past the Elizabethan-era military barracks and the town's Anglican parish church, built in 1650–52 during the Commonwealth period and for this reason lacking a spire.

Thurstaston

On the Wirral peninsula in Merseyside, Walk 62 leads through the woods and across the heathland of Thurstaston Common, a local nature reserve and a Site of Special Scientific Interest with three types of heather – common, bell and cross-leaved. Birdwatchers should be on the lookout for the Yellowhammer, Meadow Pipit and Long-Tailed Tit. From Thurstaston Hill, 298ft (91m) in height, there are fine views of the Dee Estuary and the Irish Sea.

Grange-over-Sands and 'Hampsfell'

An attractive coastal town situated between the fells of the Lake District and Morecambe Bay, Grange-over-Sands developed from a fishing village into a grand late Victorian and Edwardian resort after the arrival of the Furness railway in the 19th century. Walk 66 leads from the town onto Hampsfield Fell or 'Hampsfell', and to the 'Hospice of Hamspfell', a limestone tower around 20ft (6m) in height built in 1846 by a local minister as a shelter for travellers. According to the inscription on the hospice, 'The Roof will Show a Prospect Rare' – climb up to use the compass pointer and viewpoint to determine whether you agree.

Bamburgh

On a breathtakingly beautiful stretch of Northumberland coastline, Walk 60 delivers stirring views of seemingly endless beaches, cliffs and dunes, of the romantic Cheviot Hills, of the offshore Farne Islands – once home to saintly Christian hermits, but now a haven for seabirds – and of the majestic Bamburgh Castle. Now a small village, Bamburgh was, from the 7th century, capital of the kingdom of Northumbria, and was a political and religious centre of international importance, with trading links to Byzantium (modern Istanbul, Turkey) and regular religious links to the papacy in Rome. Today in the village you can pay your respects at the museum dedicated to Grace Darling, a lighthouse keeper's daughter who with her father William defied the odds to save seven survivors from the wreck of the SS *Forfarshire* in 1838 and became a nationally known heroine before dying from tuberculosis.

55 Gristhorpe Man and his Landscape

This walk in North Yorkshire's eastern extremity follows part of the long-distance Wolds Way, passing through land in which a prehistoric chieftain lived and died

A little inland from the rocky peninsula of Filey Brigg, which marks the end or start of both the Cleveland Way and the Wolds Way, is peaceful pasture and arable land bounded on the south by the first slopes of the chalk escarpment of the Yorkshire Wolds. It is fertile land, once wet with bog but long-since drained and farmed. The local name for this landscape – 'Carr' – is from an Old Norse word meaning boggy ground.

Some of Britain's earliest inhabitants lived around here – not, like their successors, on the Wolds themselves, but in refuges among the reeds and willows. Most of the details of their civilisation have disappeared, with burial sites vanishing under the plough. Fortunately, however, we know a good deal about one inhabitant, now known as Gristhorpe Man, whose remains, along with the artefacts associated with him, are displayed in the Rotunda Museum in Scarborough.

Gristhorpe Man

In 1834 workmen, employed by local landowner William Beswick in Gristhorpe, dug into an ancient burial mound on the Carrs near the village. Under a covering of oak branches they uncovered a coffin lid carved with a face, which they later trampled on and made unrecognisable! The coffin was made from a single oak log, with lichened bark still adhering to it. Within was the complete skeleton of a man, more than 6ft (1.8m) tall, with his legs drawn up to his chest. His body had been wrapped in animal skin, secured by a bone pin. With him were a bronze dagger head and a bone pommel for it, as well as a flint knife. By his side was a bark dish stitched with strips of animal skin or sinew. It is believed that he is probably more than 4,000 years old, and is likely to have been a Bronze Age chieftain, who died in his forties.

You will get a fine view of Gristhorpe Man's homeland from the first part of the walk as you ascend from Muston on to the slopes of Flotmanby Wold. This is part of the Wolds Way, which runs 79.5 miles (128km) from Hessle Haven on the banks of the Humber to Filey Brigg. In good weather, you can see the Brigg to the north-east and Scarborough further to the north.

The walk descends along an ancient hollow way route, perhaps once part of a prehistoric route from the Wolds on to the watery peat landscape of the Carrs. Today the Carrs are crisscrossed with drainage ditches that include the evocatively named Old Scurf and the channelled River Hertford, cut in 1807. To the north is the Hull-to-Scarborough railway line; there was a station just southwest of Gristhorpe village. The walk continues by the Main Drain and alongside Muston Bottoms to the village, which is worth exploring for its vernacular houses, many built of chalk with typical pantiled roofs.

Below: Coastal pleasures at Filey – with the trees and fields of Gristhorpe Man's domain beyond

55 Gristhorpe Man and his Landscape

Climb for views of Gristhorpe Man's domain – as well as Scarborough and the coast

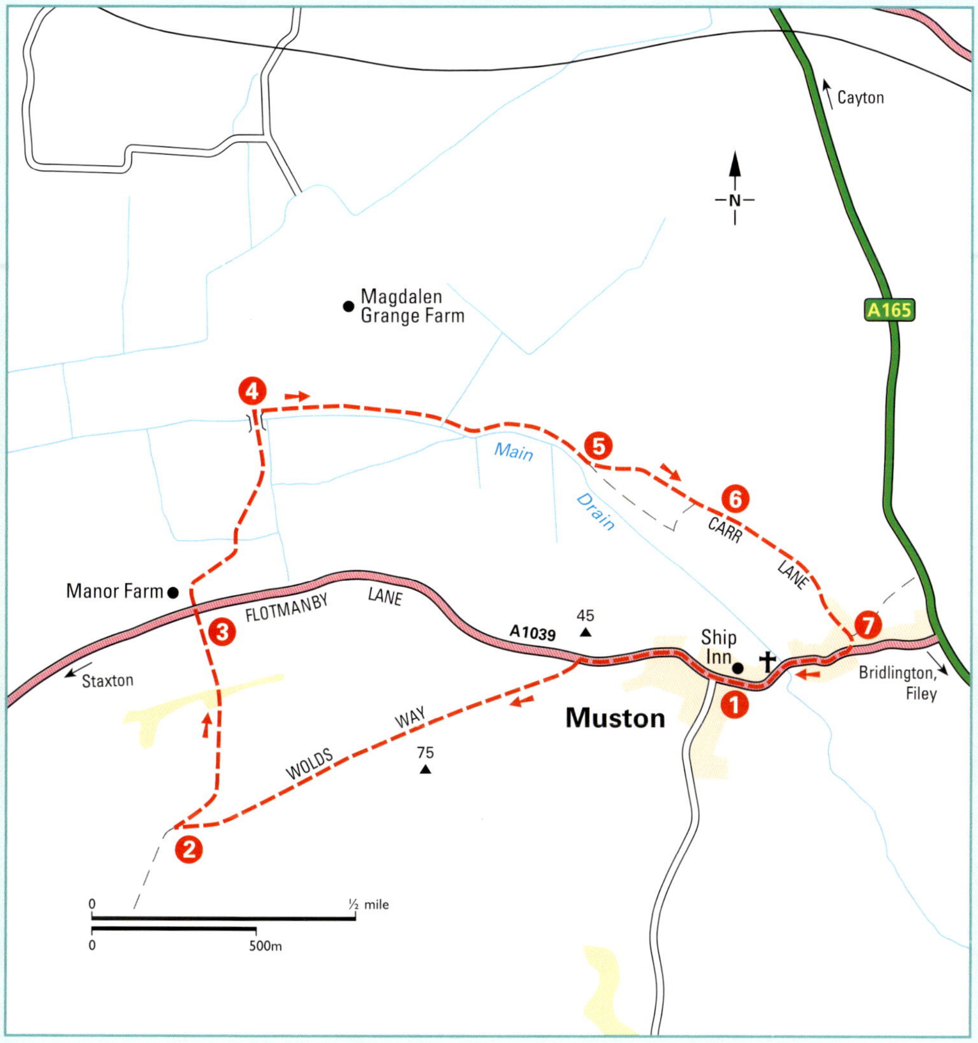

Distance 3.75 miles (6km)

Minimum Time 2hrs

Ascent/Gradient 249ft (75m) ▲▲▲

Level of Difficulty ●●●

Paths Field paths and tracks, muddy after rain, 4 stiles

Landscape Hillside, then flat farmland

Suggested Map OS Explorer 301 Scarborough, Bridlington & Flamborough Head

Start/Finish Grid reference: TA 096796

Dog Friendliness Live stock in fields, so dogs on lead

Parking Street parking in Muston, near the Ship Inn

Public Toilets None en route

1 From the Ship Inn, walk in the direction of Folkton. After the houses end, and just before the stone holding the Muston village sign on the right, take a waymarked stile in the hedge on your left, signed 'Wolds Way'. Go forward with the hedge on your right. The path becomes a track. Follow the 'Wolds Way' signs uphill over two waymarked stiles, passing two disused stiles on the ascent. At the top right-hand corner of the next field go over a stile and continue ahead to the next signpost.

2 Go over the embankment then turn right down the track, following the bridleway sign. Continue downhill, in this hollow way. When it comes into a field, walk straight across to reach a main road, Flotmanby Lane.

3 Cross the road and walk through the farm buildings of Manor Farm, bearing right along the track by a barn. The track eventually bears left and crosses a stream, then reaches a drainage channel that is crossed by a concrete bridge with metal rails.

4 Cross the bridge and turn right at the end, along the side of the channel. Follow the track to the next bridge. Do not cross, but continue straight ahead, still following the channel. Go through a waymarked gate and continue ahead; the drainage channel eventually swings right, away from the path. Continue through two more waymarked gates.

5 Before you reach another waymarked gate, turn left. Walk up the field side with the hedge to your right. Follow the hedge as it bends round to the right. The path reaches a waymarked gate. Go through the gate into a track called Carr Lane.

6 Follow Carr Lane between the hedges and past farm buildings. Eventually the lane becomes metalled and passes a row of houses to reach a T-junction before a green.

7 Turn right, then right again at the main road. Follow the main street of Muston as it winds through the village, past All Saints' Church, to the Ship Inn.

57 Smugglers and the Famous Souter Lighthouse

A walk full of historical interest leads along the Durham coast near South Shields to a smugglers' den-turned-pub and the world's first electric lighthouse

The coast of Durham south of the Tyne was long renowned for its smugglers. The natural caves at the base of the cliffs of Marsden Bay provided hiding places for illicit goods. Most famous of the smugglers was Jack the Blaster, who in 1792 used explosives to increase the size of one of the caves, built steps down from the cliff top, then used the space to sell refreshments to other smugglers. In the 19th century an underground ballroom was created here, and in the 1930s a lift was installed. It is now a pub and eating place called the Marsden Grotto.

The Sneak's Punishment

Another local 18th-century smuggler turned informer to the customs men. His fellows discovered his treachery and the smugglers' ship was prevented from landing its cargo. As punishment the man was hanged in a basket in a shaft, now called Smugglers' Hole, near the Grotto, where he starved to death. On stormy nights, according to local tradition, his shrieks can still be heard in the howling of the wind.

On the walk you will pass two windmills. The first, in Marsden, is a squat building that retains its sails. The other, higher on Cleadon Hills, was built in the 1820s, and survived until the end of the 19th century, when it was damaged in a storm. In the Second World War it housed Royal Observer Corps members who scanned the sea for enemy aircraft.

Looking south from the tower you see the Penshaw Monument, a half-sized replica of the Temple of Theseus in Athens built to commemorate the 1st Earl of Durham, 'Radical Jack' Lambton, who was first Governor of Canada in 1838–39. As you cross the golf course beyond the windmill there are views north to Tynemouth, with its castle and priory on the headland.

First Electric Lighthouse

The red-and-white striped Souter Lighthouse was opened in 1871 to protect ships from the notorious rocks called Whitburn Steel, just off the coast. It was the first light in the world to be electrically powered, by electric alternators. Originally it was nearly 0.25 mile (400m) from the sea, but erosion has brought the cliff edge much nearer.

Now decommissioned and in the care of the National Trust, the lighthouse and its surrounding buildings reward exploration. You can visit the former lighthouse keeper's living quarters. The grassy area north of the lighthouse, The Lees, was farmed until the 1930s, and then given to the local council as a park. The industrial buildings by the road are the remains of the lime kilns used by the local limestone quarries. South of the lighthouse, where Whitburn Coastal Park now lies, was from 1873 to 1968 the site of Whitburn Colliery.

Above: At Souter lighthouse, now a National Trust attraction, you can climb the 76 steps to the top for spectacular views

Below: The Old Mill on Cleadon Hills was used for as a target by First World War gunners

Below left: This sea stack in Marsden Bay is named 'Lot's Wife' after the woman turned to a salt pillar in the Book of Genesis

57 Smugglers and the Famous Souter Lighthouse

Take in local sights and beautiful views of North Sea cliffs and stacks

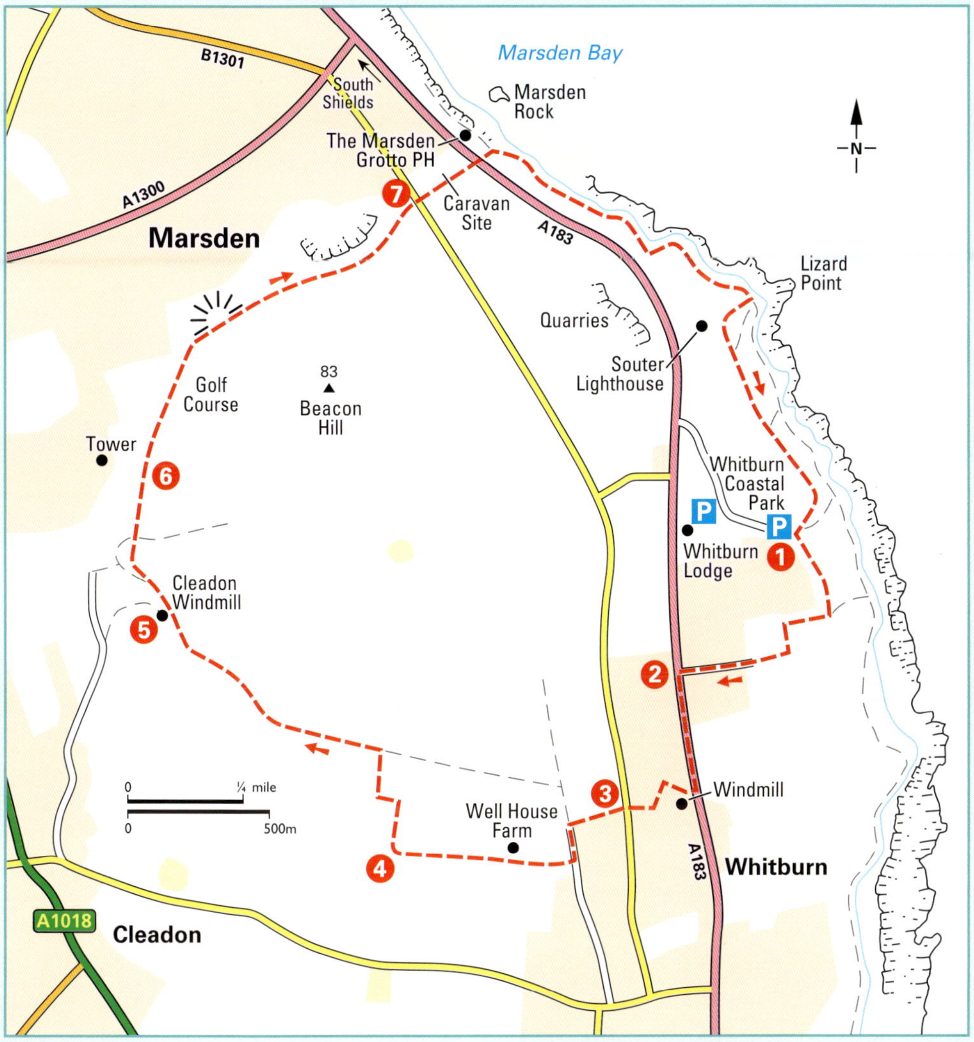

Distance 5.5 miles (8.8km)

Minimum Time 2hrs

Ascent/Gradient 246ft (75m) ▲▲▲

Level of Difficulty ●●●

Paths Roads, tracks, field and coastal paths

Landscape Views to sea, with offshore rocks, rolling countryside

Suggested Map OS Explorer 316 Newcastle upon Tyne

Start/Finish Grid reference: NZ 412635

Dog Friendliness On leads on inland section of walk

Parking Whitburn Coastal Park car park, signed off A183 – turn right after entrance and drive to southern end of road. If this National Trust car park is closed, use the municipal car park next to the Whitburn Lodge pub

Public Toilets None en route

1 Leave the car park at its southern end, following the gravel track toward the houses. The path winds and goes past a sign for Whitburn Point Nature Reserve. Follow the track ahead to go through a gap in a wall and turn right. The path bends right, left and right again to join a road into houses. Go straight ahead to join the main road.

2 Cross the road and then turn left. Walk down the road until you reach the windmill. Turn right to enter the grounds of the windmill. Go up the slope on the path, then between houses. Bear left, then turn right to reach a T-junction.

3 Go straight ahead on a path that goes to the right of house No. 99. When you reach another road, turn left. Just after the first bungalow on the right, turn right along a signed track. Follow the track towards the farm. Go through the farmyard over two stiles and follow the lane beyond, with a hedge to your right. Where it ends, turn right over a stile.

4 Follow the path along the field-edge. Go over another stile, gradually ascending. The path bends left then goes to the right, still following the field edge. Go over another two stiles. The path will bring you to the foot of the tower of Cleadon Windmill.

5 Go to the right of the windmill, following the wall on your right. Go right through a kissing gate, then bear slightly right with a brick tower to your left. Go parallel with the wall on your right. Cross a track and go through a wire mesh fence at right angles to the wall. Follow the path through scrubland to emerge by a yellow post by the golf course.

6 Cross the course, following the yellow posts and looking out for golfers. Go over a stone stile and turn right along a signed footpath, following the wall on your right. The path descends beside houses to a road.

7 Cross and take the footpath almost opposite, to the right of a caravan site, heading towards the sea. Carefully cross the busy A183, then turn right, following the sea edge. Marsden Rock is near by, and the Marsden Grotto to your left as you cross the road. Follow the coast as it bends left to Lizard Point. After a visit to Souter Lighthouse, continue ahead on a path slightly inland from the coast, which returns you to the car park.

58 Around Druridge Bay

A delight for birdwatchers, this walk explores the sands of Druridge Bay and a nature reserve created from craters left by opencast mining operations

Above: A grey heron (*Ardea cinerea*) snacks on a freshly caught eel

Main image: Big skies, empty beach at Druridge Bay

The story of Druridge Bay's pools begins 300 million years ago, when the area basked in a warm climate and was cloaked in a dense, forest swamp. The gradual accumulation of decaying vegetation eventually gave rise to extensive coal deposits, which today extend far out to sea. Although coal was dug from shallow drifts or bell pits from the medieval period onwards, mining only began here in earnest during the Industrial Revolution. Pits were sunk ever deeper, and mining developed as a major industry along the northeast coast, with villages such as nearby Broomhill springing up to house miners and their families.

As the 20th century progressed, many pits became worked out or uneconomic, yet with the onset of the Second World War the need for coal had never been greater. A new approach was tried, with the country's first opencast operation beginning on Town Moor near Newcastle. This proved cheaper and simpler than deep mining, and the scale increased as the equipment needed to excavate and move immense quantities of rock was improved. Work began on the Radcliffe site in September 1971, and a staggering 100 million tons of overlying rock was removed to extract some 2.5 million tons of coal. Within seven years, all the coal was out, leaving behind a crater 170ft (52m) deep. The Northumberland Wildlife Trust bought part of the site in 1983 and has turned the wasteland into the nature-rich lakes and islands we see today.

Nature Reserves

Hauxley Pool is typical of the several flooded workings along the coast. As the fertility of the once-barren land has been improved, many species have become established on the banks and, in spring and summer, the place is alive with colour from bloody cranesbill, yellow wort, kidney vetch and a host of other flowers. Look carefully and you'll spot the delicate pink petals of ragged robin, a rare sight in today's countryside.

The attraction for many visitors, however, is the variety and number of birds that visit these coastal lakes, providing an ever-changing spectacle that is captivating at any time of year. Resident populations are joined by birds migrating between the summer feeding and breeding grounds in the far north and the warmer climes of Africa, where many spend the winter. Dunlin, whimbrel and sanderling are amongst the many species passing through, whilst redshank, plover and bar-tailed godwit are some that winter here. You will also see whooper and Bewick's swans as well as favourites such as tits, finches, blackbirds and robins.

58 Around Druridge Bay

Tour a nature reserve, country park and beach

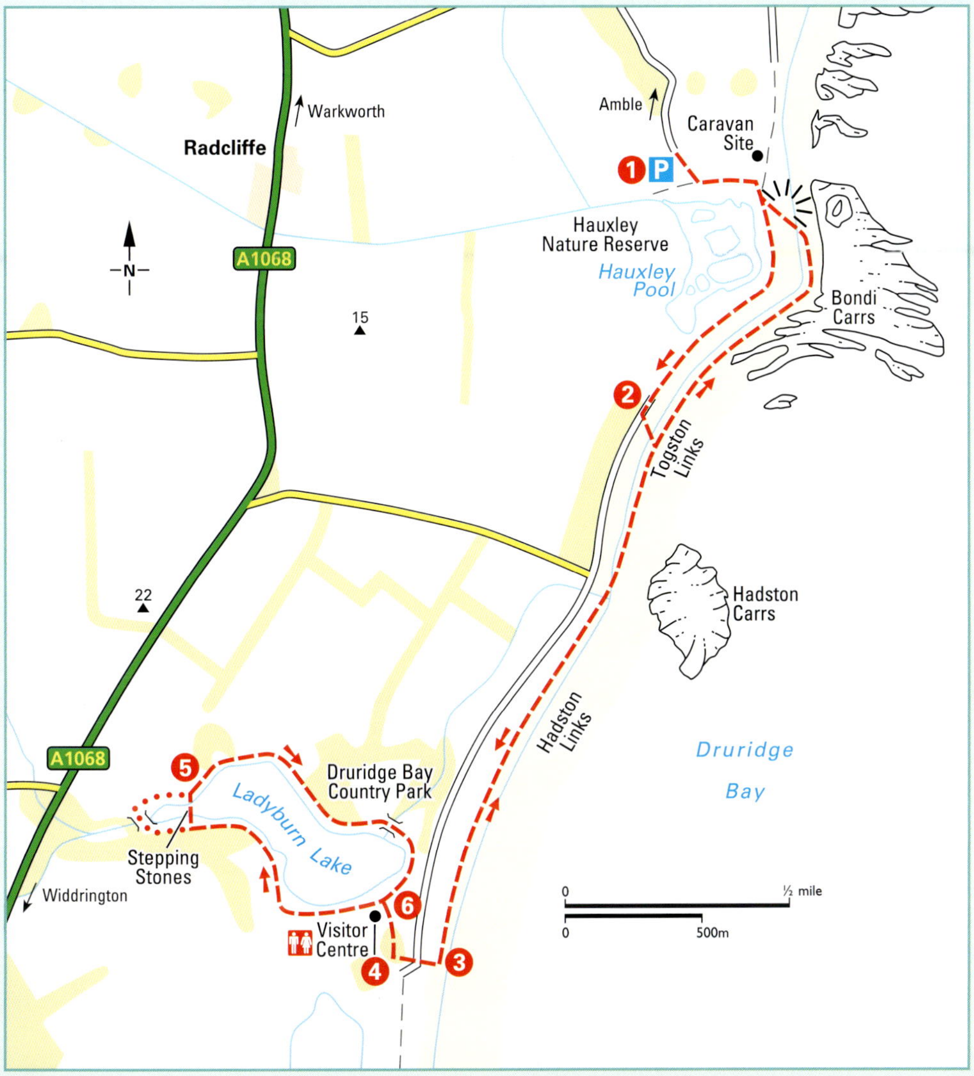

Distance 5.5 miles (8.8km)

Minimum Time 1hr 45min

Ascent/Gradient Negligible ▲▲▲

Level of Difficulty ●●●

Paths Paths and tracks, with good walk on beach, no stiles

Landscape Dunes, seashore and lakeside

Suggested Map OS Explorers 325 Morpeth & Blyth; 332 Alnwick & Amble

Start/Finish Grid reference: NU 282024 (on Explorer 332)

Dog Friendliness On lead within nature reserve

Parking Car park at Hauxley Nature Reserve

Public Toilets At Hauxley Nature Reserve and Druridge Bay Country Park visitor centre

Note Check tides before setting out; complete coastal section not always passable at high water

1 A waymarked footpath beside the car park entrance winds between the nature reserve and a caravan site towards the coast. Through a gate at the bottom, turn right on a track. This shortly passes two gates that give access to bird hides overlooking the lake.

2 Leaving the reserve, continue along a tarmac track to an informal parking area on the left, where there is access to the beach. Now, follow the shore past Togston Links, across a stream and on below Hadston Links.

3 After 1.25 miles (2km), wooden steps lead off the sands on to the dunes. Cross a tarmac track and a marshy area into pinewood. Beyond the trees, emerge by a car park and walk across to the Druridge Bay Country Park visitor centre, where there is a café and toilets.

4 A footway to the left winds around Ladyburn Lake, soon passing an area for launching boats. Keep to the lower path, which soon leads to stepping-stones across the upper neck of the lake. If you would rather not cross here, continue around the upper edge of a wooded nature sanctuary above the water to a footbridge higher up. Over the bridge, turn immediately right, through a gate into a nature sanctuary. Follow the river bank back though another gate to reach the far side of the stepping-stones.

5 This side of the lake has a more 'natural' feel, the path winding through trees to emerge beside a lushly vegetated shoreline where swans like to feed. After crossing a bridge over the lake's outflow, carry on back to the visitor centre.

6 Retrace your steps to the beach and turn back towards Hauxley, but when you reach the point at which you originally dropped on to the sands, remain on the shore towards Bondi Carrs. Seaweed can make the rocks slippery, so be careful clambering over them as you round the point, where Coquet Island then comes into view ahead. Not far beyond there, after passing a look-out post and approaching large rocks placed as a storm defence, leave across the dunes, retracing your outward path the short distance back to the car park and the start of the walk.

59 Craster and a Ruined Castle

This coastal excursion leads from a Northumberland fishing village famous for its kippers to dramatic medieval ruins that inspired Romantic artist J. M. W. Turner

Main image: The wide sands of Embleton Bay with Dunstanburgh Castle on the headland beyond

Below: The remains of Lilburn Tower at the castle

Standing in dramatic isolation on a craggy outcrop of whinstone cliff, and overlooking the vast emptiness of the North Sea, is one of England's most spectacular medieval ruins, Dunstanburgh Castle. Its lonely silhouette has inspired several artists, including the great landscape painter J. M. W. Turner, and the castle's atmospheric shell featured as a set in the 1991 film version of *Hamlet* starring Mel Gibson and Glenn Close.

Lancaster's Stronghold

Building began around 1313 by Thomas, Earl of Lancaster, the richest and most powerful baron of his day and a fierce opponent of his cousin, King Edward II. Edward upset many at the royal court through his devotion to Piers Gaveston, son of a Gascon nobleman. After Edward created Gaveston Earl of Cornwall, Lancaster mustered an opposition that contrived the execution of the king's favourite for treason. However, Lancaster's popularity amongst the other barons waned and he met his own sticky end after leaving the security of his Dunstanburgh stronghold to venture south in an ill-conceived alliance with the Scots. Meeting the king's forces at Boroughbridge, his army was routed and Lancaster captured. Rank brought him no protection from the regal wrath and, six days later, the king avenged the death of Gaveston by executing Lancaster, also on charges of treason.

The outer curtain walls of the castle cover more than 9 acres (3.6ha), exploiting the natural defences of a high, sheer sea cliff to the north and a craggy coast to the east. The steep western flank of the outcrop presented its own difficulties for would-be assailants. Part of the original construction, the outer wall is 10ft (3m) thick in places and was entered by a massive three-storey gatehouse protected by two towers rising high above.

Undone by Warwick

Additions include the Lilburn Tower on the western wall, serving as a look-out and defence against land attack from the north, whilst the south and east were protected by the Constable's and Egyncleugh towers. The mighty fortress must have appeared an impregnable defence but it was not designed to withstand cannon. The castle was besieged during the 1460s in the Wars of the Roses as the Yorkists moved to gain control in Northumberland, and it suffered a pounding at the hands of Richard Neville, Earl of Warwick. It was never re-fortified and quietly crumbled to become a splendid ruin.

59 Craster and a Ruined Castle

Tramp past a romantic ruin and enjoy stirring views

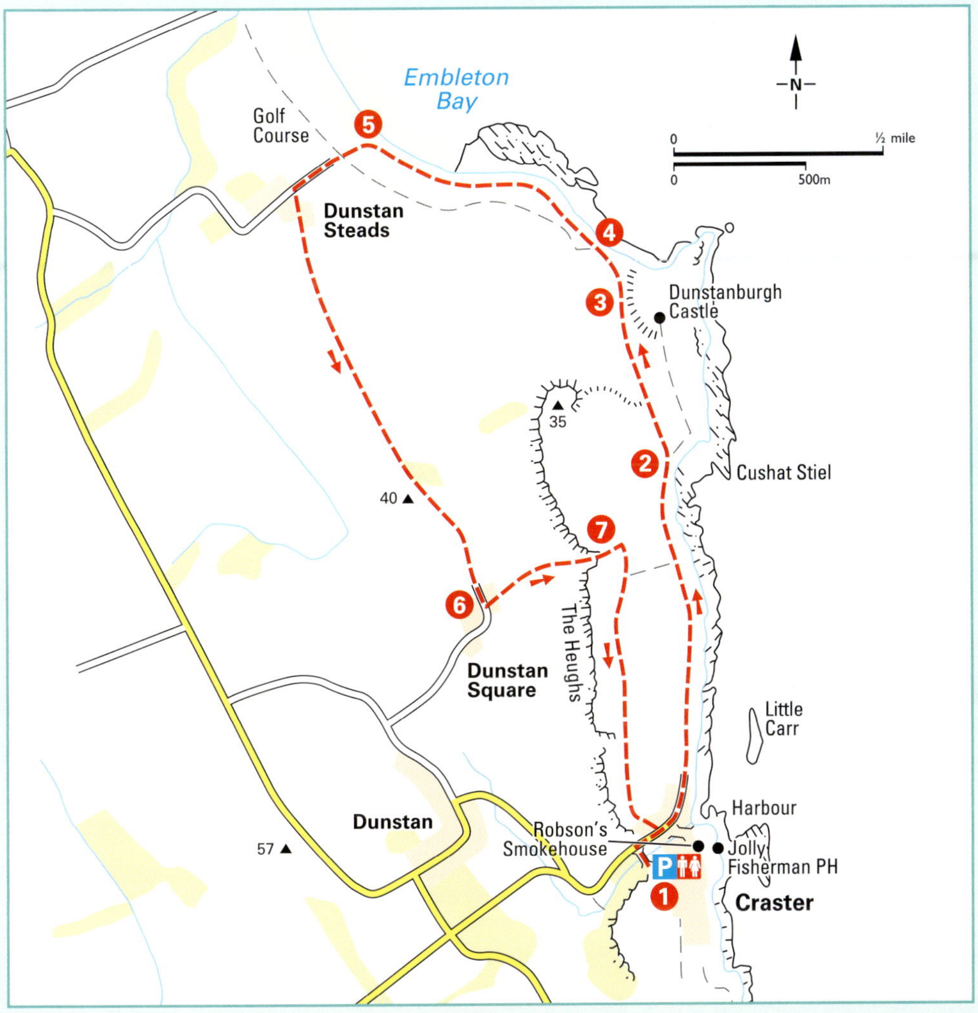

Distance 5 miles (8km)

Minimum Time 1hr 45min

Ascent/Gradient 275ft (84m) ▲▲▲

Level of Difficulty ●●●

Paths Generally good tracks, some field paths tussocky, 1 stile

Landscape Coastal pasture and dunes

Suggested Map OS Explorer 332 Alnwick & Amble

Start/Finish Grid reference: NU 256198

Dog Friendliness On lead through village and by coast; sheep grazing

Parking Pay-and-display behind Craster tourist information centre

Public Toilets Beside information centre

1 From the car park, turn right towards the village. Immediately before the harbour, go left into Dunstanburgh Road, signed 'Castle', and carry on through a gate at the end above a rocky shore, heading towards the castle.

2 After two more gates, if you want to visit the castle keep to the main track, which winds around to its entrance. Otherwise, bear left on a less-distinct path through a shallow gorge on the landward side. Continuing below the castle, pass the ruins of the Lilburn Tower; perched dramatically on top of a rocky spur outcrop, these are an impressive feature.

3 Beyond, as you pass above a bouldery beach, glance back to the cliffs protecting Dunstanburgh Castle's northern aspect, which, in the early summer, echo to the screams of innumerable seabirds, squabbling for nesting sites on the narrow ledges.

4 Through a kissing gate at the edge of a golf course, bear right to remain above the shore, where dramatic folding of the rocks is plainly evident. Ahead stretches the sandy expanse of Embleton Bay and, if the tide permits, you can continue along the beach.

5 Shortly, look for a prominent break in the dunes, through which a path leads across the golf course to meet a lane. Follow it up to Dunstan Steads, turning left immediately before on to a drive, signed 'Craster'. Where this bends behind the buildings, bear left across an open area to a gate and continue over the open fields on a farm track.

6 After 1 mile (1.6km), at Dunstan Square, pass through two successive gates by a barn, then turn left through a third gate, signed 'Craster'. Walk down the field edge, through another gate at the bottom, then on along a track rising through a break in the cliffs ahead, The Heughs. Keep going across the top to the field corner and through a gate on the right.

7 Walk away, initially beside the left-hand boundary, but after 150yds (137m), by a gate, bear right to follow the line of the ridge higher up. Eventually meeting the corner of a wall, continue ahead beside it. Shortly after crossing a track, go on over a stile, beyond which the path becomes more enclosed. Approaching the village, the path turns abruptly left behind a house and emerges on to a street. Follow it down to the main lane and turn right, back to the car park.

60 Bamburgh's Coast and Castle

A delightful walk leads across a fine beach and dunes, and through rolling countryside, offering superb views to Bamburgh Castle and the Farne Islands

Main image: A glorious vista from Budle Point

Inset: A formidable aspect – Bamburgh Castle

For as long as people have sailed this coast, the Farne Islands have been a hazard, claiming countless lives on their treacherous rocks. The most easterly outcrop of Northumberland's whinstone intrusion, they form two main groups and comprise around 30 tilted, low-lying islands, some barely breaking the waves. Their harsh environment and isolated position attracted the early Christian saints, who sought seclusion for a life of prayer and meditation. On Inner Farne, the largest of the group, is a restored 14th-century chapel dedicated to St Cuthbert, who spent the last years of his life there.

The first attempt to mark the Farne Islands for shipping was around 1673, when a signal fire was lit on a 16th-century tower, built by the Bishop of Durham, on Inner Farne. Later, other beacon towers were built, first on Staple Island, then, in 1783, on Brownsman. The first modern lighthouse was erected on Inner Farne in 1809 and was quickly followed by another on Brownsman. However, the latter actually proved a danger and was replaced in 1826 with one on Longstone. Sadly, even these efficient lights were unable to prevent every disaster, and ships continued to founder on the dangerous reefs. The event that caught the imagination of the country was the wreck of the SS *Forfarshire* in 1838, because of the heroism of the Longstone keeper and his daughter in rescuing the survivors. The Darlings had been keepers of the Farne lights since 1795, when Robert was appointed to the Brownsman beacon. He later took over the new lighthouse and was followed by his son William in 1815, who then moved to the new light on Longstone when it opened.

Heroic Rescue

A storm was raging before dawn on 7 September 1838 when SS *Forfarshire* struck Big Harcar, just southwest of Longstone. William's daughter, Grace, was keeping watch with her father and spotted the wreck. At first neither could see any survivors, but at first light they sighted men clinging to the wave-washed rock and launched their tiny boat to attempt a rescue. They found nine survivors, including a woman, but were only able to bring five back on the first trip. William returned with two of them for those remaining, whilst his daughter helped the others recover from their exposure.

Grace became a national heroine, but remained with her parents at Bamburgh. Sadly, she died of tuberculosis at the age of 26. A museum in the village tells the story; in the churchyard opposite, there is a replica of the memorial effigy that was placed near her grave, the original having been removed inside the church for protection.

60 Bamburgh's Coast and Castle

Pay your respects to Grace Darling, then explore the coast she loved

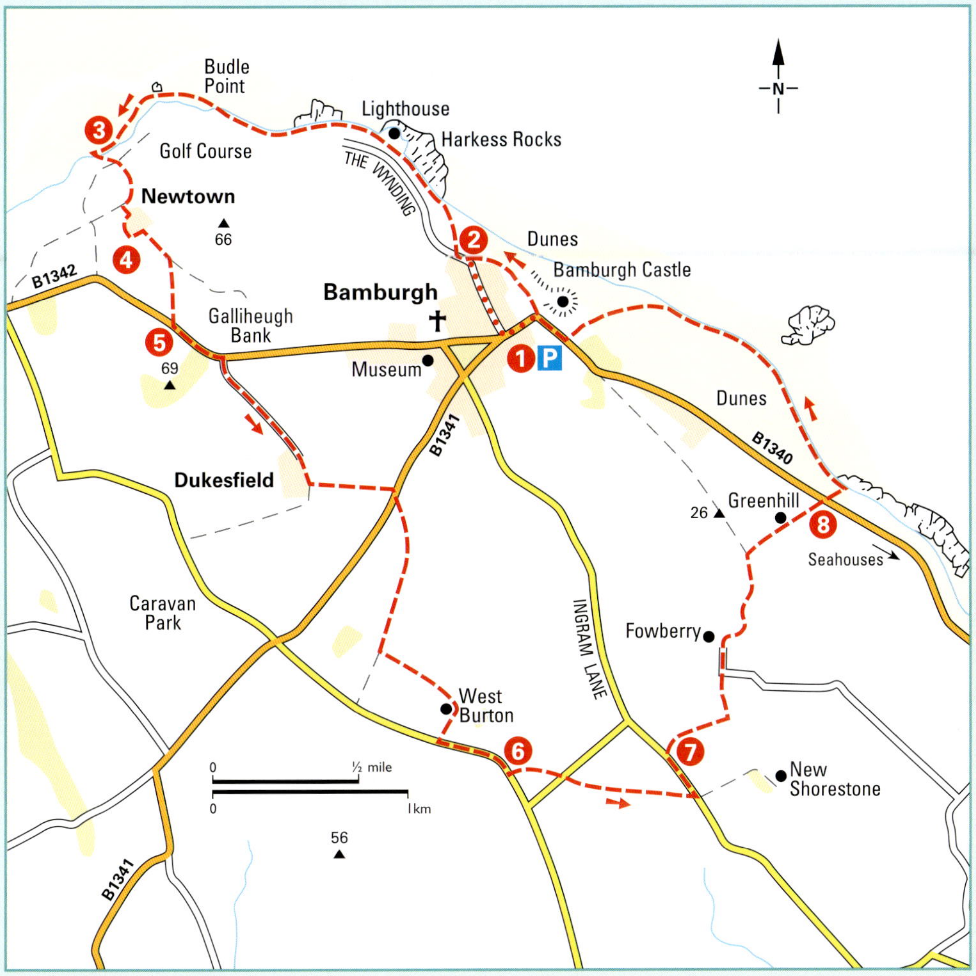

Distance 8.5 miles (13.7km)

Minimum Time 3hrs 15min

Ascent/Gradient 450ft (137m) ▲▲▲

Level of Difficulty ●●●

Paths Field paths, dunes and beach, 11 stiles

Landscape Coastal pasture and dunes

Suggested Map OS Explorer 340 Holy Island & Bamburgh

Start/Finish Grid reference: NU 183348

Dog Friendliness Can be off leads on dunes and beach

Parking Pay-and-display parking by Bamburgh Castle

Public Toilets Bamburgh

1 Walk towards Bamburgh village, where you'll find the museum and church. Our route, however, continues along the beach, reached either across the green below the castle or by following the Wynding, just beyond, then crossing the dunes behind.

2 To the left, the sand gives way to Harkess Rocks. Carefully pick your way round to the lighthouse at Blackrocks Point, which is more easily negotiated to the landward side. Continue below the dunes, soon regaining a sandy beach to pass around Budle Point.

3 Shortly before a derelict pier, climb the dunes towards a World War II gun emplacement, behind which a waymarked path rises on to a golf course. Continue past markers to a gate and along a track above a caravan park. At a bend, go through a gate on the left with a 'Coast Path' marker and on along the field edge to reach the cottages at Newtown.

4 Beyond, follow a field boundary on the left to regain the golf course through a kissing gate at the top field corner. Bear right to pass left of a look-out and continue on a grass track to the main road.

5 Turn left and walk down Galliheugh Bank to a bend and turn off to Dukesfield. Approaching the lane's end, go left over a stile and walk past a house, crossing two stiles in the field's far corner. Then continue by a hedge to a road. Cross to follow a green lane opposite and eventually, just after a cottage, reach a stile on the left. Make for West Burton Farm, turn right through the farmyard to a lane, then go left.

6 Beyond a bend and over a stile on the left, signed 'New Shorestone', bear half-right across a field. Emerging on to a quiet lane, go over another stile opposite and continue in the same direction to Ingram Lane.

7 Some 300yds (274m) to the left, a gated track on the right leads away, then around to the left towards Fowberry. Meeting a narrow lane, go left to the farm, then turn right immediately before the entrance on to a green track. In the next field, follow the left perimeter around the corner to a metal gate. Through that, remain beside the right-hand wall to a double gate, there turning right across a final field to Greenhill. Keep ahead to the main road.

8 Continue across to the beach and head north to Bamburgh. Approaching the castle, turn inland, over the dunes, where a cattle fence can be crossed by one of several gates or stiles. Work your way through to regain the road by the car park.

61 Berwick and the Tweed

The town walls, built at great cost by Queen Elizabeth I, are just one of many attractions in this historic Border town, much disputed by the Scots and English

Top: Royal Border Bridge (1847–50) designed by Robert Stevenson

Above: Berwick Castle walls

Overlooking the Tweed Estuary, Berwick is a true Border town and, despite it standing on the river's northern bank, is actually in England. Yet in the 12th century it was a Scottish royal burgh and the country's most prosperous port, busy with the export of grain from a richly fertile hinterland. The town first fell into English hands in 1174 and, for the next 300 years, was repeatedly attacked by English or Scottish troops as the two sides tried to wrest control. It changed ownership so many times that the long-suffering inhabitants must have wondered just whose side they were on.

When the political shuttlecock finally came to rest in 1482, Berwick found itself in England, although it retained the status of an independent state until 1836. However, the Scottish threat remained and, cut off from the surrounding countryside that had once made it rich, prosperity continued to be elusive until renewed threats of the 'Auld Alliance' prompted Queen Elizabeth I to commission new fortifications in 1557.

Wiping away a large part of the town's medieval walls, which were no longer effective against modern artillery, she spent £128,000 to enclose the town within thick ramparts and projecting bastions, from which defensive artillery could rake attacking forces. She probably wasted her money because the expected attack never came and the economic boost to the town was short-lived.

Berwick Boom Time

It was not until the succession of James VI of Scotland to the English throne as King James I in 1603 that the town embarked on its road to recovery. The graceful bridge was built in 1611–24 and the harbour developed and, by the middle of the 18th century, there was a regular packet service to London carrying both passengers and cargo. For the first time the salmon, for which the River Tweed is still renowned, appeared in the capital's markets, kept fresh during the voyage by ice produced on the quayside. The boom continued well into the 19th century. Berwick saw a spate of elegant new building that catered for the civil, military, religious and domestic needs of the town.

After the Railway

The spanner that brought the economic wheel to a halt was the arrival of the railway – the very thing that one might have been expected to do just the opposite. While it opened up new areas and industries by providing cheap, fast and convenient transport for freight and people, it did no good at all for the coastal seafaring trade. The port, previously the key to the town's success, gradually dwindled. Yet Berwick continues to be an attractive market town, with much of interest to see as you wander around its Elizabethan defences, unique for their completeness.

61 Berwick and the Tweed

Explore old Berwick, then take a longer ramble beside the Tweed

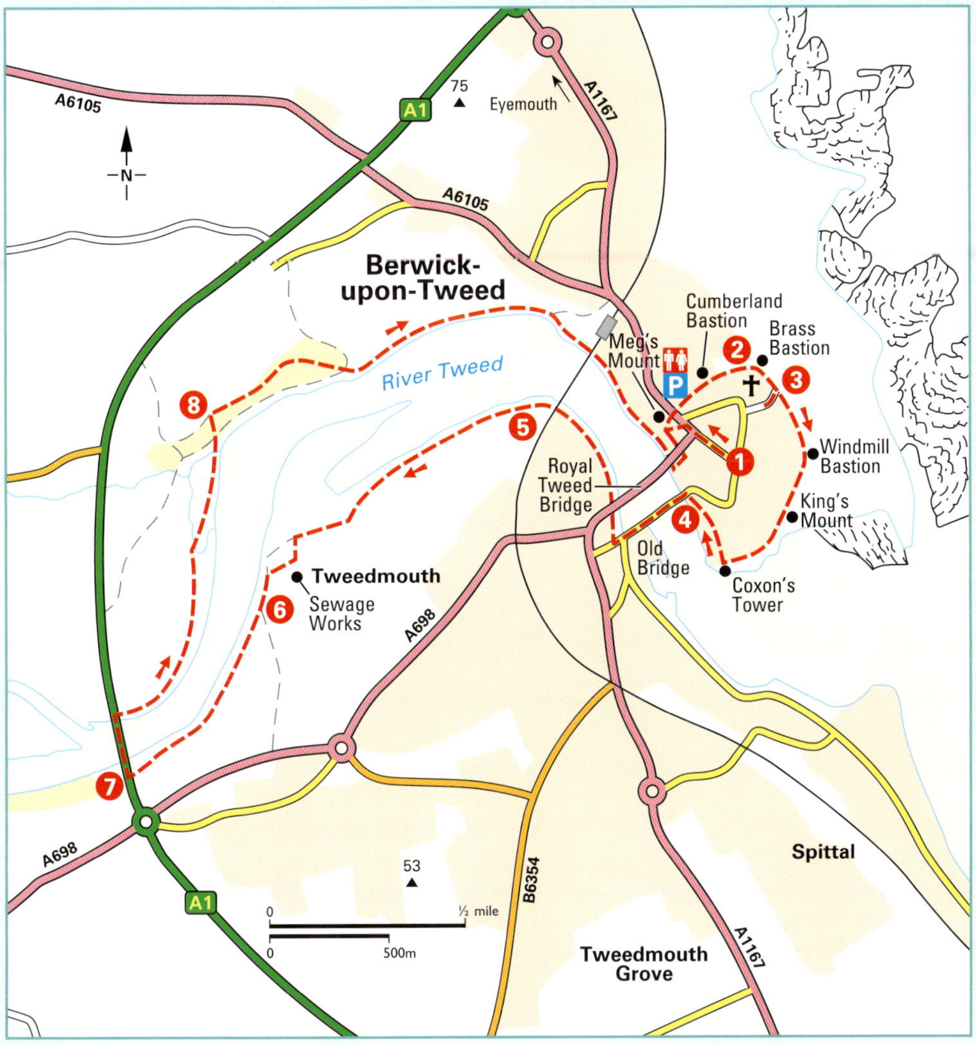

Distance 6.5 miles (10.4km)

Minimum Time 2hrs 15min

Ascent/Gradient 98ft (30m) ▲▲▲

Level of Difficulty ●●●

Paths Paved pathways and field paths; flood-meadows may be wet and muddy, particularly around high tide, 4 stiles

Landscape Town, riverside and woodland

Suggested Map OS Explorer 346 Berwick-upon-Tweed

Start/Finish Grid reference: NT 998529

Dog Friendliness On leads in town and near livestock

Parking Below ramparts outside Scots Gate

Public toilets At car park, below ramparts

Note Sheer, unguarded drop from outer edge of town walls and bastions, keep to marked pathways

1 From the old Town Hall, walk west along Marygate to Scots Gate. Immediately before it, turn left to find a gateway on the right, where you can climb on to the walls by Meg's Mount. Follow the wall back over Scots Gate and on past the Cumberland Bastion.

2 The next battery, Brass Bastion, lies at the northern corner of the town. Some 100yds (91m) beyond, a path descends inside the wall to meet The Parade by the corner of the parish church graveyard. Turn right past the barracks to the church; both are worth visiting.

3 Return to the walls and go on, passing Windmill Bastion and the site of the earlier Edward VI fort. Beyond King's Mount, the walls rise above the Tweed Estuary before turning upriver at Coxon's Tower, past elegant Georgian terraces and on above the old quay.

4 Leave the walls at Bridge End and cross the Old Bridge. Turn right past the war memorial, go beneath the modern Royal Tweed Bridge and remain by the river beyond, shortly passing below Stephenson's railway viaduct.

5 The way continues upstream along a path. Where the bank widens to a rough meadow, pick up a track on the left, leading through a series of kissing gates to an open hide. A further gate leads out on to the next section of river bank. Beyond another gate, a contained path skirts a water treatment plant. Turn left through a second gate on to a tarmac track and turn right.

6 At a bend 40yds (37m) on, bear off right along a field-edge above the steep river bank. Continue walking in the next field but, towards its far end, look for a stepped path descending the bank to a stream. Rising to a stile beyond, bear right to the main road.

7 Cross the Tweed and drop right on to a path, signed 'Berwick via Plantation', which crosses a couple of stiles to a riverside pasture. Walk away beside the left boundary for about 0.5 mile (800m). After crossing the head of a stream, move away from the hedge, aiming to meet the river below a wooded bank. Over a side bridge, bear right to a stile and continue through the trees beyond to a path at the top of the bank.

8 Go right, eventually dropping from the wood by a cottage, where a riverside promenade leads back to Berwick. Just beyond the Royal Tweed Bridge, turn sharp left, climbing back beneath it and continue beside the town walls to return to Meg's Mount.

62 Uncommon Delights at Thurstaston

This walk leads across wooded common land out to a crest commanding views of the Dee estuary, before descending to sea level to follow part of the Wirral Way

This is a walk of two distinct halves. You start near to the shoreline but, saving that for the end, climb long straight Station Road. This is an uninspiring opening but easy and quick so don't let it put you off. The grand Church of St Bartholomew signals the end of the beginning and once the main road is crossed you are on Thurstaston Common.

On Common Ground

Many people expect 'common' land to be open but the name really refers to common grazing. Where this right is no longer exercised, unless the land is managed in some way, it's quite normal for it to revert to woodland. In fact most of the common is wooded but there are still good open stretches where heathland survives. It's obviously difficult for trees to gain a foothold in the thin sandy soils of the more exposed parts.

Most of the ground is dry but there are a few damper hollows. One such hollow is skirted early on in the walk: in summer it is marked by the white tassels of cotton grass. The wet patches are also home to cross-leaved heath, not the ling and bell heather of the drier areas; its flowers grow in clusters rather than spikes. Also found are sundews, low-growing plants with reddish, hairy, sticky leaves. These trap insects from which the plant gains nutrients that are lacking in the poor soils.

Just below the summit you break out on to a bare sandstone crest which gives a view over the Dee Estuary and out to sea. On a clear day the Great Orme behind Llandudno stands out boldly, as does an offshore wind farm out in the Irish Sea. From the summit itself the view spreads to include the Liverpool cathedrals. The Forest of Bowland and Winter Hill rise to their left, and you can also identify Formby Point. After retracing your steps as far as the church, the second half of this walk begins innocuously across farmland, but as you descend towards the sea, there's an unexpected moment of drama as you arrive at the ravine of the Dungeon, complete with tiny waterfall.

Along the Wirral Way

Below this you join the old railway, which is now the Wirral Way. Past ponds, home to water-lilies and moorhens, you soon reach the brink of the slope, about 50ft (15m) above the estuary. It's stretching it a bit to call it a cliff, but it's steep enough to be no place to slip. There's little solid rock exposed in these 'cliffs', which are composed of boulder clay. You may want to linger and savour the view across the wide estuary to Wales.

Above: Pause a moment to enjoy the view

Right: Colourful heather and golden grasses on the common

62 Uncommon Delights at Thurstaston

Enjoy panoramic views from a heathland crest, and the edge of a grand estuary

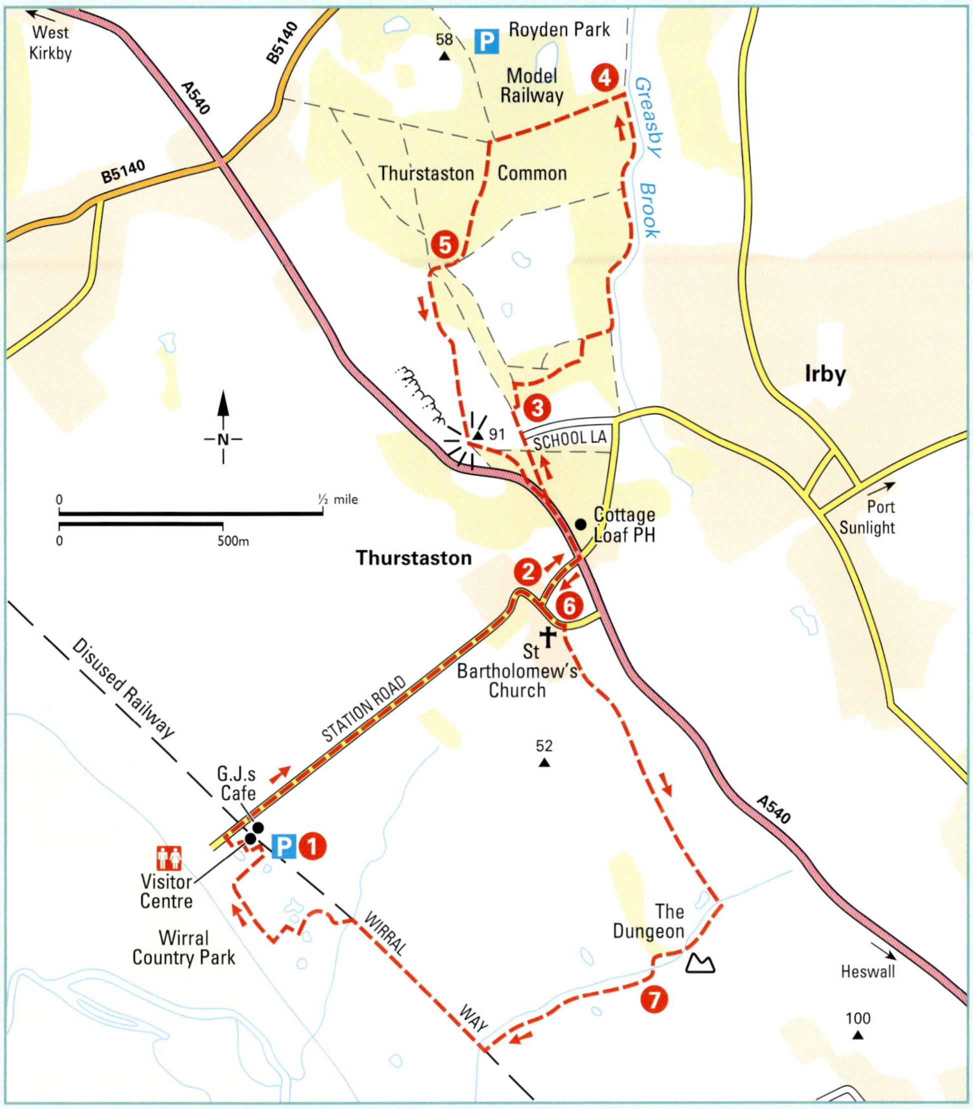

Distance 5.25 miles (8.4km)

Minimum Time 1hr 45min

Ascent/Gradient 345ft (105m) ▲▲▲

Level of Difficulty ●●●

Paths Some road walking, sandy tracks and bare rock, then field paths, 2 stiles

Landscape Woodland and heath, farmland, seashore

Suggested Map OS Explorer 266 Wirral & Chester

Start/Finish Grid reference: SJ 238834

Dog Friendliness Dogs have several opportunities to roam

Parking Wirral Country Park at bottom of Station Road, Thurstaston

Public Toilets In Country Park Visitor Centre adjacent to car park

1 From the car park, loop round past the visitor centre and wildlife pond, go out to Station Road and go straight up for 0.5 mile (800m). At the top the road swings right.

2 Turn left before the church and go up to the A540. Go left, past the Cottage Loaf, then right through a kissing gate. Follow the track past a school to the end of a cul-de-sac.

3 Go through a kissing gate to a broad path then right on a smaller path. Cross a track near a cattle grid then, beyond a gate, go left on another track. This follows Greasby Brook.

4 A boundary wall appears ahead. Turn left alongside it. Where it ends keep ahead, passing the model railway. Alongside Royden Park the wall resumes. At its end turn left by a sign and map. Cross a clearing to a junction.

5 Twenty yards (18m) further on is a kissing gate. Turn right before it, on a narrow path. At a T-junction turn right again, then at the end of this go left on a broader path. Beyond a marker stone continue over tree roots and bare rock, then at a junction of paths among light woodland and with a drop ahead go left. Follow the wide and soon open edge of the rocky escarpment up to a sandstone pillar with a map/view indicator and then the trig point. Continue the short distance to the end of the ridge and take the left fork. Descend a broad path that rejoins the outward route. Retrace your steps past the Cottage Loaf and down the top section of Station Road.

6 Turn left past the church. When the road swings round to the left, a lane continues straight ahead. Cross a stile and follow a well-marked footpath. In a dip cross a stream and turn right at a footpath sign. After recrossing the stream, zig-zag your way down a steeper slope into The Dungeon.

7 Cross the stream again and then follow it down. Climb on to an old railway embankment and go right. When green gates bar the way, sidestep to the left. Continue for another 220yds (201m) to reach a gap in the hedge. Follow a path, winding past a couple of ponds then out to the cliff tops above the estuary. Go right for 240yds (219m), then bear right across grass towards the visitor centre and the car park.

63 Wildlife and Sand at Formby Point

The effort is minimal yet the rewards are great on this engaging walk through an area of great natural beauty and of major significance for wildlife

It has to be said that most of the Cheshire and Lancashire coast is fairly urbanised. As you approach through the town of Formby there's little to suggest that the area through which this walk leads will be any different – it seems to be somewhere to retire to, or perhaps a place from which to commute to Liverpool. Tall, shady pine woods form your first impression of Formby Point. They may appear ancient but were planted less than 100 years ago, to help stabilise the sand dunes. They became an important haven for red squirrels.

The dark, peaty soils that occur inland of the dunes produce a variety of crops, but a particular local specialty is asparagus. You may still see this growing in the fields that border the reserve early in the walk. On the way out towards the shore you pass a lake, natural in origin, where swans, ducks, coots and moorhens breed.

The sand dunes at Formby form the largest dune system in England and a vulnerable and precious habitat for wildlife. The line of dunes immediately behind the beach is partly stabilised by the rough-edged marram grass, but high tides and high winds can still change their shape in a matter of hours. The feet of visitors also erode the fragile dunes.

The beach itself is littered with patches of shell debris. Under the sand there are many invertebrates that attract wading birds. One of the easiest birds to recognise is the oystercatcher, which is black and white apart from its bright orange eyes, beak and legs. As you walk along below the dunes, you will see some darker layers exposed by erosion of the sand. These sediments were formed around 4,000 years ago, when the shape of the coast was somewhat different. In places they have been found to preserve the tracks of animals and birds; human footprints have also been found. These suggest that people hunted and fished here, but the most evocative report is of a medley of small prints suggesting children at play.

Above: Marram grass on the dunes

Right: Red squirrels have made the pine woods on Formby Point their home

A Haven for Wildlife

From the end of the beach you wind through the sand hills again, past pools where natterjack toads – one of Britain's rarest animals – breed. Two other rarities also found here are great crested newts, around the pools, and sand lizards, in the drier areas.

63 Wildlife and Sand at Formby Point

Explore England's largest system of dunes

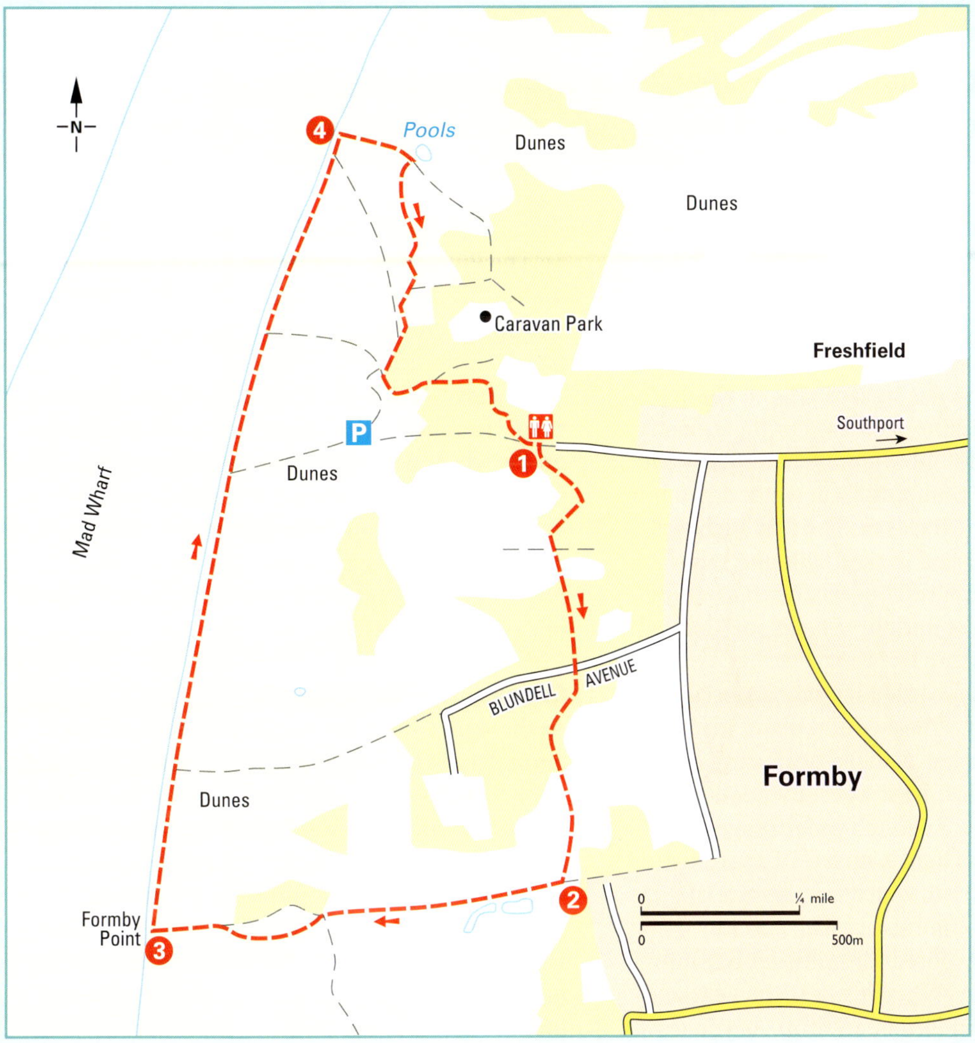

Distance 3.5 miles (5.7km)

Minimum Time 1hr 30min

Ascent/Gradient 50ft (15m) ▲▲▲

Level of Difficulty ●●●

Paths Well-worn paths through woods and salt marsh, plus long stretch of sand

Landscape Pine forest, sand dunes and a vast sweep of beach

Suggested Map OS Explorer 285 Southport & Chorley

Start/Finish Grid reference: SD 278082

Dog Friendliness On lead in nature reserve but can run free on beach

Parking Either side of access road just beyond kiosk

Public Toilets At start

1 Start just left of the large notice board. Follow the 'Squirrel Walk', with its wooden fencing, to the left and then round to the right. Keep straight on at several crossroads. There are many subsidiary paths but the main line runs virtually straight ahead to Blundell Avenue. Cross the avenue to a fainter path almost opposite, with a 'No Cycling' sign and traces of bricks in its surface. Follow this, skirting around the edge of a field (brick traces are still a useful guide). Go up a slight rise then across sand hills to a line of pines on a rise ahead. Skirt left round a hollow and you will see houses on the edge of Formby ahead.

2 Just before reaching the houses, turn right on a straight track. This swings left slightly, then forks. Go right, down steps, then straight on down the side of a reed-fringed pool. Go straight on, over a crossroads towards the sand hills. When you reach them, swing left then right, picking up a boardwalk, to skirt the highest dunes and so out to the beach.

3 Turn right along the open and virtually level sand. The firmest walking surface is usually some way out from the base of the dunes. Walk parallel to these, heading north, for more than 1.25 miles (2km). The shoreline curves very gently to the right but there are few distinctive landmarks apart from yellow-topped signs to various approach paths. Watch for a sign for the Gipsy Wood Path.

4 A distinct track winds through sand hills, then swings more decisively to the right near some pools, where there's a sign board about natterjack toads. Follow the track back into woods and, at a junction, go right. The route curves round between woods and sand hills then joins a wider track by a Sefton Coastal Footpath sign. Go right through a patch of willows, then bear left to a line of pines on a rise. From these drop down to a broad path with a gravelly surface and follow it left into woods again. Stick to the main path, with timber edgings and white-topped posts, then bear right by a large 'xylophone', and continue quickly back to the start of the walk.

65 Around Silverdale

An undemanding walk through an Area of Outstanding Natural Beauty offers delightful changes of scenery, through woods, country lanes and along the coast

Right: The Jack Scout promontory at Silverdale

Below: Lime kiln on the tumbledown shore

The Arnside–Silverdale Area of Outstanding Natural Beauty covers a mere 29 square miles (75sq km) yet includes rocky coastline, salt marsh, wetland, pasture, woodland, heathland, crags and quarries, and some attractive villages – principally Silverdale in Lancashire and Arnside in Cumbria. With such a mosaic of habitats, it's no surprise that the area is rich in wildlife – more than half of all British flowering plant species are found here.

There's a fine start to this walk, through Eaves Wood – with its yew trees and impressive beech ring. Then the route sidles through the back lanes of Silverdale before reaching the coast. The channels of Morecambe Bay shift over time and so does the shoreline. The band of salt marsh around the Cove has shrunk drastically in the last few years. At high tide the rocky foreshore may be impassable, in which case follow an alternative footpath across the open fields of The Lots safely above the shore.

It's a Bore

The route avoids a tricky section of the coast south of Silverdale, returning to the shore near Jenny Brown's Point. A breakwater running out to sea recalls a failed 19th-century land reclamation scheme. Just around the corner stands the tall chimney of a copper-smelting mill that operated around 200 years ago. Nearby is Jack Scout promontory, owned by the National Trust. From here you can watch the tidal 'bore', a wave formed by the tide running against the water current in the channel, and enjoy splendid views of Lakeland.

After Heald Brow comes Woodwell, the first of three springs on the walk. At Woodwell the water issues from the crag above the square pool. This was used for watering cattle but now you're more likely to see dragonflies. Woodwell and the other 'wells' around Silverdale are found where the water-permeable limestone is interrupted by a band of impermeable material such as clay. Rainfall generally sinks quickly into limestone and there are no surface streams over most of the area, so the springs were of vital importance. This rapid drainage also means that few of the footpaths are persistently muddy, even after heavy rain.

Lambert's Meadow, however, is usually damp. It sits in a hollow where fine wind-blown silt (known as 'loess') accumulated after the last Ice Age. The soil is dark and acidic, very different from that formed on the limestone, and the plant community is different too.

65 Around Silverdale

Take a pleasant stroll through an area rich in flowering plants

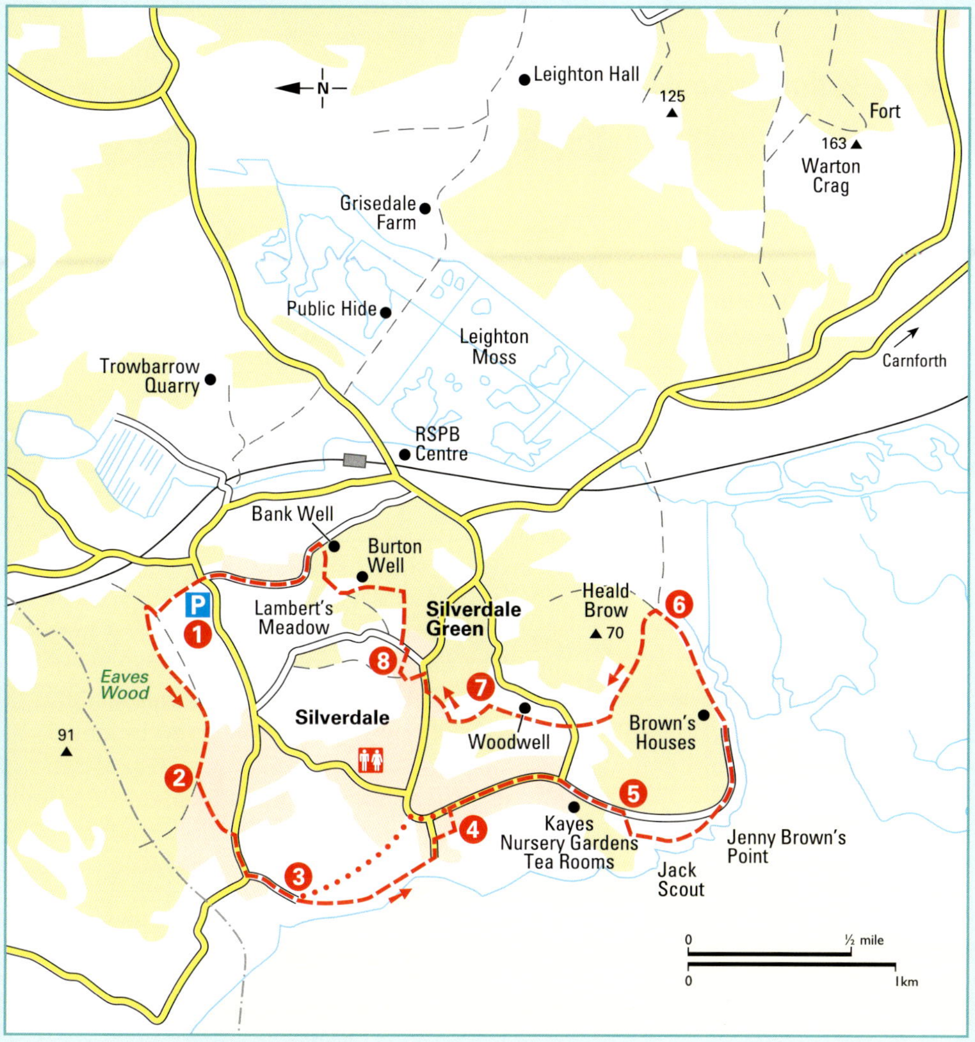

Distance 5.5 miles (8.8km)

Minimum Time 2hrs

Ascent/Gradient 426ft (130m) ▲▲▲

Level of Difficulty ●●●

Paths Little bit of everything, 9 stiles

Landscape Pot-pourri of woodland, pasture, village lanes and shoreline

Suggested Map OS Explorer OL7 The English Lakes (SE)

Start/Finish Grid reference: SD 472759

Dog Friendliness Can run free on shore and in woods

Parking Small National Trust car park for Eaves Wood

Public Toilets In Silverdale village

1 From the end of the National Trust car park at Eaves Wood, follow the footpath to reach a T-junction. Go right for a few paces and then turn left, climbing gently. Keep left to the beech ring, then carry straight on. Just beyond a junction veer left to a wall and then continue walking on this line to reach a lane.

2 Cross on to a track signed 'Cove Road'. Keep ahead down a narrow path (Wallings Lane), a drive, another track and then another narrow path to a wider road. After 200yds (183m), go left down Cove Road.

3 From the Cove walk leftward, below the cliffs, to the shore. Walk up the road to Beach Garage then take the footpath alongside. (If high tide makes this route impassable, follow the easy footpath across the fields above instead.)

4 At the next road turn right for 600yds (549m), then bear right down Gibraltar Lane for 350yds (320m). Enter the National Trust property of Jack Scout.

5 Descend left to the lime kiln then follow a narrowing path directly away from it. This swings left above a steep drop and descends. Follow a broad green path to a gate. After 150yds (137m), another gate leads into the lane. At its end continue below Brown's Houses along the edge of the salt marsh to a stile. Go up slightly, then along to a signpost.

6 Turn left, climbing to a gate. The gradient eases, over rock and through a wooded area into the open. Go left to a stile, follow a wall down into a wood. Follow a track down right. Cross the road to a wall gap, descend, then walk below the crags to Woodwell.

7 The path signed 'The Green via cliff path' leads to a rocky staircase. At the top of the stairs go ahead to join a broader path. Follow it to the left, slant right, and then continue walking into woodland. A stile on the right and a narrow section of path leads to a road. Go right for 150yds (137m), then left into The Green. Keep right at a junction then join a wider road.

8 Go left for 75yds (69m) then right, signposted 'Burton Well Lambert's Meadow'. The track soon descends then swings left, passing Burton Well on the right. Cross a stile into Lambert's Meadow, then go right, over a footbridge to a gate. Climb up, with some steps, and continue more easily to a fork. Go left alongside a pool (Bank Well) into a lane. Go left and at the end the car park is virtually opposite.

66 Over Hampsfell Above Grange-over-Sands

This relaxing walk leads through mixed woods and over open fell above a charming seaside resort, to a travellers' shelter that commands a splendid vista

Grange-over-Sands was for many years a popular seaside resort, attacting visitors with its neat and tidy white limestone buildings, colourful gardens, sunny aspect and seaside disposition. It thrived particularly after the arrival of the Furness Railway in the town in 1857, and day-trippers would also arrive by steamer via the waters of Morecambe Bay and would disembark at the Claire House Pier, which was dramatically blown away by a storm in 1928.

Today the sea is somewhat distanced from the sea wall and the town, despite past popularity, has fallen from grace with many holidaymakers, and now retains a refined air of quiet dignity. Grange has many fine and interesting buildings and its ornamental gardens, complete with ponds, provide suitable solitude in which to relax and enjoy a picnic or read the newspaper. The gardens rise to Hampsfell (Hampsfield Fell on the map) via the charming mixed woods of Eggerslack, which add yet another dimension to this pleasant area.

The Hospice of Hampsfell

The neat square tower that adorns the top of Hampsfield Fell is known as the Hospice of Hampsfell. Built of dressed limestone blocks and around 20ft (6m) high, it was built in 1846 by a minister from nearby Cartmel Priory for 'the shelter and entertainment of travellers over the fell'. Enclosed by a fence of chains supported by small stone pillars to keep cattle out, and with an entrance door and three windows, it provides a convenient shelter should the weather take a turn for the worse. On its north face stone, steps guarded by an iron handrail provide access to the top of the tower and a resplendent view.

On the top, a novel direction indicator, consisting of a wooden sighting arrow mounted on a rotating circular table, lets you know which distant point of interest you are looking at. Simply align the arrow to the chosen subject, read the angle created by the arrow and locate it on the list on the east rail.

Below: Open, airy spaces – the view from Hampsfell

66 Over Hampsfell Above Grange-over-Sands

Drink in marvellous views from a 'hospice' on high ground

Distance 4 miles (6.4km)

Minimum Time 2hrs

Ascent/Gradient 790ft (241m) ▲▲▲

Level of Difficulty ●●●

Paths Paths and tracks, can be muddy in places, 7 stiles

Landscape Town, woods and open fell, extensive seascapes

Suggested Map OS Explorer OL7 The English Lakes (SE)

Start/Finish Grid reference: SD 410780

Dog Friendliness Busy lanes and open fell grazed by sheep

Parking Car park below road and tourist office in central Grange

Public Toilets At Ornamental Gardens, north end of car park

1 Join the main road through Grange and go right, heading north, to pass the ornamental gardens. Cross the road and continue along the pavement to the roundabout. Go left along Windermere Road rising to go round the bend, and find steps up to a squeeze stile on the left, signed 'Routon Well/Hampsfield'.

2 Take the path rising through Eggerslack Wood. Cross directly over a surfaced track and continue to pass a house on the left. Steps lead on to a track. Cross this diagonally to follow a track, signed 'Hampsfell'. The track zig-zags to the right (with a house to the left) and continues up through the woods to a stile over the wall.

3 Cross the stile to leave the wood and follow the path directly up the hillside. Pass sections of limestone pavement and little craggy outcrops until the path levels and bears left to a stile over a stone wall. Cross the stile and go right along the wall. Continue in the same direction, following a grassy track, to pass ancient stone cairns and up to the obvious square tower landmark of the Hospice of Hampsfell.

4 Take your time to enjoy the view, using the direction indicator, then leave the tower, head south and follow the path over the edge of a little limestone escarpment – take care here. Continue over another escarpment and descend to find a stile over the wall. Descend to the bottom of the dip and rise up the green hill beyond. Cross over the top and descend to find a stile over the wall. Although the path bears diagonally left at this point it is usual to continue directly to the little cairn marking Fell End, with fine views over the estuary. Turn sharp left and descend to pick up a grassy track leading left round a little valley of thorn bushes to a gate leading out on to a road.

5 Cross the road, take the squeeze stile and descend diagonally left across the field to a gate on to a road by the front door of Springbank Cottage. Descend the surfaced track to enter a farmyard and continue left over a stone stile. Go over the hill, following the path that is parallel to the wall and then take the stile into a narrow ginnel. Follow this down, with a high garden wall to the right, round the corner and descend to a junction of roads. Go left on a private road/public footpath, and then bear right at the fork. At the next junction turn right to descend the track and at the following junction go left down Charney Well Lane. When you get to another junction, turn left below the woods of Eden Mount to a junction with Hampsfell Road near the bottom of the hill and turn right. At the junction with a larger road go left and pass the church before descending to pass the clock tower and junction with the main road (B5277). Go left and then right to the car park.

67 Far Back in Time on Birkrigg Common

This engaging ramble provides a good outing on the characterful expanse of Birkrigg Common, which is strewn with Bronze and Iron Age remains

Birkrigg Common is a wonderful open expanse of bracken, grass and low limestone scars, rising between the shores of Morecambe Bay and the gentle valley containing Urswick Tarn. Although only a lowly height, it offers splendid views encompassing the whole of Morecambe Bay and most of the Furness Peninsula, with Black Combe and the Coniston Fells prominently in view. Other Lakeland fell groups, the Yorkshire Dales and Bowland feature more distantly. A network of paths and tracks allows an intimate exploration of the countryside, which turns out to be remarkably varied and interesting.

Below: The walk's inland loop passes the charming parish church of Great Urswick

Bottom: The Bronze Age Druid's Circle on Birkrigg Common overlooking Morecambe Bay

An Ancient Sea

The bedrock of Birkrigg Common is Carboniferous limestone. It outcrops only on the margins of the Lake District, most notably around Morecambe Bay and Kendal, but also around Shap and above Pooley Bridge. It was laid down in a shallow sea and once covered the whole of the Lake District, before the area was pushed up into a vast dome by earth movements. Subsequent erosion largely removed the limestone layer, exposing the volcanic core of the Lake District, leaving only a few outcrops of limestone around the fringes.

Birkrigg Common is dry, as most limestone areas are. In the low-lying valley at Urswick, however, water has pooled to form the lovely little reed-fringed Urswick Tarn, which is a haven for waterfowl. Some ground water contained in the limestone layer reaches the surface as freshwater springs out on the sands of Morecambe Bay.

Bronze Age Settlements

The area around Birkrigg Common was always fairly dry and fertile, compared to the higher Lakeland fells, so it attracted the attention of early settlers. Little remains to be seen, though the most notable feature is an early Bronze-Age small stone circle of limestone boulders on the seaward slopes. A standing stone at Great Urswick, known as the Priapus Stone and thought to be associated with fertility rites, has been forced into a recumbent position at the base of a roadside wall.

A few tumuli are dotted around the countryside and a rumpled series of low, grassy earthworks represent the remains of an ancient homestead site. Above Great Urswick, a low hill encircled by a limestone scar bears a hill-fort, probably dating from the Iron Age, in the centuries preceding the Roman conquest. It's interesting to wander around and let your imagination run free at the ancient settlement sites. Very little is known about them, but there has been a continual human presence in the area for more than 4,000 years.

67 Far Back in Time on Birkrigg Common

Climb to an old standing stone and an ancient fort

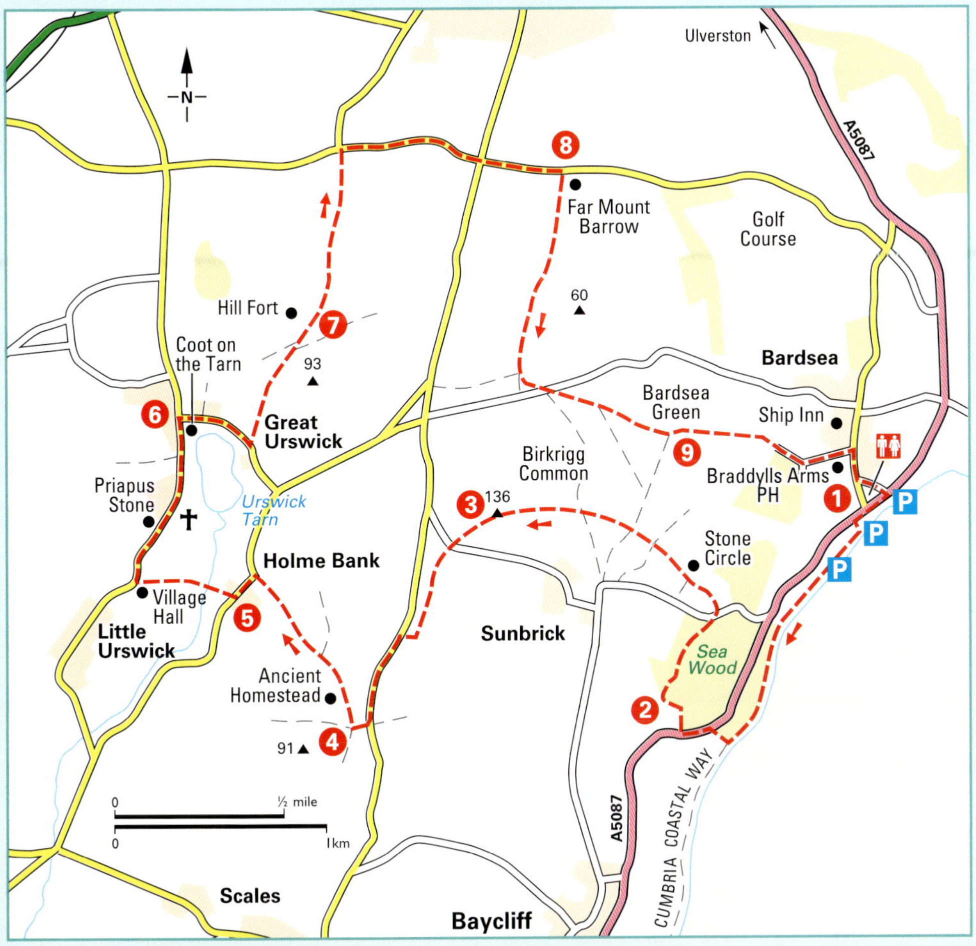

Distance 8 miles (12.9km)

Minimum Time 3hrs

Ascent/Gradient 577ft (176m) ▲▲▲

Level of Difficulty ●●●

Paths Paths and tracks, some field paths may be muddy, 10 stiles

Landscape Low-lying, rolling limestone country, with coastal margin, woodlands, open common and enclosed pastures

Suggested Map OS Explorer OL6 The English Lakes (SW); OL7 The English Lakes (SE)

Start/Finish Grid reference: SD 301742 (on Explorer OL7)

Dog Friendliness Under close control on roads and where livestock grazing

Parking Small car parks between coast road and shore at Bardsea

Public Toilets On coast road below village of Bardsea

1 Follow the shore along to Sea Wood. At the far end of the wood turn right, up through its inside edge to the road. Turn left up the road for about 400yds (366m), then right at a gate into another part of Sea Wood.

2 Turn left to follow a path around the top edge of the wood, then go left again to leave the wood at a gate. Cross a road and follow a grassy path through bracken on Birkrigg Common. Turn left to reach a wall corner and then walk a few paces to a stone circle on your right. Follow any grassy path through the bracken to the high skyline. Birkrigg Common bears a trig point at 446ft (136m) and commands fine views.

3 Pass a bench and take a path to the right down to a road. Cross over the road and walk parallel to another road as the common tapers out to a cattle grid. Continue along the road and then make a sharp right turn to go along a walled track.

4 Cross a stile at the end of the track and bear right past a stone trough and the site of an ancient homestead. Keep left of a wall to cross a stile at a gate. Bear left to find a path down a valley to a gate. Turn right before the gate, cross a stile, then follow a hedgerow across a slope to a house. Cross a stile leading down to a road, and then turn left to pass farm buildings at Holme Bank.

5 Turn right signposted 'Public Footpath Church Road'. Cross a ladder stile and footbridge, then take a path to a village hall and road. Cross the road and turn right to pass a school. Just after the entrance, look out for the Priapus Stone, which is incorporated into a wall. Pass the parish church and village store in Great Urswick.

6 Turn right at the Coot on the Tarn to follow another road. Watch for Clint Cottage on the left and Tarn House on the right, then turn left up a steep track. This is flanked by hedgerows and reaches two gates. Go through the gate on the left and walk straight ahead, keeping to the right of a low hill; this is the site of an ancient, probably Iron Age, fort.

7 A wall leads to another gate, then straight on again. Cross a stile on the right, and on the other side of a gate, cross a stile on the left. Walk straight on, crossing two more stiles to reach a road junction. Turn right, walk through a crossroads and to the next farm.

8 Turn right at Far Mount Barrow along a track signposted 'Bardsea Green'. Cross a stile by a gate and keep left to cross a road on Birkrigg Common. Turn left again for Bardsea Green, along an obvious path parallel to the road, then parallel to a wall.

9 At a corner of the wall, go through a gate on a track down to a road; cross a dip. Keep left up into Bardsea, right at the Braddylls Arms and follow a road down to the shore.

68 The Commanding Black Combe

This tough but energising walk scales Black Combe, an isolated peak rising between sea and higher fells that commands wide-ranging views

Black Combe's steep slopes rise to a domed summit that often wears a woolly cap of cloud. Moist air rising from the Irish Sea has to cross this hill before reaching the higher fells of the Lake District, so tends to leave a puffy cloud tethered to the summit as water vapour starts to condense. Bear this in mind when attempting to climb the fell; the whole idea is to enjoy the view from Lakeland's last fell and cloud cover will confound the plan. Also bear in mind that this is one of the more remote walks in the book. Black Combe is not a place to be caught out in foul weather.

Britain's Widest View

Poet William Wordsworth praised the view from Black Combe, claiming that 'the amplest range of unobstructed prospect may be seen that British ground commands', though lamenting 'we have seen into Scotland, Wales, the Isle of Man… but alas we have still failed to see Ireland as we have been promised'. He seems to have been drawing on comments made by the 18th-century surveyor Colonel Mudge, who said that the summit offered a more extensive view than any other point in Britain. Mudge saw Ireland several times, though only before sunrise and after sunset.

Grouse, Snipe, Curlew

Black Combe is made of friable Skiddaw slate, which outcrops, naturally, around Skiddaw and also on the Isle of Man. It is the oldest exposed rock in the Lake District, belonging to the Ordovician period of 450–500 million years ago and weathers to produce domed summits covered in patchy scree and thin, poor soil. Bracken covers the lower slopes of the fell, giving way to bilberry and heather on the higher slopes, although the summit is a delightful swathe of short, green grass. Tree cover is sparse and confined to the lower slopes. Grouse, introduced for sport, flourish on the slopes along with snipe and the ubiquitous curlew.

Abandoned Mills

Several streams have carved deep little valleys in the flanks of Black Combe. Whit Beck was once used to turn a waterwheel at Whitbeck Mill. The present building, restored as a dwelling, dates from the 18th century, but may stand on an earlier mill site. The dilapidated wheel last turned in 1916. Too many old farms and cottages lie derelict or disused on the flanks of the hill, victims of wavering farm economies. Black Combe is one large sheep-grazing range today.

Below: The mighty Black Combe dominates this quiet corner of the Lake District. There are excellent views out over the Irish Sea

68 The Commanding Black Combe

Climb out on a limb, far removed from the higher Lakeland fells

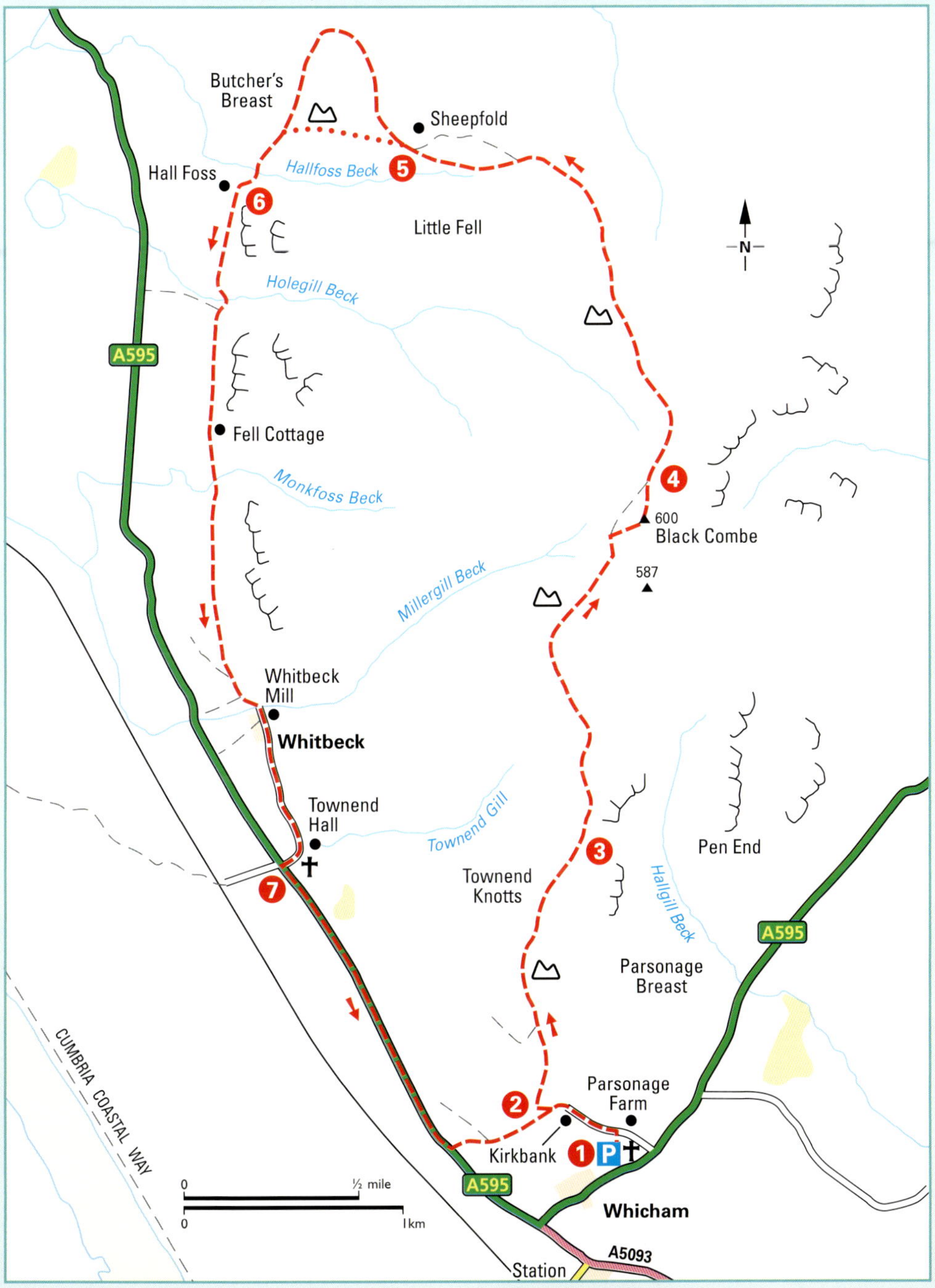

Distance 8.5miles (13.7km)

Minimum Time 4hrs

Ascent/Gradient 1,883ft (574m) ▲▲▲

Level of Difficulty ●●●

Paths Clear path to top, rather vague beyond, no stiles

Landscape Broad, open, whaleback hill covered in bracken and heather

Suggested Map OS Explorer OL6 The English Lakes (SW)

Start/Finish Grid reference: SD 136827

Dog Friendliness On lead or under close control on grazing land and on road

Parking Car park at Whicham Church or lay-by at Whitbeck Church

Public Toilets None en route; nearest at Silecroft beach

Note Not advised in poor visibility

1 Leave the car park at Whicham Church on a short path to a lane. Turn left behind Kirkbank on a good track. At the corner of a wall, go right turn up a path and on through a gate on to the slopes of Black Combe.

2 The fellside is covered in bracken, but a broad, grassy path leads straight up a little valley. Avoid a path to the left. Towards the top of the valley, bracken gives way to grass and bilberry. Look back for fine coastal views.

3 The broad path slices up across a heathery slope, levelling out near the summit. In mist, watch carefully for a right turn on to the broad, domed top of Black Combe. A trig point is enclosed by a circular wall at 1,970ft (600m).

4 You can turn around and retrace your steps to Whicham, or enjoy a circuit of the fell. Head north from the summit to join a path onwards. Turn left downhill at a small cairn. The path can be vague in places.

5 Swing left just before an old sheepfold. The path is grassy. Keep left at a fork for a steep descent, or right for a gentler descent. Either way, the path later swings left and runs beside a fence on Butcher's Breast then beside a wall, fords Hallfoss Beck and runs close to the ruined farm of Hall Foss.

6 Keep to the path beside the wall, fording Holegill Beck near a solitary larch. Pass abandoned Fell Cottage and cross Monkfoss Beck. When a fork is reached, keep left to follow a grassy path across a slope of bracken. A track leads past Whitbeck Mill, continues past the buildings of Whitbeck, and then reaches the main road at Whitbeck Church.

7 Turn left along the main road. Follow the road until a wooden footpath sign points left up a slope. The path climbs beside a wall, and then runs gently down to a track. The track passes Kirkbank and leads on to the narrow lane followed at the start. A short path on the right leads back to Whicham Church.

69 Over Muncaster Fell

A fine linear walk leads from Ravenglass past a castle and Roman remains to Eskdale Green, from where you can return on the 'La'al Ratty' steam railway

Below: Pulling into Ravenglass station

Bottom: Splendid Lake District views from the terraced gardens at Muncaster Castle

Muncaster Fell is a long and knobbly fell of no great height. Its summit rises to 758ft (231m), but is a little off the route of this walk. A winding path negotiates the fell from end to end and this can be linked with other paths and tracks to offer a fine walk from Ravenglass to Eskdale Green. This is a linear walk, but when the Ravenglass and Eskdale Railway is in full steam, a ride back on the train is simply a joy.

Steam Power

Affectionately known as 'La'al Ratty', the Ravenglass and Eskdale Railway has a history of fits and starts. It was originally opened as a standard gauge track in 1875 to serve a granite quarry and was converted to narrow gauge between 1915 and 1917. After a period of closure it was bought by enthusiasts in 1960, overhauled and re-opened, and is now a firm favourite. The line runs from Ravenglass to Dalegarth Station, near Boot at the head of Eskdale. The railway runs almost all year, but there are times in the winter when there are no services. Obtain a timetable and study it carefully. When the trains are running, there are few Lakeland journeys to compare with a trip both ways.

The Romans operated an important port facility at Ravenglass. Fortifications were built all the way around the Cumbrian coast to link with Hadrian's Wall and a Roman road cut through Eskdale, over the passes to Ambleside, then along the crest of High Street to link with the road network near Penrith. Some people think the Romans planned to invade Ireland from Ravenglass, although this is a subject of debate. The mainline railway sliced through the old Roman fort in 1850, leaving only the bathhouse intact, though even this ruin is among the tallest Roman remains in Britain.

Surrounded by luxuriant rhododendrons, Muncaster Castle is almost completely hidden from view. It has been the home of the Pennington family since about 1240, though they occupied a nearby site even earlier than that. The estate around the castle includes a church founded in 1170, as well as a network of paths and tracks to explore. Owls are bred and reared at Muncaster, then released into the wild.

69 Over Muncaster Fell

See one of Britain's tallest Roman ruins at Ravenglass

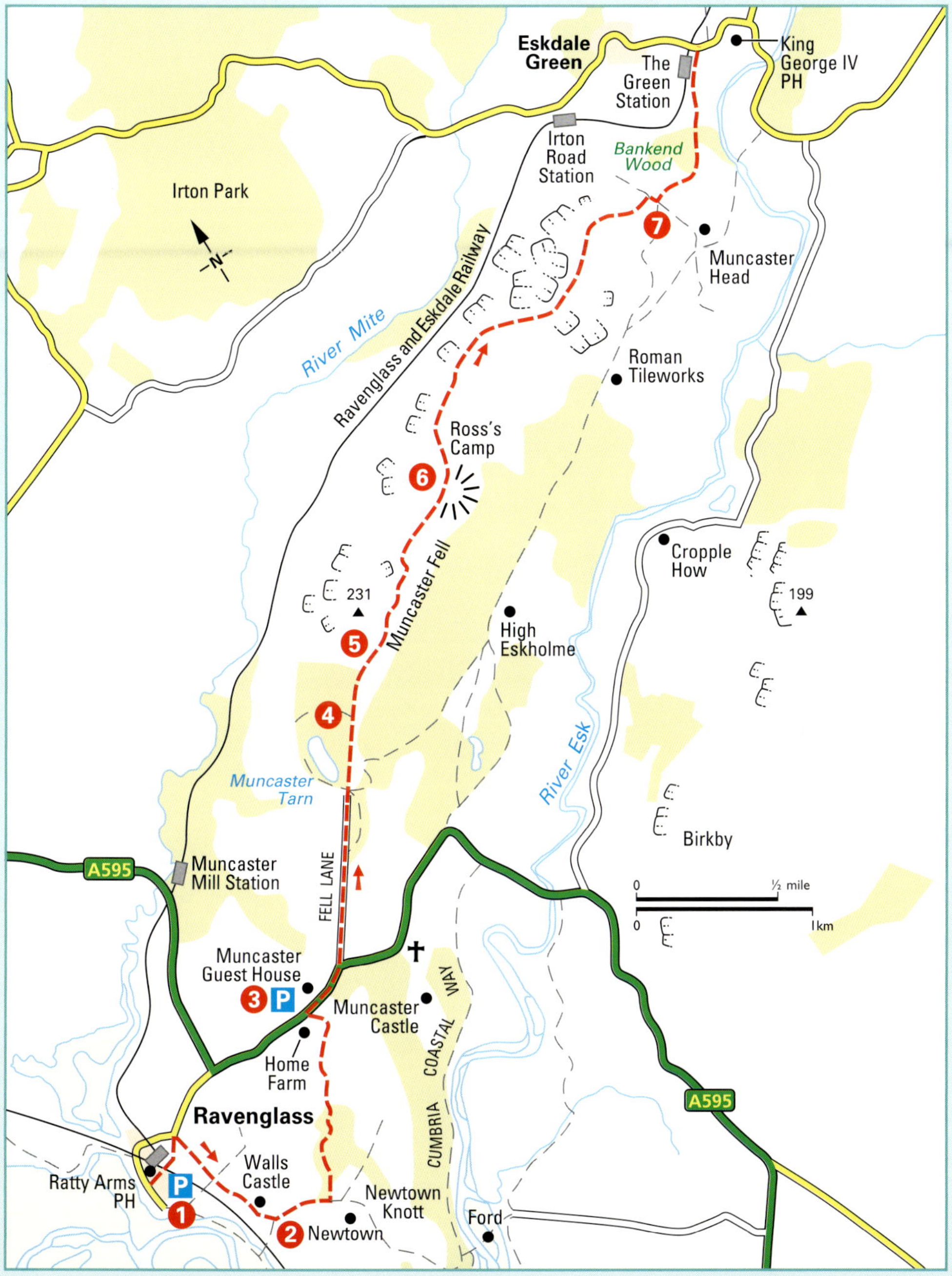

Distance 6 miles (9.7km)

Minimum Time 2hrs 30min

Ascent/Gradient 730ft (220m) ▲▲▲

Level of Difficulty ●●●

Paths Clear tracks and paths, muddy after rain, 1 stile

Landscape Woodlands, moderately rugged fell and gentle valley

Suggested Map OS Explorer OL6 The English Lakes (SW)

Start Grid reference: SD 085964

Finish Grid reference: SD 145998

Dog Friendliness Under close control where sheep are grazing

Parking Village car park at Ravenglass, close to station

Public Toilets Ravenglass village and Ravenglass and Eskdale Station

1 Leave the car park across the mainline and miniature railway line, using footbridges, then take a path to a road junction. Turn right on a path by the side of a road, signed 'Walls Castle'. The bathhouse is soon on the left.

2 Continue along the road and turn left on a track signed 'Newtown'. Turn left before the cottage and go up a wooded valley. Go through four gates, following the track from the wood, across fields and into another wood. Turn left to Home Farm and a busy main road.

3 Cross the road and turn right, passing Muncaster Castle car park and the Muncaster Guest House. The road leads up to a bend, where Fell Lane is signposted uphill. Ascend the track, cross a little wooded dip, then fork right and left. Go through a gate at the top of the lane to reach Muncaster Fell.

4 A path runs through boggy patches on the edge of a coniferous plantation, then crosses Muncaster Fell. A path rising to the left leads to the summit, or keep right to continue.

5 Views develop as the path winds about on the slope overlooking Eskdale. A panorama of fells opens up as a curious structure is reached at Ross's Camp. Here, a large stone slab was turned into a picnic table for a shooting party in 1883.

6 Continue along the footpath, looping round a broad and boggy area to reach a corner of a dry-stone wall. Go down through a gateway and bear in mind that the path can be muddy. There is a short ascent on a well-buttressed stretch, then the descent continues on a sparsely wooded slope, through a gate, ending on a track near another gate.

7 Go through the gate and turn left, crossing a field to reach a stone wall seen at the edge of Bankend Wood. Walk on, keeping to the right side of the wall, to reach a stile and a stream. A narrow track continues, becoming better as it draws close to a road. Turn left at the end of the road to reach The Green Station.

Wales

Wales

The coastline of Wales, ranging from the Glamorgan Heritage Coast and Gower peninsula in the south through the sometimes wild, wind-battered stretches of Pembrokeshire in the far west to the estuaries and coastal towns of the north, offers wide variety as well as profound natural beauty.

Walkers in this region encounter rugged headlands with tumbling cliffs, maritime heath, peaceful woods, flower-strewn downlands and sudden peaks rising dramatically just inland, as well as coastal resorts, beautiful bays and fine sandy beaches with sweeping surf. There are views of estuary, islands and sea stacks, and plentiful opportunities to admire rare plants and native trees, to watch seabirds and spot marine life.

On Anglesey just off the coast of North Wales, Walk 82 leads to a Royal Society for the Protection of Birds (RSPB) seabird centre, from where you may be able to see the rare mountain chough, which nests locally, as well as wrens, stonechats, guillemots and puffins. The walk crosses maritime heathland, where western gorse and bell heather grow, and perhaps you'll find another rare species – the spotted rock rose. Nearby you may encounter Welsh mountain ponies, introduced as part of a return to traditional land management methods.

In North Pembrokeshire Walk 78 from St Justinian's leads along the coast opposite Ramsey Island and past waters where you may see seals, dolphins and harbour porpoises. This beautiful

Previous pages: Miles and miles of unspoilt headlands, cliffs and bays in Pembrokeshire

Insets: Powerful waves at Broad Haven and peaceful waters at Stackpole Quay, both in Pembrokeshire

Opposite page: Another slice of Pembrokeshire beauty, on the cliff path near St Justinian's

Below: Dunraven Bay on the Glamorgan Heritage Coast

nature walk treads in the footsteps of St Justinian. According to rather colourful tradition, he was a nobleman from Brittany who settled as a hermit on Ramsey Island in the 6th century, then became Abbot in the Cathedral at nearby St David's; he later returned to the island with his followers, but they revolted against his strict rule and beheaded him. The saint's body is said to be buried in a ruined chapel on the cliffs opposite Ramsey Island.

Saintly Encounter

Another tradition has it that on Ramsey Island – known in Welsh as *Ynys Dewi* ('St David's Isle') – the patron saint of Wales, St David, once met the patron saint of Ireland, St Patrick. Wales is a land rich in legend and local tradition, and many walks in this chapter visit ruins and places of natural beauty with sacred associations. Further up the Pembrokeshire coast from Ramsey Island, Walk 80 passes through the coastal town of Newport (Dyfed), and climbs the mountain of Carn Ingli that rises behind it. The name means 'Mount of Angels' and by tradition St Brynach ascended the peak to commune with heavenly messengers.

At Greenfield near Holywell, North Wales, Walk 85 goes to St Winefrede's Chapel and Well. It is said that in the 7th century Winefrede rebuffed the romantic advances of local leader Caradoc, who

Best of the Rest

Conwy

On the west bank of the River Conwy estuary, the castle and walled town of Conwy were built in 1283–88 by King Edward I's brilliant military architect Master James of St Georges as part of a series of fortified settlements intended to impose English rule on the Welsh. The fortifications are impressive: a castle with eight drum towers and walls 15ft (4.5m) thick in places and town walls more than three-quarters of a mile (0.5km) in length that contain 21 defensive towers. Walk 83 climbs from the town onto Conwy Mountain behind and past the 10-acre (4ha) Iron Age fort of Castell Caer at the summit. If you're a photographer, pack your camera – the walk delivers breathtaking views of the coast, the Carneddau mountains, the Conwy estuary and the town and castle.

St David's and St Non's Bay

The pretty village of St David's is in fact a city, due to the presence of its majestic 12th-century cathedral in the Transitional Norman architectural style. According to tradition, the patron saint of Wales, St David, founded a church and monastery on the banks of the River Alun in the spot where the cathedral now stands. Walk 77 leads from the city out to St Non's Bay, named after David's reputed mother, St Non or Nonita. The walk leads to a ruined chapel marking the spot at which David was born, supposedly at the height of a storm in c.AD500, and to the holy spring said to have arisen on the night of its birth, now marked by St Non's Well.

Broad Haven

From the North Pembrokeshire resort of Broad Haven on St Brides Bay, Walk 76 leads through coastal woodland and passes the remains of an Iron Age fort on Black Point, as well as a small standing stone, Harold's Stone, said to mark the spot at which Earl Harold of Wessex won a military victory in the 11th century. If you arrive at low tide, try also a ramble along the beach to see Den's Door, the Sleek Stone and other intriguing rock formations.

Swanlake Bay and Manorbier Castle

A relaxing walk (73) leads across farmland in a lush corner of Pembrokeshire praised by a celebrated local, the medieval clergyman Giraldus Cambriensis, as 'the pleasantest spot in Wales' to the beautiful white sands of Swanlake Bay. The walk begins in the village of Manorbier near the ruins of the Norman castle in which Giraldus was born in *c.*1146. The castle, well preserved and with chapel, crypt and lovely gardens, is well worth a visit and commands fine views of the coast and unspoilt countryside nearby. Fans of CS Lewis's *The Chronicles of Narnia* (published 1950–56) will be interested to know that Manorbier Castle was used as Cair Paravel in the BBC TV adaptation of the books (1988–90).

St David's Head

Dominated by the 594ft (181m) peak of Carn Llidi, St David's Head contains ancient remains including the partially collapsed Neolithic burial chamber of Coetan Arthur. Its massive capstone measures 8.5ft by 19ft (2.6m by 5.9m) and is supported at one end by an orthostat (upright stone) 5ft (1.5m) tall. There are also remains of an Iron Age hillfort on the headland, and views up and down the coast are breathtaking. The walk (79) begins and ends at the splendid Whitesands Beach. Time for a swim?

Dunraven Bay and the Ogmore Estuary

A varied walk (70) leads from Dunraven Bay, with its fossil-rich red sandstone cliffs, inland over farmland and through woods to St Bride's Major, then through dunes past the white Portobello House and along the estuary of the River Ogmore to Ogmore-by-Sea. From this village on the Glamorgan Heritage Coast there are views of the once notorious Tusker Rock, which is submerged at high tide and caused many shipwrecks.

Barmouth

William Wordsworth and J. M. W. Turner were among those attracted by the beauty of this former port that became a 19th-century resort. Walk 81 commands wonderful views across the estuary of the River Mawddach of the peaks of Cadair Idris.

Rhossili Bay

Walk 72 in the Gower peninsula, South Wales, leads along the 633ft (193m) ridge of Rhossili Down behind the breathtakingly beautiful 4-mile (6.4km) sands of Rhossili Bay. The walk passes the Anglo-Norman Church of St Mary the Virgin in Rhossili and the megalithic burial site of Sweyne's Howes. There are lovely views of Worm's Head at the southern end of the bay.

in his fury attacked and beheaded her; when her head fell to the ground a holy spring broke from the place it landed. She was later brought back to life by St Beuno, and the spring waters were found to have healing powers; the Well, not far from the 12th-century Basingwerk Abbey that is also visited on the walk, became a place of pilgrimage. It is mentioned by name in the medieval poem 'Sir Gawain and the Green Knight' (late 14th century) and kings Richard I and Henry V both visited the shrine, the first in 1189 to pray for success on the Third Crusade (1189–92) and the second to give thanks for victory at the Battle of Agincourt in 1415. The chapel in the late Perpendicular Gothic style was built in the early 16th century.

Remains of Industry

As well as visiting ancient sites of religious significance, Walk 85 tours local remains of 18th- and 19th-century industry, for Greenfield Valley was home to a range of mills and factories, including brass and copper mills manufacturing bowls, and cotton mills producing textiles. Today the area has been turned into the 70-acre (28ha) Greenfield Valley Heritage Park.

Another former industrial site visited in this chapter is a onetime centre of quarrying, copper- and lead-mining near Prestatyn, North Wales (see Walk 84), now overgrown with native trees including dogwood and whitebeam, hawthorn, sycamore and sessile oak. You may also see orchids, dog violets and bluebells on what is a relaxing wander across limestone hillside with views of the Dee Estuary, the mountains of Snowdonia, the resort of Prestatyn and the North Wales coast.

Sands and Fossils

Of course, parts of Wales remain important centres of modern industry, which creates much-needed local employment, and far away to the south Walk 75 runs within sight of some of Milford Haven's smoking oil refineries and power stations as it leads into Angle Bay and a refreshing taste of the wildness of the Atlantic coast. At low tide Angle Bay is an expanse of mud and sands where you will see redshank, dunlin and red plover. On the headland above is evidence of medieval strip farming. West Angle Bay has pretty sands, and fine rock pools and low cliffs and is a good spot for viewing fossils.

Angle Bay is just one of many beautiful beaches on these coasts. Walk 71 visits Oxwich Bay on the Gower peninsula, where the 2.5-mile (4km) beach, the Sands, was voted the most beautiful in Britain in 2007, and is centre for swimming, diving and water sports. The place is typical of the richness of the Welsh coasts in combining these attractions with access to a national nature reserve behind the dunes, and to the 13th-century St Illtyd's Church on the site of a 6th-century hermitage.

Far left: Follow the acorn

Left: Pale sands and crags at Swanlake Bay, Pembrokeshire

Below: You can break many of the walks for a beach picnic, a paddle or even a swim

70 An Easy Stroll Along the Heritage Coast

Beginning as a pleasant foray across farmland, this charming walk leads through dunes, along the Ogmore estuary and back over impressive cliffs

Most visitors to South Wales overlook the chunk of land that lies south of the M4 motorway between Cardiff and Swansea. Yet smack bang between the two cities and overshadowed by the huge industrial complexes of Port Talbot, there lies an unspoilt strip of coast. The Glamorgan Heritage Coast, the 14-mile (22.5km) stretch of coastline that runs between Ogmore and Gileston, stands defiant against progress – just as its cliffs defy the huge ebbs and flows of the tides in the Bristol Channel. Sandy beaches, often punctuated by weathered strips of rock, break up an otherwise formidable barrier of limestone and shale cliffs that rise and dip gracefully above the turbulent grey waters. It's fair to say that the scenery doesn't quite match the breathtaking beauty of the Gower Peninsula or Pembrokeshire, but somehow the unkempt wildness has an appeal all of its own.

Down to the Ogmore

The walk starts at Dunraven Bay, which houses the Heritage Centre, offering interesting displays and information about the area. The centre makes an appropriate starting point for a walk that gives an intriguing taster of this unique landscape. The early stages of the walk track inland, through woodland and farmland before heading coastwards, at the small village of St Bride's Major.

From here, the path sneaks between dunes and drops to the Ogmore River. Following the estuary downstream through bracken that simply teems with wildlife, and passing the white Portobello House, you meet the coast at Ogmore-by-Sea and pick up the coast path above one of many beautiful beaches in the local area. With glittering ocean views to your right and the dunes arrayed to your left, you now climb easily back up above Dunraven where, if you time it right, you witness the cliffs reflecting the pastel shades of sunset as you make the final drop to the beach. If you've been lucky enough to see this, you'll agree that it is a wonderful way to finish off an evening stroll.

A Protected Landscape

The Glamorgan Heritage Coast was one of three pilot schemes set up in 1972 to protect the country's unique coastal landscapes and environments from destructive development. There are now 43 such areas in England and Wales, and in Wales they account for more than 40 per cent of the total coastline. The aims of the scheme are fourfold: to maintain the ecological diversity; to provide public access and encourage recreational use; to protect the needs of the local population, including farmers and landowners; and to preserve the quality of the coastline. The Glamorgan Heritage Coast is managed by the Countryside Council for Wales, which employs a professional ranger service to take care of the day-to-day running of the area.

Below: Limestone cliffs between Ogmore-by-Sea and Southerndown

70 An Easy Stroll Along the Heritage Coast

Explore a little-known part of the South Wales coast

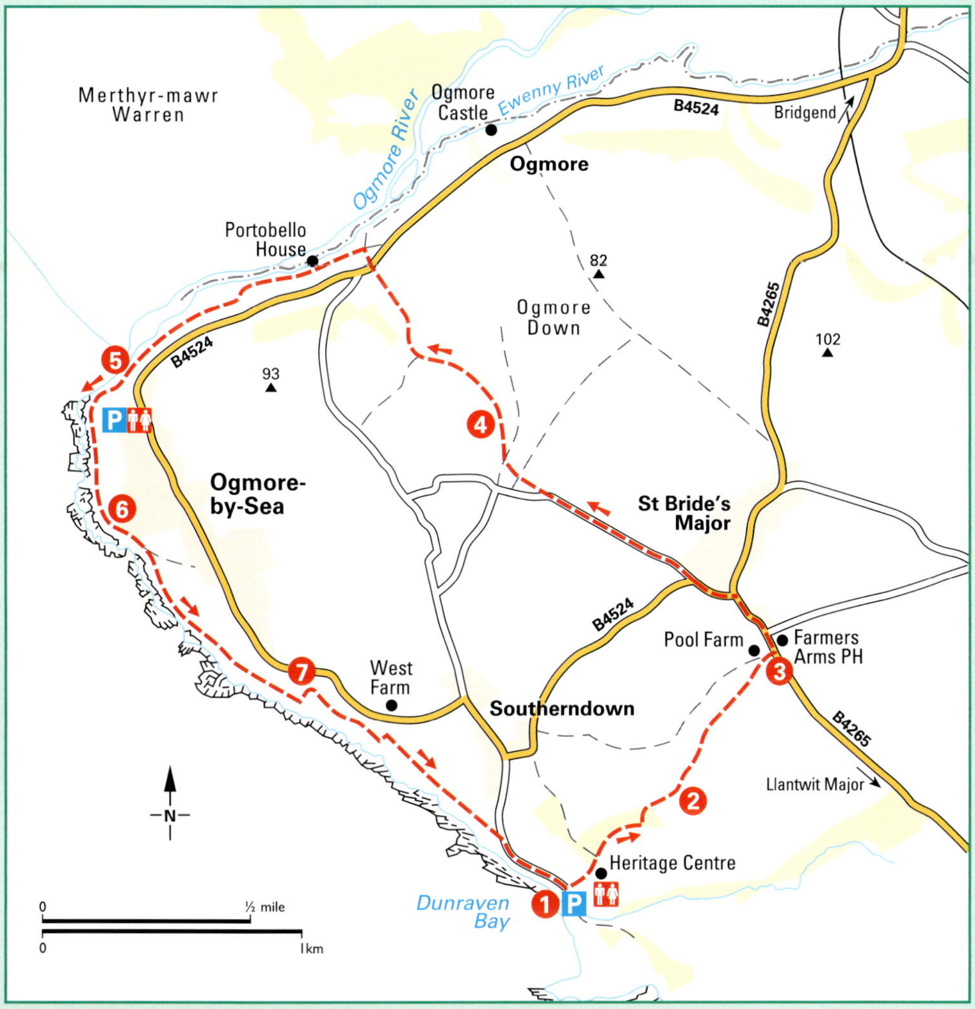

Distance 6 miles (9.7km)

Minimum Time 2hrs 30min

Ascent/Gradient 460ft (140m) ▲▲▲

Level of Difficulty ●●●

Paths Easy-to-follow across farmland and coastline, 5 stiles

Landscape Deciduous woodland, farmland, bracken-covered sand dunes and rocky coastline

Suggested Map OS Explorer 151 Cardiff & Bridgend

Start/Finish Grid reference: SS 885731

Dog Friendliness Some difficult stiles; total ban on beach at Dunraven in summer

Parking Large car park at Heritage Centre above Dunraven Beach

Public Toilets Heritage Centre, also at Ogmore

1 From the car park, head up the lane at the back of the car park and pass the Heritage Centre on the right. Keep walking straight ahead as the track swings left and go through a gate to duck into woodland. Continue to a fork, where you keep left to reach a stile. Cross this stile and walk along the edge of the field to reach a gate on your left. Go through the gate, then cross a stone stile on your right to keep ahead with hedge to your right.

2 Cross into another field and keep to the left-hand side, following the hedgerow, which is now on your left. When you reach the next stile, continue ahead, go past a gate on the left, to reach another stone stile on the left. Cross this stile and head right over another stile, next to a gate, to another stone stile between the house and the farmyard.

3 Turn left on to the road and walk into the village. Keep left into Southerndown Road then fork right into Heol-y-slough. Follow this road for 0.75 mile (1.2km) then, as the road bends left, continue across the common. Keep ahead where a bridleway crosses the track. As you join another track, maintain your direction along the valley floor.

4 The path winds its way down through sand dunes, passing a tributary valley on the left, and eventually emerges on the B4524. Cross the road and continue towards the river until you locate one of the many paths that lead left, parallel to the river, towards Portobello House. Keep left on the drive then, once above the house, bear left to follow a clear path through the bracken, again parallel to the Ogmore River.

5 Make sure you stay above the small cliffs as you approach the mouth of the estuary and you'll arrive at a car parking area above the beach. From here, follow the obvious track along the coast around to the left.

6 You'll come to a dry-stone wall, which will funnel you through a gate marked 'Coast Path'. Continue along the coast path until, 1.25 miles (2km) from the gate, you meet with a very steep-sided valley. Turn left into this valley then turn immediately right, on to a footpath that climbs steeply up the grassy hillside.

7 Stay with the footpath as it follows the line of a dry-stone wall around to West Farm. Keep the wall to the left to continue to the upper car park. A gap in the wall, at the back of this, leads you to a grassy track that follows the road down into Dunraven.

71 Woodland and Family Wars at Oxwich Point

A short but exhilarating ramble leads through woodland past a 6th-century church then along a delightful stretch of coastline and to a Tudor mansion house

The Gower contains fewer headlands than nearby Pembrokeshire, and this makes it much more difficult to fashion short but interesting circular walks. This excursion stands out for a couple of reasons. Firstly, it can be combined with a visit to Oxwich National Nature Reserve, a treasure trove of marshland and sand dunes in a wonderful beachside location. And secondly, the wonderful coastal scenery includes the beautiful and usually deserted beach known as 'The Sands'.

Once a busy port that paid its way by shipping limestone from quarries on the rugged headland, Oxwich is now one of the prettiest and most unspoilt Gower villages. The name is derived from Axwick, Norse for 'water creek'. It is best visited away from the main holiday seasons.

Founded in the 6th century AD, and tucked away in a leafy clearing above the beach, St Illtud's Church is particularly significant for its stone font, which is said to have been donated by St Illtud himself. The grounds are tranquil, with an atmosphere that comes in stark contrast to the summertime chaos of the beach below. Behind the building is the grave of an unknown soldier who was washed up on the beach during the Second World War. It's certainly a spooky spot and the graveyard is said to be haunted by a half-man/half-horse creature. St Illtud (or St Illtyd) was a Welsh-born monk who founded the nearby abbey of Llan-Illtut (Llantwit Major). He is perhaps most famous for his fights against famine, which included sailing grain ships to Brittany, where he died in AD505.

Oxwich Castle

Really a 16th-century mansion house built by Sir Rhys Mansel on the site of the 14th-century castle, Oxwich Castle occupies an airy setting above the bay. Sir Rhys, in common with many Gower locals, wasn't above plundering the cargo of ships that came to grief in the bay and was quick to take advantage of a French wreck in late December 1557. The salvage rights, however, belonged to a Sir George Herbert of Swansea, who quickly paid Mansel a visit to reclaim his goods.

A fight broke out and Sir Rhys's daughter Anne was injured by a stone thrown by Herbert's servant. She later died from her injuries. Court action against Herbert proved ineffective and a feud continued for many years until eventually the Mansel family moved to Margam, east of Swansea. Part of the mansion was leased to local farmers, but most of the fine building fell into disrepair.

Right: Gentle light at sunrise over beautiful Oxwich Bay

71 Woodland and Family Wars at Oxwich Point

Take a tour of a Gower headland

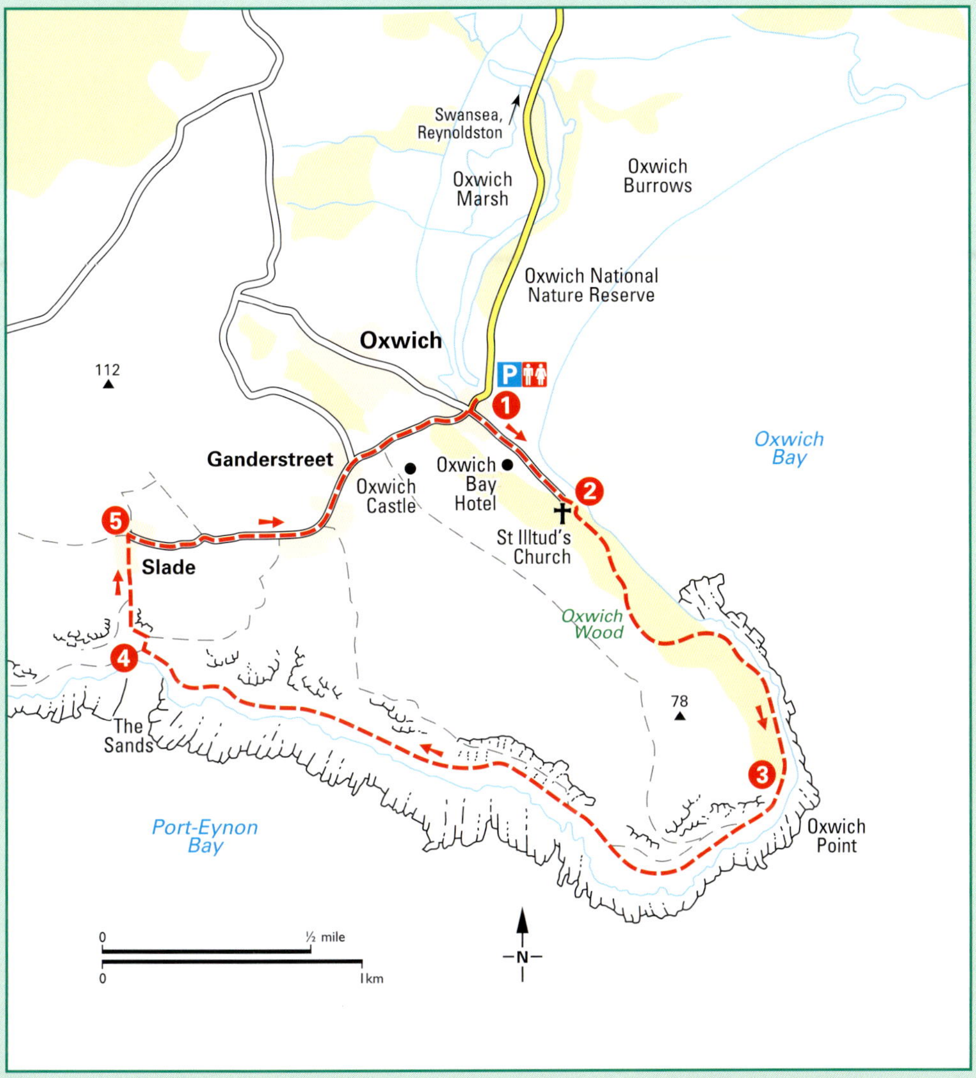

Distance 4.5 miles (7.2km)

Minimum Time 2hrs

Ascent/Gradient 480ft (146m) ▲▲▲

Level of Difficulty ●●●

Paths Clear paths through woodland, along coast and across farmland, quiet lane, 4 stiles

Landscape Mixed woodland and rugged coastline

Suggested Map OS Explorer 164 Gower

Start/Finish Grid reference: SS 500864

Dog Friendliness Can mostly run free but watch steep cliffs and livestock

Parking Oxwich Bay

Public Toilets At car park near start

1 Walk back out of the car park and turn left to a crossroads. Turn left here (waymarked 'Eglwys') and go on past the Woodside Guesthouse and the Oxwich Bay Hotel, leaving both on your right. The lane you are following leads into the woods and up to the fine 6th-century St Illtud's Church, where a gate marks the end of the road and the start of a path leading out on to Oxwich Point.

2 Join the path that runs a little way beneath the church, and follow it for a few paces before going up wooden steps that climb steeply into the wood. Keep going until the footpath levels out, when you should bear to the left and drop back down through the wood and then around the headland until the path comes out into the open above the beautiful headland of Oxwich Point.

3 The path now drops through gorse and bracken to become a grassy coast path running easily above a rocky beach. Keep the sea on your left and ignore any tracks that run off to the right. After walking for approximately 1 mile (1.6km), you will pass a distinct valley that drops in from your right. Continue past this valley and you will be funnelled into a narrow, fenced section of the path, with a field to your right. Follow this, and go across a succession of stiles, and you will eventually reach a path diversion that points you to the right, away from the beach.

4 Follow this to a stile and a broad farm track, where you turn left. Continue up and around to the right until you come to a kissing gate. Go through this and keep right up a lane past some houses to a crossroads.

5 Turn right and follow the road along to a fork, where you keep right. Drop down to reach the entrance of Oxwich Castle on the right. After looking at or exploring the castle, turn right, back on to the lane and walk down into Oxwich village. Keep straight on to reach the car park.

72 The Highs and Lows of Rhossili Bay

A tramp over high ground on the Gower Peninsula offers views of beach, cliffs and sea and the chance to visit a sea-washed nature reserve once likened to a dragon

Of the many walks on the Gower Peninsula this is one of the very best – although rather oddly, for all the coastal views your feet won't leave a single footprint in the sand in the walk's short form. The lofty heights of Rhossili Down show the magnificent arc of sand in its best light and offer a feeling of spaciousness that's difficult to describe and almost impossible to equal in this part of the world. The ancient stones that define the ridge line only add to the captivating atmosphere.

The Gower Peninsula is a 15-mile (24km) finger of land that points westwards from Swansea. Its southern coast boasts dune-backed beaches of surf-swept, clean, yellow sand and magnificent limestone cliffs, chiselled in places into deep gullies and knife-edge ridges. The northern coast forms the southern fringes of the marshy Loughor Estuary. It's nothing like as dramatic as the southern coast, but it's an important habitat for wading birds and other marine life. Between the two coastlines, the land rises into a series of whaleback ridges, or downs, covered with gorse, heather and bracken and littered with prehistoric stones and remains. Scattered around the windswept landscape are a number of impressive castles. In 1957, the peninsula was designated Britain's first Area of Outstanding Natural Beauty.

On Rhossili Down

None of the Gower beaches are blessed with quite the untamed splendour of Rhossili Bay. It owes much of its wild nature to the steep-sided down that presides over its waves and provides a natural and impenetrable barrier to development. The down is a 633ft (193m) high, whaleback ridge that runs almost the full length of the beach. The path that traces the ridge is one of the fairest places to walk in the whole of South Wales, especially in late summer when the heather tinges the hillsides pink. From The Beacon, at the southern end of the ridge, the views stretch a long way and it's often possible to see St Govan's Head in Pembrokeshire and even the North Devon coastline on a very clear day.

The string of islets that thrust into the Atlantic at the bay's southernmost tip are known as Worms Head. This is a derivative of the Old English *Orm*, 'dragon' or 'serpent'. The likeness can be seen. It is now a nature reserve, but can be reached at low tide by scrambling across a rocky causeway. Check the tide timetables before making such a sortie, as it's easy to be cut off by the rising tides.

Below: Looking down on Worms Head

Below left: The golden sands of Rhossili Bay run for more than 4 miles (6.4km) from Worms Head to the outcrop of Burry Holmes

72 The Highs and Lows of Rhossili Bay

Wonder, as you walk, at the stunning views over one of Wales's finest and wildest beaches

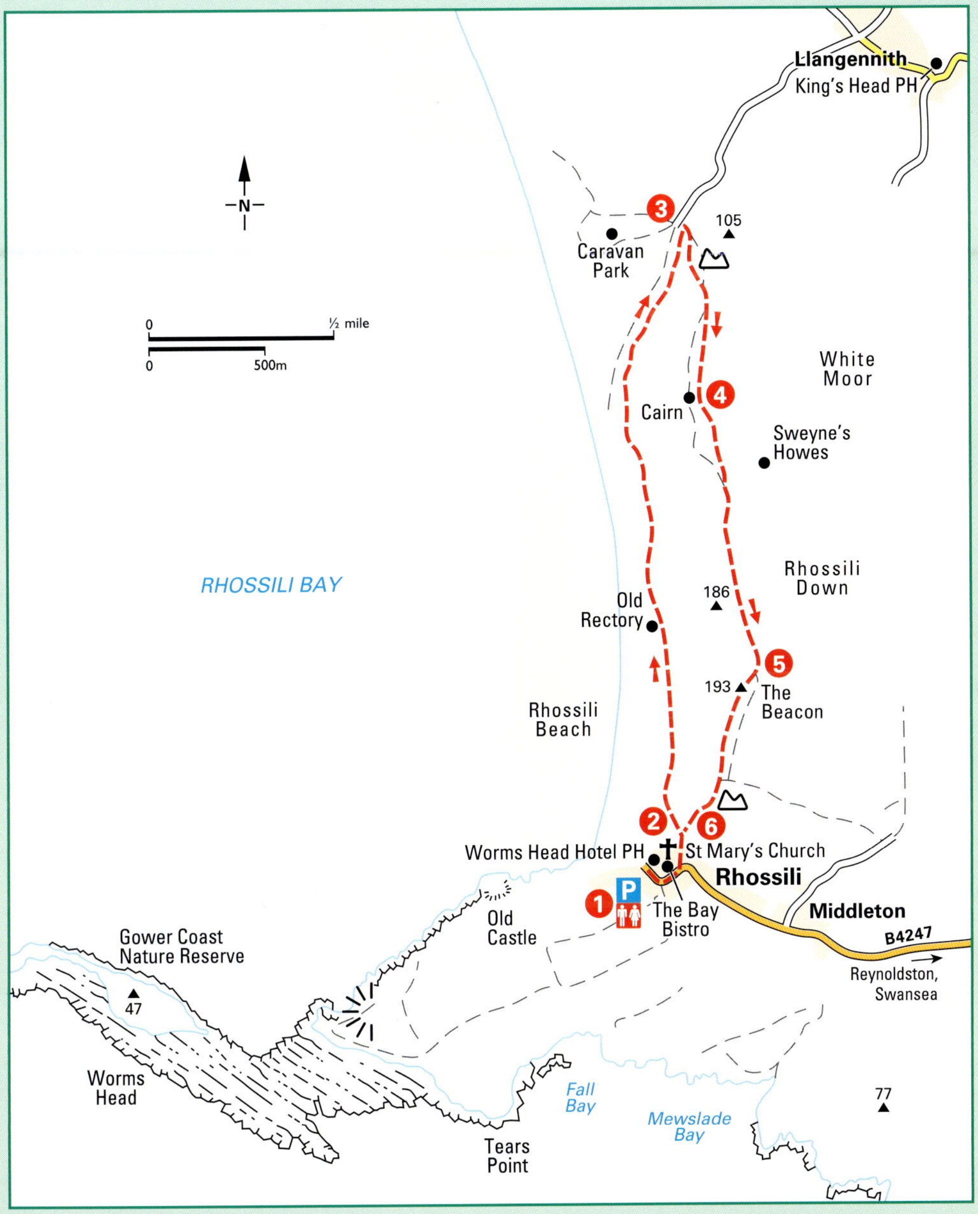

Distance 4 miles (6.4km)

Minimum Time 1hr 45min

Ascent/Gradient 590ft (180m) ▲▲▲

Level Of Difficulty ●●●

Paths Easy-to-follow footpaths across grassy downs, 2 stiles

Landscape Rolling downland, rocky outcrops and views over gorgeous sandy beach

Suggested Map OS Explorer 164 Gower

Start/Finish Grid reference: SS 416880

Dog Friendliness Care needed near livestock

Parking Large car park at end of road in Rhossili

Public Toilets At start

1 From the car park, head out on to the road and continue uphill as if you were walking back out of the village. Immediately after passing St Mary's Church bear left down on a broad track to a gate at its end. Go through this and keep left to follow a grassy track that snakes along the steep hillside.

2 Follow this through the bracken, passing the Old Rectory on your left, and eventually you'll reach a sunken section with a wall on your left and a caravan park situated behind. Don't be tempted to break off right just yet; instead, keep going until you come to a gate on the left.

3 Don't go through the gate; turn sharp right and follow the grassy track steeply up on to the ridge. At the top of the steep section keep to the top track that follows the crest.

4 You'll pass some ancient cairns and drop slightly to pass a pair of megalithic cromlechs, or burial chambers. These are known as Sweyne's Howes and are more than 4,000 years old. Continue on a broad track up to the high point of The Beacon.

5 Keep straight ahead on a clear track that starts to drop easily then steepens to meet a dry-stone wall. Continue walking down the side of the wall and you'll eventually come to the gate you passed through on the way out.

6 Follow the lane out to the road, turn right and pass St Mary's Church on your right to return to the car park.

73 Magnificent Manorbier and Swanlake Bay

A delightful outing leads across open farmland before taking in beautiful sands and breathtaking coastal scenery near the 'pleasantest spot in Wales'

Above: The green hills give on to the beach at Manorbier Bay

Above right: Manorbier Castle - the grounds contain beautiful walled gardens

This is a delightful short walk that runs along the heads of some magnificent cliffs and visits a wonderful and remote sandy cove. The outward leg isn't particularly inspirational, but the narrow lane provides convenient access to the highest ground and the section across farmland is open and breezy, with fine views over the coast. Once reached, the narrow belt of white sand that makes up Swanlake Bay provides ample reward for your efforts. Flanked on both sides by impressive sandstone crags and cut off from easy road access by the farmland that you've just traversed, it sees few visitors and provides a stunning setting for a picnic and, perhaps, a paddle.

Gerald's Pleasant Spot

Once lauded by its most famous son, Giraldus Cambrensis, alias Gerald of Wales, as the 'pleasantest spot in Wales', Manorbier is these days best described as an attractive but sleepy coastal village dominated by a mighty castle and set among some of South Pembrokeshire's prettiest and most unspoilt countryside. Giraldus was born Gerald de Barri, the grandson of Odo, the first Norman Lord of the Manor, in 1146. He is best known for his attempts to set up an independent Church for Wales (a movement denied by Henry II) and for his chronicles of everyday life.

The village name derives from 'Maenor of Pyrrus' or 'Manor of Pyr'. Pyrrus was the first Celtic abbot of Caldey, a nearby island first inhabited by monks in the 6th century AD and known in Welsh as Ynys Pyr, or Pyr's Island. Its landscape is wild and unspoilt and its buildings are inspirationally simple. There is a working Benedictine monastery and a number of ornate churches, including 12th-century St Illtud's, with its ancient sandstone cross.

Manorbier Castle

Despite the profusion of well-preserved castles in this corner of Pembrokeshire, it still comes as a surprise to discover such an impressive edifice tucked away in this tiny village. The original castle was raised in the late 11th century, but the stone building that stands tall and proud over the beach and village these days was constructed in the early 12th century. Since the time of Gerald of Wales and the de Barris, the castle has passed through many hands, including the Crown.

The castle is now privately owned, but is open to the public for tours. As well as the splendid views over the bay from the top of the castle walls, you will also see many stately rooms, occupied these days by waxwork models of various figures, including Gerald, hard at work on his accounts.

73 Magnificent Manorbier and Swanlake Bay

Explore the coastal landscape loved by Gerald of Wales

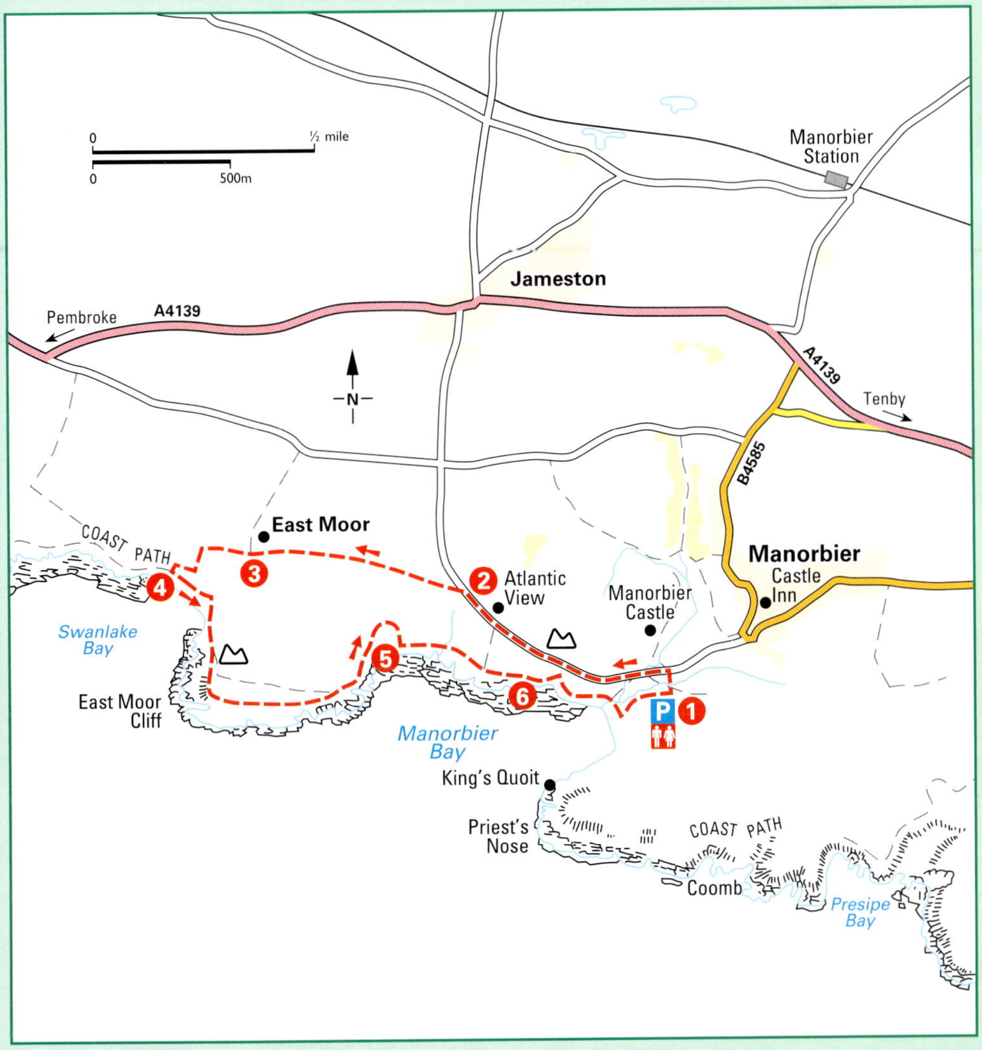

Distance 3 miles (4.8km)

Minimum Time 1hr 30min

Ascent/Gradient 290ft (88m) ▲▲▲

Level of Difficulty ●●●

Paths Coast path, clear paths across farmland, 3 stiles

Landscape Sandy coves and dramatic coastline

Suggested Map OS Explorer OL36 South Pembrokeshire

Start/Finish Grid reference: SS 063976

Dog Friendliness Difficult stiles, poop scoop on beaches. Keep on lead and off grass near house on The Dak

Parking Pay-and-display car park by beach below castle

Public Toilets At start

1 Walk out of the car park entrance and turn left towards the sea. Stay on the road as it bears to the right and climbs steeply above the coast. Pass Atlantic View cottage on your right before reaching a double gate on your left.

2 Cross the stile and walk along the field edge, with a bank and fence on your right, to reach a stone step stile. Cross the stile and head in the same direction to a wooden stile close to the farm, which you also cross. Continue to a gate by the farmhouse, which brings you into a small enclosure, then to a wooden stile that leads away from buildings.

3 Continue again along the edge of the field to another gate. Go through and turn left to drop down the field edge to a zig-zag that leads on to the coast path. Access to the beach is more or less directly beneath you.

4 Turn left on to the coast path and follow it over another stile and steeply uphill. You'll eventually reach the top on a lovely airy ridge that swings east and then north to drop steeply down into a narrow dip above Manorbier Bay.

5 Cross another stile and climb out of the dip to continue walking easily above the rocky beach. This path leads to a drive, beneath a large house.

6 Continue beneath The Dak and uphill slightly to a gate, where the coast path drops off to the right. Follow this as it skirts a small car park and then winds down through the gorse and bracken to the beach. Cross the stream and turn left to follow a sandy track back to the car park.

75 Two Faces of the Haven

A tramp around the headland to Angle Bay leads away from the industry of the Haven's inner shore to the unspoilt beauty of the Atlantic coast

Above: Industrial landscape – Rhoscrowther oil refinery can be seen from West Angle Point

Right: Unspoilt West Angle Bay

The narrow finger of land that juts out between Freshwater West and Angle Bay forms the eastern wall of the mouth of Milford Haven. On the northern edge of the peninsula, the waters are passive, lapping against a coastline that's gentle and sloping, but as you round the headland, a radical transformation takes place: here cliffs defiantly resist the full brunt of a considerable Atlantic swell. There are other differences, too. While the views along the seaward coast are wild and unspoilt, the inner shores of the Haven reveal the ugly scars of industry. Smoking oil refinery chimneys dominate the eastern skyline.

The narrow-necked shape of the peninsula lends itself to a challenging circular walk that shows both sides of the coin. The outward leg, as far as the sands of Freshwater West, is about as tough as coast-path walking gets – constantly dipping and climbing on narrow, often quite exposed paths. The return leg is a little more civilised, tracking easily around the curve of Angle Bay and following field edges back out on to the headland.

Refuge for Massachussetts Whalers

Milford Haven is the name of both a huge natural inlet, once described by Admiral Nelson as 'the finest port in Christendom', and the small town that nestles on its northern shores. Despite the obvious advantages of the sheltered waterways, the Haven saw only limited development until the 20th century. Although there is evidence of earlier settlements and shipping activity, the town as it is now and the original dock sprang up in the late 1700s to house a small whaling community that had fled from Nantucket, Massachusetts, during the American War of Independence. The military saw the potential for shipbuilding, but lack of funding at the time prohibited expansion. Various enterprising ideas followed, but by the end of the 19th century, the whaling had all but declined and the Navy had moved to nearby Pembroke Dock.

Lifelines and Modern Controversies

Large-scale fishing off the Pembrokeshire coast threw the port a lifeline in the early 1900s and then, as this too declined, mainly due to over-fishing and subsequent smaller catches, energy production took over as the area's main industry. There were once three refineries and a power station at the head of the Haven. One of the refineries has now closed and the original oil-fired power station was also closed after bowing to considerable public pressure against its plan to burn Orimulsion, a controversial fuel with a contested safety record. More recently, a LNG (Liquid Natural Gas) terminal was opened and in March 2009 plans for a new £1 billion gas-fired power station were approved.

75 Two Faces of the Haven

Escape 21st-century industry on timeless cliffs above Atlantic breakers

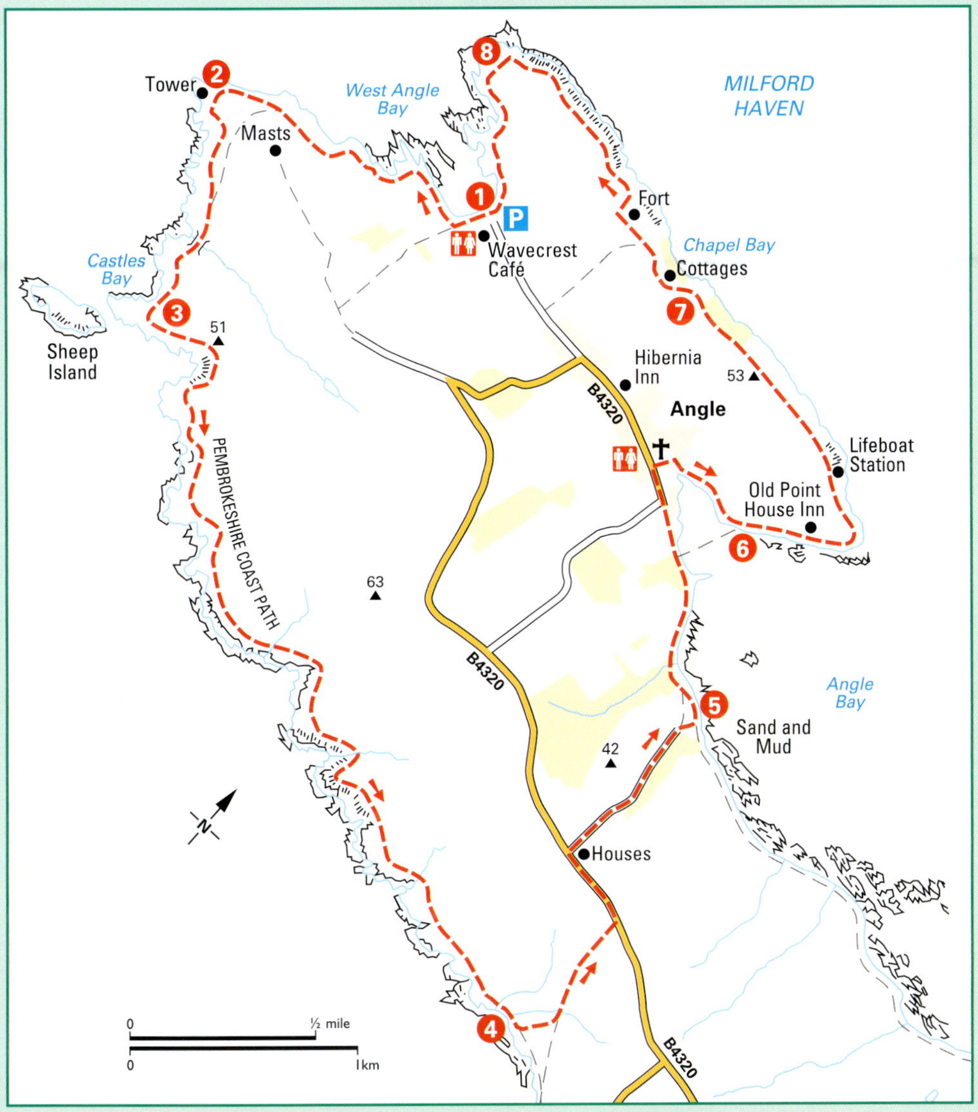

Distance 9 miles (14.5km)

Minimum Time 4hrs

Ascent/Gradient 1,017ft (310m) ▲▲▲

Level of Difficulty ●●●

Paths Coast path and easy tracks over agricultural land, short road section, 9 stiles

Landscape Rugged coastline, magnificent beach and sheltered harbour

Suggested Map OS Explorer OL36 South Pembrokeshire

Start/Finish Grid reference: SM 854031

Dog Friendliness Care needed on cliff tops and near livestock

Parking Car park at West Angle Bay

Public Toilets At start and just off route in Angle village

1 Facing the sea, walk left out of the car park and pass between the café and the public conveniences to a waymarked gate. Follow the field edge along, passing through further gates, and eventually leading out on to the coast, where a right fork drops to a ruined tower on a slender headland.

2 Continue back up from this, pass through further gates and then go down to a footbridge. Climb up from this and pass Sheep Island on your right.

3 Continue along the coast, dropping steeply into a succession of valleys and climbing back up each time. As you reach the northern end of Freshwater West, keep your eye open for a footpath waymarker to the left.

4 Cross a stile and walk up the floor of the valley, swinging left to a stile at the top. Carry on across the next field, and cross another stile, then continue to the road (B4320). Turn left on to the road and walk on past a cluster of houses as far as a right-hand turn. Follow this road all the way down to the coast and turn left on to the coast path to merge on to a drive.

5 Take the drive to a bridleway sign on the right. If the tide is low, you can cross the estuary here and continue along the bank of pebbles to the road on the other side. If it is not low tide, carry on along the drive to join a road that leads into Angle village and bear right by the church to follow a dirt track over a bridge and around to the right.

6 Continue around, pass the Old Point House Inn on your left and follow field edges to the gravel turning point above the lifeboat station on your right. Keep straight ahead, through a gate, and continue through a succession of fields into a wooded area.

7 You will join a broad track that runs around Chapel Bay cottages and fort. Keep straight ahead to follow the narrow path back above the coast. This eventually rounds the headland by Thorn Island.

8 As you descend into West Angle Bay, the path diverts briefly into a field to avoid a landslide. Continue downwards and then bear right on to a drive that drops you back with no further diversions to the car park.

76 Broad Haven and the Haroldston Woods

This charming walk follows a winding path through mixed woodland then provides an easy stroll on the Haroldston cliffs and on past Iron Age remains

Below: Low tide on Little Haven

Main image: The sea sweeps in onto the gentle sands of Broad Haven and Little Haven beaches

Woodland walking is something of a rarity along the Pembrokeshire Coast Path, so this short stretch of permissive path, which sneaks through a narrow strip of woodland separating Broad Haven from Haroldston, makes a refreshing diversion from the usual salty air and the cries of the seabirds. This is the easiest of the Pembrokeshire walks in the book, with an almost billiard table-level section of coast path, some of which has been surfaced for access by wheelchair users. The artificial path, however, takes nothing away from the magnificent scenery.

Eroding Cliffs

The cliffs here are of softer shales and millstone grit, making them prone to erosion and subsidence – as you'll witness firsthand along the way. Amazingly, this whole stretch of coast sits on top of huge coal reserves, but the last colliery, which was situated further north in Nolton Haven, actually closed down in the early 1900s.

As you progress southwards, you'll pass the crumpled remains of an Iron Age fort on Black Point – although this is rapidly becoming separated from the main cliff by a landslide – and also a diminutive standing stone, known as the Harold Stone, which is tucked away in a field on the left as you approach Broad Haven. It's said to mark the spot where Harold, the Earl of Wessex, defeated the Welsh in the 11th century, but it's actually more likely to be a remain from the Bronze Age.

Coastal Resort

Broad Haven is about as close as you'll get to a traditional seaside resort in North Pembrokeshire. The town's popularity as a holiday destination blossomed in the early 1800s, but recent years have seen an acceleration in development that has resulted in almost wall-to-wall caravan parks and a significant rise in the number of residential properties. The beach is beautiful, with gently sloping sands encased in brooding dark cliffs.

As well as the usual selection of family holidaymakers, it's a popular place with windsurfers. This is due partly to a shop and rental centre behind the beach, and because the prevalent south-westerlies that blow across and onshore from the left make it a safe but fun place to play in the sometimes sizeable surf.

At low tide it's possible to walk south along the beach to the charming village of Little Haven. A walk northwards will reveal some fascinating rock formations beneath the headland. These include Den's Door, an impressive double arch in a rugged sea stack; the Sleek Stone, a humpback rock forced into its contorted position by a geological fault; and Shag Rock and Emmet Rock. Contorted layers of rock are also clearly visible in the main cliffs.

76 Broad Haven and the Haroldston Woods

A stone reputedly marks the spot where Earl Harold of Wessex triumphed in battle

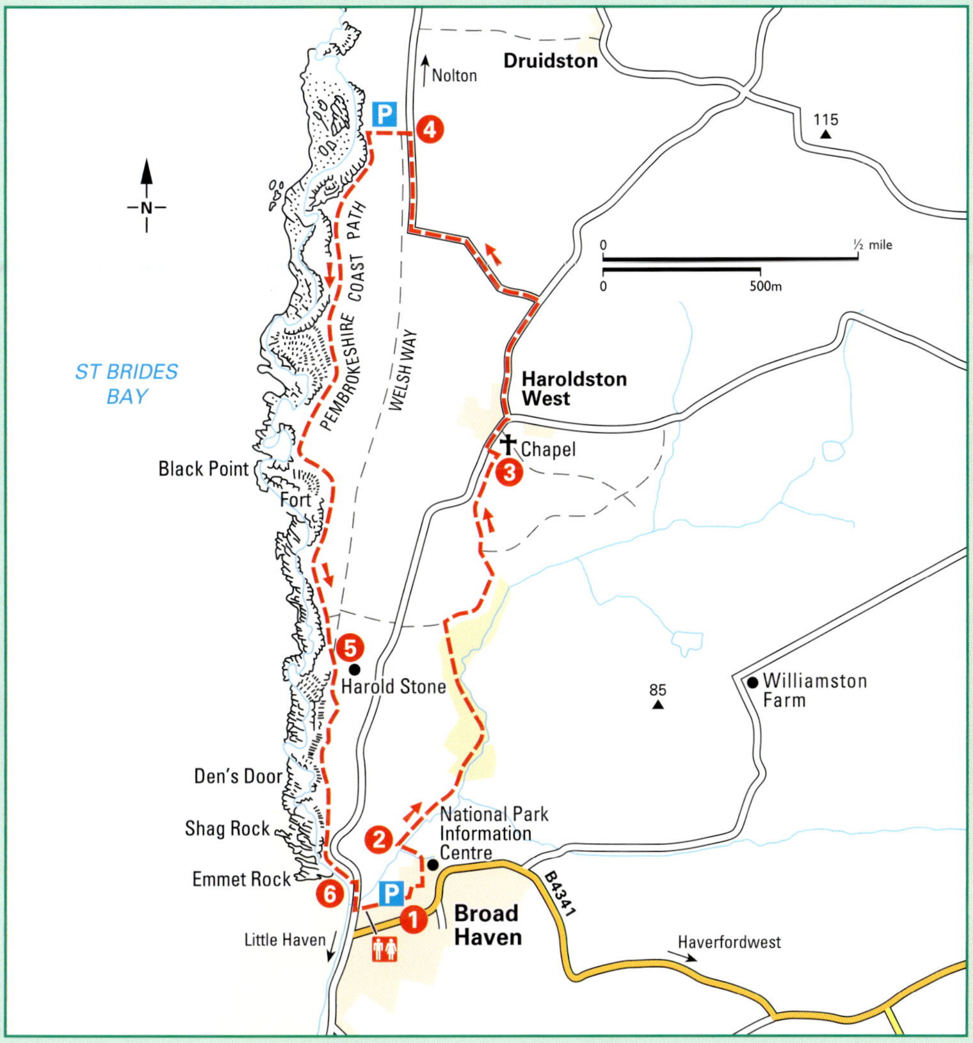

Distance 3.5 miles (5.7km)

Minimum Time 1hr 30min

Ascent/Gradient 290ft (88m) ▲▲▲

Level of Difficulty ●●●

Paths Woodland trail, country lanes and coast path, no stiles

Landscape Mixed woodland and lofty cliffs above broad beach

Suggested Map OS Explorer OL36 South Pembrokeshire

Start/Finish Grid reference: SM 863140

Dog Friendliness Poop scoop around car park and beach, care needed on cliff tops

Parking Car park by tourist information centre in Broad Haven

Public Toilets Between car park and beach

1 From anywhere in the car park, walk towards the National Park information centre and follow a waymarked path that runs between the information centre and the coastguard rescue building. Fork left at the junction with the holiday park path and continue to a kissing gate, where you cross a small footbridge to another junction with a path from the holiday park. Turn half-right, through a kissing gate, to continue with the stream on your left.

2 Cross the stream by another bridge and now, with the stream and valley floor to your right, continue easily upwards until you reach a T-junction of paths by a fingerpost. Turn right here, past a bench on the right, and then swing left to continue upwards to another junction of paths by a small chapel.

3 Turn left to the road and then right on to it to walk uphill, with the church on your right. Keep ahead at the T-junction, then take the first left, towards Druidston Haven. Follow this road over a cattle-grid as far as a sharp right-hand bend. Continue for another 300yds (274m) to the Haroldston Chin parking area and a gate on the left.

4 Go through the gate and follow the well-surfaced track down towards the coast. On reaching the cliff tops, bear around to the left and continue past Black Point.

5 After passing the Harold Stone on your left, the path starts to drop, generally quite easily but there is one steep step. Follow the path down to meet the road and keep right to drop to the walkway above the beach.

6 Cross over the bridge and then, just before the road you are on merges into the main road, turn left on to a tarmac footpath that leads through a green back to the car park.

77 A Pilgrimage Around St Non's Bay

From the cathedral city founded by Wales' patron saint, this magical walk leads to the ruined chapel and holy well said to mark his birthplace

Main image: Pembrokeshire at its best – beautiful St Non's Bay

Above: St Non's Well

This walk makes a great evening stroll. The paths that lead from the city are pleasant and easy to follow, but they're quickly forgotten as you step out into the more glamorous surroundings of the coast. The all-too-short section of towering buttresses and jagged islets leads easily to a spot that can claim to be the very heart of spiritual Wales – the birthplace of St David. The serenity of the location soothes the mind in readiness for the short jaunt back to the compact little city he founded.

Birth of a Patron Saint

Considering the immense influence he has had on Welsh culture, little is known about the patron saint himself. His mother is said to be St Non, derived from Nun or Nonita, who was married to a local chieftain called Sant. They settled somewhere near Trwyn Cynddeiriog, the rocky bluff that forms the western walls of the bay named after her.

Legend suggests that David was born around AD500, in the place where the ruined chapel stands today. Although a fierce storm raged throughout his birth, a calm light was said to have lit the scene. By the morning, a fresh spring had erupted near by, becoming the Holy Well of St Non and visited on this walk. St David went on to be baptised by St Elvis at Porthclais, in water from another miraculous spring. Judging from his parentage, David would have been well educated. According to tradition, he made a number of religious journeys, including one to Jerusalem, before finally returning to his birthplace in around 550. He then founded a church and monastery at Glyn Rhosyn, on the banks of the River Alun, on the site of the present St David's Cathedral, where he set about trying to spread the Christian word to the mainly pagan locals. St David's Day is celebrated on 1 March and St Non, who saw out her life in Brittany, is remembered on the following day.

St David's is little more than a pretty village, though it boasts the title 'city' due to its magnificent cathedral. It's a wonderful place that doesn't seem any the worse for the amount of tourism that it attracts. Known as Tyddewi – 'David's House' – in Welsh, the city grew as a result of its coastal position at the western extreme of the British mainland: it would have been linked easily by sea to Ireland and Cornwall. As well as the cathedral and the ruins of the Bishop's Palace, it houses a plethora of gift shops and the National Park information centre, close to the car park, is one of the finest in the country.

77 A Pilgrimage Around St Non's Bay

Enjoy easy walking around the wonderful coastline that gave birth to St David

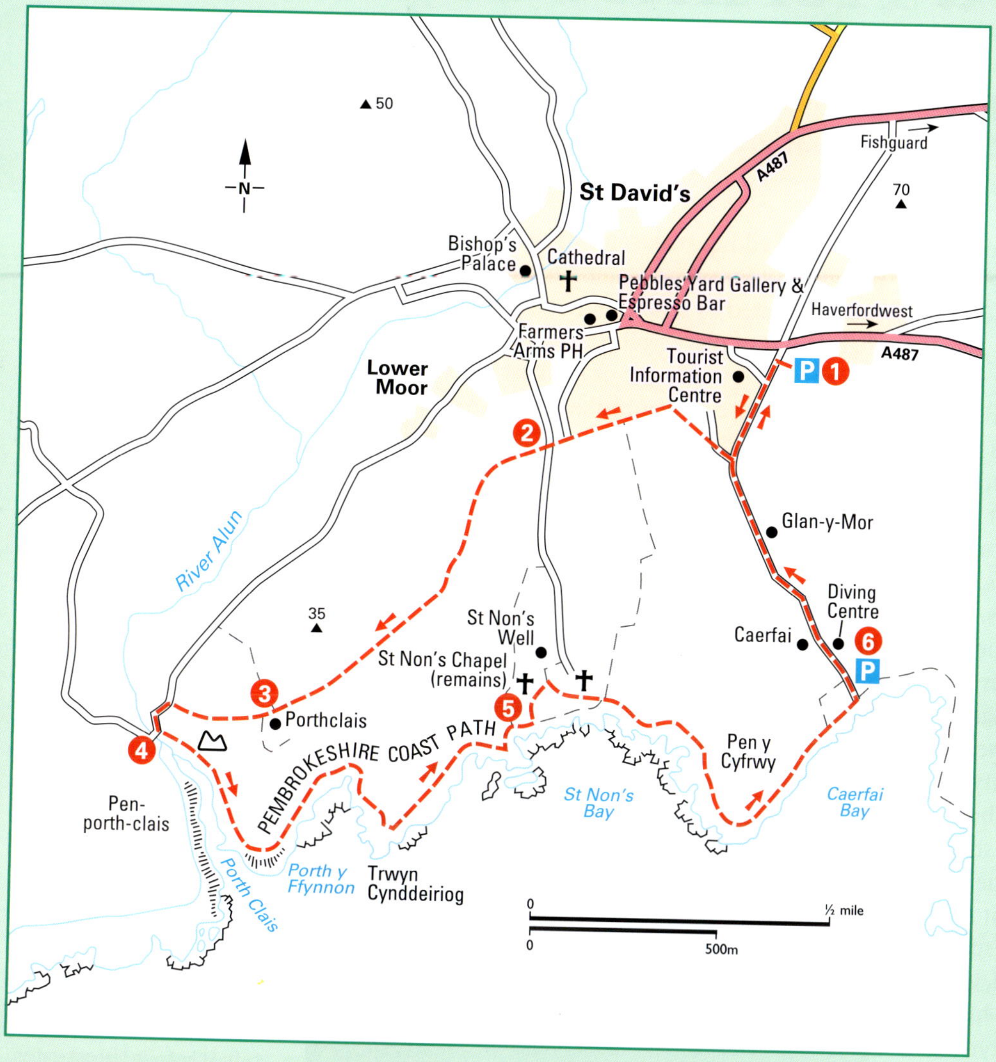

Distance 3.5 miles (5.7km)

Minimum Time 1hr 30min

Ascent/Gradient 262ft (80m) ▲▲▲

Level of Difficulty ●●●

Paths Coast path and clear footpaths over farmland, 2 stiles

Landscape Leafy countryside and dramatic cliffs

Suggested Map OS Explorer OL35 North Pembrokeshire

Start/Finish Grid reference: SM 757252

Dog Friendliness On lead around St Non's Chapel and well

Parking Pay-and-display car park in St David's

Public Toilets Next to tourist information centre

1 Turn left out of the car park in St David's and walk down the road, as if you were heading for Caerfai Bay. As the houses thin out, you'll see a turning on the right that leads to more dwellings. Take this turning, and turn left on to a waymarked bridleway. Follow this between hedges, past the end of a road and on to reach a junction with another road.

2 Walk straight across and take the waymarked path to a fork, where you keep right to continue to a stile. Cross and keep to the left of the field to another stile, where you keep straight ahead again. This leads to a farmyard, which is also a caravan park.

3 Go through the gate and turn left towards the farmyard and then right. As the drive swings left, keep straight ahead with the hedge to your right. Continue across this field and drop down between gorse bushes, keeping straight ahead at a crossroads of paths, to the road at Porth Clais. Turn left to the bottom of the valley and then, before crossing the bridge, turn left on to the coast path.

4 Climb up steeply on to the cliff tops and bear around to the left towards Porth y Ffynnon. The next small headland is Trwyn Cynddeiriog, where there's a grassy platform above the cliffs if you fancy a rest. Continue into St Non's Bay and look for a footpath on the left that leads to the ruined chapel.

5 From the chapel, head up to a gate that leads to St Non's Well and, from there, follow the path beneath the new chapel and back out on to the coast path. Turn left to climb easily on to Pen y Cyfrwy, continue around this and drop down towards Caerfai Bay.

6 You'll eventually come out beneath the Caerfai Bay car park where you turn left on to the road. Follow this past the Diving Centre to St David's and the start of the walk.

79 A Rocky Ramble Around the Head

This inspiring walk is an easy stroll around dramatic cliffs and past ancient remains on one of mainland Britain's most westerly points

Steeped in legend, peppered with the evidence of civilisations past, and scenically stunning, it would be difficult to imagine a more atmospheric place than St David's Head. For full effect, visit at sunset and watch the sky turn red over the scattered islets of the Bishops and Clerks.

Carn Llidi, a towering monolith of ancient rock that has all the attributes of a full-blown mountain, yet stands only 594ft (181m) above sea level, dominates the headland. Its heather- and gorse-covered flanks are alive with small heathland birds, which chatter from the swaying ferns and dart for cover in the hidden crannies of dry-stone walls.

The coast, when you meet it, is at its intricate finest; a succession of narrow zawns (clefts), broken up by stubborn headlands that thrust defiantly into the ever-present swells. The Head itself is magnificent and a few minutes spent exploring will uncover rocky terraces that offer shelter from the wind and stunning views to Ramsey Island.

The Warrior's Dyke

Despite its hostile demeanour, St David's Head was once home to a thriving Iron Age community whose members lived in huts and kept their livestock in a field system, the remains of which are still visible.

The headland, naturally guarded by the ocean on three sides, was also defended by the Clawydd-y-Milwry (the Warrior's Dyke) at its eastern edge. The dyke is actually formed by three ditches and two ramparts that cut across the neck of the headland. The main bastion, a dry-stone wall that would once have stood around 15ft (4.6m) tall, is still easily visible as a linear pile of stones and rocks. Within the fort there are a number of standing stones, stone circles and the remains of basic huts. These impressive defences are thought to have been built around AD100.

Burial Chambers

At least 3,000 years older, but well worth seeking out, is Coetan Arthur, a Neolithic quoit, or burial chamber, which stands directly above a narrow zawn, bounded on its eastern walls by the red-coloured crags of Craig Coetan, a popular climbing venue. Coetan Arthur consists of a 12ft (3.7m) long capstone, propped up on a smaller rock. The quoit would have originally been covered with earth to form a mound, but this has long since been eroded away. There is evidence of several more burial chambers near the summit of Carn Llidi.

Happily, both St David's headland and Carn Llidi are in the care of the National Trust and you are free to wander at will to investigate. However, you should bear in mind that these fascinating sites are Scheduled Ancient Monuments and so are protected by law from interference.

Main image: The walk leads out to St David's Head from behind the wide beach of Whitesands Bay

Inset: Looking back from St David's Head down the coast to St Justinian's and Ramsey Island

79 A Rocky Ramble Around the Head

Climb from Whitesands Beach to explore an atmospheric headland

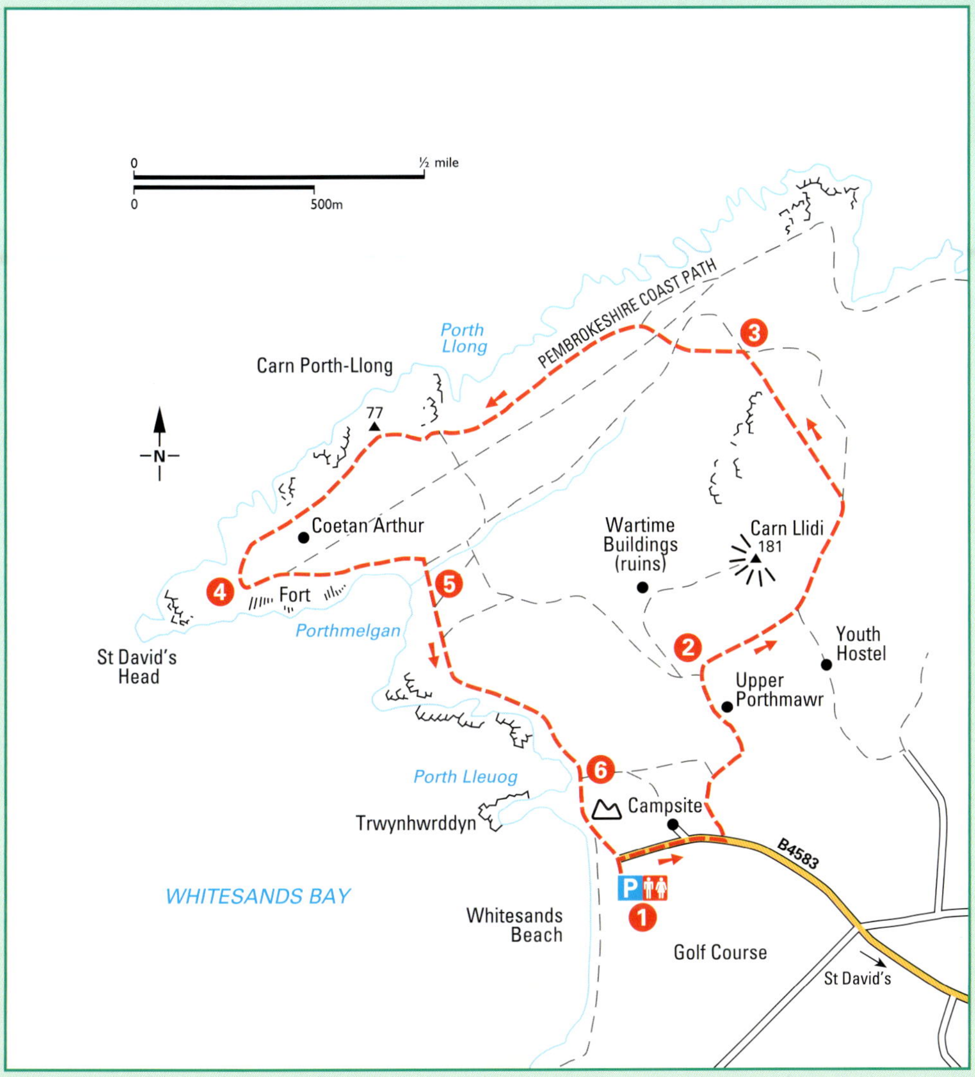

Distance 3.5 miles (5.7km)

Minimum Time 2hrs

Ascent/Gradient 425ft (130m) ▲▲▲

Level of Difficulty ●●●

Paths Coast path, clear paths across heathland, 1 stile

Landscape Dramatic cliffs, heather- and gorse-covered hillsides

Suggested Map OS Explorer OL35 North Pembrokeshire

Start/Finish Grid reference: SM 734271

Dog Friendliness Care needed on cliff tops and near livestock

Parking Whitesands Beach

Public Toilets At start

1 From Whitesands Beach head up the road, pass the campsite and take the second track on the left. Bear right where this track splits and continue around a left-hand bend to walk up to the buildings. Keep left to walk between the houses, then carry on to a gate.

2 Turn right on to the open heathland and follow the footpath along the wall beneath Carn Llidi. Keep going past the track that drops to the youth hostel on the right, and continue around to where the path splits. Take the higher track and carry on in the same direction until, at the corner of a wall, a clear track runs diagonally left towards the coast.

3 Follow this to the coast path, where there's a large fingerpost, and turn left to hug the cliff tops. At Porth Llong, the path bears right to climb to a cairn. The headland is a labyrinth of paths and tracks – for maximum enjoyment, stick as close to the cliff tops as possible. The official coast path doesn't go as far as the tip of the peninsula, but plenty of other tracks do, so you are free to follow one as far out as you wish.

4 From the tip, turn left and make your way through the rocky outcrops on the southern side of the headland. As you approach Porthmelgan you will see an obvious path that traverses the steep hillside; pick up this path and follow it down into a valley, which shelters a small stream.

5 Cross the stream and climb up the steps on the other side. Continue to a kissing gate where the National Trust land ends and here maintain your direction. Pass above Porth Lleuog and the distinctive rocky promontory of Trwynhwrddyn, which is worth a visit in its own right if you have a few moments to spare.

6 The path then drops steeply down to the road at the entrance to Whitesands Beach.

80 Walk with Angels Above Newport

A coastal exploration of the Pembrokeshire town of Newport is followed by a stiff climb on to Carn Ingli, one of Britain's most sacred hilltops

The domination of Newport's skyline by the bold, rock-capped summit of Carn Ingli seems to make the two inseparable, so it makes sense to explore both in one walk. The walk's coastal section is easy to follow and thoroughly enjoyable, as the path traces a varied line along the Nyfer Estuary, at one stage following the actual sea wall. The tracks that cross the common on the other hand are rough. In late summer, when the bracken is fully grown, they can be difficult to follow in places. They're worth sticking with though, for the views from the jagged rocks of the peak are among the best in the Pembrokeshire Coast National Park.

Once a thriving port immersed predominantly in the wool trade, Newport was the former capital of the Marcher Lordship of Cemmaes, the only one to escape the abolition imposed by King Henry VIII in the 16th-century Acts of Union. William Fitz-Martin, who moved to Newport from nearby Nevern, granted a number of privileges to the town, including the right to elect its own mayor, something it still has to this day. There is also the beating of the bounds on horseback by the mayor, which takes place every August. The local castle, which was once the home of the aforementioned lord, has since been incorporated into a grand mansion house and is now in private ownership.

The Rock of Angels

Often described as one of the most sacred sites in Britain, the lofty heights of Carn Ingli were well known by the mystical St Brynach, who scaled them in order to commune with angels. After a life of persecution – the Irish-born saint was made most unwelcome by the Welsh when he returned from his pilgrimage to the Holy Land – he finally settled in Nevern, where he built his church. It remains one of the most visited in Pembrokeshire due to its ancient Celtic cross and a yew tree that appears to bleed. A second cross, carved into the rocky hillside, has seen so many visitors that the stones beneath it are now as smooth as glass.

Judging from the remains of Iron Age fortresses and Bronze Age huts, there was human activity on Mynydd Carningli long before Christianity. The size of these settlements suggests that the hillside would once have supported fairly large communities. Perhaps the existence of standing stones nearby demonstrates that early settlers were also aware of the mountain's special powers.

Below: Carn Ingli looms behind Newport

80 Walk with Angels Above Newport

See where an Irish saint communed with heavenly beings

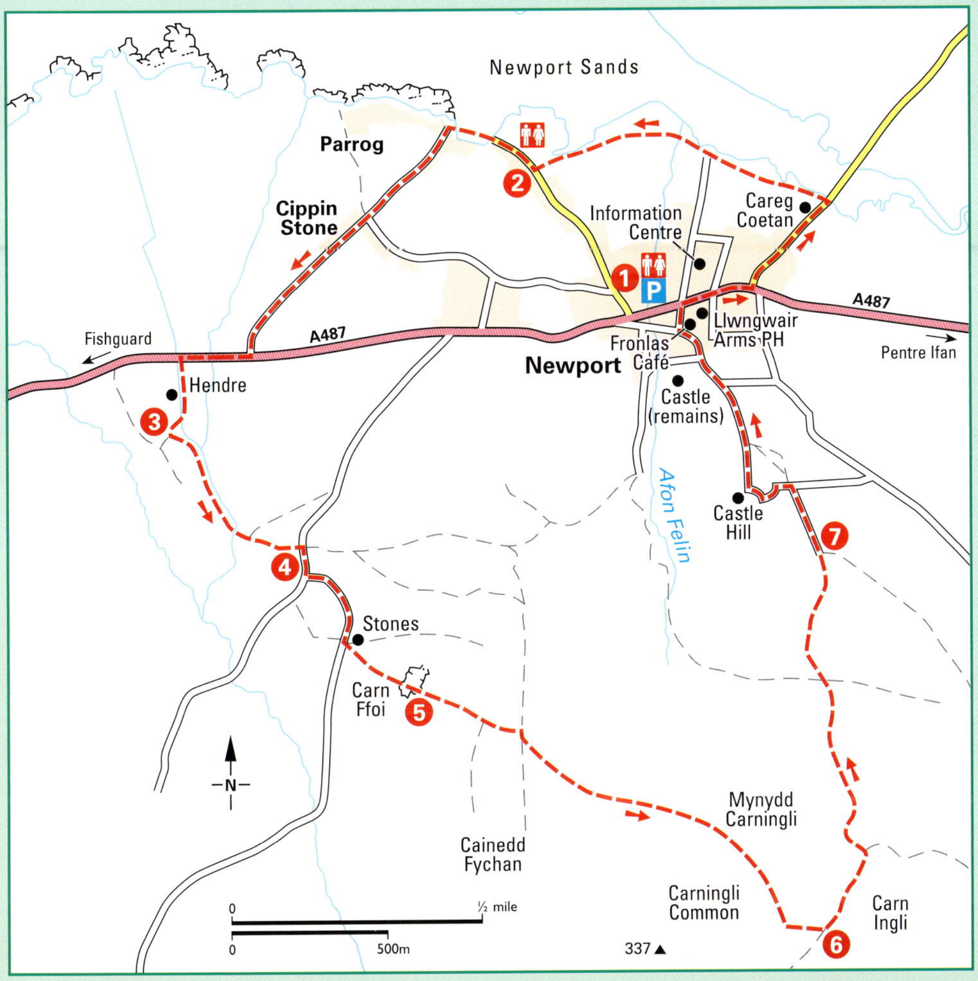

Distance 5.5 miles (8.8km)

Minimum Time 3hrs 30min

Ascent/Gradient 1,080ft (329m) ▲▲▲

Level of Difficulty ●●●

Paths Easy coastal footpaths, boggy farm tracks, rough paths over bracken and heather-covered hillsides, 2 stiles

Landscape Attractive harbour, farmland and rock-capped moor

Suggested Map OS Explorer OL35 North Pembrokeshire

Start/Finish Grid reference: SN 057392

Dog Friendliness Care on roads, poop scoop on coast path section

Parking Free car park opposite information centre, Long Street

Public Toilets At start and near Parrog

1 Turn right out of the car park and left on to the High Street. Fork left into Pen y Bont and continue to the bridge, where a waymarked footpath leads off to the left. Follow this along the estuary to a small road.

2 Turn right on the road and walk past the toilets to its end, where the path then follows the sea wall. Continue to another lane (signed 'Coast Path' as this is diversion for high tide) and turn left to follow it up to the A487. Turn right on to this road, then turn left to continue walking up the drive of Hendre Farm.

3 Go through the gate, to the left of the buildings, and follow the track to a gate where you bear left to follow a small stream. The path emerges on to open ground and hugs the left edge of the field to reach another gate. Continue in the same line along a hedged section, boggy for most of the year. Keep ahead at the stile to climb up to the road.

4 Turn right on to the road and then fork left to continue past some houses to a pair of huge stones on the left. Pass through these stones and follow the faint track up to a rocky tor. Head up from this towards the larger tor of Carn Ffoi. From the top of here you'll be able to pick up a clearer path that leads through an old field system that is defined by small, ruined walls. Continue as far as the obvious corner of a fenced-off field.

5 Now bear half right on to a clear footpath that leads across the hillside, aiming towards the obvious top of Carn Ingli, which rises ahead of you. Fork left after 50yds (46m) and then continue across the hillside beneath the high point of Carningli Common. The path bears right to climb into the saddle between Carningli Common and the rocky top of Mynydd Carningli. Continue to the far end of the rocky ridge and then bear left to follow a faint path up on to the ridge top.

6 Follow the ridge line northwards and drop down, again on faint footpaths, to join a good, clear track that runs straight down the hillside. Continue on this, keeping straight ahead at two crossroads, then turn left and then right when you get to the next junction. This drops you down to a gate in a corner, which leads on to a lane.

7 Take the lane to a crossroads and turn left to the road head, where you turn right. Follow this down to a junction in College Square, where you turn left. Then turn right, on to Church Street. Continue into the centre and turn right into Market Street to the main road, which you cross into Long Street.

81 The Sublime Mawddach

This walk treads in the footsteps of William Wordsworth, J. M. W. Turner and Charles Darwin, who all visited beautiful Barmouth to work and explore

Below: Sandbanks are visible in the estuary at low tide

Bottom: Wild flowers on a hillside above the Mawddach Estuary

Barmouth (once better known in Welsh as *Y Bermo*), used to be a seaport, trading the coarse woollen goods of Merionydd with the Americas. In those days the village cottages were strung out across terraces in the cliffs and there was one pub, the Corsygedol Arms, for the traveller. There wasn't enough room to squeeze the main road from Harlech between those rocks and the sea, so it bypassed the village and instead went inland, over the Rhinog mountain passes.

In the mid-19th century all this changed. Barmouth built a main street on the beach; visitors became more frequent and the resort's sea and sand attracted gentry from the Midlands. Barmouth also came to the notice of the famous: the poet William Wordsworth said of the Mawddach Estuary that it was 'sublime' – and equal to any in Scotland. Artists like J. M. W. Turner and Richard Wilson came to capture the changing light and renowned beauty of estuary and mountainside. In 1867 the railway came, and a new bridge was engineered across the estuary sands. It was half a mile (800m) long and had a swing section across the main channel to allow shipping to pass.

Glorious Setting

Today you can see that Barmouth is not as smart as it was in its heyday. It is still in the most wonderful situation, though, and as you step on to the wooden boards of that half-mile foot and railway bridge you may feel exactly what Wordsworth felt.

The view is best when the sun's shining and the tide's half out. That way the waters of the Mawddach will be meandering like a pale blue serpent amid pristine golden sandbars. Across the estuary your eyes cannot help but be drawn to mighty heights of Cadair Idris. As you get to the other side and look back to Barmouth, you will see how this town has been built into the rocks of the lower Rhinogs. Once across the bridge you're ready to explore those wooded foothills. Through Arthog the path climbs enchantingly between oak trees and you find yourself looking across to waterfalls that thunder into a wooded chasm. Then at the top you are presented with a unified view of all that you have seen little by little so far: the estuary, the sandbars, the mountains and the yawning bridge. By the time you return to Barmouth you will have experienced that 'sublime' Mawddach.

81 The Sublime Mawddach

Cross the Mawddach Estuary by historic footbridge for grand views of mountains, sand and water

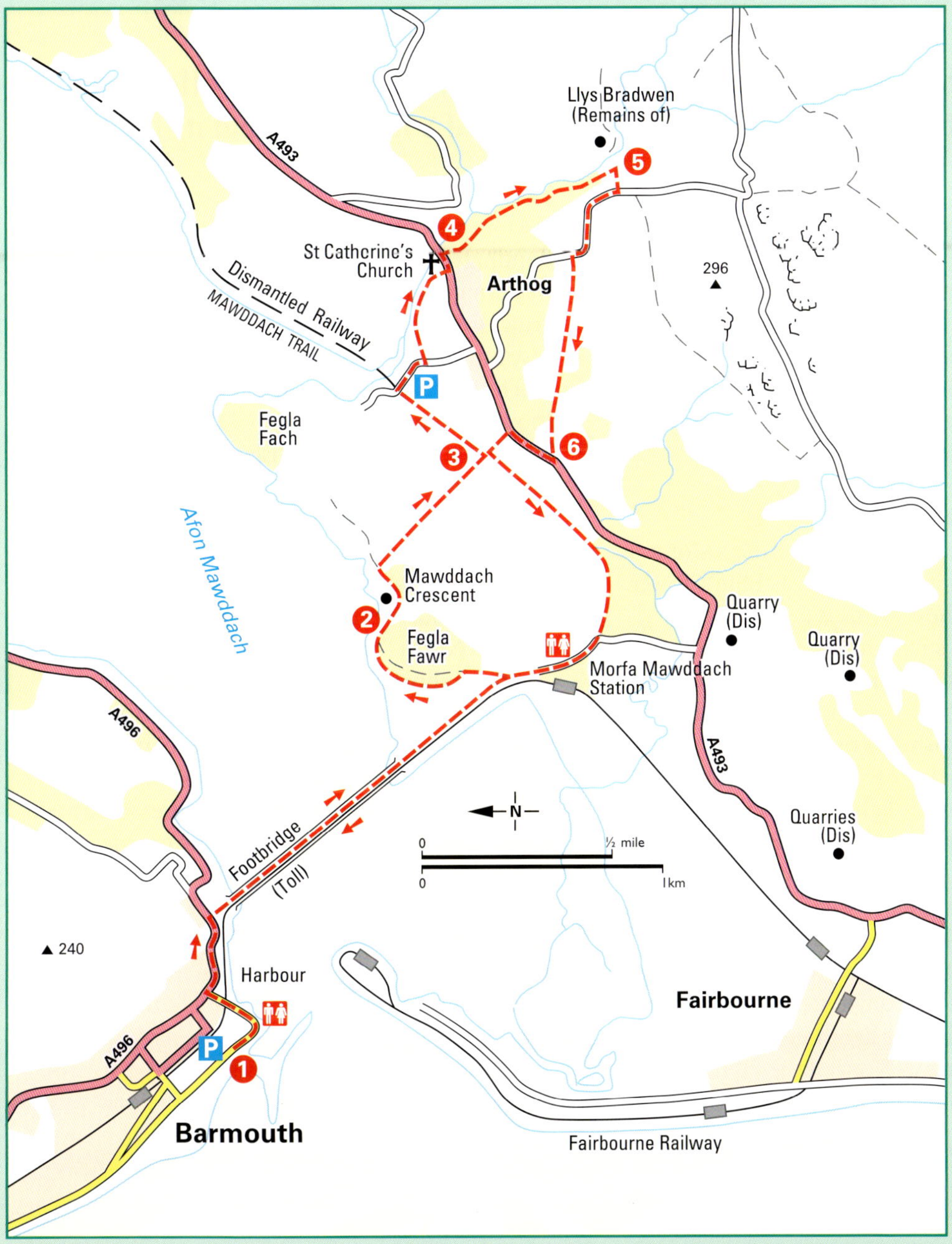

Distance 6 miles (9.7km)

Minimum Time 4hrs

Ascent/Gradient 656ft (200m) ▲▲▲

Level of Difficulty ●●●

Paths A bridge, good tracks and woodland paths, 6 stiles

Landscape Estuary and wooded hills

Suggested Map OS Explorer OL23 Cadair Idris & Llyn Tegid

Start/Finish Grid reference: SH 613155

Dog Friendliness Dogs should be on lead at all times

Parking Car park on seafront

Public Toilets At Barmouth's car park, or near Morfa Mawddach Station

1 Follow the promenade around the harbour, then go over the footbridge across the estuary; you will have to pay a toll to make the crossing. On reaching the path along the south shore, turn left along the grassy embankment to a track rounding the wooded knoll of Fegla Fawr on its seaward side.

2 At the houses of Mawddach Crescent, take the track passing to their rear. Rejoin the track along the shoreline until you reach a gate on the right marking the start of a bridleway heading inland across the marshes of Arthog.

3 Turn left along the old railway track, then leave it just before the crossing of the little Arthog Estuary and turn right along a tarmac lane beside a small car park. Bear left over a ladder stile and then follow a raised embankment to a wall, which now leads the path to the main Dolgellau road next to St Catherine's Church.

4 Directly opposite the church gate is a footpath beginning with steps into woodland. From there a waymarked path climbs by Arthog.

5 Beyond a stile at the top of the woods, turn right to a lane and right along the lane, then left along a track by the cottage of Merddyn. The track gets narrower and steeper as it descends into more woodland, beneath the boulders of an old quarry and down to the Dolgellau road by Arthog Village Hall.

6 Turn right along the road, then left along a path back to the railway track and the Mawddach Trail. Turn left along the trail and follow it past Morfa Mawddach Station and back across Barmouth's bridge.

83 Conwy: Castle High and Castle Low

Conwy's magnificent castle lies at the foot of the Carneddau, but up in the foothills this walk also visits the Iron Age or Roman remains of Castell Caer

Below: Heather-covered slopes looking from Conwy Mountain towards Penmaen-bach

Main image: The imposing Conwy Castle has eight drum towers and a high curtain wall

Conwy is special. Approaching from Llandudno Junction, three fine bridges (including Thomas Telford's magnificent suspension bridge of 1822) cross the estuary beneath the mighty castle, allowing the road and the railway into this medieval World Heritage Site. The fortress dates back to 1283–88, when King Edward I of England built it as part of his 'iron ring' to repress the rebellious troops of Llewelyn the Great. Great town walls with gates and towers still encircle old Conwy. You should walk these walls – for they offer fine views of the castle, the Conwy Estuary and the rocky knolls of Deganwy.

From the Quayside

The walk description begins at the quayside, not the car park, as you will probably want to take a good look around this medieval town. The route starts on a shoreline path under the boughs of Bodlondeb Wood. Not long after passing through Conwy's suburbs you're walking the hillside, on a path threading through gorse and small wind-twisted hawthorns. If you liked the views from the castle walls, you'll love the view from the Conwy Mountain ridge. Looking back you can see the castle, towering over the town's roof tops; but now added to the scene are the Carneddau, the limestone isthmus of the Great Orme and, across the great sands of Lafan, Anglesey.

There is quite a network of paths criss-crossing the ridge and usually the best course is the highest: you'll need to be on the crest path to see the remains of Castell Caer. This 10-acre (4ha) fort has been linked to both Roman and Iron Age settlers – it has formidable defences, with clearly visible artificial ramparts that overlook spectacular sea cliffs on one side, and a wide view of the land to the south. Beyond the fort, the path misses out the peaks of Penmaen-bach and Alltwen. Instead you should descend to the Sychnant Pass, a splendid, twisting gorge that separates Conwy Mountain from the higher Carneddau peaks.

It's all downhill from here, but the scenery becomes more varied and still maintains interest. As you descend you can see the tidal River Conwy, twisting amongst an expanse of chequered green fields. Little hills present themselves to you, on your way back north. One last one has pleasant woods with primroses and bluebells, and it gives you another fine view of Conwy Castle to add to your collection before returning to base.

83 Conwy: Castle High and Castle Low

Take a tour from historic Conwy up to an outpost of the Celtic era

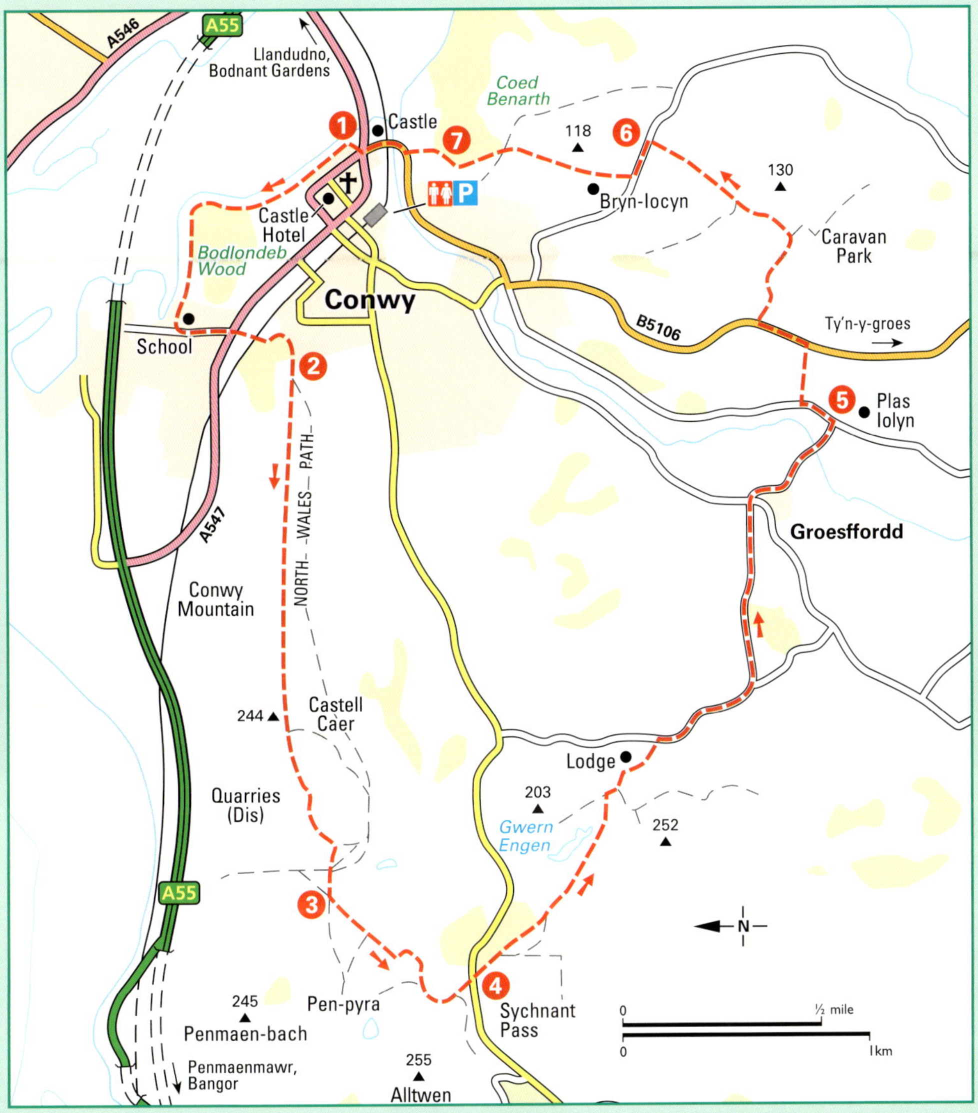

Distance 6.75 miles (10.9km)

Minimum Time 4hrs

Ascent/Gradient 1,493ft (455m) ▲▲▲

Level of difficulty ●●●

Paths Good paths and easy-to-follow moorland tracks, 5 stiles

Landscape Town, coastline, high ridge, farmland and copse

Suggested Map OS Explorer OL17 Snowdon

Start/Finish Grid reference: SH 783775

Dog Friendliness OK on high ridges, but keep on lead elsewhere

Parking Large car park on Llanrwst Road behind Conwy Castle

Public Toilets At car park

1 From Conwy Quay head north-west along the waterfront, going past the Smallest House and under the town walls. Next fork right along a tarmac waterside footpath that rounds Bodlondeb Wood. Turn left along the road, past the school and on to the A547. Cross the road, then go over the railway line by a footbridge. The track beyond the railway skirts a wood in order to reach a lane, and at this point you should turn right.

2 At a fork bear right past a house to a waymarked stile, from which a footpath makes its way up the wooded hillsides on to Mynydd y Dref (Conwy Mountain). Follow the undulating crest of Conwy Mountain and continue past the remains of the 10-acre (4ha) Castell Caer fortress.

3 Several tracks converge in the high fields of Pen-pyra. Here, follow signposts for the 'North Wales Path' along the track heading to the south-west over the left shoulder of Alltwen and down to the metalled road traversing the Sychnant Pass.

4 Follow the footpath from the other side of the road, skirting the woods on your left. Climb over a stile, then carry on past Gwern Engen to meet a track. Go right on the track and then bear left, dropping above the Lodge to reach a lane. Turn right along the lane, then turn left, when you reach the next junction, into Groesffordd village. Cross the road, then take the road ahead that swings to the right past a telephone box, then left (south-east) towards Plas Iolyn.

5 Turn left at the end then opposite a white house take a path up to a cottage. Cross a track and go upfield to the B5106, then left to Conwy Touring Park. Follow the drive to a hairpin, take a waymarked path through trees, recrossing the drive. Through a kissing gate, go up the field-edge, then left along a ridge above successive pastures, finally meeting a lane.

6 Turn left, then right along a track past a communications mast to Bryn-locyn. Continue to a stile by Coed Benarth, from which a path drops beside the wood.

7 Go over a ladder stile on your left-hand side and across a field to a roadside gate. Turn right on to the B5106 to quayside, or turn left to get back to the main car park.

85 How Grey was my Valley

This instructive walks leads through more than 1,500 years of history in a place where industry has given way to a green and pleasant heritage park

A good head of water has served the Greenfield Valley well over the centuries – and this water gushes out from a spring high on the limestone hillsides beneath Holywell. Geologists will tell you that this is a natural phenomenon, but romantics tell a different story. They say St Winefride's Well dates back to the 7th century when St Beuno set up a church here. His daughter Winefride taught in the convent and caught the eye of Caradog, the local chieftain. After being spurned by the young nun, the vengeful Caradog drew his sword and cut off her head. Immediately, a spring emerged where her head hit the ground. Since then, pilgrims have been coming to this 'Lourdes of Wales' to take the healing waters. In 1499 Margaret, the Countess of Derby and mother of Henry VII, financed the building of an ornate chapel around the well.

Basingwerk Abbey

The religious connections also played a prominent role in the 12th century, when the Savignac Order, which was later to be combined with the Cistercians, set up Basingwerk Abbey at the bottom of the hill. The abbey is the first thing you see at the start of the walk and, although it has been in ruins since the Dissolution of the Monasteries, a couple of fine sandstone arches remain in good condition.

The Industrial Revolution

The monks were the first to utilise the power of the stream when they built a corn mill. It was to be one of many industrial buildings that occupied the whole valley from the mid-17th century onwards. Brick chimneys, mill pools, reservoirs and waterwheels sprung up, and steam from those chimneys billowed up through the trees. Thomas Williams of the Parys Mine Company established a rolling mill and the Abbey Wire Mill here, while in the Battery Works up the hill the workforce hammered out brass pots and pans used in the slave trade – ships would leave Liverpool laden with brassware for West Africa, where they would load up with slaves for the Caribbean, returning to Liverpool with sugar, tobacco and cotton.

In 1869 the railway came and by 1912 a full passenger service was operating from Greenfield to Holywell. At a gradient of 1 in 27 it was the steepest conventional passenger railway in Britain, and remained so until its closure in 1954. One by one, the mills shut down. Some were demolished, others left to crumble. Today the valley is a heritage park and relics of the old industries sit among pleasant gardens. As you cross the high fields later in this walk, you can see the new century's industries along the coastline of the Dee Estuary far below.

Below: St Winefride's Well, where pilgrims seek healing

Below right: Handsome sandstone ruins of Basingwerk Abbey

85 How Grey was my Valley

Follow in the footsteps of monks, martyrs and merchants

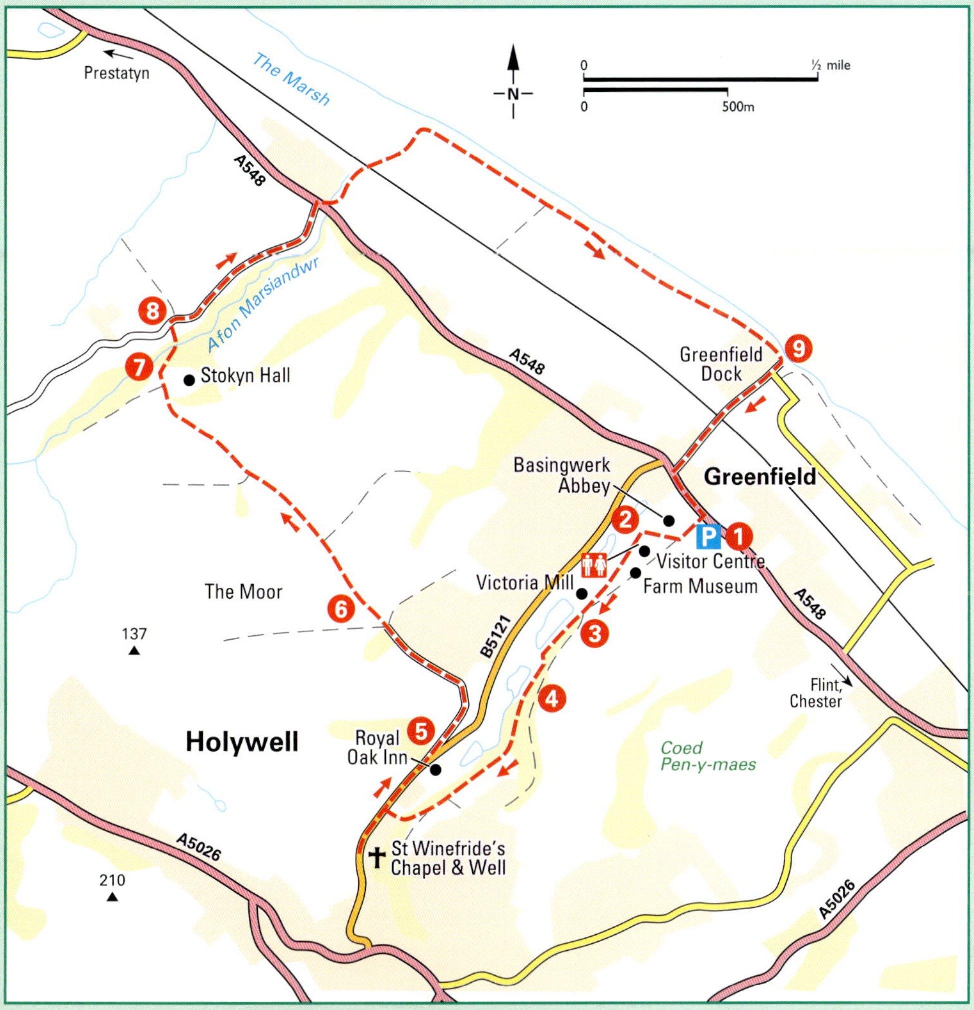

Distance 5 miles (8km)

Minimum Time 3hrs

Ascent/Gradient 558ft (170m) ▲▲▲

Level of Difficulty ●●●

Paths Woodland paths and tracks, lanes, field paths and coastal embankment, 9 stiles

Landscape Wooded former industrial valley, pastured hillside and coast

Suggested Map OS Explorer 265 Clwydian Range

Start/Finish Grid reference: SJ 197775

Dog Friendliness Dogs should be on lead

Parking Just off A548 at Greenfield

Public Toilets By visitor centre

1 Take the footpath that emerges from the back of the car park on the left-hand side and follow it around the abbey.

2 Turn left between the visitor centre and the old schoolhouse on a track that passes Abbey Farm. Take the left fork by the brick walls of Abbey Wire Mill, following the sign to the Fishing Pool, a lily-covered pond.

3 Beyond Victoria Mill take the lower right-hand fork then bear right past some fixed iron gates to pass the crumbling remains of Meadow Mill. Beyond the mill turn left up some steps, climbing up by a weir and back on to the main track.

4 Turn right along the lower track, eventually passing above Hall's soft drinks factory. Beyond a brick chimney, fork off right down to a kissing gate and wind out to the road. Turn left along the road as far as St Winefride's Chapel and Well. When you've viewed these, go back down the road to the Royal Oak Inn.

5 Climb the lane, called Green Bank, that begins from the opposite side of the road. Beyond the houses bear off right along a waymarked track. Keep ahead past the entrance to a small housing estate on a sunken path. Enter a field over a stile at the top.

6 Head out to the distant right corner and continue at the edge of the next field. Maintain your northwesterly direction to a stile and keep going to another, part-way down the boundary. Walk on with a hedge on your right, exiting over a stile onto a track.

7 Leave the cart track where it swings round to the right for a second time and follow a signed footpath across a meadow and then through trees to the banks of Afon Marsiandwr. After crossing the stream the path climbs out of the woods and crosses a field to a lane.

8 Turn right along the lane, following it down to reach the coast road (A548). Cross the road with care. The continuing footpath to the seashore lies opposite, over a step stile. Cross a field and then a railway track, again with care as trains are not infrequent, and continue walking until you get to the inner flood embankments. Turn right.

9 The footpath comes out by Greenfield Dock. Turn right here along the lane back into Greenfield. Turn left to the car park.

Scotland

WALK

Scotland

A country of dramatic natural beauty, Scotland has a long and rugged coastline – much of it unspoiled. With a single land border facing England to the south, the country is otherwise bounded by the North Sea to the east and by the Atlantic Ocean to the west and north and, remarkably, incorporates almost 800 islands.

Scotland consists of roughly the northern third of the island of Great Britain and has a land area of 30,414 square miles (78,772 square kilometres). The islands are in four principal groups – Shetland, Orkney and the Inner and Outer Hebrides – and greatly extend the coastal length. Exact calculations of the length of its coastline, including that of the islands, vary but most agree on a total of more then 8,000 miles (13,000 kilometres).

Many of the islands are no more than sea-lashed rocks but others have been a setting for key events in Scottish history or today play an important role as a natural habitat for rare or endangered species. On the Isle of Arran off Scotland's southwest coast, Walk 90 leads us far back into history to visit Middle Stone Age remains and three dramatic Bronze Age standing stones on Machrie Moor. These stones, of weathered red sandstone, are of considerable size – the largest is 18ft (5.5m) tall – and were once part of a larger circle, and stand close to other stones and circles, the whole area probably a religious centre of some kind.

On the 'holy island' of Iona in the Inner Hebrides walk 91 visits 'Coracle Bay', where St Columba – the man credited with bringing Christianity to Scotland – is said to have landed after his emigration from Ireland in AD563. On Iona, Columba and his 12 disciples founded an oak-log church and a simple monastery that proved to be a key base for the spread of their faith.

English man of letters Dr Samuel Johnson, author of the *Dictionary of the English Language* (1755), was greatly moved by the spiritual impact of the remains on Iona during the visit he made to

the Western Isles in August-November 1773 with his friend and eventual biographer James Boswell. Both men published accounts of their trip, Johnson writing *A Journey to the Western Islands of Scotland* (1775) and Boswell describing his experiences in *The Journal of a Tour to the Hebrides with Samuel Johnson LLD* (1785). Walk 94 also follows in the footsteps of this illustrious couple, to the island of Raasay, where Boswell was entertained by the local laird, Macleod, with strenuous walking, dancing the Highland reel and the drinking of whisky.

A Restorative Drink

On the mainland, walk 102 visits Leith, now a suburb of Edinburgh, but for centuries an important port at the point where the Water of Leith (the principal river that flows through Edinburgh) meets the Firth of Forth (the estuary of the river Forth). In the 1st century AD the Romans stored wine for their legions at Leith and thereafter the port became rich on the trade in claret, once the national drink of Scotland and drunk patriotically by the Jacobites who supported the restoration of James Stuart to the throne. Our walk leads past a mineral water well discovered in 1760, and at its conclusion provides opportunities to enjoy a restorative pint or a couple of drams in one of the many and varied pubs of Leith.

Preceding pages: The pretty village of Crail in Fife was once Europe's largest fish market

Left: Dunnottar Castle perches on a dramatic clifftop near Stonehaven, south of Aberdeen

Far left, inset: Lighthouse at St Abb's Head, Berwickshire

Main image: Beach and hills at Loch Shieldaig, Ross-shire

Below: The quay at Port Logan in the Rhins of Galloway

Far right: Up from Moonen Bay on the Isle of Skye

Main image: 'I'll take the low road' – this one leads down to Loch Diabaig, Ross and Cromarty

Below: Bronze Age standing stones on Machrie Moor, Isle of Arran

Learning and Traditions

There are plenty of pubs on offer, too, in the university town of St Andrews. Walk 100 visits this small town on the Fife coast in which Scotland's oldest university was established in 1410, and provides an opportunity to drink in the charming atmosphere, watch the students wandering about in their distinctive scarlet gowns, and perhaps become acquainted with some of the university traditions that were established in the medieval period – such as the flour and egg fight in St Salvator's Quad on 'Raisin Monday' in November. The walk also leads past the clubhouse of the Royal and Ancient Golf Club, founded in 1754 and one of the most venerable and prestigious clubs for a sport that was established in Scotland in the 15th century.

Other walks also provide insights into Scottish history and traditional ways of life. A short distance to the southeast of St Andrews, Walk 101 visits the East Neuk of Fife, leading through traditional fishing villages including Crail and Anstruther (once so busy as a centre of the herring trade that you could walk right across the harbour stepping from one boat to another).

Far away in the southwest of the country, Port Logan in Galloway is another picturesque village with a past as a centre for fishing, but here all is not as it first appears – for the village was used as the fictional 'Ronansay' in the BBC television series *Two Thousand Acres of Sky* about a mother who begins a new life far away from the inner city. Walk 87 takes in sights that will seem familiar if you watched the series, and also delivers views of magnificent Galloway scenery.

Fish, Dolphins and Birds

Port Logan is not the only place in this chapter where the modern world has left its mark on a traditional setting. Walk 92 along the shores of beautiful Loch Alsh provides views of the Isle of Skye and also of a local salmon farm. The fish farms of Scotland now produce salmon with a fish-counter value of £1 billion each year. They employ 8,500 people and produce 160,000 tonnes of fish a year, enough to give every Briton a 4oz (100g) steak every week. Another successful modern industry in Scotland is marine tourism, now worth £9 million a year. Walk 97 beside Loch Gairloch, a

sea loch in northeastern Scotland, is close to waters that are among the best in the country for seeing dolphins, whales and porpoises. Elsewhere there are wonderful opportunities to see birds. On Walk 103 to St Abb's Head in Berwickshire a birdspotter might see razorbills, guillemots, kittiwakes, herring gulls, shags, fulmars and puffins. This is a bracing walk with wonderful sea and cliff views and a sighting of the dramatically situated St Abb's lighthouse perched on a cliff's edge.

On Orkney, Walk 98 leads past the remarkable 100ft (30m)-deep collapsed sea cave of the Gloup (from a Norse word meaning 'chasm') and onto land on the Brough of Deerness, where in the Mull Head Nature Reserve you'll find high sandstone cliffs on which fulmars, razorbills, guillemots and kittiwakes nest. Watch out also for skuas and gulls, which nest on the heath. Visit in summer and you'll also see beautiful bell heather and purple ling.

Best of the Rest

Arbigland, Birthplace of John Paul Jones

Walk 86 runs along the shore of the Solway Firth and visits Arbigland House and estate in Dumfries and Galloway. This was the birthplace of John Paul Jones, a Scot who emigrated to Virginia and became a key figure in the early years of the United States' Continental Navy. He is celebrated above all for his victory in 1779 in a four-hour naval battle off Flamborough Head against HMS *Serapis* and HMS *Countess of Scarborough*. The walk leads to a museum housed in the cottage on the Arbigland estate in which the naval hero was born plain John Paul on 6 July 1747.

Ardstinchar Castle

From the village of Ballantrae, Walk 88 leads along a stretch of Ayrshire coast past the ruins of Ardstinchar Castle, setting of a dramatic 16th-century family feud involving the local Kennedy family. The quarrel is described in the 1896 novel *The Grey Man* by S R Crockett. Looking out to sea you will be able to drink in views of the beautiful Ailsa Craig, an island in the Firth of Clyde.

Glenashdale Falls, Isle of Arran

From Whiting Bay on the Isle of Arran, Walk 89 is a forest ramble that leads past a wealth of native trees including alder, ash, downy birch, hazel, oak and rowan, as well as more unusual species including the Siberian crab and the Douglas fir, to the beautiful Glenashdale Falls. If it's been raining then your luck's in – the waters, which tumble over a 140ft (43m) drop, look at their very best when the Glenashdale Burn is running fast. You will pass signs to nearby 'Giants' Graves', a group of Neolithic cairns, so you can make the detour to visit this interesting site if you wish.

Glendale, Isle of Skye

Over crofting land, Walk 93 takes you along cliff tops up to Waterstein Head, at 971ft (296m) above sea level the second-highest cliff on Skye. There are wide and magnificent views, and you can see the Neist Point lighthouse, 142ft (43m) above sea level and 62 ft (19m) tall. Film fans may recognise Neist Point and its lighthouse from the 1996 movie *Breaking the Waves*, directed by Danish director Lars von Trier and starring Emily Watson. A graveyard created for the film is still visible on Neist Point.

Diabaig

An enchanting coastal ramble, Walk 96 leads from Torridon village up towards Diabaig past a series of lochs through land associated with water spirits, ghosts and the *Duine Sithe* or fairy folk. One local threat is said to be a water spirit that appears in the form of a white horse, but bears you to a watery death if you fall under its spell and climb up for a ride. You are advised not to make too much noise when you pass the *Cnoc nan Sithe* ('Fairy Knoll').

Loch Shieldaig

Walk 95 introduces you to a cannon salvaged from one of the many ships of the Spanish Armada of 1588 that sank along the Scottish coastline. The walk embarks from Shieldaig village through a birch wood and across a peat bog that is a sea of heather and cotton grass in summer. You pass onto higher ground with views of loch and sea and of the islands of Skye and Raasay.

Dunottar Castle

In a dramatic setting atop sheer 165ft (50m) cliffs above the North Sea, the ruined Dunnottar Castle near Stonehaven in northeastern Scotland was once the hiding place of the country's crown jewels. When Oliver Cromwell's army invaded Scotland in the 17th century the jewels were hidden in the castle by George Ogilvie. Cromwell's troops under General Overton besieged the castle in 1651 but when they finally took the fortress after a siege of eight months, the jewels were missing – they had already been smuggled out. Walk 99 leads from the attractive coastal town of Stonehaven up along the breathtaking cliffs to the inspiring castle ruins and back. Take your binoculars if you have some: there are wonderful sea views and the cliffs are a haven for nesting birds.

86 The Solway Shore from Carsethorn to Arbigland

A bright walk along the seashore leads to the cottage birthplace of John Paul Jones, the 'father of the American Navy', on the Arbigland estate

Above: Humble beginnings – John Paul's father was a gardener on the Arbigland estate

Right: The cottage, now a museum, contains a bronze bust of 'the father of the American Navy' made in 1780

The man hailed in the United States as the 'father of the American Navy' was born John Paul in a poor gardener's cottage at Arbigland, on the Solway coast in 1745. At the age of 13 years old, John signed up as an apprentice seaman journeying to Virginia on the *Friendship of Whitehaven*. He later signed on as third mate on a slave ship, the *King George of Whitehaven*. He lasted two years and advanced to first mate before he quit in disgust with the slave trade. On his passage home he acquired his first command when the captain and mate of his vessel died of fever. As the only qualified man left, John took control and brought the ship safely home. The owners rewarded him with permanent command.

He had a reputation for a fiery temper and was once charged with murder but found not guilty. In 1773 he fled the West Indies, after killing the ringleader of a mutiny, and went to Virginia. It was around this time that he changed his name to John Paul Jones.

In the lead up to the War of American Independence, when the US Congress was forming a Continental Navy, Jones offered his services and was commissioned as a first lieutenant on the *Alfred* in 1775. Later, as captain of the *Providence*, he advised Congress on naval regulations. In 1778, after a daring hit-and-run raid on Whitehaven, he sailed across the Solway to Kirkcudbright Bay with the plan of kidnapping the Earl of Selkirk and ransoming him for US captives. However, the earl was not at home – and the raiding party had to be content with looting the family silver.

Famous Battle

In September 1779, as commodore of a small squadron of French ships, John Paul Jones engaged his ship the *Bonhomme Richard* with the superior HMS *Serapis* and HMS *Countess of Scarborough* off Flamborough Head. After a dreadful four-hour fight, in which Jones was injured and his ship sunk, he eventually won the battle, transferred his crew to the *Serapis* and sailed for Holland with his prisoners and booty. John Paul Jones died in France in 1792 and his body lay in an unmarked grave for more than 100 years. His remains were eventually taken back to the United States amid great ceremony and he was laid to rest in the chapel crypt of the Annapolis Naval Academy in 1913.

The walk leads from Carsethorn along the coast past the delightful 'House on the Shore', built in 1936 as the dower house for Arbigland House; the principal house on the estate had been built in 1755 by gentleman-architect William Craik. After a stretch along the shore, and a chance to inspect an intriguing natural rock arch called the Thirl Stane, you make your way on to the estate road to the cottage in which John Paul was born. The return route leads along inland road and track before going back to the coast for a final stretch along the beach to the car park. Another locally born man who rose to a significant position in the United States was James Craik, who became personal physician to George Washington, first US President.

87 In Port Logan – or is it Ronansay?

Walk into the world of a hit BBC TV drama

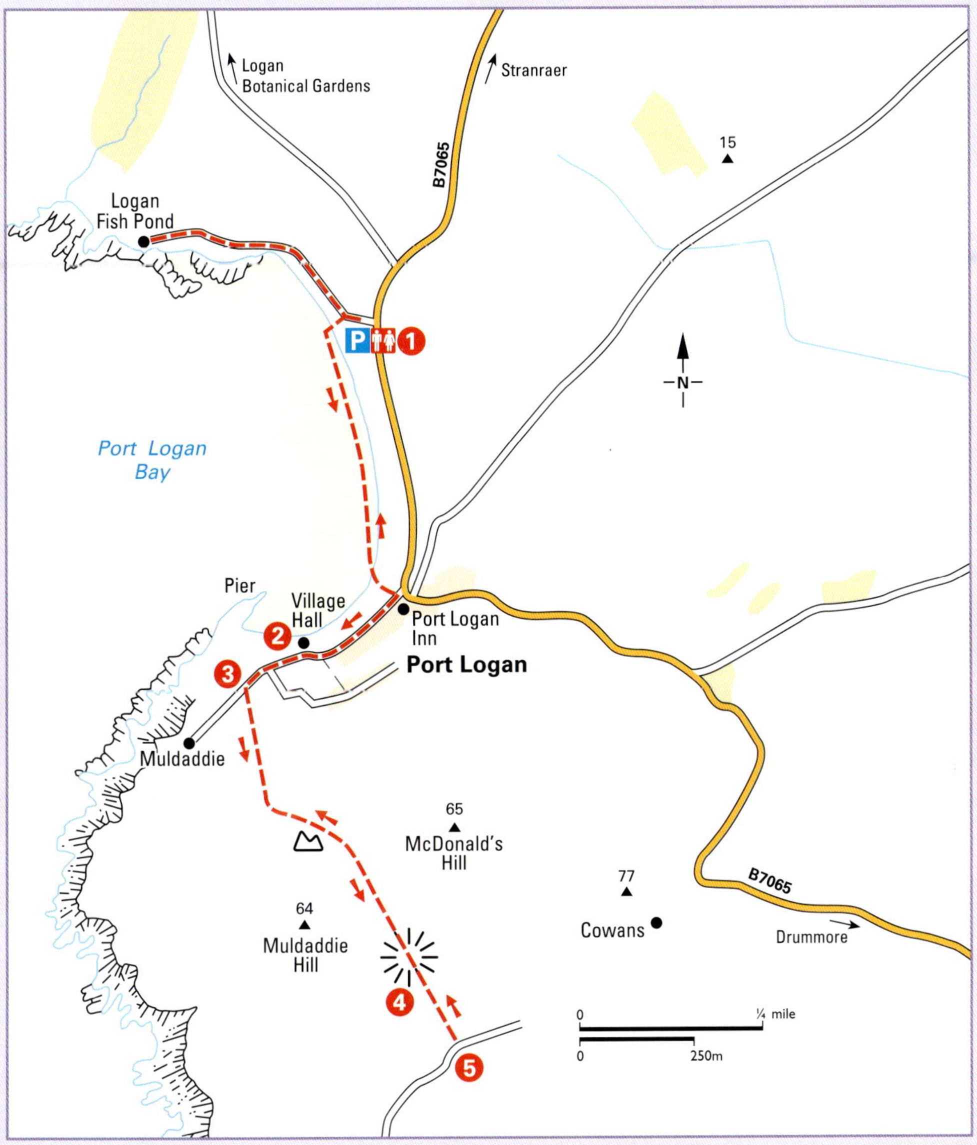

Distance 2.5 miles (4km)

Minimum Time 2hrs

Ascent/Gradient 492ft (150m) ▲▲▲

Level of Difficulty ●●●

Paths Shoreline, country lanes and hill tracks, 1 stile

Landscape Hill, pasture and shoreline

Suggested Map OS Explorer 309 Stranraer & The Rhins

Start/Finish Grid reference: NX 097411

Dog Friendliness Keep on lead near livestock

Parking Public car park on road to Logan Fish Pond

Public Toilets At car park

1 From the car park go across a wooden walkway, down some steps on to the sand and turn left to walk along the beach. When you reach the start of the village, climb on to the road in front of the Port Logan Inn. Turn right and then continue walking along the main street, passing the war memorial to reach the village hall. In *Two Thousand Acres of Sky* the village hall featured as the village school, and had a school sign fixed to the front. There was also a timetable for Caledonian MacBrayne ferries displayed on a notice board on the wall. Opposite the village hall is a small but picturesque harbour with a rather unusual lighthouse. Nowadays, Port Logan harbour is used only by a few pleasure craft.

2 Port Logan was a thriving fishing port in the past and during the filming of the television series, the pier was festooned with fishing gear, gas bottles and sacks of coal, but they were just props. Move away from the harbour area and continue along the road to the farm of Muldaddie.

3 Just before the farm turn left on to an old hill track and head uphill. Near the top, look back downhill for a magnificent view back to the village and across Port Logan Bay to the Mull of Logan. The track is heavily overgrown here, and is blocked by a barrier made from gates, but this can easily be crossed by going over a stile at the side.

4 Continue along the track to a T-junction, following the public footpath sign.

5 Retrace your steps to Port Logan then go back on to the beach, turn right and retrace your steps to the car park. From here you can continue along a rough road to the Logan Fish Pond. It's right at the end on the left and is by the only building there.

88 The Murderous Tale of Ardstinchar Castle

This walk leads past the ruins of a castle that was at the centre of a bloody tragedy in the 16th century, and delivers sea views of the beautiful Ailsa Crag

Main image: In these fields the drama was played out – looking out from Ballantrae across the bay to the rock of Ailsa Craig

Above: Ballantrae was once a thriving fishing village

If the ruins of Ardstinchar Castle could speak, they would tell a tale of murder most foul and of a series of intrigues designed to wipe out one branch of Ayrshire's most powerful family – the Kennedys. The events were described in an ancient manuscript found in a basement in an Edinburgh library; although anonymous, it is believed to be the work of John Mure of Auchindrain House, near Ayr. The writing of S R Crockett, religious minister turned novelist, brought this story to the attention of a wider public. Crockett used the dramatic story as the basis of his novel *The Grey Man*, which was published in 1896. Woven through the book is the factual thread of tragic events that occurred in Ayrshire at the end of the 16th century.

Kennedy Feud

Crockett's novel opens with the fictional burning of Ardstinchar Castle, but he uses this event to outline the origins of the Kennedy feud. This was an attempt by the Earl of Cassillis, the senior Kennedy, to acquire the lands of Crossraguel Abbey. All efforts to persuade Allan Stewart, the Commendator of Crossraguel, having failed, Cassillis seized him, carried him off to his stronghold at Dunure Castle and there 'roasted the hapless Stewart over a slow fire until he signed'. Stewart was rescued by his brother-in-law, Kennedy of Bargany, and Cassillis was brought before the High Court and made to compensate his victim. But Cassillis was allowed to keep the lands for which he had committed the crime.

Moreover, Cassillis was thereafter intent on destroying the house of Bargany – and various plots, intrigues and bloodlettings took place, culminating in the murder of Bargany near Maybole in 1601. Bargany was interred in the family vault at Ballantrae and Cassillis escaped justice once again. But Bargany's ally John Mure, the 'Grey Man' of Crockett's tale, took revenge by having an uncle of Cassillis assassinated.

Suspicion immediately fell on Mure, but he had an alibi. However, there was one witness who could tie Mure to the crime. A young boy had delivered a letter from the intended victim to Mure, who read it then told the boy to return it and say he had not found Mure. To protect himself, Mure and his son strangled the boy and threw him into the sea. When the boy's body washed ashore a few days later, both Mures were arrested, tried and found guilty of murder and also of being involved in the assassination. Sentenced to death, they were executed at Edinburgh in 1611, thus ending the feud and leaving Cassillis free of any retribution.

88 The Murderous Tale of Ardstinchar Castle

Tramp a stretch of the Ayrshire coast that was the setting for a violent feud

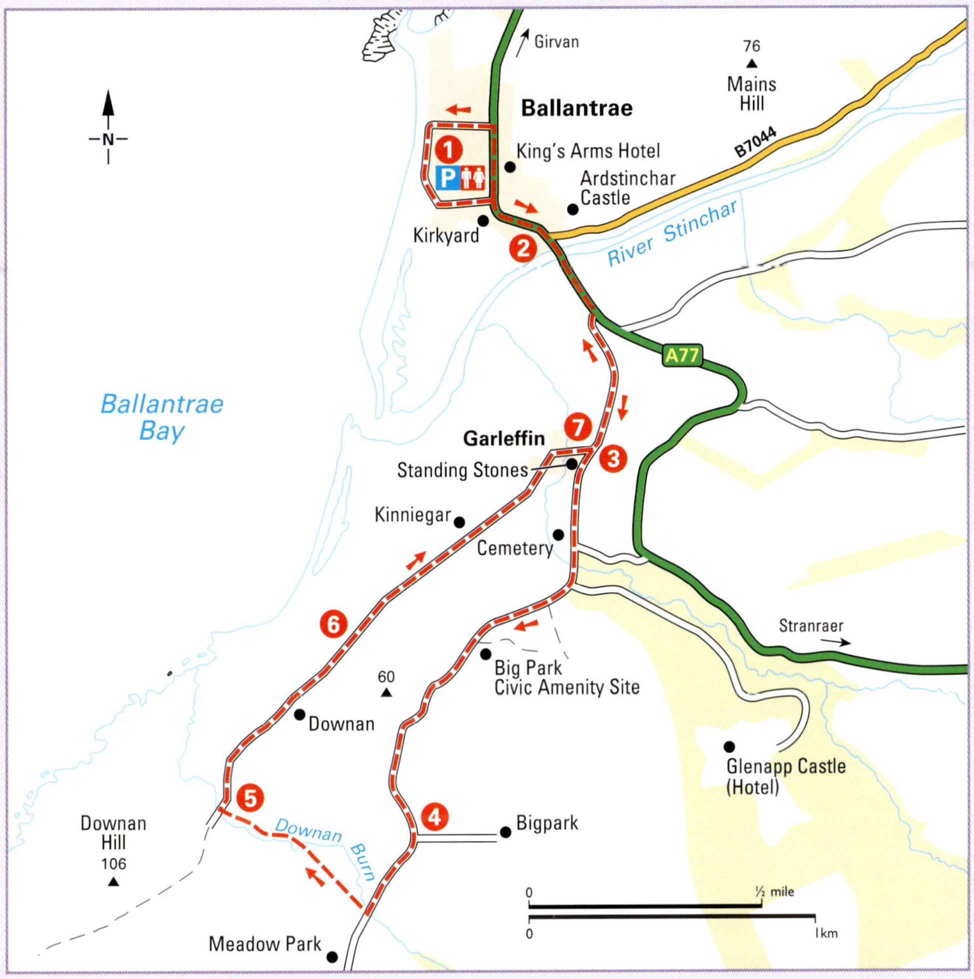

Distance 3 miles (4.8km)

Minimum Time 2hrs

Ascent/Gradient 295ft (90m) ▲▲▲

Level of Difficulty ●●●

Paths Country lanes and farm tracks

Landscape Hillside, pastures and seashore

Suggested Map OS Explorer 317 Ballantrae, Barr & Barrhill

Start/Finish Grid reference: NX 082824

Dog Friendliness Mainly farmland, so keep on lead near livestock

Parking Car park near school on Foreland, Ballantrae

Public Toilets Beside car park

1 Leave the car park and turn left on to the Foreland. At the T-junction with Main Street, cross the road and turn right. Near the outskirts of the village, just before the bridge over the River Stinchar, look up to your left to view the ruins of the former stronghold of the Bargany Kennedy's Ardstinchar Castle. As the castle walls are considered unstable, it is not advisable to go any closer.

2 From here cross the Stinchar Bridge and take the first turning on the right, heading uphill on a narrow country lane and past a row of cottages. At a junction in the road keep to the left but look out for one of the Garleffin Standing Stones in the rear garden of the bungalow at the junction.

3 There's another stone in the front garden of this house but you will see this later in the walk. In the meantime continue uphill, passing the cemetery on your right, then going past Glenapp Castle gates on your left. A little further on you come to the Big Park Civic Amenity Site, on the left.

4 The next landmark on the left is the farm road leading to Bigpark. Continue past this road, and look out for the next farmhouse on the right. Approximately 300yds (274m) before this house, the road dips and there is a stream beside the road. At this point, turn right on to a farm track and follow it as it heads downhill between two high hedges.

5 Near the bottom of the hill, just as you have passed a large barn on your left, the road splits. Turn right at this point and then continue along this road, through a farm steading, past Downan farmhouse and on uphill. When the road levels out, look to the horizon in front of you for the distinctive outline of Knockdolian Hill, often referred to by local mariners as the 'false Craig'.

6 Look over to your left at the same time to see the real Ailsa Craig away to the northwest; looking along the beach towards Ballantrae you can see Shellknowe. Continue along this road, past the farm of Kinniegar and through the hamlet of Garleffin. Note that some of the houses have names like Druidslea and Glendruid.

7 In the front garden of Druidslea is another standing stone. Turn left, go downhill on this country lane, turn left on to the main road and return to Ballantrae. Go through a gate on the left-hand side and into the kirkyard. The Kennedy crypt can be found by going up some steps on the right. If the door is locked you can still see inside through a small window on the door. Return to Main Street and turn left, go along the street and take the first turning left past the library. Walk along this street to reach the T-junction and turn left into Foreland and return to the car park where you started.

89 Spectacular Falls at Glenashdale

A short, scenic woodland outing leads to the dramatic Glenashdale Falls and provides the chance to examine the Isle of Arran's ancient bedrock

Below: One of the intriguing Giants' Graves – a Neolithic cairn. You can detour from Point 2 on the walk to see these

Bottom left: Glenashdale Falls

Bottom right: Looking across Whiting Bay to Holy Island, today home to a Buddhist retreat

Millions of years ago this area was a hot and barren desert. During what geologists refer to as the Permian period, 270 million years ago, the underlying red sandstone formed from sand dunes. On top of this a sill (layer) of igneous rocks was laid down in the Tertiary period, 210 million years later. The Tertiary sill at Glenashdale is about 100ft (30m) thick and composed of several types of igneous rock, the major part being quartz-dolerite. When this is harder than the surrounding rock, it stands proud as the softer rocks are eroded. At Glenashdale continual erosion has created spectacular waterfalls and, where the stream and the waterfall have cut into the Glenashdale sill, it is easy to examine the exposed structure of the rocks.

Following the stream up from the waterfall the banks and bed of the stream reveal dark- and medium-grained igneous rocks with a few specks of pyrites – a shiny yellow mineral. Southwest of the falls there are veins of a dark basalt. Bring a small geological field guide in your pocket – the photographs will help identify the different rocks.

A field guide to trees could also prove useful, although several of the trees have been conveniently labelled. There is an abundance of native trees such as the alder, hazel, downy birch, oak, ash and rowan. The latter, also called the mountain ash, has bright red berries in the autumn and in Scottish folklore was used for warding off witches.

Exotic Trees

You will also find a wide variety of exotic trees in the glen. The Siberian crab has white flowers and small green berries, which may turn into bright red fruits. You'll also come across large specimens of the Douglas fir. This evergreen native of North America is extensively planted in Europe to provide high-grade timber but seldom reaches its maximum height of 328ft (100m); most European specimens tend to be around 180ft (55m).

Other North American species include the Great fir and the Sitka spruce. The Sitka spruce is a fast-growing conifer that often reaches heights of 197ft (60m), and although it thrives in a range of soils it is particularly suited to the mild, wet Scottish climate. On the edge of the path look out for the heart-shaped leaves of wood sorrel with its white, bell-like flowers in April and May. There's a profusion of red campion and the scent of wild honeysuckle and wild garlic mingle with the pine tang of the wood. Look out for yellow pimpernel, with its star-like flowers, in May and August.

89 Spectacular Falls at Glenashdale

Get a close-up view of Glenashdale trees, flowers, rocks – and tumbling waterfalls

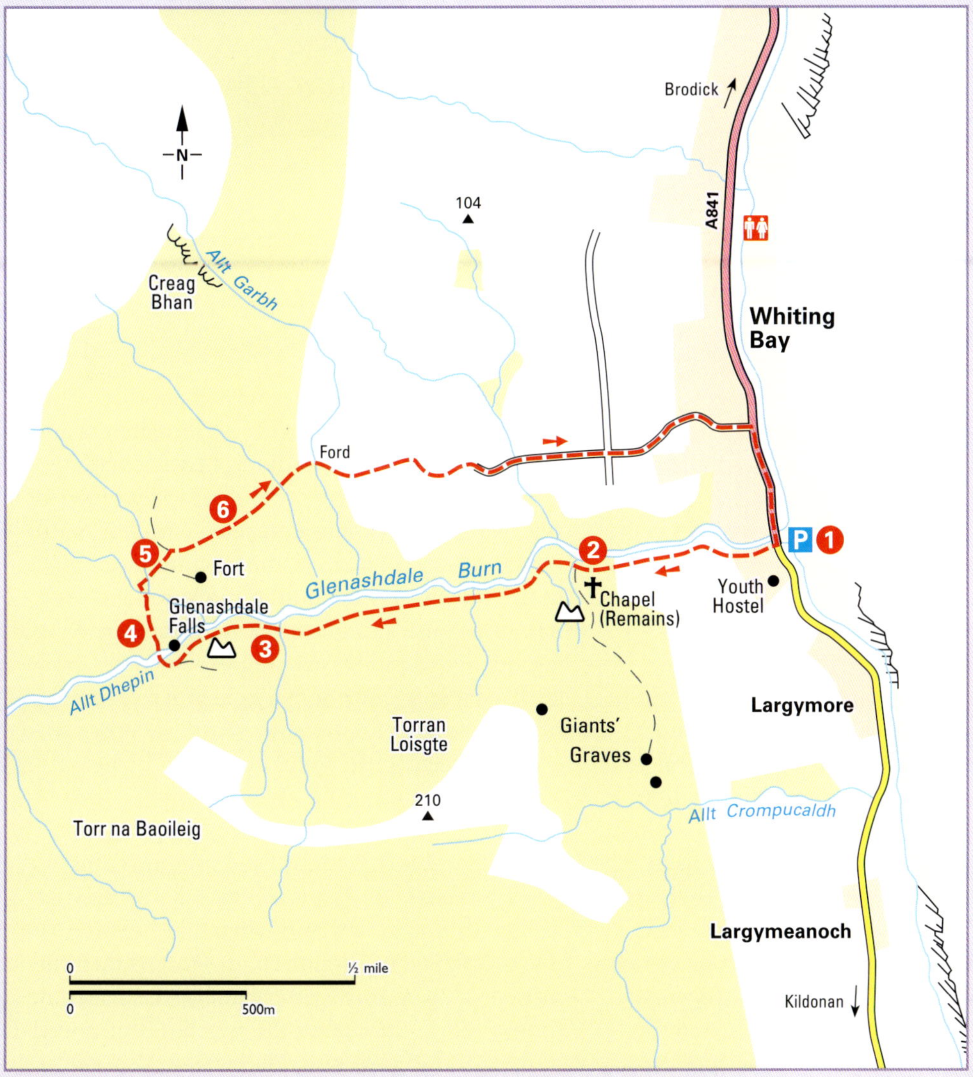

Distance 2.75 miles (4.4km)

Minimum Time 2hrs

Ascent/Gradient 442ft (135m) ▲▲▲

Level of Difficulty ●●●

Paths Forest paths and forest roads

Landscape Woodland, waterfalls, rock

Suggested Map OS Explorer 361 Isle of Arran

Start/Finish Grid reference: NS 047252

Dog Friendliness Good, locals walk their dogs here

Parking Car park opposite youth hostel in Whiting Bay

Public Toilets None en route; nearest at Shore Road, Whiting Bay

1 From the car park turn right on to the road, cross it and turn left on to the footpath, signposted 'Giants' Graves and Glenashdale Falls'. Follow this leafy lane until it reaches the rear of a house, then continue on the path along the river bank. Go through a gate, pass a forest walks sign and then continue until you reach a signpost pointing in the direction of the Giants' Graves.

2 The path forks here. Take the right fork, following the sign to 'Glenashdale Falls'. The path continues, rising gently through a wooded area, where several of the trees are helpfully identified by small labels fixed securely to the trunks. Continue uphill, keeping to this path, which is marked by the occasional waymarker, crossing a bridge and then fording a shallow section of the burn.

3 Eventually the path starts to climb steeply uphill and continues to some steps and then forks once again. Keep right, and follow this path until you reach the falls. Keep on the path past the falls and continue uphill until you cross a bridge. A picnic table situated on the river bank here is a good spot to stop for refreshment and a short rest.

4 From here follow the path into an area planted with Sitka spruce. Keep to the track marked by the green waymarkers as it heads through this dark part of the walk, going through a gap in a wall and eventually arriving at a place where a sign points off the main route to an Iron Age fort. Turn off to look at the remains of the Iron Age ramparts, if you wish, then retrace your steps to the sign and continue your route along the path.

5 Cross over a bridge by another waterfall and then follow more waymarkers to a clearing and a viewpoint. Sit on the bench here and enjoy the panoramic view across the wooded glen. From here you can see the full extent of the Glenashdale Falls as the water cascades over the top. A waymarker points uphill through a densely wooded area before ending at a T-junction with a forest road.

6 Turn right on to the forest road and continue, crossing water at a ford and going through three kissing gates until the route continues on a metalled road. Continue along this road, over a crossroads and downhill. Turn right at a T-junction and walk 200yds (183m) back to the car park.

90 Back in Time on Machrie Moor

An instructive walk leads to imposing standing stones and one of Scotland's best early settlements

Arran is famous for archaeological remains dating from the Mesolithic or Middle Stone Age period, and the greatest concentration of these can be found on the wild, windswept Machrie Moor. There are remains of hut circles, chambered cairns and standing stones. The circles of grey granite boulders and tall, weathered red sandstone pillars are an impressive sight against a winter sun on the wide expanse of moor.

The earliest inhabitants settled here some 8,000 years ago and, across the millennia, settlements were created and the first simple monuments erected. Within this small area of moor there are more than 40 stone circles, standing stones, chambered tombs and hut circles – making it the finest Neolithic and Bronze Age site in Scotland.

Most visitors head straight for the three large red sandstone pillars, the tallest standing slightly over 18ft (5.5m). These stones were once part of a much larger circle; the other stones have fallen or been removed. No one is certain what function these Bronze Age circles performed, but it is likely that they had a religious significance. Many stone circles are precisely aligned to particular celestial events, such as the rising of the midsummer sun, and they possibly also fulfilled seasonal functions, indicating when to carry out certain rituals or to plant and harvest crops. A survey of the area by archaeologist John Barnatt in 1978 revealed that four of the circles were aligned with a gap in the skyline of Machrie Glen, where the sun rises at midsummer.

Legendary Figures

Other early Arran inhabitants had another explanation for the circles. At a time when people attributed anything they did not understand to legendary figures, the standing stones on Machrie Moor became associated with the giant Fingal, a Scottish form of the Irish warrior Finn MacCumhail, and the double circle still has the name of Fingal's Cauldron Seat. According to legend, Fingal put his dog Bran in the outer circle and tied it to a stone with a hole in it to prevent it from wandering about while Fingal sat down to enjoy his meal in the inner circle.

Peat Protection

The dwellers on the moor lived in round huts, the remains of which are still visible. There is no explanation as to why and when they departed, but one theory is that climate change forced them to move to a more sheltered part of the island. In the thousands of years since, the area has been covered by a blanket of peat bog. There is surely more to discover under this protective layer, as recent excavations have uncovered even older structures.

Top right: A standing stone on Machrie Moor

Right: The small harbour at Blackwaterfoot

90 Back in Time on Machrie Moor

Explore the moorland home of Arran's Stone Age inhabitants

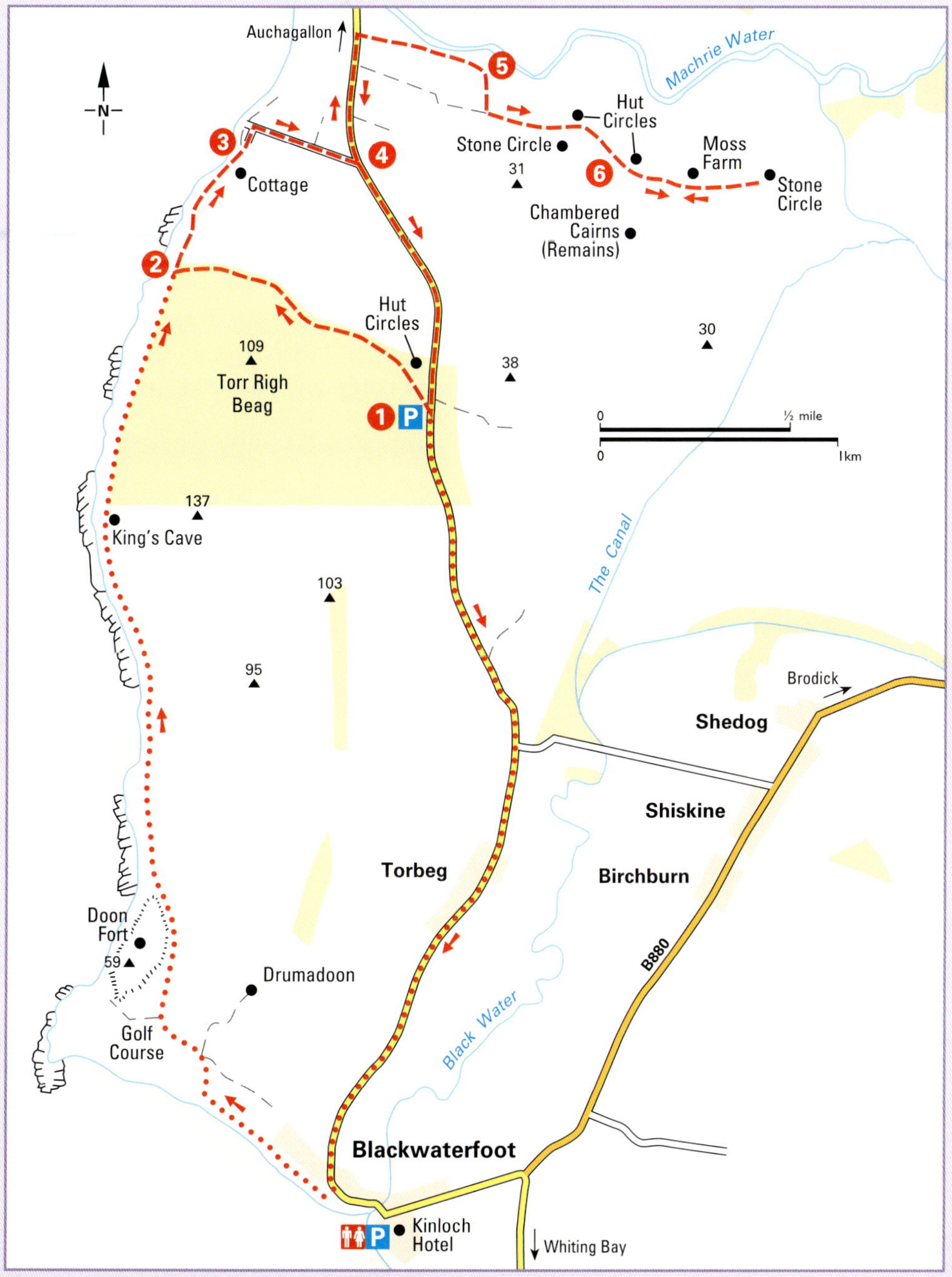

Distance 5.5 miles (8.8km)

Minimum Time 3hrs

Ascent/Gradient 114ft (35m) ▲▲▲

Level of Difficulty ●●●

Paths Footpaths, rough tracks, road, 3 stiles

Landscape Forest, seashore, fields and moorland

Suggested Map OS Explorer 361 Isle of Arran

Start/Finish Grid reference: NS 898314

Dog Friendliness Keep on lead near livestock and where requested by signs

Parking King's Cave car park

Public Toilets Car park at Blackwaterfoot

1 From the car park take the footpath signed for 'King's Cave' through woodland, past the site of some hut circles and the edge of the woods until it heads downhill towards the sea. Look out for a waymarker on the right pointing back in the direction you have just walked.

2 Turn right on to a faint path, in summer overgrown with bracken. In a short distance, climb through a wire fence. Cross this field and go through a gate, then head downhill aiming for a white cottage.

3 At the left end of the cottage go through a gate at the corner of the garden wall and along a farm road between two fences. Keep on this road, passing a cottage on the right and then keeping right at the fork.

4 When the road ends at a T-junction with the A841, turn left. Continue to the signpost for 'Machrie Moor standing stones'. At the sign turn right, climb over a stile and then follow the access road. This rough track passes through two fields.

5 In the second field, when you are nearing the far left-hand corner, you will come across a megalithic site. Nothing is to be seen above ground, actually, and the site was only identified by archaeologists after flints were found that proved to be around 7,000 to 9,000 years old. After identifying the site, continue on the road to the Moss Farm Road stone circle, which dates to around 2000BC.

6 From here the track continues, passing the deserted Moss Farm then crossing a stile to the main stone circles of Machrie Moor. After inspecting these, return to the stile and take the Moss Farm Road back to the A841. Turn left on to this and walk for approximately 1.5 miles (2km) to return to the car park.

Extending the Walk

Whether King's Cave is actually where Robert Bruce met his fabled spider is not known, but he certainly spent some time hiding there during the Wars of Independence. To extend the walk and visit the cave, continue into Blackwaterfoot then follow the coastal path north, behind Doon Fort. Once past the cave, you can either continue on the main walk from Point 2, or turn right to return to the start.

91 Around Iona, Holy Island of St Columba

This circuit of parts of the island held sacred to the memory of a Celtic saint, leads past his landing place in Coracle Bay and to a marble quarry

Above: Looking across the shore at the Sound of Iona

In the early summer of AD563, a middle-aged cleric crossed over from Ireland with 12 companions and the intention of setting up a monastic community on the remote and windswept island of Iona. Columba (in Gaelic, *Colum Cille*, 'the Dove of the Church') did not intend to bring Christianity to a new country, indeed he had left his native Ireland under a cloud.

The problems had started with a dispute over copyright: Columba had secretly copied a psalter owned by St Finnian of Clonard, and Finnian had claimed ownership of the copy. The dispute became more complicated when a young prince accidentally killed an opponent during a game of Irish hockey and claimed sanctuary with Columba. A battle followed, for which Columba felt responsible. In penance for these events he accepted 'white martyrdom', perpetual exile.

A Simple Life, Based on Prayer

At the centre of Columba's settlement on Iona was a church of oak logs and thatch and, around it, huts for the individual monks. Columba himself slept on the bedrock, with a stone for a pillow. Larger huts of wattle were used as the dining hall, guest house, library and writing room. The monks' lives consisted of prayer, simple farming and study, and here Columba composed poetry in Latin and Irish.

Celtic versus Roman Christianity

Columba's Celtic Christianity spread from Iona across Scotland and led to the Northumbrian foundation of Lindisfarne, with its rich tradition of illustrated religious books such as the Lindisfarne Gospel. Here the faith came into contact with the Roman-style Christianity of continental Europe, brought to England by Augustine in AD597. While the outward dispute was on the correct hairstyle for monks and the way to calculate the date of Easter, it seems that the Celtic Christianity was more personal and mystical, the Roman more authoritarian. The Roman version eventually dominated, but the Celtic was not fully suppressed. Columba, never officially canonised as a saint, is venerated in Scotland and Ireland to this day.

Iona Today

Columba's church vanished beneath a later Benedictine abbey, itself heavily restored in the 19th century. But the spirit of Columba still dominates the island. From the low hill called Dun I, on the day of his death, he blessed the island and community. The monks grew kale and oats at the machars (coastal lowlands) of Bay at the Back of the Ocean (Camus Cuil an t-Saimh), over what is today the golf course. At the southern tip of the island is Coracle Bay, traditionally named as the saint's landing place.

'That man is little to be envied, whose patriotism would not gain force upon the plain of Marathon, or whose piety would not grow warmer among the ruins of Iona,' wrote the renowned English writer and critic Samuel Johnson, who visited the island in 1773. Today's Iona Foundation is ecumenical – tied to no single denomination of Christianity – and has restored the buildings within a tradition of simple craftsmanship and prayer. The grave of John Smith, Labour leader in the 1990s, lies in the northeast extension of the burial ground.

91 Around Iona, Holy Island of St Columba

See the ruins that so moved Samuel Johnson – and the hill from which Columba gave his last sermon

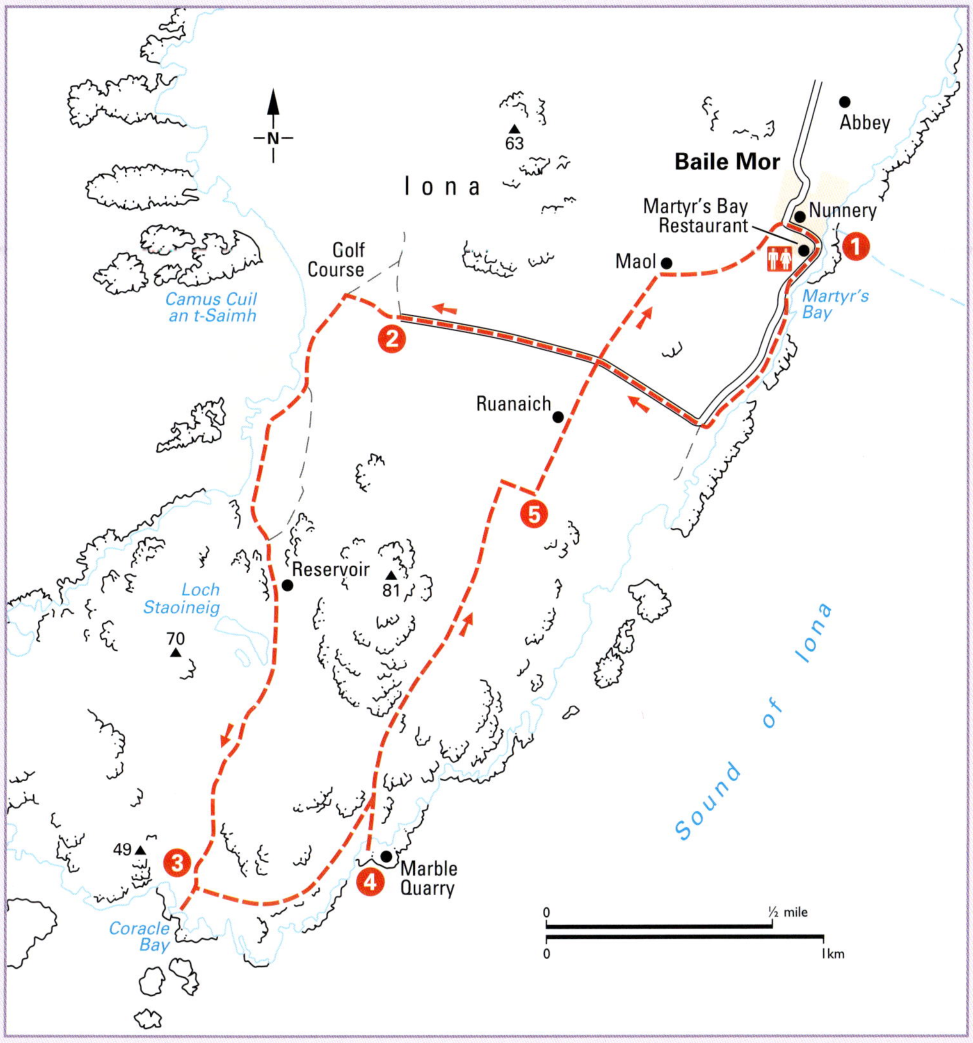

Distance 5.25 miles (8.4km)

Minimum Time 3hrs 30min

Ascent/Gradient 650ft (198m) ▲▲▲

Level of Difficulty ●●●

Paths Tracks, sandy paths, some rugged rock and heather

Landscape Bare gneiss rock and Atlantic Ocean

Suggested Map OS Explorer 373 Iona, Staffa & Ross of Mull

Start/Finish Grid reference: NM 286240

Dog Friendliness Keep on lead near sheep

Parking Ferry terminal at Fionnphort on Mull

Public Toilets Beside Martyr's Bay Bar

1 Ferries cross to Iona about every hour. Once on the island, take the tarred road on the left, passing Martyr's Bay. After a second larger bay, rejoin the road as it bends right. Follow the road across the island to a gate on to the Iona golf course (dogs on leads).

2 Take the sandy track ahead, then bear left past a small cairn to the shore. Turn left along the shore to a large beach. At its end, bear left up a narrow valley. After 100yds (91m), you pass a small concrete hut to join a stony track. It passes a fenced reservoir and drops to the corner of Loch Staoineig. Walk along to the left of the lochan on a path, improved in places, that runs gently down to Coracle Bay. You cross to the left of an area that shows the furrows of lazybed cultivation – fields drained to improve crop yields – and reach the shore just to the left of a rocky knoll.

3 Take the route ahead, following an indistinct path. If your ferry to the mainland leaves in 2 hours' time or earlier, return by the outward route and leave exploring the marble quarries for another visit. Otherwise, return inland for approximately 200yds (183m) and bear right into a little grassy valley. After 100yds (91m), go through a broken wall and then bear slightly left, past another inlet on the right. Cross heather to the eastern shoreline of the island. Bear left, above the small sea cliff, for 0.25 mile (400m). Turn sharp right into a little valley descending into the remnants of the marble quarry.

4 Turn inland, back up the valley to its head. Pass the low walls of two ruined cottages and continue in the same direction for about 200yds (183m) to a fence corner. Keep the fence on your left, picking a way through heather. Dun I with its cairn appears ahead – aim directly for it to reach the edge of fields, where a fence runs across ahead. Turn right along it to a small iron gate.

5 This leads to a track that passes Ruanaich Farm to the tarred road of the outward walk. Cross on to a farm track, which bends to the right at Maol. It reaches Baile Mor (Iona village) at the ruined nunnery. Just ahead is the abbey with its squat square tower, or turn right directly to return to the ferry pier.

92 Sight of Salmon and Skye on Loch Alsh

A coastal walk along Loch Alsh delivers delightful views of the Isle of Skye and of the sea and leads past a fish farm, part of a thriving local industry

Two hundred years ago, Scotland's rivers were full of salmon, and smoked salmon was the crofter's winter food store. When wild salmon became scarce it began to be considered a luxury food, and today, if you buy salmon, it's almost certainly from a fish farm.

A fish farm should be sheltered from storm waves, but in water at least 30ft (9m) deep so that fish droppings don't poison the fish. There should be a vigorous tidal flow to carry oxygen-rich water into the pens, no pollution and the water should be cool, but should not freeze. In other words, it should be in a Scottish sea loch.

Tough Tasks of a Fish Farmer

Fish farming is a tough life. Mending a net that's 3ft (90cm) underwater is not comfortable when the water is still, and is even harder when – as is almost invariably the case – the water is not still. The very day when it's blowing half a gale tends naturally to be the one on which the nets break.

Hauling the cages out of the water for cleaning is the toughest job of all – seaweed grows on fish farms just as it does on the shoreline, and after two years it starts to hinder the flow of water. And a single storm, or even a passing whale, can tear the nets and lose the work of two years.

During its first 40 years, fish farming tried to produce as much as possible, as cheaply as possible. Salmon were stocked like battery hens and fed a high-fat diet. Antibiotics are used to keep the salmon alive if they are not altogether healthy, and dyes give the fishes' flesh a marked pink colour. One result has been pollution from their droppings poisoning nearby shellfish beds.

Fish farms act as reservoirs of disease, in particular of the parasitic sea-lice. There are many reasons for the decline of the wild salmon and infection from fish farms is one of them. Scottish fish farming has now reached the point where it has to clean up its act. A recent development is the organic fish farm, where the fish are stocked less densely and are fed a more natural diet.

Round and Round

Fish pens are circular because the salmon prefer to swim round and round. If they were put in a square enclosure, the corners would be wasted. More importantly, the fish would hit the sides, and this would damage their scales.

Below: Sea waters in Loch Alsh, an inlet between the Isle of Skye and the mainland

92 Sight of Salmon and Skye on Loch Alsh

Tour the loch side – and, if you have the energy, climb Glas Bheinn for the view

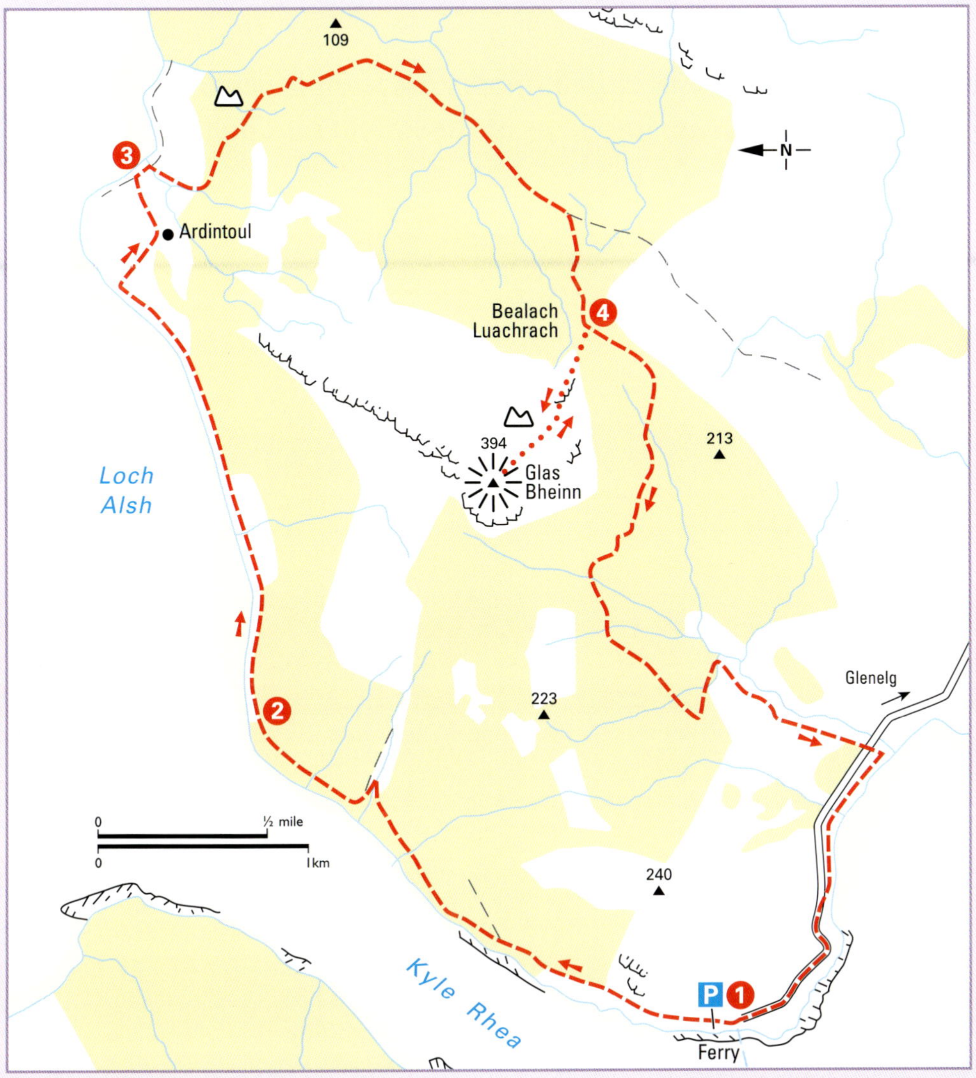

Distance 8.5 miles (13.7km)

Minimum Time 4hrs

Ascent/Gradient 1,000ft (300m) ▲▲▲

Level of Difficulty ●●●

Paths Tracks, grassy shoreline, minor road, 4 stiles

Landscape Wooded coast, moorland pass, stony paths

Suggested Map OS Explorer 413 Knoydart, Loch Hourn & Loch Duich

Start/Finish Grid reference: NG 795213

Dog Friendliness Off lead most of walk

Parking Above pier of Glenelg ferry

Public Toilets None en route or near by

1 A track runs out of the car park, signed for Ardintoul and Totaig. It descends gently through two gates, then goes up through a third into a plantation. With high power lines just above, the track forks. Take the left-hand fork, running downhill and passing an arrow made of stones. The track goes between the feet of a tall pylon and then climbs again to contour through a birch wood. It runs in and out of a tiny stream gorge, then gently descends towards the shore. On the other side of Loch Alsh, the white houses of Balmacara are directly ahead.

2 At the shoreline, the track disappears into an open field strip. Follow the short grass next to the shingle beach, passing a salmon farm just offshore. When the trees once more run down to the sea, a green track passes next to the shore to reach an open field below a small crag with birches. Keep along the shore, outside field walls, and sometimes taking to the stripy schist shingle, towards a square brick building on the point ahead. As you pass the end of the birch crag, you come to a wall gap. Here a track that's simply a pair of green ruts runs directly inland through a grey gate to meet a gravel track. Turn left, away from the abandoned Ardintoul farm to pass sheds and a house to regain the shoreline at Ardintoul.

3 The track runs along the shoreline, then turns inland to climb the hill behind. The steeper uphill sections are tarred. Below on the left, the Allt na Dalach runs into Loch Alsh, with, at low tide, a clear example of a gravel spit where river debris runs into tidal water. The track enters plantations, crosses a stream and bends right to complete its climb to the Bealach Luachrach. Here you may see fresh peat workings on the left.

4 The energetic can make a diversion on to Glas Bheinn – a tough little hill, but a fine viewpoint. The grading and timing given for this walk don't take account of this side-trip. From the road's high point, turn right up a wet tree gap to reach open hillside. Follow the remains of an old fence up the first rise. Where it bends right, continue straight uphill to the summit, returning by the same route. The old fence makes a useful guide back into the tree gap. Continue downhill from Point 4 on the unsurfaced road, which reaches the tarred public road 1 mile (1.6km) north of Glenelg village. Grassy shoreline, then the road, leads back to the ferry pier.

93 Crofters' Country near Waterstein Head

A tramp through crofting land and over peat moors leads on dramatic sea cliffs to the magnificent Waterstein Head, for views of the Neist Point lighthouse

Top: Big cliff scenery on the Isle of Skye

Above: Triangular piles of peat, stacked to dry

After the defeat of Bonnie Prince Charlie's Jacobite Uprising by the army of King George II in 1746, the Scottish clan system was swept away. The clansmen were transformed into crofters. Rents rose, partly to support the landlords' new London lifestyles. Crofting lands were cleared to make way for sheep, and the crofters were forced to relocate, first to the shore and later right out of the country to Canada and Australia. By the late 1800s, however, they were starting to fight back. In 1882, crofters at the Braes, south of Portree, resisted an eviction. Fifty Glasgow policemen were sent to restore order, and in the 'Battle of the Braes' the crofters retaliated with sticks and stones.

In Glendale, land-starved crofters deliberately let their cattle stray on to neighbouring farms. Government forces and the gunboat *Jackal* were defied by 600 crofters. There were four arrests, including John Macpherson, the 'Glendale Martyr', and a minister, the Reverend D MacCallum. The 'martyrs' received two-month prison sentences. The public outcry that followed saw a newly formed 'Crofters' Party' send four MPs to Westminster. The first of the Crofting Acts, passed by Gladstone's government, led to fairer rents and security of tenure for the crofters.

Crofters Today

Today, thanks to those battles of long ago, Glendale and the Braes are inhabited lands where so much of Highland Scotland is empty. Crofters now have the right to buy and enjoy subsidies and grants from the government. Few crofts provide enough to live on, without a part-time job on the side: as a result, there's a series of small-scale enterprises along the Glendale Visitor Route. Peat became the crofters' fuel supply and in a few places it is still being worked today. Above Loch Eishort on this walk you'll see triangular stacks, each made from four peats, drying in the wind – and, of course, getting wet again in the rain. When it burns, it brings the smell of the wild bog-moss right into the house.

93 Crofters' Country near Waterstein Head

Drink in clifftop views on Skye – and get a close look at some peat-cutting

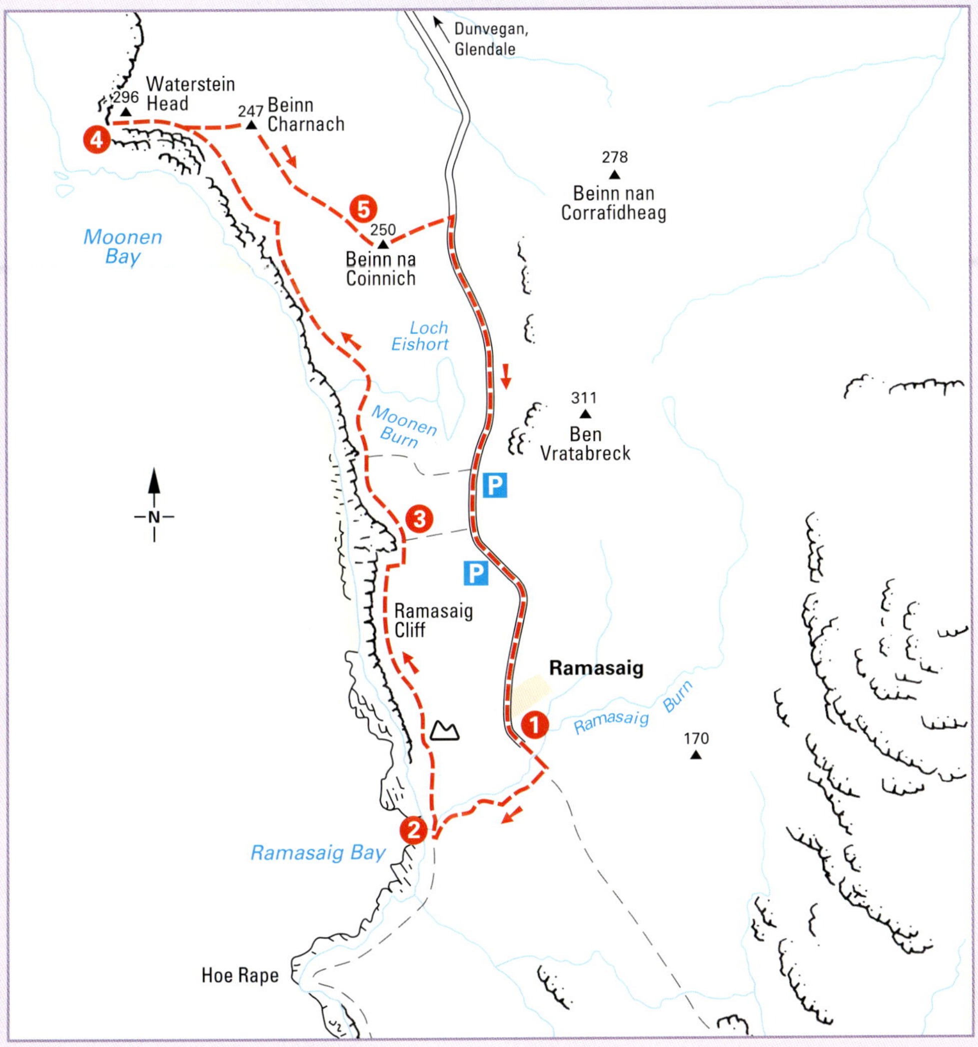

Distance 5.75 miles (9.2km)

Minimum Time 3hrs 30min

Ascent/Gradient 1,500ft (457m) ▲▲▲

Level of Difficulty ●●●

Paths Grassy clifftops and moorland, 2 fences and 1 gate

Landscape Cliff tops high above Atlantic Ocean

Suggested Map OS Explorer 407 Skye – Dunvegan

Start/Finish Grid reference: NG 163443

Dog Friendliness On short lead – risk of scaring sheep over cliff edges

Parking Ramasaig road end or pull-ins at pass 0.75 mile (1.2km) north

Public Toilets Glendale village hall

1 From the end of the tarmac, the road continues as a track past farm buildings, with a bridge over the Ramasaig Burn. After a gate it reaches a shed with a tin roof. Bear right and follow the left bank of Ramasaig Burn to the shore.

2 Cross the burn at a ford and head up a very steep meadow beside the fence that protects the cliff edge. There's an awkward fence to cross halfway up. At the top, above Ramasaig Cliff, follow the fence on the left. It cuts across to the right to protect a notch in the cliff edge. From here, you could cut down to the parking areas at the nearby road pass.

3 Keep downhill along the cliffside fence. At the bottom, a turf wall off to the right provides another shortcut back to the road. The clifftop walk now bears slightly right around the V-notch of the Moonen Burn. A small path crosses the stream and slants up left to rejoin the clifftop fence, which soon turns slightly inland around another cliff notch. The cliff-edge fence leads up and to the left, to reach Waterstein Head. Here there is a trig point, 971ft (296m) above the sea – the second highest cliff on Skye. Below, you will see Neist Point lighthouse.

4 Return for 0.25 mile (400m) down to where the fence bends to the right, then continue through a shallow grassy col for the slight rise to Beinn Charnach. Here bear right to follow a gently rounded grass ridge-line parallel with cliffs. The highest line along the ridge is the driest. A fence runs across, with a grey gate at its highest point where it passes through a col. Climb over the gate and on up to a cairn on Beinn na Coinnich.

5 Continue along the slightly rocky plateau for 300yds (274m) to the southeast top. Now the Ramasaig road is visible 0.25 mile (400m) away on the left. Go down to join a quad-bike track heading towards the road. Just before reaching the road, the bike track crosses a swampy col. This shows old and recent peat workings. Turn right, along the road, passing above Loch Eishort to the start.

94 A Raasay Roundabout

A seaside and woodland walk treads in the footsteps of James Boswell and Dr Johnson on the island that sheltered Bonnie Prince Charlie

In his *Journal of a Tour to the Hebrides with Dr Johnson* (1773), Scottish biographer James Boswell described the island of Raasay: 'It was a most pleasing approach to Raasay. We saw before us a beautiful bay, well defended with a rocky coast; a good gentleman's house, a fine verdure about it, a considerable number of trees, and beyond it hills and mountains in gradation of wildness. Our boatmen sung with great spirit.' Boswell found Raasay a delight. He enjoyed the company of Macleod the laird and his ten beautiful daughters; he was impressed by the fine food and the two pet parrots; he enjoyed the landscape; and he very much enjoyed his walk.

Below: Mermaid statue at the Battery, a former cannon emplacement on Raasay

Main image: The walk starts from East Suisnish pier on Raasay

On Dun Caan

Boswell rose before six and, after a light breakfast of dry bread and whisky, set off with the laird. The aim was the island's highest point, Dun Caan. Once there, they lunched on cold mutton and brandy, and danced a Highland reel on its flat summit. They returned by way of Beinn a' Chapuill, and in the afternoon 'there came a heavy rain, by which we were a great deal wet'. Their walk totalled 24 miles altogether (nearly 40km). By way of a warm-down, Boswell 'exerted himself extraordinarily in dancing, drinking porter heavily'.

'If I had my wife and little daughters with me, I would stay long enough,' said Boswell. And today Raasay, with its 22 well-laid paths, its woodlands and moors and small beaches, offers walking for everyone, with none of the mainland's turgid bog and skin-shredding gabbro. Boswell and his companion Dr Johnson felt highly honoured by the boatman who ferried them to Raasay, for just 27 years before the sailor had carried the Bonnie Prince in the opposite direction. Prince Charles Stuart had sheltered on Raasay for as long as was safe, then crossed to the mainland and walked across the moors to Strath. The boatman told Boswell that the prince had been a stronger walker than himself, but that he had had to dissuade him from littering the countryside with his empty brandy bottle. Even today, unfortunately, some walkers need similar education.

As punishment for sheltering the prince, the island was stripped of its cattle and every house burnt. The restoration of Raasay House was almost complete when Boswell visited. He had just one complaint. While the ruins of the former castle boasted an ancient garderobe, the new house had no such 'convenience', and Johnson reproached the laird accordingly. 'You take very good care of one end of a man, but not of the other!'

94 A Raasay Roundabout

Investigate the remains of Raasay's old iron mine and works railway

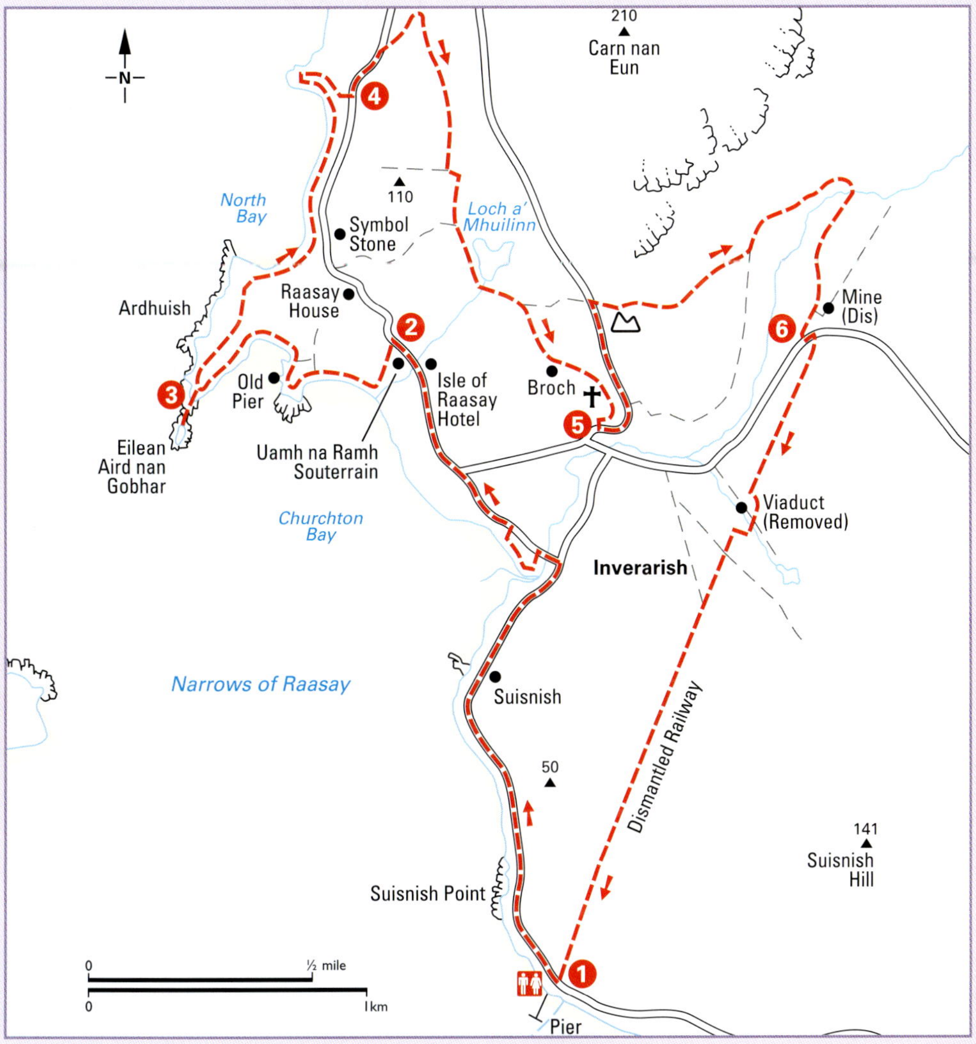

Distance 7.75 miles (12.5km)

Minimum Time 3hrs 45min

Ascent/Gradient 820ft (250m) ▲▲▲

Level of Difficulty ●●●

Paths Small but clear paths, some tracks, 1 stile

Landscape Shingle beaches, woodland and moorland

Suggested Map OS Explorer 409 Raasay, Rona & Scalpay or 410 Skye – Portree & Bracadale

Start/Finish Grid reference: NG 555342

Dog Friendliness Close control in woodland and moor, keep on lead near livestock

Parking Ferry terminal at Sconser, Skye (or lay-by to east)

Public Toilets Sconser ferry terminal and start of walk

1 CalMac ferries run roughly hourly during the day to the island of Raasay. Turn left on the island's small road. At Inverarish, turn left over a bridge and divert left past cottages and along the shore. After a playing field you then rejoin the road, which leads past the Isle of Raasay Hotel to another road junction.

2 Uamh na Ramh souterrain is over a stile on the left. Continue ahead past the superb but neglected stable block – ahead is Raasay House, now an outdoor centre. At the corner of the stable, turn left, signed 'Clachan'. A track continues below the ramparts of an old gun battery decorated with two stone mermaids. From the pier, follow a path around the bay, until a gate leads to a pleasant shoreline path to Eilean Aird nan Gobhar. Check the tides before crossing the rocks to this tidal island.

3 Head inland over a rock knoll, then pass along the left-hand edge of a plantation on a muddy path overhung by rhododendron. Continue along the shore of North Bay, with a pine plantation on your right, round to a headland. Go up briefly through the low basalt cliff and return along its top. Head along the left edge of the plantation, to emerge through a decorative iron gate on to a road.

4 Turn left for 180yds (165m) to a grey gate on the right. A green track leads up and to the right into a craggy valley. At a walled paddock, the track turns left and then right to join a tarred track. Follow this down past a lily lochan (Loch a' Mhuilinn) and turn left across its dam. Join a path running up under larch and rhododendron then in 100yds (91m) bear right, waymarked 'Temptation Hill Trail'. Look for a path on the right that leads up to Dun Bhorogh Dail, the remains of an Iron Age broch (tower). The main path leads down past a white church, then bends right and drops to a tarred road.

5 Turn sharp left up the road for 0.25 mile (400m), then right at a signpost for Burma Road. The track shrinks to a path, bends left and climbs quite steeply. It becomes a forest track, passing waymarkers, finally reaching the abandoned buildings of an old iron mine.

6 When you get to the tarred road beyond, turn left to a signpost for the Miners' Trail, then right on the green track of a former railway. Where a viaduct has been removed, a new-built path descends and then climbs to regain the railbed. The blue-waymarked Miners' Trail turns off, but your route follows the railway onwards, across a stretch of moor and down to the ferry terminal.

95 The Shores of Loch Shieldaig

Through birch woods, over peat bogs and across grassy meadows, this peninsula walk offers marvellous views up Loch Torridon and down Loch Shieldaig

Above: Cannon at Shieldaig lost by one of the ships of the Spanish Armada

Main image: Perfect calm on Loch Shieldaig

The Shieldaig peninsula separates inner and outer Loch Torridon, and at every turn there's a new view – up the loch to Liathach and the lesser-known hills to the south, out across the sea to Skye and Raasay, or into a sheltered bay with a cluster of eider or the sleek head of a seal. But on a warm, grey summer's day you may wish to complete the walk quickly and not linger too long.

The reason? In Gaelic she's *meanbh-chuileag* ('the tiny fly'), but she's better known as the mighty midge, Scotland's scourge. I say 'she' as the male is an altogether weaker creature, content with a suck of bog myrtle, a brief dance in the summer haze and death among the heather stalks. It's the female that needs a blood meal in order to lay her eggs. The blood host could be a deer, a sheep, a grouse – or, of course, you. The larvae hatch in wet peat moss, which is all too common in western Scotland. They have the evil ability to absorb oxygen even from such waterlogged surroundings.

A Prince Discomfited

Bonnie Prince Charlie, wandering Scotland in the damp summer of 1746, was mildly inconvenienced by the pursuing redcoats. But his real enemy was the midge. On Benbecula, crouching under a rock in the rain, on a muggy June day, he lost his customary poise and gave way to 'hideous cries and complaints'. His remedy was brandy when brandy was to be had, and otherwise whisky. During his flight through the heather he got through as much as a bottle a day. Indeed, his alcoholism in later life can in part be blamed on the midge.

Later Victims of the Midge

There's a historical mystery over the midge. Dr Johnson, touring just 27 years after the time of Bonnie Prince Charlie, didn't notice the midge at all. Then the poet Samuel Taylor Coleridge, walking the Great Glen in 1803, found them mildly annoying, but said the bed-bugs were much worse.

By 1872 the midges were bad enough to completely ruin one of Queen Victoria's picnics. This increase in the midge may be down to the Highland Clearances. Glens formerly farmed became their bog breeding grounds. But the worst midge story of all is said to have happened at Gairloch. A replacement minister, the Revd John Morrison, was sent to the Presbyterian church there in 1711, and the congregation so disapproved of his sermon that they stripped him naked, tied him to a tree and left him overnight for the midges!

95 The Shores of Loch Shieldaig

Explore some of the many inlets of the Shieldaig peninsula

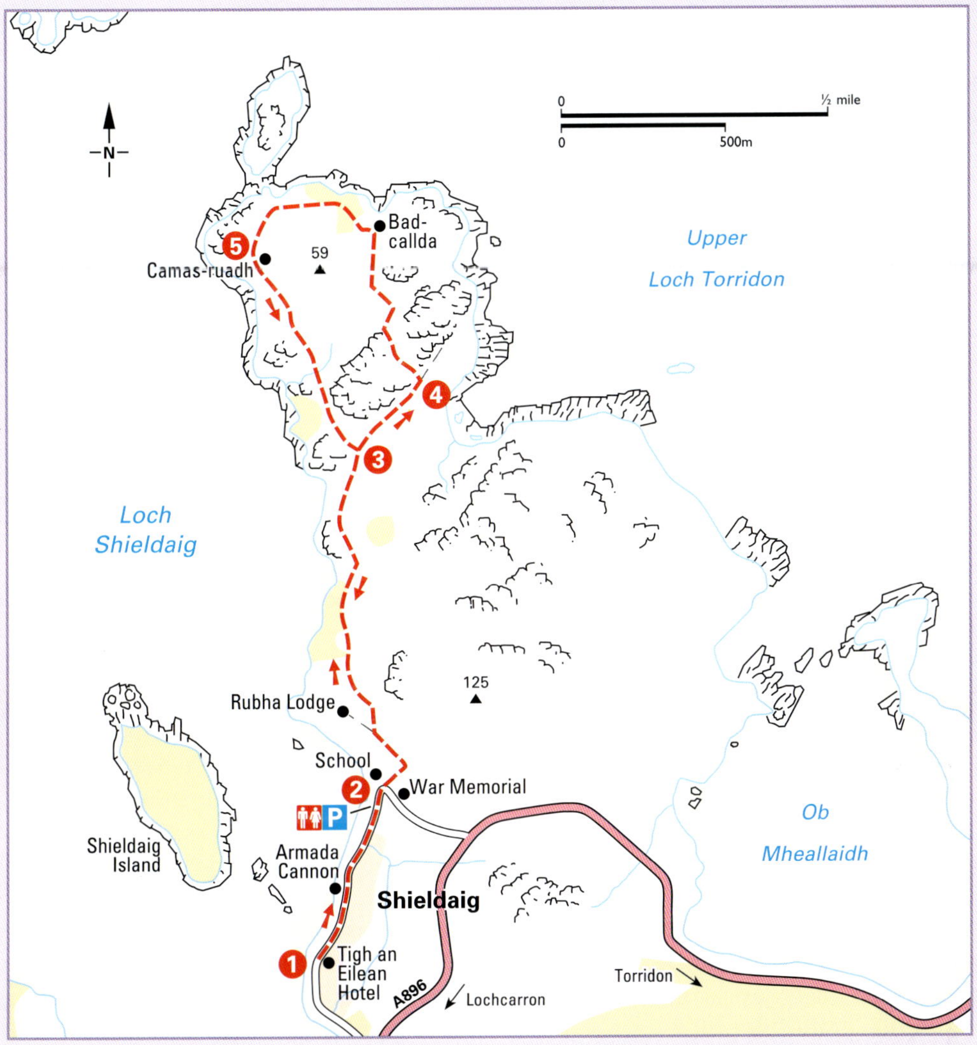

Distance 3.25 miles (5.3km)

Minimum Time 1hr 45min

Ascent/Gradient 500ft (152m) ▲▲▲

Level of Difficulty ●●●

Paths Well-made old paths, 1 rough section

Landscape Saltwater views up Loch Torridon and down Loch Shieldaig

Suggested Map OS Explorer 428 Kyle of Lochalsh

Start/Finish Grid reference: NG 814538

Dog Friendliness Keep on lead in village and when passing livestock

Parking South end of Shieldaig village, opposite shop and hotel

Public Toilets North end of village (another car park)

1 Follow the street along the shoreline past a cannon salvaged from the Spanish Armada of 1588. At the village end the street rises slightly, with another parking area, and a war memorial above on the right.

2 In front of the village school, turn right up a rough track. The track passes a couple of houses to turn left. In another 100yds (91m) the track divides; here the main way to Rubha Lodge forks off left, but your route bears right, passing to the right of a glacier-smoothed rock knoll. The terraced path runs through birch woods at first, with the peaceful waters of Loch Shieldaig visible below on the left. Running on, the path passes above two rocky bays, then strikes across a peat bog, bright in mid-summer with bell heather and the fluffy white tops of cotton grass. In the middle of this flat area it divides at a cairn.

3 The right-hand path runs along the edge of the peaty area, with rocky ground above on its left, then next to birch trees for 50yds (46m). Look out for the point where its pink gravel surface becomes peaty, with a rock formation like a low ruin on the right, because here is an easily missed path junction.

4 What seems like the main footpath, ahead and slightly downhill, peters out eventually. The correct path forks off to the left, slanting up to the higher ground just above. The path is now clear, crossing slabby ground in the direction of the peninsula's trig point, 0.25 mile (400m) away. After 220yds (201m) it rises slightly to a gateway in a former fence. Aiming right of the trig point, it crosses a small heather moor. At a broken wall, the path turns down right through a gap to the top of a grassy meadow. The first of the two shoreline cottages, Bad-callda, is just below. Rough paths lead to the left across the boggy top of the meadow and above a birchwood, with the trig point just above on the left. Keep going forward at the same level to a heather knoll, with a pole on it. Just below you is a second cottage, Camas-ruadh.

5 The footpath zig-zags down to the right between rocks. White paint spots lead round to the right of the cottage and its shed. Turn left behind the shed to join a clear path coming from the cottage. The return path is easy to follow, mostly along the top of the slope dropping to the right to Loch Shieldaig. After 0.5 mile (800m) it rejoins the outward route at the cairn, Point 3.

96 Following the Diabaig Coast Path

An enchanting ramble above Loch Torridon leads through reputedly haunted places and in the footsteps of the 'fairy folk' – the legendary *Duine Sithe*

New Year's Eve in Wester Ross is a time when old songs are sung, whisky is drunk – not all of it approved by the exciseman, either – and tales are told in both English and Gaelic. Over the years, these stories grow and also change location, so that the tailor who lost his hump to the fairies lived not only in Scotland, but also in Ireland and even Italy. Today the story is categorised as 'folktale type 503'.

Fairy Tales and Ghosts

Many of the tales told in Alligin take place in the knolly, magical ground on the way to Diabaig. One story concerns two villagers who were bringing whisky for the New Year from Gairloch by way of the coast path. They heard wonderful music and came upon a cave in the hill, where the fairy people had started their Hogmanay celebrations a few hours early. Fascinated, the man with the keg crept closer and closer until he was actually inside, whereupon the cave closed up and disappeared. A year later the other man came back, found the cave open and dragged his friend out across the threshold. The friend thought he'd been in there only a few minutes, but of the whisky he carried there was no trace. At the top of the hill road is tiny Lochan Dearg, and here there is traditionally said to be a ghost who appears only to people bearing his own name, Murdo Mackenzie. The kilted spirit, identified as one of the Mackenzies of Gairloch, was apparently slain by a Torridon MacDonald and then buried somewhere near by.

Horse Tales and Fairy Folk

Loch Diabaigas Airde (at Point 3 on the walk) is reputedly haunted by the water spirit called the 'kelpie'. This appears as a magnificent white horse, but if you mount it, the horse gallops rapidly into the loch and you're never seen again. That is, unless you just happen to have a bridle made of pure silver to tame it. Another kelpie is said to live in the Lochan Toll nam Biast, the Lochan of the Beast Hole, at the back of Beinn Alligin.

Fairy music has – it is said – been heard above the gorge of the Alligin burn. So to protect yourself from the *Duine Sithe* (fairy folk), be polite but don't accept food from them. At best it will be cow dung, at worst it will enslave you for ever. Carry iron, oatmeal or a groundsel root for protection and a cry of *am monadh oirbh, a' bheistein* ('back to the hill, you wee beastie') is effective. Approaching Alligin Shuas, walk carefully past Cnoc nan Sithe, the Fairy Knoll, so as not to disurb them.

Right: Water and rocks, green fields and clean air – Lower Diabaig, overlooking the loch

96 Following the Diabaig Coast Path

Be on your guard – especially if your name is Murdo Mackenzie

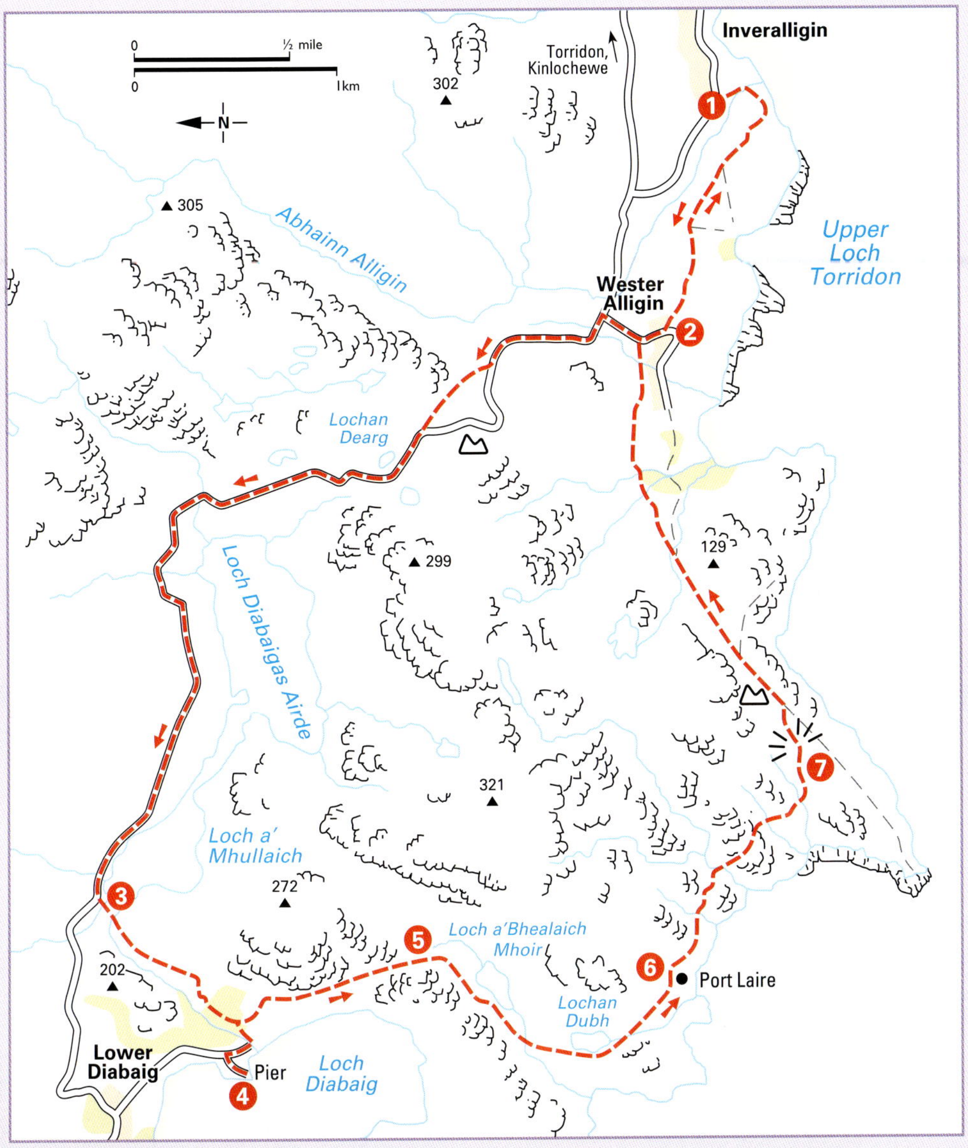

Distance 9.5 miles (15.3km)

Minimum Time 6hrs

Ascent/Gradient 1,805ft (550m) ▲▲▲

Level of Difficulty ●●●

Paths Narrow, rough and wet in places, no stiles

Landscape Rocky knolls and small lochans

Suggested Map OS Explorer 433 Torridon – Beinn Eighe & Liathach

Start/Finish Grid reference: NG 842073

Dog Friendliness Keep on lead passing Alligin Shuas and near sheep

Parking Wester Alligin, pull-off on side road near Alligin River

Public Toilets Torridon village

1 From the parking place, follow the road over the Abhainn Alligin river. A path leads along the shore for 100yds (91m), then goes up to the right, among outcrops. Bear left underneath a power line to the corner of a driveway. Keep ahead to reach Wester Alligin.

2 Turn up the road and then left, on the road for Diabaig. As the road steepens, take a path to the right of power lines, rejoining the road across a high pass and then down past two lochs, Loch Diabaigas Airde and Loch a'Mhullaich, which are linked.

3 Turn off left, crossing the outflow of Loch a'Mhullaich on a footbridge. A clear path leads out along the high wall of a stream valley, then zigzags down to a grey gate. Go down through woods to a white house, No 1 Diabaig. Turn right to reach the old stone pier.

4 Return up the path you just came down to pass a stone shed. Here a sign indicates a turn to the right, under an outcrop and between boulders. The path heads up to a small rock step with an arrow mark and a conveniently situated tree root you can hold on to; it then leads up to a gate in a fence and zig-zags into an open gully with a large crag on the right. At the top of this, the path then turns right along a shelf, with still more crag above before it slants gently down along the foot of another crag, then up to a col, with a last view of Diabaig.

5 From here the path is small but clear. It bends right to Loch a' Bhealaich Mhoir, and then turns left below it to Lochan Dubh. Cross its outbound slant down left towards the cottage of Port Laire.

6 Pass above the house, then slant gradually up, away from the sea. The path crosses the head of a bracken valley with a ruined croft house into a bleak knolly area out of sight of the sea. Cross two branches of a stream and go up to a cairn that marks where the path bears left up the spur. It now contours across a heathery meadow among the knolls, at the end of which it climbs pink rocks over a final spur. Just ahead is a gate in the deer fence.

7 The path leads along a level shelf with views to the head of Loch Torridon, then crosses a steep heather slope. When the path forks, take the upper branch to go through a wide col then down towards Wester Alligin. From a gate above the village, a faint path runs down in the direction of a green shed. It descends through a wood, then contours just above the village to reach the road above Point 2. Retrace your steps to the walk's start.

97 In Gairloch Waters

This excursion provides a chance to see porpoises and dolphins along the Gairloch shore, before leading past the Flowerdale Waterfall and up a picturesque valley

On a calm day in 1809, three fishermen drowned in Loch Ewe when their small boat was attacked and sunk by a whale. These waters are among the best in Europe for cetaceans (whales, dolphins and porpoises). The Gulf Stream brings warm, plankton-rich water and the swirling currents around the islands bring nutrients to the surface. The plankton flourish; the fish eat the plankton; the whales and dolphins eat the fish.

Porpoise or Dolphin?

The strongest currents are at headlands and narrow sea passages, so these are good places to look for marine wildlife. Early morning is best of all when looking west, as the low sunlight shines off the creatures' wet backs. On most summer days, with a little patience you may see the harbour porpoise or common dolphin in Loch Gairloch. But which is which? At 6ft (2m) or less in length, the porpoise is smaller. It has a short, stubby fin compared with the dolphin's more elegant one. Harbour porpoises are normally shy, but the ones at Gairloch are unusually friendly, often approaching boats. Endangered in the world as a whole, the ones at Gairloch are doing well and a Special Area of Conservation has been proposed for them here.

The whaling industry in Scotland ended in 1951, but serious threats remain. Dolphins and porpoises are accidentally caught in fishing nets and floating plastic rope and old nets are another danger. Pollution from agriculture and forestry releases heavy metals and pesticides into the ocean. Fish farming is also probably damaging the dolphins. More fish sewage than human sewage goes into the Hebridean seas, all of it untreated, and anti-fouling paint on fish farms contributes more chemicals, pesticides and antibiotics.

Cetaceans use sound signals for finding fish, as well as for communication. Interference comes from ships, dredging nets, seismic oil exploration and seal scammers – underwater beepers fitted to fish farms. We don't know how well the dolphins and porpoises are doing.

The growth of the whale-spotting industry means that we are just starting to discover how the populations are growing or declining. Marine tourism is now a £9 million concern with 400 jobs and by going on one of these trips, you'll contribute to crucial research. A responsible boatman will not pursue the animals or steer into the middle of a group, but will wait for the dolphins to approach.

Left: Common dolphin

Below inset: At Charlestown, calm days are best for seeing marine life in these waters

Below: On Gairloch beach

97 In Gairloch Waters

Be on the lookout for the unusually friendly Gairloch porpoises

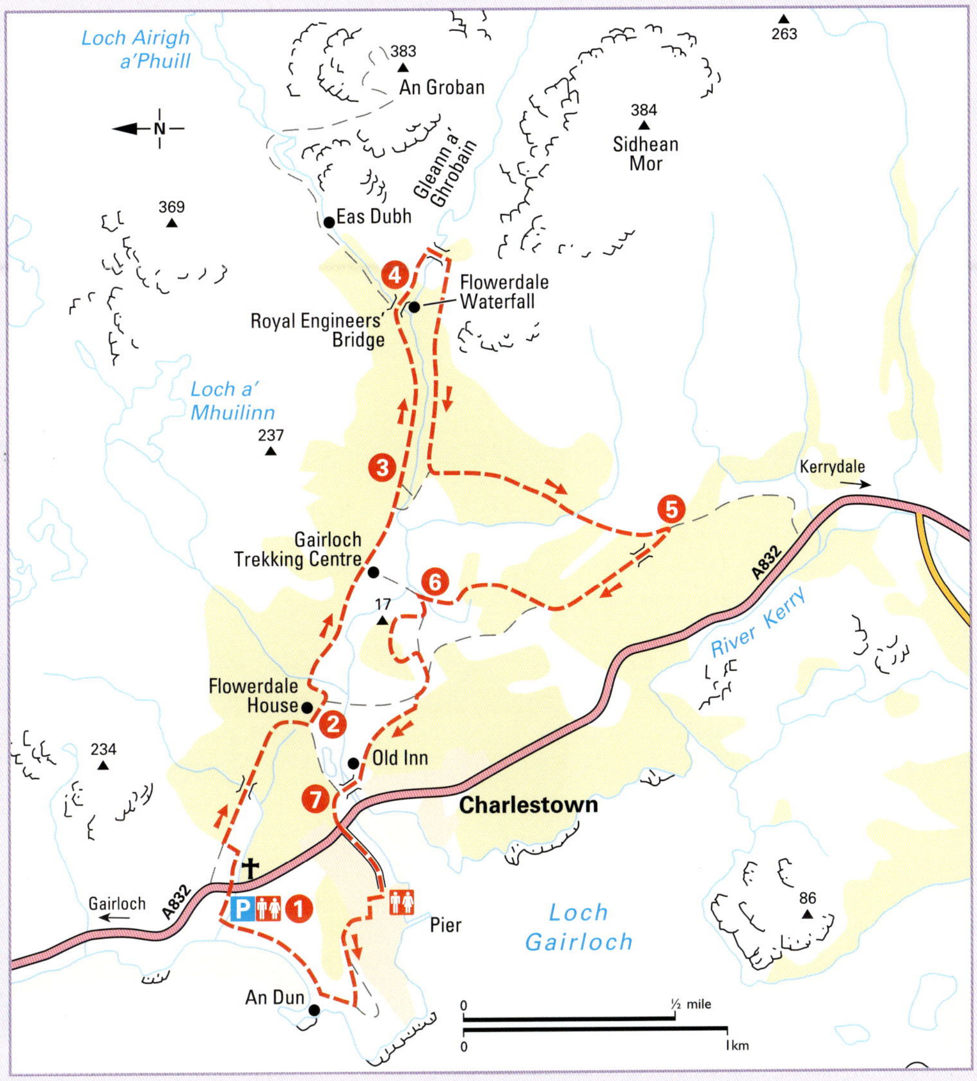

Distance 5.25 miles (8.4km)

Minimum Time 2hrs 45min

Ascent/Gradient 800ft (244m) ▲▲▲

Level of Difficulty ●●●

Paths Tracks and smooth paths, mostly waymarked, no stiles

Landscape Gentle river valley and rocky coast

Suggested Map OS Explorer 433 Torridon – Beinn Eighe & Liathach or 434 Gairloch & Loch Ewet

Start/Finish Grid reference: NG 807756 on OS Explorer 433

Dog Friendliness Keep on lead past Flowerdale House (as signs indicate)

Parking Beach car park, southern end of Gairloch

Public Toilets Walk start and Charlestown pier

1 Cross the road and head up to the right of the newer cemetery. Turn left at its corner, going into trees to a path above. Turn right until a footbridge leads on to a wide path that soon runs downhill. The main path bends right (green-top waymarker) and runs down to a tarred driveway.

2 Turn left along a tarred track to pass Flowerdale House.The track passes to the left of a lovely old barn and turns right at a sign for the waterfall to pass Gairloch Trekking Centre. In about 0.25 mile (400m) you pass a timber-surfaced bridge on the right.

3 Follow the main path ahead, still to the left of the stream to reach a footbridge built by the Royal Engineers, just before you get to Flowerdale Waterfall.

4 The path leads up past the waterfall to cross a footbridge, runs up into a pine clump, then turns back down the valley. After another footbridge it joins a rough track. You pass a memorial to the blind piper of Gairloch, just before a forest road beside Point 3. Turn left through felled but regenerating forest.

5 A blue-topped pole marks a path to the right. It leads through scrub birch and bracken with waymarker poles. The path bends right at an old cornerpost and down above and left of a field. Turn right underneath two oak trees and cross a stream to an earth track.

6 Turn left for a few steps, until a small bracken path runs up to the right past a power pole. The path bends left under oaks, then drops to rejoin the earth track. This soon meets a larger track, the old road from Loch Maree to Gairloch. Turn right along this, through gates, to the Old Inn at Charlestown.

7 Cross the old bridge, and the main road, towards the pier. Turn right at the signpost for the beach to a stepped path to the left of Gairloch Chandlery. The tarred path passes to the left of a pinewood, then turns right into the trees. It bends left and emerges to run along the spine of a small headland. Just before being carried out to sea it turns sharp right, and crosses above a rocky bay to the fort (An Dun). A duckboard path runs along the back of the beach, then turns right to the car park.

98 The Gloup Loop

A fascinating circular walk leads past a collapsed sea cave and around the Mull Head Nature Reserve, where you can inspect ancient rocks and varied plant life

The Gloup – named from the Old Norse word *gluppa*, 'chasm' – is not the only collapsed cave in Orkney, but at 100ft (30m) deep it is the most visited. This remarkable feature was formed by the force of the North Sea. The parish of Deerness in which it lies is a peninsula joined to Orkney's mainland by a very narrow spit. The land has been altered repeatedly by the people and the climate. This walk follows the story of the landscape.

Centuries of Settlement

The *Orkneyinga* saga (compiled 1192–1206) mentions Deerness several times and nearby excavations by archaeologists have turned up an Iron Age settlement, a Pictish farm, obvious Norse remains and a hog-back gravestone in the kirkyard dating from AD1100. The first people to have an impact on Mull Head were Neolithic. The ancient scrubland was grazed by animals, then Norsemen played their part, followed in their turn by locals 'paring' – stripping off the top soil for use elsewhere – during the 18th century. Mull Head has been continuously grazed, creating a mature heather heath and very impoverished soil.

In 1993 Orkney Islands Council declared Mull Head a Local Nature Reserve, the ninth in Scotland. Because it has been spared agricultural 'improvement' it is now very rich. The rocks themselves, which you will see as you walk the headland, are 350 million years old. There are two types: Eday flags, which are coarse red sandstone, and Rousay flags at the south end of the reserve, both formed from conditions when Lake Orcadie covered this land. Visible ripples in the stone are characteristic of formation in shallow flowing water. The plants that survive here are determined by the location, too – how close to the sea they are, how fertile the soil is where they grow, how marshy it is and how influenced by humans. Plants that have to withstand the salt spray at the cliff edge, such as sea pink or thrift, will hug the ground. As well as salt tolerators and salt haters, plants that prefer marshy conditions, such as grass of Parnassus, grow here.

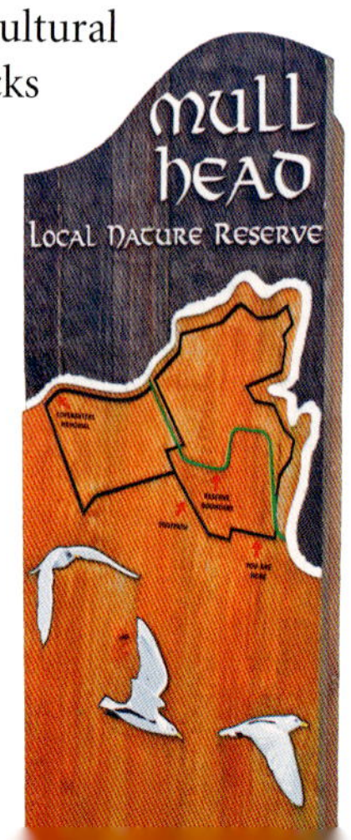

Mull Head has never been ploughed, although Clu Ber, the first range of cliffs you will see, has been burned, cultivated and fertilised to allow grazing for stock, and even though this was done generations ago, the heather's destruction means that grass and different herb species thrive. The final influence on the plants are the activities of some of the birds. Islands of lush grass found on the heath are where great black-backed gulls roost each night, the grasses benefiting because they fertilise the soil.

Top left: Sandstone cliffs and wild heath in the Mull Head Nature Reserve

Top right: Ancient rocks are visible along the Orkney shore

Right: The nature reserve is a haven for nesting birds including razorbills, kittiwakes and fulmars – as well as for skuas and gulls

98 The Gloup Loop

Walk where Vikings built a settlement around 1,000 years ago

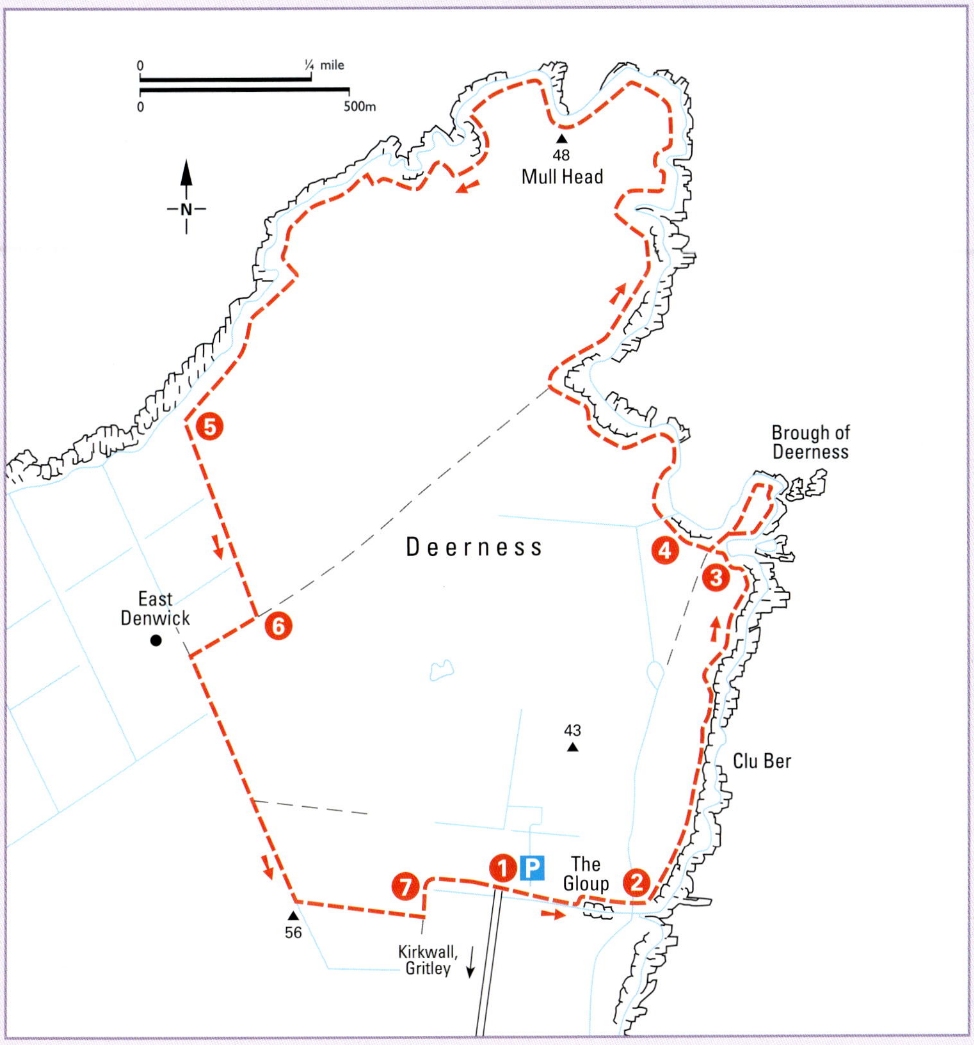

Distance 4 miles (6.4km)

Minimum Time 2hrs 30min

Ascent/Gradient 93ft (28m) ▲▲▲

Level of Difficulty ●●●

Paths Continuous, 6 kissing gates

Landscape Moorland, cliff edge

Suggested Map OS Explorer 461 Orkney – East Mainland

Start/Finish Grid reference: HY 590079

Dog Friendliness Dogs must be kept under control due to wildlife

Parking Mull Head car park

Public Toilets Nearest are 4 miles (6.4km) away at Sandi Sand

1 Leave the car park at its right-hand corner, by the information plaque. Follow the direction sign along the path to The Gloup, where you will find two viewing platforms.

2 Past The Gloup you will see a red-painted kissing gate and a directional sign pointing left; this will lead you along a grassy footpath to the Brough (pronounced 'broch') of Deerness, but a more interesting route, perhaps, is straight ahead and then left along the cliff edge, also following a grassy path.

3 At the Brough is another information plaque and, in the cliff edge, a precipitous stone staircase that takes you down the cliff and, by turning right at the beach, into a sheltered stony bay, Little Burra Geo. You will see in the edge of the Brough wall a steep dirt path you can climb with the help of a chain set into the rock. This path will take you to the top of the Brough so that you can explore the ancient site there.

4 Having climbed back to the main route, another red-painted kissing gate on your right shows the footpath leading along to the cairn at Mull Head. From the cairn the path turns left and becomes much narrower, taking you along the northern cliff edge.

5 The path turns sharp left just before a wire fence and climbs uphill through moorland to another red-painted kissing gate.

6 Turn right here and go down to a red kissing gate you can see in the fencing above a farmhouse, East Denwick. Here turn left along a wide hill track. Just above the farmhouse, you pass through another red kissing gate and the track becomes very overgrown. At the top a left turn leads downhill to a red kissing gate on your left.

7 The narrow grass path through the gate and between wire fences turns sharp right and leads back into the car park.

99 The Hidden Treasures of Dunnottar

A bracing walk along the cliffs leads to the dramatic remains of Dunnottar Castle, which once housed Scotland's crown jewels in a time of need

Above: Harbour and marina at Stonehaven

Below: Dunnottar Castle occupies a gloriously picturesque setting on a clifftop above the North Sea

There's more than a dash of romance on this windswept walk to Dunnottar Castle, one of Scotland's lesser known fortresses. Now a glowering ruin precariously situated above chilly northern seas, in the 17th century it was the setting for one of the most fascinating and little known episodes in Scotland's history when it was used as a hiding place for the country's greatest treasures – the 'Honours of Scotland' or crown jewels.

Symbols of Independence

Scotland's crown jewels, which comprise a crown, a sword of state and a silver sceptre, are among the oldest in Europe. The crown was created in 1532 for King James V. It is made of gold encrusted with precious stones and pearls, and rimmed with ermine. The sword was fashioned in 1507 for King James IV and has a silver-encrusted scabbard lined with red velvet, while the sceptre, made in 1494 and lengthened in 1536, has a pearl-topped globe of rock crystal that some say has magical properties. Together they are powerful symbols of Scotland's independence, on display at Edinburgh Castle.

However, you can only see them thanks to the bravery of a few patriotic Scots. When Oliver Cromwell invaded Scotland in 1650, he had every intention of destroying the regalia, as he had done with the English crown jewels, but they were spirited away from Edinburgh for safe keeping and given to George Ogilvie at Dunnottar Castle.

Cromwell's army came to Dunnottar the following year and besieged the castle for eight months, but when they finally took it, they discovered the jewels had gone. They had been smuggled out by the wife of the Revd James Granger, the minister of nearby Kineff, and her maid. These two intrepid patriots had visited a friend in the castle and managed to leave with the jewels hidden in their clothes. They took the Honours to Kinneff, further down the coast, where they hid them, sometimes stashing them under the church floor, sometimes under their bed.

The jewels remained there for eight years, and although Cromwell's men tried everything they could to find them – imprisoning the Grangers, and even torturing Ogilvie's wife – no one gave the secret away. Go to Kinneff Old Church and you'll see a memorial to the Grangers.

The crown jewels were returned to Edinburgh after the Restoration in 1660 and, following the Act of Union with England in 1707, were walled up in a sealed room in a tower in Edinburgh Castle. People eventually forgot where they were and many believed they had been stolen by the English. It was Sir Walter Scott who rediscovered them, in 1818, locked inside a chest covered with dust.

99 The Hidden Treasures of Dunnottar

See where Scottish patriots outwitted English besiegers

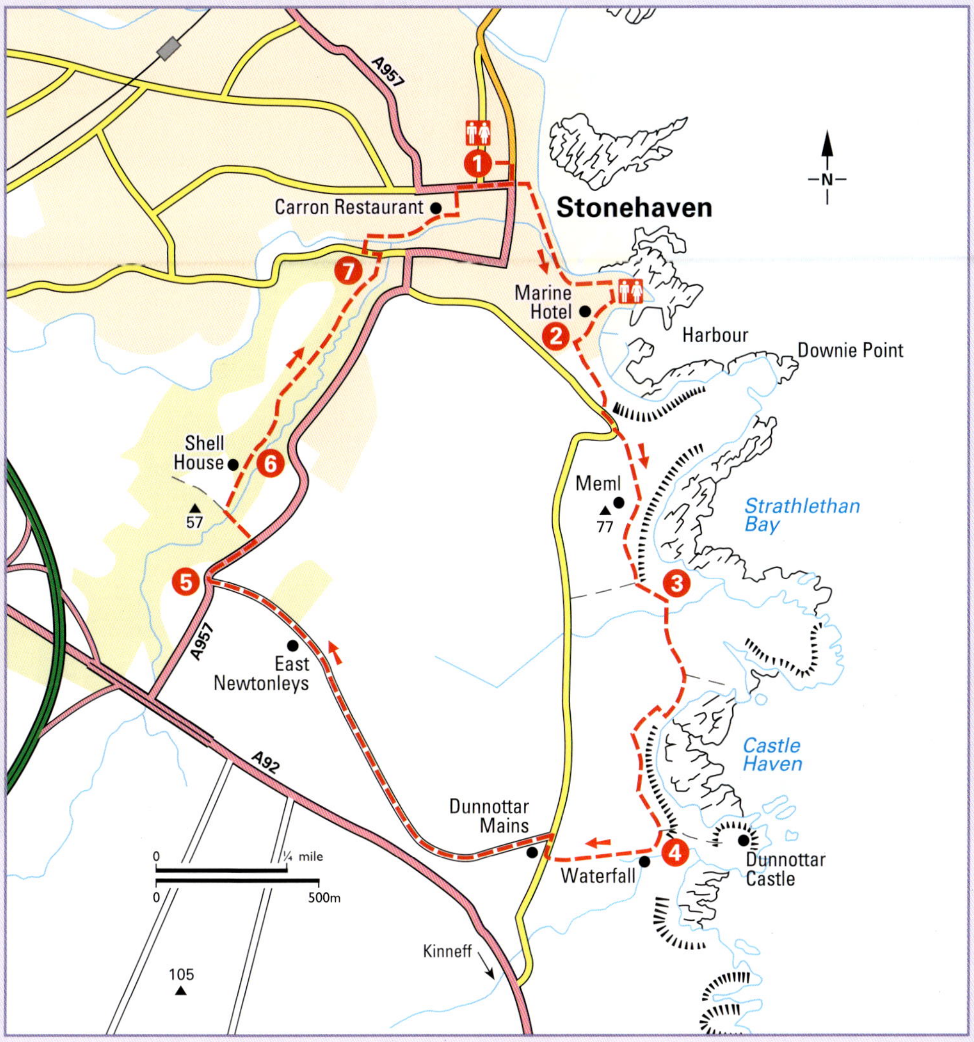

Distance 3.5 miles (5.7km)

Minimum Time 1hr 30min

Ascent/Gradient 377ft (115m) ▲▲▲

Level of Difficulty ●●●

Paths Cliff edges, metalled tracks, forest paths

Landscape Striking seascapes, ancient castle

Suggested Map OS Explorer 396 Stonehaven & Inverbervie

Start/Finish Grid reference: NO 874858

Dog Friendliness Keep on lead along cliffs

Parking Market Square, Stonehaven

Public Toilets Market Square and harbour, Stonehaven

1 From the Market Square in Stonehaven, walk back on to Allardyce Street, turn right and then cross over the road. Turn left up Market Lane and, when you come to the beach, turn right to cross over the footbridge. Turn right at a sign to Dunnottar Castle to reach the harbour. Cross here to continue down Shorehead, on the east side of the harbour. Go past the Marine Hotel, then turn right into Wallis Wynd.

2 Turn left into Castle Street. This becomes a steep path, and when it emerges at the main road maintain your direction, carrying on walking along the road until it starts to bend. Continue ahead here, following the enclosed tarmac path, going between arable fields and past a war memorial standing on the right-hand side. Go across the middle of the field, then carry on above Strathlethan Bay.

3 The path turns right across the middle of a field and then over a footbridge. You now pass a path going down to Castle Haven and continue following the main path around the cliff's edge. Cross another footbridge and bear uphill. You'll soon reach some steps on your left that run down to Dunnottar Castle.

4 Your walk bears right here, going inland and past a waterfall, through a kissing gate and then up to a house. Pass the house to the road into Stonehaven by the Dunnottar Mains, turn right then take the first turning on the left and walk alongside the farm. Follow this wide, metalled track past East Newtonleys on the left-hand side, to the main A957.

5 Turn right and walk downhill, then take the first road on the left, signed 'Dunnottar Church'. Follow this over the Burn of Glaslow to a path on the right, signed 'Carron Gate'. You take this path into the woods but at once fork right, following the lower path that runs along by the burn. Continue in this direction until you reach the Shell House on the left.

6 Just past the Shell House, carry on along the lower path, which then turns uphill to join a higher path. Bear right at this point, to reach the end of the woods at Carron Gate. Walk through a housing estate to join Low Wood Road and the River Carron.

7 Turn left, then go right to cross the footbridge with the green railings. Turn right and walk along by the water. You'll soon pass the striking art deco Carron Restaurant on the left-hand side, and then come to a cream-coloured iron bridge. Bear left here, then turn first right to return to the Market Square.

101 A Fishy Trail in Fife

A linear coastal walk leads through the villages of Fife's East Neuk, including what was once the largest fishmarket in the whole of Europe

King James II of Scotland described the East Neuk of Fife as 'a fringe of gold on a beggar's mantle'. This corner of the East Coast is dotted with picturesque fishing villages that nestle close together while each retains its own distinctive character. Crail is perhaps the prettiest of these villages, with a neat little harbour that attracts many artists and photographers. It was once the largest fishmarket in Europe and, like all the East Neuk villages, used to trade with the Low Countries and Scandinavia; you can see the Dutch influence in the houses with their crow-stepped gables and charming pantiled roofs.

Below: Harbour and seafront at Anstruther or 'Enster'

Below right: Lobster pots in Crail

Herring Capital

Further down the coast is Anstruther (known locally as 'Enster'), the largest and busiest of all the East Neuk villages and home of the local lifeboat. Fishing has always been the focus of life here. The village was the capital of the Scottish herring trade and the harbour was once so busy that you could cross it by stepping over the boats. Look at the houses as you pass and you'll see that many of them have spacious lofts with a pulley outside – designed to store fishing gear and provide an area for mending the nets.

Fishing dominated the lives of people in the past and each of the East Neuk villages was a closely knit community. It was rare for people to marry outside their own village and local women were as heavily involved in the work as the men. They prepared the fish, baited the hooks, mended the nets and took the fish to market for sale, carrying enormous baskets of herrings on their backs. They certainly needed to be strong – they also used to carry their husbands out to sea on their backs so that the men could board their boats without getting wet.

Don't Mention the Minister!

Fishing has always had its dangers and many local superstitions are attached to the industry. Women aren't allowed aboard when a boat is working, and it is considered unlucky to utter the word 'minister' on a boat – he had to be referred to as 'the fellow with the white throat' or 'man in the black coat'. Other words to be avoided are 'pig', 'rat' and 'salmon'. These are known as 'curlytail', 'lang-tail' and 'red fish' (or 'silver beastie'), respectively. If these words were spoken on a fishing boat the men would cry 'cauld airn' (cold iron) and grab the nearest piece of iron. It's the equivalent of touching wood and is meant to break the bad luck.

101 A Fishy Trail in Fife

Tramp the coast from Crail to Anstruther

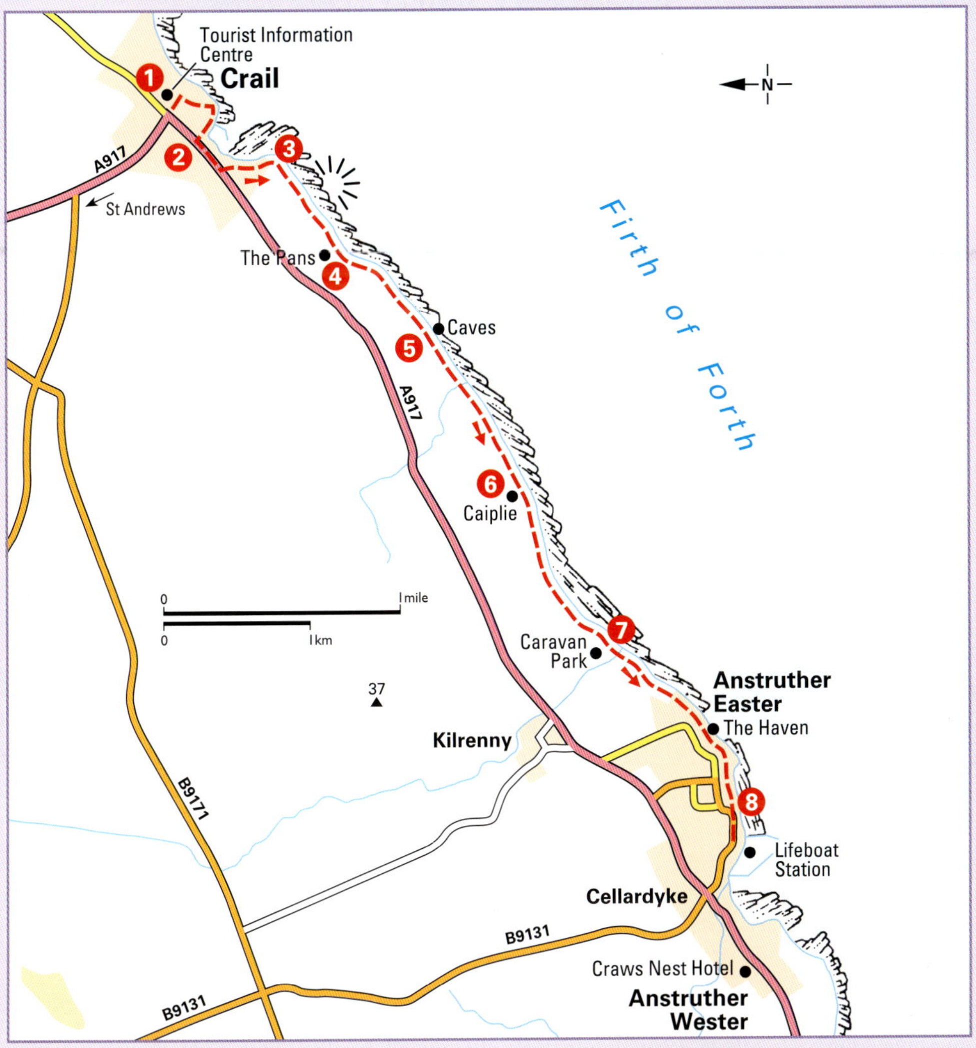

Distance 4 miles (6.4km)

Minimum Time 1hr 30min

Ascent/Gradient 49ft (15m) ▲▲▲

Level of Difficulty ●●●

Paths Well-marked coastal path, 3 stiles

Landscape Picturesque fishing villages and extensive sea views

Suggested Map OS Explorer 371 St Andrews & East Fife

Start Grid reference: NO 613077

Finish Grid reference: NO 569034

Dog Friendliness Good, but keep on lead near cattle

Parking On street in Crail

Public Toilets Route passes plenty both in Crail and Anstruther

1 From the Tourist Information Centre in Crail, walk down Tolbooth Wynd. At the end, turn right and, where the road divides, bear left (a sign says 'no vehicular access to harbour'). You'll now be walking beside the old castle wall to a lookout point, which gives you a grand view of the harbour. Bear right and walk on to reach the High Street.

2 Turn left and walk along the road out of the village, passing two white beacons that help guide boats into the harbour. Turn left and walk down West Braes, following signs for the Coastal Path. At Osbourne Terrace, turn left down a narrow path go down steps through a kissing gate and on to a track by the shore.

3 From here you follow the path as it hugs the shoreline. You should soon see cormorants perched on rocks to your left and will also get views of the Isle of May. Go down some steps, over a slightly boggy area, and continue walking until you reach two derelict cottages – an area known as The Pans.

4 Walk past the cottages and continue along the shore, then hop over a stone stile. You'll now pass flat rocks on the left, which are covered with interesting little rock pools. Cross the burn by the footbridge – you'll now be able to see the Bass Rock and Berwick Law on your left and the village of Anstruther ahead, and will soon reach some caves.

5 Pass the caves, then cross a little stone stile on the left-hand side and go over a footbridge. Your track is narrower now and takes you past fields on the right, then some maritime grasses on the left. Stone steps lead to another stile. Climb over it to reach Caiplie.

6 Go through the kissing gate to pass in front of houses, follow the wide grassy track, then go through another kissing gate to walk past a field. The path now runs past a free-range pig farm and up to a caravan park.

7 Continue along the shore, on a tarmac track to reach a play area and war memorial on the right. Maintain direction now as you enter the village of Cellardyke and continue to the harbour. Pass the harbour and The Haven restaurant and continue along John Street, then James Street.

8 At the end of James Street maintain direction, then follow the road as it bends down to the left. You'll walk past a guiding beacon and will come into Anstruther's busy harbour. You can either walk back to Crail or take the bus that leaves from the harbour.

102 Intoxicating History along the Leith Shore

A gentle walk along the Water of Leith leads to the site of Edinburgh's ancient port, where claret once flowed in freely to become the Jacobites' drink of choice

Visitors often forget to come to Leith, yet Edinburgh's ancient seaport is full of history. Even though the docks have been spruced up and become rather trendy, Leith retains an edgy, maritime atmosphere – like an old sea dog who'll spin you a yarn for a pint.

There has been a port at Leith, where the Water of Leith meets the Forth, from at least the 1st century AD when the Romans stored wine for their legions here. Over the ensuing centuries the port grew, and by medieval times it was facilitating valuable trade with France. Ships would leave loaded with dried local fish and return laden with wines, which were landed by the French monks of St Anthony who were based in Edinburgh.

One of the main imports was claret, which rapidly became Scotland's national drink when the most popular drink in England was port. One old verse sums up its popularity, beginning with the words: 'Guid claret best keeps out the cauld an drives awa the winter soon'. When cargoes arrived, some would be sent on a cart through Leith and anyone who fancied a sample simply turned up with a jug, which would be filled for 6d. It didn't seem to matter how large the jug was.

The quality of the claret imported and bottled in Leith was extremely good. One historian said it 'held in its day a cachet comparable to that which one now associates with chateau-bottled wines'. Claret drinking was seen as a symbol of Scotland's national identity and Jacobites drank it as a symbol of independence. During the 18th century the British government, determined to price the French out of the market, raised taxes on claret. Inevitably traders began to smuggle it into Scotland instead. It was only in the 19th century that claret drinking declined when taxes rose and the Napoleonic Wars made it scarce. While Leith claret was still drunk by the wealthiest people, whisky (a drink from the Highlands) took its place as the people's pick-me-up, going from strength to strength to reach its present state of popularity.

Costly Expedition

All this time, the Port of Leith continued to grow in importance and it was from here, in 1698, that the ill-fated Darien expedition set sail, a venture that was eventually to cost Scotland her independence.

The intention was to establish a colony at Darien on the Isthmus of Panama. It cost £400,000 to fund, but it was thought that the venture would give Scotland control of a potentially lucrative trading route. However the terrain proved hostile and the colonists rapidly died. The Scottish economy was plunged into crisis and the country was pushed inexorably towards union with England.

Right: A former barge moored on the Shore at Leith has been converted into offices

102 Intoxicating History along the Leith Shore

Pass an 18th-century 'Roman temple' on your way to the welcoming pubs of Leith

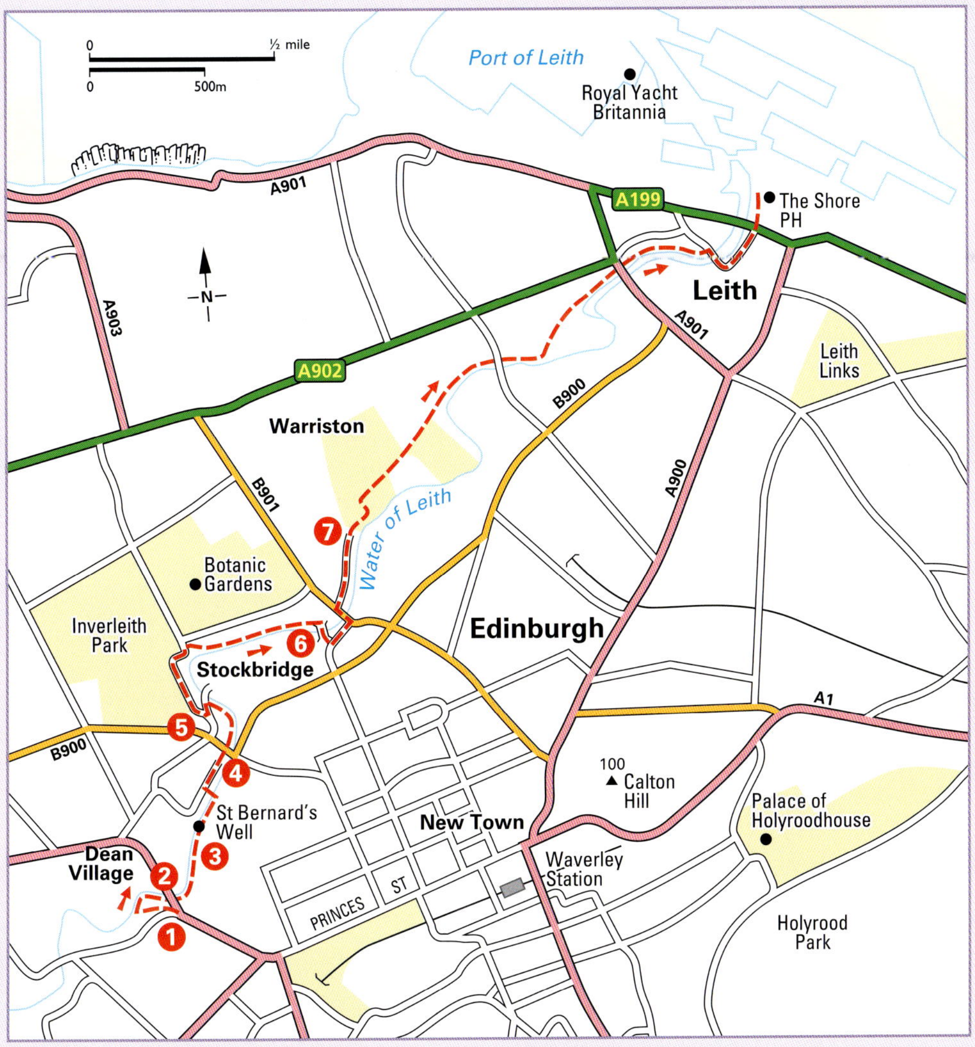

Distance 3.5 miles (5.7km)

Minimum Time 1hr 30min

Ascent/Gradient Negligible ▲▲▲

Level of Difficulty ●●●

Paths Wide riverside paths and city streets

Landscape Edinburgh's hidden waterway and revitalised port

Suggested Map OS Explorer 350 Edinburgh

Start Grid reference: NT 243739

Finish Grid reference: NT 271766

Dog Friendliness Can run free beside water, keep on lead in Leith

Parking Scottish National Gallery of Modern Art, Belford Road

Public Toilets Near Stockbridge

1 From the junction of the Dean Bridge and Queensferry Street, turn left to walk down Bell's Brae. You are now in the Dean Village, which dates back to 1128. It was once a milling centre and had 11 watermills that produced all the meal for Edinburgh. At the bottom, turn right into Miller Row.

2 Follow this to walk under the impressive arches of the Dean Bridge, which was designed by Thomas Telford and opened in 1832. Your path then runs along the bottom of the steeply sided gorge, beside the Water of Leith, and feels extremely rural. You'll pass an old well on your left, followed by the more impressive St Bernard's Well.

3 St Bernard's Well was discovered by some schoolboys in 1760. The mineral water was said to have healing properties and, in 1789, the present Roman Temple was built, with Hygeia – the goddess of health – at the centre. From here, continue along the main path, then go up the steps. Turn left, and go right on to Dean Terrace to reach Stockbridge.

4 Cross the road and go down the steps ahead – immediately to the right of the building with the clock tower. Continue to follow the path beside the river. Where the path ends, climb on to the road, turn left and then right to go down Arboretum Avenue.

5 Walk along this road, then turn right along the path marked Rocheid Path. This runs beside the river and is a popular cycleway and jogging path. Follow this, passing the backs of the Colonies. This low-cost housing was built by the Edinburgh Co-operative for artisans living here in the late 19th century. The idea was to provide houses in a healthy environment away from the dirt of the city. Walk to Tanfield Bridge.

6 Go right, over the bridge, go up the steps, then turn left, walking towards the clock tower. At the end turn left along Warriston Place, cross the road, then turn right down Warriston Crescent. This is lined with town houses. Walk to the end where you will reach the playing fields.

7 Bear right, around the edge of the park, then follow the path as it bears uphill between trees. Turn left at the top and follow the cycle track marked 'Leith 1.25'. Follow this all the way into Leith: it brings you out near the old Custom House. Cross the bridge, then turn left to walk along the shore and explore the pubs, before returning to town by bus.

103 A Windy Clifftop Walk to St Abb's Head

A tramp along the Berwickshire cliffs is a thrilling experience – and a particular treat for birdwatchers keen to see razorbills, guillemots and other seabirds

St Abb's Head is a place you only ever seem to hear mentioned on the shipping forecast – and then its name is generally followed by a rather chilly outlook, along the lines of 'north-easterly five, continuous light drizzle, poor'. In fact, you could be forgiven for wondering if it even exists or is simply a mysterious expanse of sea – like Dogger, Fisher or German Bight. But St Abb's Head does exist – as you'll find out on this lovely, windswept walk that will rumple your hair and leave the salty tang of the sea lingering on your lips, and provide plentiful opportunities for spotting seabirds.

Below inset: A shag on the rocks

Below main image: Dramatic cliffs near St Abb's Head are an ideal home for nesting seabirds

Blunt Beaks

Birds you might spot on this walk include guillemots, razorbills, kittiwakes, herring gulls, shags and fulmars – as well as a few puffins. Guillemots and razorbills are difficult to differentiate, because they're both black and white, and have an upright stance – rather like small penguins. However, you should be able to spot the difference if you've got binoculars, as razorbills have distinctive blunt beaks. Both birds belong to the auk family, the most famous member of which is probably the great auk, which went the way of the dodo and became extinct in 1844 – a victim of the contemporary passion for egg collecting.

Luckily no egg collector could scale these precipitous cliffs, which are surrounded by treacherous seas. Do this walk in the nesting season (May to July) and you may well see young birds jumping off the high cliff ledge into the open sea below. Even though they can't yet fly, as their wings are little more than stubs, the baby birds are nevertheless excellent swimmers and have a better chance of survival in the water than in their nests – where they could fall prey to marauding gulls. Neither razorbills nor guillemots are particularly agile in the air, but they swim with the ease of seals, using their wings and feet to propel and steer their sleek little bodies as they fish beneath the waves.

While the steep cliffs are home to most of the seabirds round St Abb's Head, the low, flat rocks below are the favoured nesting site of shags. These large black birds are almost indistinguishable from cormorants – except for the distinctive crest on their heads that gives them a quizzical appearance. They tend to fly low over the water, in contrast to the graceful fulmars that frequently soar along the cliff tops, hitching a ride on currents of air.

103 A Windy Clifftop Walk to St Abb's Head

Enjoy spectacular coastal views – and pack your binoculars for spotting seabirds

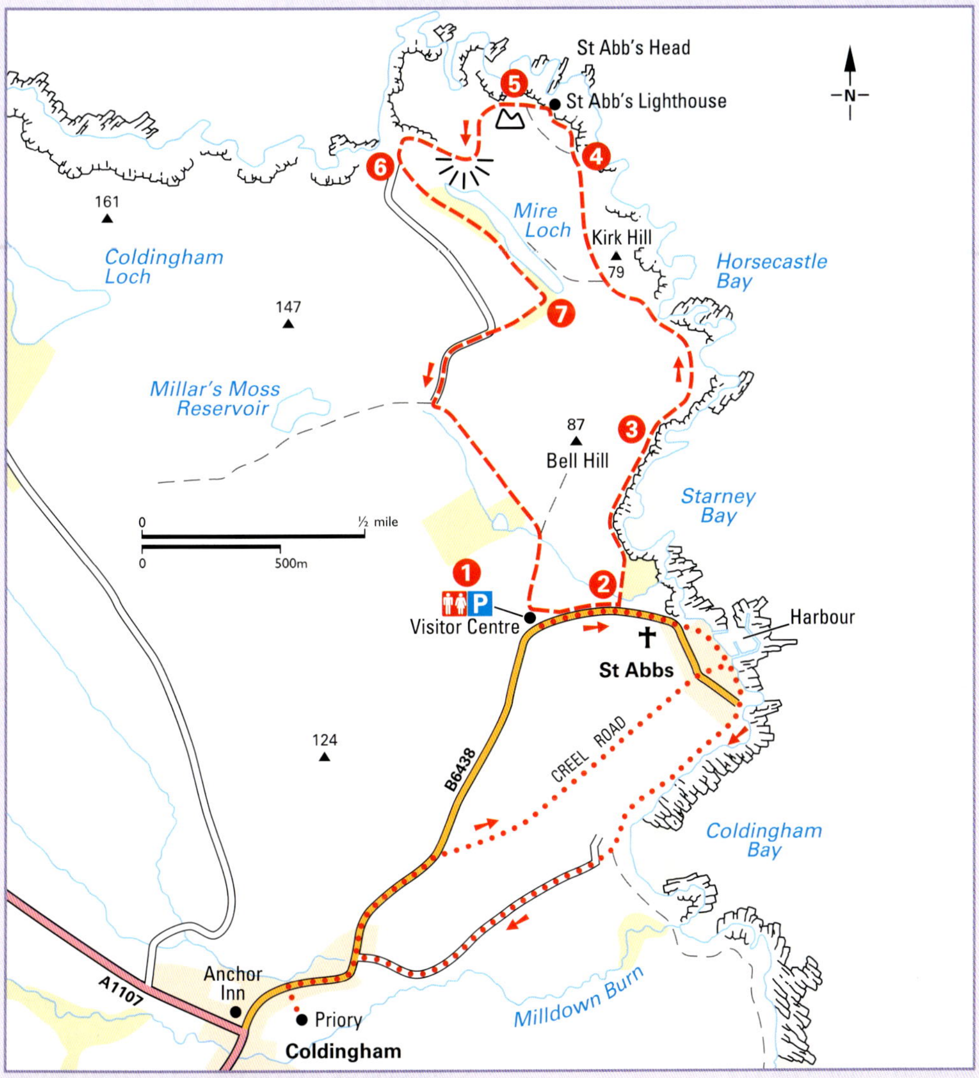

Distance 4 miles (6.4km)

Minimum Time 1hr 30min

Ascent/Gradient 443ft (135m) ▲▲▲

Level of Difficulty ●●●

Paths Clear footpaths and established tracks

Landscape Dramatic cliff tops and lonely lighthouse

Suggested Map OS Explorer 346 Berwick-upon-Tweed

Start/Finish Grid reference: NT 913674

Dog Friendliness They'll love the fresh air, but keep on lead by cliffs

Parking At visitor centre

Public Toilets At visitor centre

1 From the car park, take the path that runs past the information board and the play area. Walk past the visitor centre, then take the footpath on the left, which runs parallel to the main road. At the end of the path, turn left and go through a gate – and you'll immediately get great views of the sea.

2 Follow the track, pass the sign to Starney Bay and continue, passing fields on your left-hand side. Your track now winds around the edge of the bay – to your right is the little harbour at St Abbs. The track then winds around the cliff edge, past dramatic rock formations and eventually to some steps.

3 Walk down the steps and then follow the grassy track as it bears left, with a fence on the left. Go up a slope, through a gate and maintain your direction on the obvious grassy track. The path soon veers away from the cliff edge, past high ground on the right, then runs up a short, steep slope to a crossing of tracks, passing a butterfly haven on the right.

4 Maintain direction by keeping to the coastal path which runs up a slope. You'll soon get great views of the St Abb's lighthouse ahead, dramatically situated on the cliff's edge. Continue as far as the lighthouse and walk in front of the lighthouse buildings and then down to join a tarmac road. Take care here, as this path is steep and eroded.

5 Follow the road down to reach the bottom of the hill, then about 50yds (46m) before reaching a cattle grid, turn left to walk down a narrow path.

6 Continue along the path and over a stile. The path now runs through scrub and woodland along the edge of a loch. Continue along the path to an intersection with a track.

7 Turn right along the wide track and walk up to the road. Go left now and continue, going across a cattle grid. When you reach a bend in the road, follow the tarmac track as it bears left. You'll soon go through a gate, then pass some cottages before reaching the car park on the left-hand side.

Extending the Walk

You can add a different dimension to your walk in this area by visiting the priory ruins in Coldingham. From the harbour in St Abbs, head south along the coastal footpath towards Coldingham Bay. A lane will take you up into the village where you can visit the priory. Return to St Abbs by following the main road until you reach the Creel Road path on your right. This will take you down into the back of St Abbs, above the harbour.

Acknowledgements

The Automobile Association would like to thank the following photographers and companies for their assistance in the preparation of this book.

Abbreviations for the picture credits are as follows: (t) top; (b) bottom; (l) left; (r) right; (c) centre; (AA) AA World Travel Library.

3 AA/R Coulam; 6 AA/C Warren; 8/9 Peter Heyes/Alamy; 10/11 Adam Burton/Alamy; 12/13 Kevin Britland/Alamy; 13tr AA/N Hicks; 13cr Robert Harding Picture Library Ltd/Alamy; 14t AA/N Hicks; 14b AA/A Burton; 15 Peter Barritt/Alamy; 16t AA/A Burton; 16r AA/J Wood; 18cl Lee Pengelly/Alamy; 18bl Akiko Nagahama/Alamy; 18br AA/C Jones; 20tl Powered by Light/Alan Spencer/Alamy; 20c AA/J Wood; 20b Ashley Cooper/Alamy; 22l AA/R Moss; 22r AA/J Wood; 24l AA/N Hicks; 24tr James Davis Photography/Alamy; 24b David Newham/Alamy; 26cl AA/N Hicks; 26bl Adam Burton/Alamy; 28l Adam Burton/Alamy; 28b Adam Burton/Alamy; 30l Gillian Moore/Alamy; 30r Martin Fowler/Alamy; 32tl AA/R Moss; 32bl AA/J Wood; 32br AA/J Wood; 34l Michael Willis/Alamy; 34b Tremorvapix/Alamy; 36l AA/B Pearce; 36tr Rick Strange/Alamy; 36b Graham Bell/Alamy; 38l AA/W Voysey; 38r Rick Strange/Alamy; 40l David Chapman/Alamy; 40br Bruce Little/Alamy; 42tl AA/H Williams; 42b James Osmond Photography/Alamy; 42cr Mike Hayward/Alamy; 44bl Tony Lilley/Alamy; 44r AA/H Williams; 46tl AA/M Jourdan; 46tr AA/M Jourdan; 46br AA/M Jourdan; 48 AA/A Burton; 50b AA/A Burton; 50c dbphotos/Alamy; 52l AA/A Burton; 52r AA/A Burton; 54/55 AA/J Miller; 56 Stockpile Images/Alamy; 57 AA/A Burton; 58l David Cantrille/Alamy; 58r AA/W Voysey; 59 Howard Taylor/Alamy; 60 AA/A Burton; 62cl Malcolm McHugh/Alamy; 62b Patrick Eden/Alamy; 64tl Robin Steward/Alamy; 64b Available Light Photography/Alamy; 66 Derek Payne/Alamy; 68c AA/A Burton; 68b AA/M Moody; 70c csimagebase/Alamy; 70r PBstock/Alamy; 72t Pink Sun Media/Alamy; 72C Robert Estall photo agency/Alamy; 72bl Niall McOnegal/Alamy; 74tl Betty Finney/Alamy; 74bl Betty Finney/Alamy; 74cr Peter Lewis/Alamy; 74br Slick Shoots/Alamy; 76t AA/J Miller; 76cr AA/J Miller; 78c AA/M Busselle; 78b AA/J Miller; 80c Nick Hanna/Alamy; 80cr AA/J Miller; 80b Keith Shuttlewood/Alamy; 82bl AA/J Miller; 82tr MichaelGrantWildlife/Alamy; 84tl AA/N Setchfield; 84bl AA/N Setchfield; 84br AA/N Setchfield; 86tl Country Collection – Homer Sykes/Alamy; 86b Malcolm Fairman/Alamy; 88c AA/N Setchfield; 88bl AA/W Voysey; 88br AA/W Voysey; 90cr AA/N Setchfield; 90br AA/N Setchfield; 92b AA/J Miller; 92br terry harris just greece photo library/Alamy; 94/95 AA/T Mackie; 96 AA/T Mackie; 96/97 AA/J A Tims; 97 AA/T Mackie; 98bl PremierPS/Alamy; 98br Michael Juno/Alamy; 99 AA/T Mackie; 100tl Clynt Garnham Architecture/Alamy; 100b AA/M Birkitt; 102t AA/N Setchfield; 102bl Rodger Tamblyn/Alamy; 102br Quentin Bargate/Alamy; 104l Mark Baigent/Alamy; 104r Colin Palmer Photography/Alamy; 106 Pictures Colour Library; 108t Simon Batley/Alamy; 108b Ronnie McMillan/Alamy; 110b AA/T Mackie; 110tr AA/T Mackie; 112tl AA/M Moody; 112tc AA/A Burton; 112cl Arco Images GmbH/Alamy; 112r Clynt Garnham/Alamy; 114cl AA/T Mackie; 114bl AA/T Mackie; 114b AA/T Mackie; 116tl Clynt Garnham/Alamy; 116b Chris Herring/Alamy; 118l AA/A Baker; 118r AA/T Mackie; 120b Jon Gibbs/Alamy; 120cr Robert Estall photo agency/Alamy; 122t AA/A Baker; 122cl AA/T Mackie; 122bc AA/T Mackie; 124 AA/T Mackie; 126tr Alistair Laming/Alamy; 126cr AA/T Mackie; 128l Peter Huggins/Alamy; 128b AA/S & O Mathews; 130 AA/T Mackie; 132 AA/A J Hopkins; 134t AA/J A Tims; 134b AA/J ATims; 136/137 AA/R Coulam; 138 Christine Whitehead/Alamy; 139 AA/A J Hopkins; 140 Holmes Garden Photos/Alamy; 141tl AA/M Kipling; 141tr AA/J Morrison; 143 AA/D Clapp; 144l AA/M Kipling; 144c AA/J Morrison; 146bl AA/R Coulam; 146br Jason Friend Photography Ltd/Alamy; 146tr AA/R Coulam; 148t AA/Graeme Peacock/Alamy; 148cl katewarn images/Alamy; 150l Graeme Peacock/Alamy; 150b AA/R Coulam; 152t AA/A J Hopkins; 152r AA/J Beazley; 154t AA/J Beazley; 154l AA/J Beazley; 156l Peter T Lovatt/Alamy; 156b Lynne Evans/Alamy; 158t Peter Heyes/Alamy; 158b naturpics/Alamy; 160bl John Morrison/Alamy; 160br AA/T Marsh; 162t Peter Heyes/Alamy; 162b Dave Pilkington/Alamy; 164 John Morrison/Alamy; 166t Stan Pritchard/Alamy; 166b AA/J Sparks; 168 Jon Sparks/Alamy; 170tl AA/P Sharpe; 170b AA/T Mackie; 172/173 AA/C Warren; 174tr camera lucida lifestyle/Alamy; 174cr A Room With Views/Alamy; 174b David Angel/Alamy; 175 Realimage/Alamy; 176 AA/J A Tims; 177t Manor Photography/Alamy; 177b AA/J A Tims; 178 mkimages/Alamy; 180 Photolibrary Ltd; 182l AA/M Moody; 182t AA/H Williams; 184l AA/J Gravell; 184r AA/J Gravell; 186l AA/C Warren; 186b AA/M Sterling; 188t AA/C Warren; 188c Bryan Eveleigh/Alamy; 190l AA/J A Tims; 190b AA/J A Tims; 192c AA/C Warren; 192l joan gravell/Alamy; 194cr Christopher Nicolson/Alamy; 194br The Photolibrary Wales/Alamy; 196c AA/C Warren; 196b AA/C Warren; 198 The Photolibrary Wales/Alamy; 200l AA/W Voysey; 200b David Noton Photography/Alamy; 202l AA/G Matthews; 202bc AA/S Watkins; 204cl AA/S Lewis; 204b Jon Arnold Images Ltd/Alamy; 206tl AA/D Croucher; 206t Pearlimage/Alamy; 206cl AA/N Setchfield; 208bl The Photolibrary Wales/Alamy; 208br Glyn Thomas Photography/Alamy; 210/211 AA/M Taylor; 212tl AA/J Beazley; 212/213b AA/J Beazley; 213t AA/R Weir; 213b Robert Morris/Alamy; 214t David Robertson/Alamy; 214b David Robertson/Alamy; 215 AA/R Weir; 216t doughoughton/Alamy; 216b South West Images Scotland/Alamy; 217cl Robert Morris/Alamy; 217b Robert Morris/Alamy; 220t South West Images Scotland/Alamy; 220cl Jason Baxter/Alamy; 222cl Dave Clarke Photography/Alamy; 222bl Lynne Evans/Alamy; 222br AA/K Paterson; 224tr Celtic Collection – Homer Sykes/Alamy; 224b John Morrison/Alamy; 226 Peter Marshall/Alamy; 228 Tim Gainey/Alamy; 230t Joanne Moyes/Alamy; 230bl Jason Friend/Alamy; 232cl Jan Smith Photography/Alamy; 232b Neil Dangerfield/Alamy; 234t AA/J Beazley; 234cl Stephen Dorey/Alamy; 236 Andrew Hopkins/Alamy; 238t Graham Uney/Alamy; 238c John Peter Photography/Alamy; 238b AA/J Beazley; 240tl Graham Uney/Alamy; 240tr Les Gibbon/Alamy; 240b David Gowans/Alamy; 242t Simon Price/Alamy; 242b AA/J Henderson; 244t AA/J Smith; 244cr AA/J Smith; 246l AA/M Taylor; 246r AA/S Day; 248 AA/K Blackwell; 250cl AA/R Surman; 250b AA/D Forss.

Every effort has been made to trace the copyright holders, and we apologise in advance for any accidental errors. We would be happy to apply the corrections in the following edition of this publication.